Cricket Brach Apt 67

FISCAL ADMINISTRATION
Analysis and applications for the public sector

THE DORSEY SERIES IN POLITICAL SCIENCE
Consulting Editor   SAMUEL C. PATTERSON   The University of Iowa

JOHN L. MIKESELL
Professor of Public and Environmental Affairs
INDIANA UNIVERSITY

Fiscal Administration
Analysis and applications for the public sector

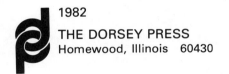

1982
THE DORSEY PRESS
Homewood, Illinois   60430

To Karen, Amy, Tom, and Daniel

© THE DORSEY PRESS, 1982

ISBN 0-256-02452-9
Library of Congress Catalog Card No. 81–70953
Printed in the United States of America

1 2 3 4 5 6 7 8 9 0 MP 9 8 7 6 5 4 3 2

PREFACE

Fiscal administration encompasses a wide range of activities vital to the operation of any government, including all portions of the budget cycle, the tax, charge, and aid processes of revenue generation, administration of the government debt, and management of idle cash, the topics examined through this book. Fiscal officers are likewise involved in collective bargaining, in developing policies for risk management and insurance, in managing purchasing and inventory policies, and so on. Those other activities are assigned because the fiscal officer is best able to integrate the effects of decisions made in those areas with the financial conditions of the government. Furthermore, the fiscal officer is not likely to be overwhelmed by quantitative manipulations needed to protect the interests of the government in such discussions. In sum, those in fiscal administration are necessarily a crucial link between policy formation and the process by which services are delivered. A world of scarcity, either severe or minimal, requires that the practitioners of fiscal administration be at the heart of the action.

This text evolved from my frustrated search of almost 10 years for a book appropriate for public finance and budgeting courses in a public affairs— public administration program. Material from economics, my academic discipline, usually ignored the practicalities of public agency operations, frequently required theoretical background beyond that of the typical student, and gave cursory attention to budget systems. Material from political science, generally limited to budgeting, concentrated on process outcomes and organizational dynamics without much development of analytic framework. Material from finance both emphasized corporate operations and required substantial theoretical background. No single approach was enough. No text or group of texts integrated all that students needed exposure to in a coherent conceptual framework with the appropriate analytical tools.

The needs of future practitioners are diverse. They need to learn about budget systems and their operation, revenue policies and their administration, public debt management, and idle fund management— because those are the responsibilities of the people doing fiscal administration. That is what this text examines—integrating materials, concepts, and approaches from several academic disciplines.

The structure of the text similarly emerges from almost 10 years of developing an integrated view of public financial administration. It seemed to me that the appropriate textbook should (1) introduce an analytic framework for public financial administration; (2) develop an understanding of fiscal institutions and the political constraints on their operation; (3) provide as many concrete examples of principles developed as possible; and (4) develop some technical skills that could be useful both immediately and over a career in public management. To put those views into action, the book contains short cases and related selections which illustrate and expand on principles developed in the chapters. Questions after each case or selection are designed only to start discussion; there is sufficient conflict in most of them to generate substantial debate. Each major section also has a series of homework exercises that require application of technical skills developed in the text. A number of the exercises are difficult and time-consuming. They will cause fewer problems, however, than would being unprepared on the job.

Chapters develop the environment of fiscal administration, cultivate the mindset appropriate for fiscal administration, and introduce a number of techniques used in fiscal administration. While it is true that the financial mechanisms—the forms, deadlines, system labels, etc.—of every government are different from that of every other, the objectives and analytic approaches are consistent. These chapters chart a path that may be followed through the cloud of institutional peculiarities regardless of local jargon.

The first chapter examines why governments exist and why there is any need for public financial administration, separate and distinct from business finance. The arguments developed there are based on the logic of public choice, an academic discipline which brings several tools of modern economics to the study of political science questions. It is a robust field of inquiry which comes as close as anything to presenting a general theory of budgeting.

The next chapters, gathered as Part One, examine how (and why) the budget process operates, what its logic is, and how practitioners try to improve that process. The chapters, along with cultivating the attitudes requisite to roles in the budget process, provide several analytic techniques used by participants in the process. The chapters do not replicate special studies of behavior in the budgetary process; some instructors will want to supplement coverage in the text with their favorite from that group.

The second major part, six chapters, focuses on the means of financing the services provided through budgetary decisions. Four chapters cover taxes, the compulsory extractions that are the foundation of government finance. One chapter is devoted to user charges, a much-discussed but little-used revenue source. Such revenue is attractive because of feared resistance to tax increases, although services provided seldom are good candidates to yield substantial charge revenue. A final chapter in the section outlines intergovernmental fiscal relations, an area including division of responsibilities between governments, tax relationships, mandates, and grant systems.

The third section contains two chapters on important areas of government finance: debt administration and cash management.

Some may argue that the revenue section ought to come before the budgeting section because government budgeting involves allocation of whatever the revenue system can produce. Others would agree that budgeting should come first because the financing function serves to acquire sufficient resources to accommodate the provision of services adopted through the budget process. It is a judgment call and makes for a lively discussion. Instructors may pursue their personal preference here, for the sections are designed to be used in either sequence. What is certain is that neither can be ignored.

ACKNOWLEDGMENTS

I owe special thanks to Jerry McCaffery of Indiana University and John Bowman of Virginia Commonwealth University. Our many discussions improved my understanding of public finance, defined what ought to be taught about public budgeting and finance, and contributed illustrations and examples used here. Thanks also to reviewers of an earlier version of the manuscript (John R. Gist of Virginia Polytechnic Institute, Marcia W. Taylor of The University of South Carolina, and series editor Samuel Patterson of The University of Iowa) for comments that improved both the logic and the clarity of the final product. Students at Indiana University tested earlier versions of the material here, probably in violation of regulations against cruel treatment of human subjects—some of the early material was really bad. Thanks are also due Mrs. Karen Evans, who miraculously converted almost incomprehensible drafts into a manuscript.

John L. Mikesell

CONTENTS

1

Fundamental principles of public finance

Governments budget, businesses budget, and, although often unconsciously, individuals budget. Budgeting, a method for deciding what actions are to be taken, is a nearly universal activity. Efforts to finance those actions are likewise universal—few valued resources are free, so any government, business, or individual must figure out some way to pay for the resources they use. Because governments, businesses, and individuals must budget and finance that budget as a necessary accompaniment to their existence, the more important initial questions for public fiscal administration are why governments exist and what sets them apart from businesses and individuals, not why budgeting and finance should be studied.

Modern public financial administration, including budgeting, borrows liberally the tools and concepts of business management.[1] That transfer of techniques cannot be complete, however, because of the basic nature of service provided by government. Private enterprise has failed to provide the appropriate level of these government services, so

---

[1] That is not new. Woodrow Wilson wrote in 1887: "The field of administration is a field of business. It is removed from the hurry and strife of politics . . . It is a part of the political life only as the methods of the counting house are part of the life of society." ("The Study of Administration," *Political Science Quarterly*, 2 [1887] as reprinted in *Classics of Public Administration, ed. Jay M. Shafritz and Albert C. Hyde.* [Oak Park, Ill.: Moore Publishing, 1978], p. 3.) The borders and distinctions have, however, grown more interesting as the following chapters will demonstrate, particularly as mechanics surrender to analysis.

some feature must distinguish them from goods and services provided privately. (The feature certainly is not importance to life, as virtually all governments, foreign and domestic, leave provision of food, clothing, and usually shelter, to the private sector.) This feature—shortly to be described as nonappropriability—both prevents private provision and limits the extent to which business management techniques can be applied in fiscal administration. Thus, this initial section examines the nature of public services that renders them the unique province of government.

THE BASIS FOR GOVERNMENT ACTION: NONAPPROPRIABILITY

Governments exist to provide services to people which businesses or individuals are unwilling or unable to provide independently. Richard Musgrave identifies three economic functions of government.[2] The first function, stabilization and growth, involves the combat against unemployment and inflation and provision for increases in the standard of living for the citizenry. The second function is distribution, the correction of perceived injustices in the distribution of wealth in society. That presumably means taking from the well-to-do and improving the conditions of the less well-to-do. The third function is allocation, the provision of public or collective goods. These are goods or services which are socially desirable but which ordinary business firms cannot be expected to provide in desirable amounts. The reasons for their reluctance to provide public goods will become apparent shortly.

Such market failure, "the failure of a more or less idealized system of price-market institutions to sustain 'desirable' activities or to estop 'undesirable' activities," is the logical basis of government actions in market economies, so our essential concern is with this allocation function.[3] What about these goods makes them public? Why can private action not be relied on to provide police and fire protection, education, national defense, and so on? Individuals do demand these services, and we expect businesses to provide services demanded. Quite simply, business will not provide them because it will be unable to charge a price for

---

[2] Richard A. Musgrave, *The Theory of Public Finance* (New York: McGraw-Hill, 1959), p. 5.

[3] Francis M. Bator, "The Anatomy of Market Failure," *Quarterly Journal of Economics,* August 1958, p. 351. Public goods are only one type of market failure, but they are the basis for budgeting, taxation, and other parts of fiscal administration. Other failures create the need for government regulation of electric utilities, railroads, and so on. Those will not be considered here.

the service sufficient to cover the cost of resources used to provide that service (including a normal profit for the firm).

The public-good problem is one of excluding those who have not paid for the good from receipt of services from that good.[4] If someone pays for a public good, everyone in the immediate area will receive the services of that public good. Thus, if Lombardi in apartment 10A pays for fire protection, Banks in adjoining apartment 10B receives some of that protection, regardless of any payment by Banks. That illustrates the nonappropriability feature: the inability of a provider to receive all returns from his purchase of a service. Nonappropriability includes two elements, as diagrammed in Figure 1–1, which distinguishes private

FIGURE 1–1
The elements of nonappropriability

| | Exhaustion | |
	Alternate use	Joint use
Feasible	Private goods	Toll goods
Not feasible	Common pool resources	Public goods

Exclusion

goods, public goods, and two intermediate kinds of goods, toll goods and common property resources. The initial element is failure of exclusion: there is no way to prevent people from receiving the service even though they have not paid for it. The other element is nonexhaustion: one person's use of the service does not preclude anyone else from concurrent full use of the service. Private goods do not have appropriability problems: one person's use eliminates the possibility of anyone else using it, and exclusion is feasible. Obviously, the full range of ordinary commodities and services (bread, milk, etc.) fall into this private-good class. The only way an individual can receive the benefits from a private good is by paying for it; there are no effects on others, and it is possible to separate payers from nonpayers.

---

[4] A more complete analysis of public goods may be found in "The Welfare Foundations of Public Finance Theory," the first chapter of John G. Head, *Public Goods and Public Welfare* (Durham, N.C.: Duke University Press, 1974).

Public goods include services, such as national defense, mosquito abatement, pollution control, and disease control. The common characteristics of these services are that once they are made available, separation of those who have paid from those who haven't paid is impossible, and any number of people can consume the same good at the same time without diminishing the amount of good available for anyone else to consume. The most obvious example of a pure public good is national defense. If one person in Detroit is protected against thermonuclear attack now, others in Detroit would be protected as well. In fact, most people in the midwestern United States and part of Canada would have exactly the same level of protection. The service, once provided, can be consumed by a large number of people without diminishing the amount of service available to others, and no mechanism is available to deny service to those not paying for it.

Some goods have one characteristic of the public good but not both (as shown in Figure 1–1) and are not public goods. These are toll goods and common pool resources. Toll goods have the nonexhaustion characteristic: one person can consume the service to its fullest while leaving the same amount of the service for someone else to consume. For these goods, however, exclusion is feasible; boundaries can separate payers and nonpayers. Examples include drive-in movies and toll roads: up to a congestion point, a larger number of people can consume these services without exhausting the service concurrently available to others. Neither are public because those not paying can be prevented from receiving the service—by fences or toll barriers.

Common pool resources are goods or services for which exclusion is not feasible, but there are competing and exhaustive uses. Examples include water from underground pools, oil deposits, gas deposits, or fisheries. There are no normal barriers allowing people to exercise normal property rights on the resource, but the resource, when used, becomes unavailable for others to use. Left to private processes, these resources may be rapidly used because the resource is valuable and in its natural state is not subject to normal ownership controls (first come, first served is a normal allocation principle).

Within the range of exclusion failure, if somebody provides the service, all receive that service. When one structure in an urban area receives fire protection, nearby structures receive protection as well, given the propensity of fires to spread. Obviously there are geographic limits to that range of nonappropriability: fire protection provided in Bloomington, Indiana, will not extend to the people in Jackson, Mississippi. Within that geographic area, however, all receive the service regardless of payment made for it, whether they want it or not. Such is the special monopoly position of governments: not only are alternate providers unavailable, but residents do not have the option of not paying for the services because revenue systems operate independently from service delivery. A governor of Kentucky recognized the difference between operating the state and operating his successful business: "Hell, governing Kentucky is easier than running Kentucky Fried Chicken. There's no competition."[5] There is no competition because only one state governs in Kentucky and because no private firms will provide the services provided by the state. The former occurs because American rules of government define geographic boundaries for government; the latter, because those services are nonappropriable and, hence, cannot feasibly be sold at market. Paying regardless of preference or consumption is, of course, a unique feature of government provision.

Provision of a good or service by a government does not render that good or service a public good; whether the good is public depends on its appropriability. Furthermore, government provision does not necessarily require government production. Provision ensures that the good is available for consumption, generally at no direct charge to the user. Private production could be through contract with the providing government. The production choice should be made according to which producer would produce the desired quantity and quality of service at least cost to the providing government.

Some cities, especially in California, have provided a full range of services entirely by contract. Such an arrangement is called the Lakewood Plan after an early contract city.[6] Production by contract is probably limited by the ability to design a contract specifying the service qualities to be delivered more than by anything else. Even parts of the judicial system may be privately produced: California permits litigants to hire private jurists when court congestion or special expertise makes such procedure attractive to both parties.[7]

Our focus primarily is with public goods, the class of goods and services for which private action will fail to provide the desired service because the private supplier cannot effectively charge for the service. Business firms provide goods and services because they intend to make money, not for the sheer enjoyment of providing the goods or services. If it is not possible to charge people for the use of the good or service, a business firm will seldom provide the service. Occasionally governments will provide private goods and almost always do a very bad job

---

[5] Governor John Y. Brown, Jr., quoted in *Newsweek,* March 30, 1981.

[6] Robert Bish, *The Public Economy of Metropolitan Areas* (Chicago: Markham Publishing, 1971), p. 85.

[7] "California Is Allowing Its Wealthy Litigants to Hire Private Jurists," *The Wall Street Journal,* August 6, 1980.

of it. Organizational problems, particularly lack of appropriate production incentives, cause high cost, undesirable production strategies, and a bland product designed by an uneasy consensus. Governments do provide toll goods (highways, bridges, etc.), and sometimes they do about as well as the private producer would do. Evidence is, however, that fewer resources will be wasted if government avoids provision of private goods.

PUBLIC CHOICES AND PUBLIC FINANCE

Building social decisions from individual preferences

The logic of moving from individual choice to choices made by society as a whole is built on a few fairly simple tenets. First, individuals are the best judges of their own well-being and will generally act to improve well-being as they see it. There is no scientific principle which leads us to reject or accept the judgments made by individuals about their own lives. Second, the welfare of the community depends on the welfare of the individuals in that community. In other words, communities are made up of the people in them. From that comes the third tenet, judging the impact of a social action on the welfare of the community. The Pareto criterion, named after a 19th century economist, holds that if at least one person is better off from a policy action and no person is worse off, then the community as a whole is unambiguously better off for that policy.[8] Does a social action harming anyone, despite improving the condition of many individuals, improve the welfare of society as a whole? It cannot be indisputably argued that such an action improves the well-being of society, regardless of the numbers made better off, because the relative worth of those harmed cannot scientifically be compared with those helped. Such a proposed policy would fail the Pareto criterion for judging social action.[9]

With those standards we can analyze the implications of nonappropriability on public provision. Suppose that only five people are influenced by construction of a harbor on a lake. The cost of that harbor is $9,000. Each individual in this community knows the maximum sacrifice

[8] Vilfredo Pareto, *Manuel d'economie politique,* 2d ed., pp. 617–18.

[9] Benefit-cost analysis, an analytic technique which will be discussed in a later chapter, employs a less restricting and somewhat less logically appealing rule than the Pareto criterion. This is the Kaldor criterion, which holds that a social action improves community welfare if those benefiting from a social action could hypothetically compensate in full the losers from that action and still have gain left over. Because no compensation need actually occur, losers can remain and the Pareto criterion would not be met.

that he or she would be willing to make to have that harbor as compared to having no harbor at all. These are the individual benefit numbers in Figure 1–2. The harbor would be a public good: each individual could use it without using up capacity available for anyone else, and exclusion of nonpayers is not feasible.

FIGURE 1–2

Individual	Individual benefit
A	3,000
B	3,500
C	2,000
D	3,000
E	2,500

First, would the harbor get built without public action (by individual action only)? The cost of the harbor is $9,000, the most that any single individual (individual B) will pay to get the harbor built is $3,500. Thus, the harbor would not be produced by any single individual. If the harbor only costs $3,250 to construct, however, we suspect individual B would build the harbor for his benefit and four other people in the community would receive benefits from the harbor without payment. Once the harbor is there, it is available for all because it has the public good features. The initially presumed construction cost is, however, such that the maximum individual benefit is less than the cost of the project, so the harbor will not be built by private action.

Is the harbor socially desired, in the sense that the value of the harbor is greater than the resources going into the construction of the harbor? The social cost is the value of the resources being used up in the construction of the harbor ($9,000). The social benefit of the harbor is the sum of the improved welfares of the individuals with the harbor ($14,000). Thus, social benefits are greater than social cost so it is a desirable project for the community.[10] A responsive government would act to provide the harbor and would raise sufficient funds through the revenue structure to finance the project. Should the government levy an equal per capita tax on the community to finance the harbor ($1,800 each), all individuals would still be better off with the harbor and the tax

---

[10] A small number of people may construct the harbor without the full coercion of government. Individuals A, B, and D could form a little yacht club: the sum of benefits to those three exceeds the cost. Those people might agree privately to build the harbor for their use, and the benefits would spill over to C and E.

than without either. Government can thus provide a desired service which public good features prevent private action from providing.

A second example yields additional insights. Presume that the community receives benefits from a project as in Figure 1–3. The cost of the

FIGURE 1–3

Individual	Individual benefit	Cost share	Individual gain
A	2,000	1,300	700
B....................	1,500	1,300	200
C....................	2,000	1,300	700
D	500	1,300	−800
E....................	200	1,300	−1100

project is $6,500. Because the sum of individual benefits ($6,200) is less than the cost of the project, the resources going into the project would be worth more in other uses than they are in the particular use being considered. Suppose, however, that the project decision will be made at a referendum among the people in the community (simple majority). The referendum also includes the method to be used to finance the project: by an equal per capita tax (project cost divided by number of people in the community, or $1,300 per person). If the people in the community vote according to their individual net gain or loss from the project (as computed in Figure 1–3), it will be approved (three for, two against). Does voter approval make the project desirable for the community? Not at all, because the project misallocates resources as it consumes resources that have a greater value in other use. The majority vote may misallocate resources when used for public decisions, as may any technique that does not involve comparisons of social cost and social return.

A third example further illustrates the limits of scientific principles in public decision making. Figure 1–4 presents individual benefits from a

FIGURE 1–4

Individual	Individual benefit	Individual payment	Individual gain
A	2,000	1,200	800
B	1,500	1,200	300
C	2,000	1,200	800
D	700	1,200	−500
E	700	1,200	−500
Total	6,900	6,000	

project with a total cost of $6,000 and an equal per capita tax method of distributing the tax burden. Total benefits do exceed total cost, so the project apparently represents an appropriate way to use scarce resources—and the project would be approved by majority vote if the people voted according to their individual gain or loss. The project does, however, leave some individuals worse off. Are the losses of D and E less important to the community than the gains of A, B, and C? That takes a value judgment about the worth of individuals to society, one which science and Pareto cannot help with.[11]

One voting rule would ensure that only projects that pass the Pareto criterion would be approved. That rule is unanimity, because we presume that people will not vote for policies contrary to their own best interest. This rule is seldom used because of the substantial cost of reaching decisions which would often result. James Buchanan and Gordon Tullock identify two elements constituting the full cost of making a community decision.[12] The first, the cost of reaching the decision, the "time and effort . . . which is required to secure agreement,"[13] rises as the percentage agreement required for the decision rises. As more of the group must agree on any issue, the investment of effort in bargaining, arguing, and discussion normally rises. That investment is a real cost because the effort could have been directed to other uses. The second element, the external costs or the cost from group "choices contrary to the individual's own interest,"[14] falls as the agreement percentage rises. (These are the costs imposed on individuals D and E in Figure 1–3 by a simple majority choice. Those costs could have been prevented by requiring a higher vote for approval.) The optimal choice percentage—the lowest combination of the two cost elements—usually would require neither unanimity nor one person rule, as the former has excessive decision costs and the latter, excessive external costs. Certain decisions are more dangerous to minorities (the losers in decisions) than others. For instance, many juries must reach a unanimous verdict because of the very high external costs that juries can place on people.

---

[11] For the project presented in Figure 1–4, it is possible to rearrange individual cost shares to compensate those losing from the project (one option: increase the payments made by A and C by 500 and reduce those made by D and E by the same amount). That is a general situation for any project in which total benefits exceed total cost. There is no possible reallocation of cost which will allow the project in Figure 1–3 pass the criterion.

[12] James M. Buchanan and Gordon Tullock, *The Calculus of Consent* (Ann Arbor: University of Michigan Press, 1962), chaps. 6–8.

[13] Ibid., p. 68.

[14] Ibid., p. 64.

For similar reasons, constitutional revision has high percentage vote requirements because of that danger of external costs.[15]

The paradox of voting

A further problem, the cyclical majority, infects the voting process. Kenneth Arrow demonstrated that individual preferences may not be combinable into a unique collective choice.[16] In other words, there may be no single "peoples' choice." For example, assume a three-person group; each person has an equal vote, with decisions made by majority rule. Suppose that there are three alternatives open (a school, a library, and a museum) and that each person has the specific preferences shown in Figure 1—5. The voting paradox emerges when options are

FIGURE 1—5
Alternatives: School, library, museum

Preferences of individual A:
  library, museum, school
Preferences of individual B:
  museum, school, library
Preferences of individual C:
  school, library, museum

considered two at a time. In a comparison of the library against the museum, the library is the preferred alternative of two of the three individuals (Figure 1— 6). If the library then competes against the school,

FIGURE 1—6
Voting results

Library versus museum—library chosen.
Library versus school—school chosen.
School versus museum—museum chosen.

the school is the choice of two of the three people. To test the consistency of the result: if now the school competes with the museum, the museum is the choice of two of the three people. Thus, there is no

---

[15] Majority votes can be structured to approve only projects that meet the social benefit greater than social cost criterion if projects are financed solely from benefit-base charges.

[16] Kenneth J. Arrow, *Social Choice and Individual Values* (New York: John Wiley & Sons, 1951).

alternative which is the consistent choice and there is no clearly preferable collective outcome: the majority choice cycles among the alternatives.

Obviously the absence of a clear winner creates a problem for the logic of democracy. If individual choices cannot be combined to generate a unique community choice, voting—the decision tool of a democracy—loses a great portion of its attractiveness. All is not lost, however: the cyclical majority will not occur if voters do not prefer either extreme policy to an intermediate policy, a property called *single peak preference.* That property may be illustrated by the following example: suppose the alternatives being considered are (*a*) raise teachers' salaries by $1,000, (*b*) raise teachers' salaries by $500, (*c*) no raise for teachers' salaries. In this instance, there is a natural ordering for preferences. The ordering *a, b, c,* and *c, b, a,* are clearly plausible (more to some to none; none to some to more). Other rankings, for instance *c, a, b,* seem less plausible because they would rank the intermediate position lower than either of the two extremes. When that apparently illogical ranking is excluded, the cyclical majority will not emerge. It should also be noticed that in any voting condition based on majority rule, the alternative finally chosen will be that preferred by the individual whose preferences are median for the group (50 percent above, 50 percent below). The effect of majority-rule decision making is thus to convert the person with median preferences into the decisive party in the community.

Complications from representation

Decisions on public expenditure and taxation typically occur through a representative process, not direct election. An understanding of some elements of the representative process are needed to understand the budget and financing functions. Anthony Downs' works provide insights into the process of representation.[17] He argues that political parties in a democracy operate to obtain votes to retain the income, power, and prestige that come with being in office. Parties are not units of principle or ideals, but are primarily seekers of votes. A second presumption is a lack of perfect knowledge in the system: parties don't always know what citizens want, citizens don't always know what the government in power or its opposition has done, is doing, or should be doing to try to serve their interests. Further, information that would

---

[17] Anthony Downs, *An Economic Theory of Democracy* (New York: Harper & Row, 1956).

reduce this ignorance is expensive to acquire. The scarcity of knowledge obscures the path from citizen preferences to their votes.

Several consequences for the representative process result. First, some people are politically more important than others because they influence more votes than they cast. Equal votes don't ensure equality of influence over government action. Democratic government won't treat everyone with equal deference in a world of imperfect knowledge. Second, specialists in influencing people will appear, and some will emerge as representatives for the people. These individuals will try to convince government that the policies they support, and which directly benefit them, are good for and desired by the electorate. In turn, they will try to convince the electorate that these policies are desirable. A rational government will discount these claims, but it cannot ignore them. Information provided will reasonably be filtered to provide only data consistent with the supported cause. Third, imperfect information makes a government party susceptible to bribery simply because the party in power needs resources to persuade voters to return it to power. Parties out of power are susceptible as well, but they currently have nothing to sell. Political influence is a necessary result of imperfect information combined with the unequal distribution of income and wealth in society. Parties have to use economic resources to provide and obtain information.

Lobbying is a rational response to the lack of perfect information, but an important imbalance of interests influences the lobbying process. Suppose a direct subsidy to industry is being considered. This subsidy is of great total value to that industry. The subsidy paid by taxpayers in total is, of course, exactly equal to the subsidy received by the industry. However, each taxpayer bears a small individual share of that total subsidy. Who will undertake the expense of lobbying on the measure? The industry, not the taxpayer, because the net benefit to lobbying is positive for the industry (comparing substantial cost of lobbying with the substantial direct benefit to the industry) and negative for any taxpayer (as the substantial lobbying cost overwhelms the small individual share of the subsidy which could be saved).

A related influence on representative government is the principle of rational ignorance. Citizen effort to acquire information to cast an informed vote is usually irrational.[18] Although the cost of obtaining information may be low, the expected return of an informed vote is even lower. If others vote in an informed manner, a citizen's uninformed vote is irrelevant because the informed majority choice wins. If others vote in an uninformed manner, a citizen's informed vote is irrelevant because the choice of the uninformed majority wins. In either case, the action of

---

[18] Ibid., chap. 13.

the majority produces the election result, so individual effort to become informed yields no return. Thus, electorate choices produce indivisible benefits or costs. Information-gathering to cast informed votes will produce no electoral benefits for an individual. That, of course, is a crucial problem in any democratic society. Fortunately, many individuals become informed for other motives.

A final important point in the process of representation deals with the intensity of preference. In ordinary voting, there is no method of representing intensity of preference on particular issues. Each vote has equal weight. In a legislative body, however, trading of votes presents a method of recognizing preference intensity because a series of votes occurs on multiple issues, not just single votes. Legislators, thus, can trade votes according to intensity of preference. For example, a member of Congress may be particularly interested in the outcome on issue B but may have little concern about issue A. That representative may trade his vote on issue A for some other congressman's vote on issue B. This process, "logrolling," can produce wasteful spending (a water project yielding marginal benefit to a small area at great national cost, for instance) but it also can make it possible to improve the responsiveness of government by ensuring that intense preferences get recognized. Furthermore, the representative process has special devices for protecting the interests of minorities. These do not appear in the general referendum process. "The required majority of those voting (in a referendum) can inflict severe costs on the rest of society with dramatic consequences for the social fabric. Their major disadvantage must emerge from the absence of minority power in the direct legislation system. An initiated referendum has no provision for executive veto, creation of political stalemates in the legislative process, or changed negotiating positions in committees, all vital positions of lawmaking which can serve to protect minorities."[19]

THE CONSTRAINTS OF FEDERALISM

Three layers of relatively independent governments, not a single government, provide public services in the United States. Some understanding of their legal powers and limits are fundamental to understanding the prevailing fiscal processes. Relations among the levels are governed by national and state constitutions. The United States Constitution delimits federal authority: Article I, Section 8 lists available powers; Section 9 lists the powers denied the federal government. Of course, court decisions over time specifically define the extent of those

---

[19] John L. Mikesell, "The Season of Tax Revolt," in *Fiscal Retrenchment and Urban Policy,* ed. John P. Blair and David Nachmias (Beverly Hills, Calif.: Sage, 1979), p. 128.

powers. The federal constitution likewise enumerates in Article I, Section 10 the powers specifically denied the states. These forbidden powers are primarily in the area of conduct of foreign affairs, production of a medium of exchange (printing money), and interference with interstate commerce. The commerce clause is particularly significant for its limitations on the taxing abilities and regulatory powers of states. Other sections of the constitution apply requirements of due process and equal protection of the states. These requirements have had substantial impact on service provision processes of states, particularly as the federal constitutional requirement has often been copied in state constitutions. For instance, the dramatic change in school finance in California generated by the court case *Serrano* v. *Priest*[20] resulted from state constitutional requirements copied after the federal requirement.

The major constitutional provision for states appears in the Tenth Amendment of the U.S. Constitution (Rights reserved to states or people): "the powers not delegated to the United States by the Constitution, nor prohibited by it to the states, are reserved to the states respectively, or to the people." The states, thus, have residual powers. The constitution does not need to provide specific authority for a state government to have a particular power: constitutional silence implies that the state can act in the area in question. States are the unique "middle layer" in the federal system. In unitary governments, the middle layer between the national government and cities may not exist, or it may be simply a department of the central government. In the United States states exist as an independent layer of government with full powers (including independent financial authority) and all residual powers.

Local governments in the United States typically appear as captive creatures of their state, unless that relationship has been specifically altered by state action. The principle was defined by Judge J. F. Dillon of Iowa:

> It is a general and undisputed proposition of law that a municipal corporation possesses and can exercise the following powers and no others: First, those granted in express words; second, those necessarily or fairly implied in or incident to the powers expressly granted; third, those essential to the declared objects and purposes of the corporation—not simply convenient, but indispensable. Any fair, reasonable, substantive doubt concerning the existence of power is resolved by the courts against the corporation, and the power denied.[21]

---

[20] 5 Cal. 3d 584, 487 P. 2d 1241, 97 Cal. Reptr. 601 (1971).

[21] John F. Dillon, *Commentaries on the Law of Municipal Corporations,* 5th ed. (Boston: Little, Brown, 1911), vol. 1, sec. 237.

Dillon's rule thus holds that if state law is silent about a particular local power the presumption is that the local level lacks that power. In state–local relationships, state government holds all powers. That is a critical limitation on local government fiscal activity.

Several states have altered Dillon's rule by granting home rule charter powers to particular local governments. Such powers are particularly prevalent in states containing a small group of large metropolitan areas with conditions substantially different from the environment in other areas of the state. The special conditions of such large cities can be handled by providing them home rule charter power to govern their own affairs. State law can thus proceed without being cluttered by numerous special enactments for the larger units. When charter powers have been provided, local governments can act in all areas unless state law specifically prohibits those actions. Many times, however, fiscal activities are included in the range of areas that are prohibited under charter powers. Thus it is better to presume limits than to presume local freedom to choose in fiscal affairs. That presumption is accurate if Dillon's rule applies or if charter powers have been constrained in fiscal activities.

Conclusion

An overview of the basis for government action certainly indicates that government choices made in budgeting and revenue raising will not be simple. Government will be unable to sell its services because these services are nonappropriable (neither excludable nor exhaustible). That means that government won't have normal market tests available to help it with choices.

Governments surely don't want to waste resources—after all, resources are scarce and most things used by government do have alternative uses—so the benefit to society from government action ought to exceed the cost to society from that action. Determining whether actions really improve the condition of the community gets complicated, however, when there is no basis for making comparisons of the worth of individuals. The Pareto criterion for judging—the welfare of a community is improved if some members are made better off by an action and no one is made worse off by it—has no logical flaws and does not require interpersonal judgments, but it leaves many choices open to political decision. Despite sophistication and rigor, science and analysis will not provide definitive answers to many government choices.

Votes, either on issues or for representatives, will settle many decisions. Direct votes will not, however, guarantee no wasteful public decisions or choices which satisfy the Pareto criterion for improving society, and can impose substantial costs on minorities. Further, the cyclical majority property can prevent a clear public choice from emerging from individual preferences. Some problems of direct choice are reduced when representatives make decisions, but there will remain imbalances of influence and posturing to continue in office rather than to follow clearly defined principles.

Finance in a representative democracy is not simple. Success ought to be judged on its general responsiveness to public preferences and on its refusal to ignore minority positions. Not all governments can meet those simple standards and not all budget systems used in the United States do much to contribute to those objectives. The U.S. structure delivers and finances services using three tiers of government—federal, state, and local. Although independent in some respects, there are important mutual constraints. The federal level has powers delimited in the U.S. Constitution; the states have residual powers. Local governments—under Dillon's rule—have only powers expressly granted by their states. Some states grant local home rule, giving localities all powers save those expressly prohibited them. Few home rule authorizations are complete, however. Thus, budget and finance occurs with much variety across the country.

A CASE FOR DISCUSSION

This article, excerpted from *The Wall Street Journal,* appeared early in New York City's battle to gain control over its finances. Use the article and the fundamentals outlined in Chapter 1 to appraise the situation.

Consider these questions:

1. What can business principles provide public financial management?
2. What choices must be left to elected officials?
3. Are there any guides to drawing that important line?

Penney's Ken Axelson Finds Running a City Is Figures and People

BY FREDERICK ANDREWS
Staff Reporter of THE WALL STREET JOURNAL

NEW YORK—Kenneth S. Axelson is the very model of a corporate money man. As the senior vice president and chief financial officer of J. C. Penney Company his life flows with calculated precision. "You plan, you organize, and you program accordingly—and it all works," he says.

But since last September Ken Axelson has been experiencing a very different kind of life. It is a world that would seem to defy planning and controls and where agonizing choices have to be made that will affect the lives of millions.

Mr. Axelson is a businessman in city government. As New York's deputy mayor for finance, on loan for a year from his company, he has been working night and day to help stave off the city's financial collapse and to scale down the city's swollen (and often chaotic) operations to help it live within its means. In the process he has become a man in the middle, caught between the disparate worlds of business and politics.

Trying to organize a city's finances has little relation to the closed, secure corporate world, he is finding. "You get to the office at 8 A.M., and by five after the whole day is shot. The mayor is calling, the governor is calling . . . and

in public life there are so many different people coming at you all the time, all with legitimate demands on your time."

New York's highly unusual action in turning to the business world for help in sorting out its tangled financial affairs is not only promising to bring order to the city's accounts but also is beginning to restore the financial world's and the public's badly shaken confidence in the effectiveness of the nation's largest municipal administration.

But should other businessmen similarly be attracted to helping out struggling city administrations, Mr. Axelson would warn them that municipal budget-cutting, unlike corporate belt-tightening, poses the most agonizing social choices. Already, with the city's financial crisis far from over, thousands of city employees have lost their jobs, all new city construction has been stopped, libraries are being closed, centers for preschoolers shut down, police patrols cut back, support for foster children frozen, and fire stations closed.

"It's a terrible responsibility making these judgments," he frets. "When you are in a position to wield enormous power, it's very easy to make enormous mistakes."

Deferring to the Mayor

Not surprisingly, the unprecedented exercising of influence by nonelected officials has stirred fears in

New York of "economic czars" riding roughshod over the democratic process and slashing services vital to the city's poor.

But the businessmen [brought into New York City government], to the disappointment of their critics, have not done this. Certainly they have pushed the city hard to meet its cost-cutting goals. But, observers say, they have consistently shown caution and have deferred to Mayor Abraham Beame and his aides in deciding which programs to cut. And because they are not politicians they try to ignore the pressures from interest groups to dictate to the mayor.

"It isn't clear that the businessmen have done any more than provide an image and some tough language," says Gary Sperling, executive director of the Citizens Union, a civic group.

Three of the most talented of these businessmen sit on the Emergency Financial Control Board, which was created by the state last September to take over the city's fiscal powers.

Although the control board has final authority over New York City's spending, it is up to the 53-year-old Mr. Axelson, the city's main spokesman before the board, to push the city to bring its spending into line. At the same time, he must protect the city from what he views as the occasionally excessive demands of the board.

The Super Bookkeeper

Mr. Axelson didn't volunteer for this exhausting job. He was brought in to placate the financial community, which had lost faith in the city's ability to organize its affairs (in fact, Mayor Beame's closest aide, James A. Cavanagh, became an anathema on Wall Street and was forced to resign).

So far, New York's creditors are mostly happy with Mr. Axelson's performance as a super bookkeeper threading his way through a morass of detail without getting bogged down. It was this ability to master fine details that won him a reputation as a meticulous money strategist during Penney's period of greatest growth. A certified public accountant, he joined the $7 billion retail company in 1963 after working for Peat, Marwick, Mitchell & Company. (Penney is continuing to pay his salary, which is in the $150,000 range, during his year with the city.)

One of his greatest assets, say his admirers, is his candor. It is generally agreed that he made Penney's annual report a model of disclosure by providing information on areas that many companies prefer to keep hidden, such as details on minority hiring. "He would get up at analysts' meetings and talk about bad news without burying it," observes one veteran financial reporter.

A major job during this year with the city has been to assemble what amounts to a massive blueprint for balancing the city's budget by 1977–78. The control board's major function is to supervise this plan. To get it under way, two deadlines were set. By last September 30 the board had to give Mr. Axelson estimates of the city's future revenues. By October 15 he had to give the board a plan for bringing the city's spending into line with these projected revenues.

(At the same time, Mr. Axelson had to develop a "doomsday" plan: the exact steps the city would follow if it fell into default. He decided he would take the pragmatic approach of shutting down much of the city, including schools, and then resuming services only as money came in.)

The three-year spending plan the city submitted to the board last October was a job of forecasting probably never before attempted by any other city. Just to predict one portion of the city's future cash needs required checking thousands of contracts to see when payments were due. Using computers to project tax revenues, it was calculated that the city's annual spending of about $12 billion had to be cut by $724 million over three years.

None of this information has been easy to get. Mr. Axelson found he had inherited an antiquated and crazy-quilt accounting system (the city's published financial reports, many say, were barely comprehensible). The city also lacked any internal machinery for matching actual outlays and receipts against budgeted amounts.

And just to add complications, no single official is responsible for the city's finances. The mayor controls the budget and thus the pace of spending. The city controller, Harrison J. Goldin (also as elected official) keeps the books, manages the cash, and pays the bills.

Before Mr. Axelson returns to Penney he feels his most important accomplishment as deputy mayor will have been to launch a modern accounting system to monitor the city's finances and to bridge the gap between mayor and controller. To help in this, American Management Systems, of Arlington, Virginia, and Touche Ross & Company, the international accounting firm, have been brought in at a cost of $600,000.

Despite his candor and transparent goodwill (one city councilman calls him "a gentle soul") Mr. Axelson has proved a keen disappointment to those city critics who want upheaval, not mind-numbing financial plans. In their view, the depty mayor fell too readily into traditional City Hall thinking. When he gave a speech pointing out how little room the city had to maneuver, one banker declared, "I was aghast. He gave a speech that could just as easily been given by Beame or Cavanagh. Another prominent financial figure asserts that "he should have gone in and taken hold much more vigorously."

Mr. Axelson replies that it is so much easier to criticize from the outside. He recalls that before he took over the job, "my wife, the doorman, and I, between us, thought we had all the city's problems solved." His major role, he insists, "is to see that the decisions are made." The decisions themselves should be left to elected officials, he says.

Part of the problem is that Mr. Axelson and the business members of the control board are being pressed to rule on the funding of many major social programs, decisions they feel unqualified to make. Thus they prefer to defer to Mayor Beame. (In fact the control board, unwilling to be caught up in politics, won't even force funding decisions on areas, such as the city university and hospitals, which are included in the city's new financial plan but are not directly controlled by Mayor Beame.)

Perhaps Mr. Axelson can't be blamed for veering away from these decisions because of the inevitable occasions when he has been exposed as a political neophyte. Early on, he became caught up in one of the most emotional issues in New York: the funding of the city university and its bitterly debated free tuition and open enrollment. Mr. Axelson sought to end the argument by pointing out the city simply couldn't afford to continue spending $100 million a year on the university.

In the corporate boardroom that observation would have brought applause and immediate action. In the city, he was faced with stubborn resistance from the university's supporters. And though the university seems destined to run out of money this spring, no final decisions on funding have yet been made.

On another occasion Mr. Axelson urged that the state legislature increase city taxes on commuters to the city. But the idea was swiftly blocked by legislators from the suburbs.

This lack of teamwork (teamwork being the essence of corporate life), still mystifies Mr. Axelson. He is shocked at the changing alliances and the cross-purposes of politics. Last fall, for example, he discovered that Gov. Carey apparently planned to propose harsher city tax increases than those agreed on only the previous evening by city and state officials. "The damn games they play," he fumed. "They never said *anything*. The world collapsing around us—you would think people would go out of their way to pull together. I just don't understand it."

Nor did Mr. Axelson appreciate being lectured by congressmen at Washington hearings on federal aid for the city last fall. "I haven't been spoken to like that since I was a kid," he says.

He considers the effort worth it. For in the process of helping change the city, he feels the city is also helping to change him and to enable him to step back from his insulated corporate world.

Recently, late in the afternoon of the final day before the state housing agency was about to default, an alarmed U.S. Treasury official told him that default would also create several problems for the city. Mr. Axelson recalls simply saying, "Relax, there are six hours yet to go." And, in fact, the state legislature passed bills to save the agency at 11:19 that night.

But, says Mr. Axelson, if that incident had happened three months before, "my heart would have stopped beating."

PART ONE

Budgeting, budget
structures, and
budget reform

The logic and process of budgets

The budget process—a formalized routine involving legislative and executive branches of government—plays a key role in the provision of public goods and services. This process fulfills tasks similar to those of an economic market as it determines what government services are provided, what individuals will receive these services, and how these services will be provided. Except for the limited number of town meeting and referenda decisions, elected representatives make the primary spending decisions. In budget preparation, nonelected public employees make many crucial decisions. While these employees enjoy employment security and may be less responsive to public demands for service than those elected, the logic of representative government presumes that such bureaucrats can be made to respond to executive or legislative dictates flowing from the citizenry. A complete understanding of public expenditures obviously requires an understanding of the budget process.

Public agencies can operate with a haphazard budget process. An effectively operating process that includes incentives for officials to respond to public demands is most likely to produce consistently good decisions. A good public decision will provide citizens with the quantity and quality of public services they desire, at times and locations they desire them, at least cost to society. At a minimum, the process must recognize competing claims on resources and should focus directly on the questions of alternatives and options. A major portion of the process will involve presentation of accurate and relevant information to individuals making budget decisions.

BUDGET LOGIC AND FORM

The market process allocates private resources without a need for outside intervention; price movements serve as an automatic signal transmission device for resource flows. In the public sector, decisions about resource use cannot be made automatically because of the special features of services typically provided by government. First, there can be no sale of government services and consequently profit can neither measure success nor serve as an incentive. The nonappropriability of public goods effectively destroys the possibility of profit. Second, public and private resource constraints differ dramatically. While individual earnings constrain spending of private entities, governments are limited only by the total resources of the society.[1] There are obviously political limits to tax extractions, but those limits differ dramatically from revenue limits on a private firm. Third, governments characteristically operate as perfect monopolies. Consumers cannot purchase from an alternate supplier and, more importantly, the consumer must pay whether or not the good provided is used. And finally, public actions are undertaken in an environment of mixed motives. In many instances, not only the service provided but also the recipients of the service (redistribution) or the mere fact of provision (stabilization) are important. For example, free school lunches may be provided to improve the living standard of families with school children or to increase the income of food producers, even though more economical methods may be available to achieve these objectives. Accordingly, more may matter in the provision of a public service than simply the direct return from the service compared to its cost. Because these multiple and mixed objectives cannot be weighted scientifically, the budget process will be political, involving both pure bargaining strategies and scientific analysis.

Budgeting allocates resources among government activities and between government and private use. While those allocations are being made, the budget process erects a framework for control, accountability, and evaluation of government activity. Systems of budget and revenue raising are separable planning processes because nonappropriability ensures that payment for a service cannot be a precondition for receipt of service. Budgeting is a process of allocating resources to

---

[1] Few have dared suggest natural limits to the ability of governments to extract resources from society since Colin Clark's proposition of several years ago: "25 percent of the national income is about the limit for taxation in any nontotalitarian community in times of peace." ("Public Finance and Changes in the Value of Money," *The Economic Journal* 55 [December 1945]: 380.) That limit has been exceeded by Western nations for years, although in fairness to Clark, his limit was based on zero inflation—so it may not have been truly tested.

prevent waste of scarce resources: setting the size of the public sector and deciding what government activities are supported from that pool of public resources. The budget process establishes what gets produced, how it gets produced, and who gets the production. Revenue raising, then, is a planning process that determines how private individuals will share the burden distribution of the public sector. Revenue planning determines whose real income will be reduced by extraction of resources to deliver the budgeted services.[2] The total resources used must equal total resources raised, but the profile of government expenditure does not establish the appropriate distribution of the cost of government services. Our first focus is on budget process. Revenue planning will be examined in later chapters.

Some terminology of the budgeting and spending process

Budgets are simply plans denominated in dollar terms. They get developed as a means for establishing executive branch plans, for providing legislative branch approval of those plans, and for providing a control and review structure for executive implementation of approved plans. The language of budgeting and spending includes a number of concepts which often get confused, with resulting errors in understanding. These concepts need to be clarified before starting formal consideration of the budget process. Budgets begin as *agency requests.* The agency request is built on an agency *plan* for service in an upcoming year (the agency response to public demands for service) and an agency forecast of conditions in the upcoming year (the group of conditions influencing the agency but not subject to agency control).[3] For example, a state department of highways' request for funds for snow removal would involve a *forecast* of the number of snowy days and a *planned response* for handling that snow. Some agencies build their plans on inputs (the highway department bought 120 tons of road salt last year, so it will request about that amount for the budget year); this approach makes changes in service delivery difficult. The public service demands will be forecasts, but agency responses will be plans formulated from decisions and forecasts.

The *budget document,* or executive budget, incorporates all agency requests into a government-wide request or plan. The requests by the agencies have been accumulated and aggregated according to the pol-

---

[2] John L. Mikesell, "Government Decisions in Budgeting and Taxing: The Economic Logic", *Public Administration Review* 38 (November/December 1978).

[3] These are *forecasts,* or best estimates of conditions in the future; they are not necessarily *projections,* or simple extensions of prevailing conditions to the future.

icy directives of the chief executive. Agency requests will almost always be reduced by the chief executive to produce an overall executive plan. As will be discussed later, the substantial changes made in agency requests even before the proposals are seen by the legislature reflect differences in attitudes and service clienteles of the agencies and the chief executive.

The budget document is transmitted to the legislature for debate and consideration. The outcome of the legislative process are *appropriations,* laws which provide funds for operating agencies to spend in a specified fashion in the budget year. The initial requests by the agency reflect the plans of that agency; appropriation converts these plans (or portions of them) into legal intentions of the government.

Appropriations provide agencies with resources to make *expenditures,* the acquisition of resources by the agency during the year. Expenditure occurs when the unit pays for goods or services delivered by some supplier. Expenditure (or spending) is the direct result of appropriations made to carry out the service delivery envisioned in the agency's initial budget plan. Because, however, expenditures can involve the acquisition of resources for use both in the present period and in the future, it would not generally be correct to view the amount of expenditure to be exactly equal to the current cost of providing government services. Some of expenditure now will provide services in later periods. (In simplest terms, part of the road salt purchased this year may be used next year, but much of the difference between expenditure and service cost will be caused by capital assets, such as buildings, trucks, computers, and so on.) The cost of government would equal the amount of resources used or consumed during the period, some resources coming from expenditure in that period and some from expenditures made in earlier periods. Focus on expenditure will thus not render an entirely accurate view of the cost of government.

At the federal level, only appropriation and historical reports of spending and revenue are mentioned in the Constitution:

> Article 1., Sec. 9 [7]   No money shall be drawn from the treasury, but in consequence of appropriations made by law; and a regular statement and account of the receipts and expenditures of all public money shall be published from time to time.

Budgeting procedures have developed in practice and through a handful of laws passed to improve the decision process. The foundation for the federal budget process came from the Budget and Accounting Act of 1921, the Act which produced the first federal executive budget and established both the General Accounting Office and the Bureau of the Budget (now the Office of Management and Budget).

Orientations of a budget

Provision of services is the sole reason for governments. The budget period provides a time for examination of the public services desired by the public and of the options available to the government for providing these services. If governments budget simply to prevent public officials from stealing (a traditional attitude toward budgeting), the implication is that government does nothing useful and is little more than an expensive nuisance. A mental inventory of services to individuals, business, and the environment should lead to rejection of that implication and the associated attitude toward budgeting. Public financial managers recognize that properly designed budget procedures serve three important functions: (1) expenditure control; (2) management and efficiency; and (3) planning for service requirements.[4]

The expenditure control function in budgeting involves legality of transactions conducted by the agency. Expenditures must be in agreement with appropriation: they cannot exceed appropriation nor be for purposes different from appropriation. They must coincide with the intent of the legislature. The control function helps develop information for cost estimates used in preparation of new budgets and in preserving audit trails after budget years are over. (An audit trail is a sequence of documents—invoices, receipts, canceled checks, etc.—which allows an outside observer to trace transactions involving appropriated money: when the money was spent and who received it, when purchases were delivered and what price was paid, how the purchases were cared for and used, and what the final disposition of those purchases was.) Budgets were initially developed at the municipal level in the United States to prevent thievery, pure and simple. Budgeting and appropriating given amounts of dollars for the purchase of given quantities of inputs simplified the determination of whether legislative intent had been carried through during the year: were payments made according to appropriation? If the appropriation was for the purchase of 10 tons of gravel, was that gravel actually purchased?

Budgets also serve as a tool to increase managerial control of operating units and improve efficiency in agency operations. This function focuses on the performance activities of governments and does not dwell on inputs or resources purchased by the unit. The important concern is the relationship between the resources used by a department and the public services performed by that department. The public

---

[4] Allen Schick, "The Road to PPB: The Stages of Budget Reform," *Public Administration Review*, 26 (December 1966): 243–58.

budget—as in ordinary business—serves as the control device for the government and points up the efficiency in operation of departments. For this purpose, the unit must consider what measurable activities it performs—an often difficult, but seldom impossible, task.

The final budget function recognizes that governments face many opportunities for provision of services and that present actions both influence and are influenced by development of the community. The budget formulation period presents an ideal opportunity to consider these implications in an organized framework. Any budget item that has clear implications for spending patterns in the future (a new sewage treatment plant that will require operating expenses in the future, for instance) ought to be considered as an element of long-range plans during budget deliberation. The planning orientation uses the budget as a decision tool concerning continuation of activities, development of new programs, and allocation of resources between activities of government.

Each of these are potential uses of a public budget and each can have a role in the budget procedures of public units. The process used by state, local, and federal governments are subject to substantial individual peculiarities. The treatment here will focus on elements common to most public budget processes with special mention only of the most important peculiarities.

Budget decisions and the provision flow

Budgets can focus on three different points in the flow of government activity from the purchase of resources through the provision of the services desired by the general public. Governments seek to improve the general standard of living of citizenry by using resources in reasonable fashion. Their operations in this respect are not dissimilar to those of private business: resources are acquired for use in a process to produce a valued output. Figure 2–1 outlines that flow of service provision. The government buys asphalt, crushed stone, and so on. These inputs are used to fill chuckholes and resurface streets. Those activities improve road quality to reduce commuting time, lessen damage to vehicles from driving over roads in poor condition, and reduce vehicle accidents. That output improves the well-being of members of the community. Thus, the inputs acquired are used to the ultimate benefit of the community.

Some budget structures and procedures focus on *inputs* (the resources—labor, machines, supplies, buildings, etc.—acquired) in the flow of service provision. Object-of-expenditure, or line-item, budget classifications are structured for that focus. The budget in Figure 2–2—the budget for the Office of Historical Preservation, a small seg-

FIGURE 2–1

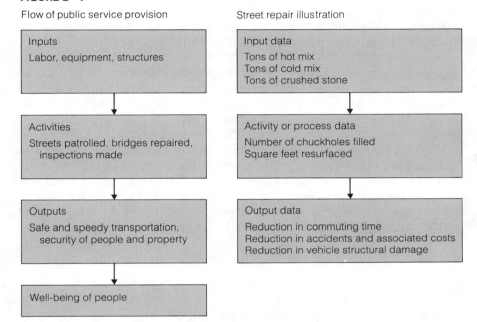

Flow of public service provision

Street repair illustration

Inputs
Labor, equipment, structures

Input data
Tons of hot mix
Tons of cold mix
Tons of crushed stone

Activities
Streets patrolled, bridges repaired, inspections made

Activity or process data
Number of chuckholes filled
Square feet resurfaced

Outputs
Safe and speedy transportation, security of people and property

Output data
Reduction in commuting time
Reduction in accidents and associated costs
Reduction in vehicle structural damage

Well-being of people

FIGURE 2–2
Object-of-expenditure budget classification for an office of historic preservation in a municipal department of metropolitan development

Element class	Request
1. Personnel services:	
1.1 Regular employees	$17,050
1.6 Holiday pay	525
2. Contractural services:	
2.1 Utilities	
2.1.2 Water and sewer........................	5,000
2.1.3 Electricity...............................	9,600
2.2 Communications	
2.1.1 Telephone	360
2.7 Printing and advertising	1,000
2.8 Subscriptions and memberships	1,200
3. Supplies:	
3.2 General	
3.2.1 Postage and office supplies..............	875
4. Capital expense and outlay:	
4.5 Lease	4,800
5. Other charges:	
5.2 Personnel expenses	
5.2.3 Employee benefits	3,520
Total	$43,930

ment of the Department of Metropolitan Development in a large city—
illustrates that classification. All request entries are for items to be purchased by the organizational unit. (An example of object classification
structure appears in an appendix to this chapter.)

While traditional budgets organize by administrative departments
and inputs acquired, some governments attempt greater emphasis on
later points in the provision of service. Some organize requests around
the *activities* of government (the functions performed using resources).
Governments use the inputs that it has acquired to pave roads, to patrol
streets, to record forms, and so on. Performance budget classifications,
to be examined in a later chapter, concentrate on that level in the flow.
Activities are not, however, conducted for their own sake but in combinations to produce *outputs* of government. These outputs, a third way
of organizing requests, include provision of safe and speedy transportation, safety and security of people and property, and so on. Program
budget classifications, also examined in a later chapter, are organized
around these outputs. These outputs when received by individuals improve the standard of living for individuals in society.

THE BUDGET CYCLE

A cycle is a complete set of events or phenomena recurring in the
same sequence. Recurring (and overlapping) events in the budgeting
and spending process constitute the budget cycle. While specific activities differ among governments, any government with separation of
powers between the executive and legislative branches shows many
elements outlined here.[5] The four major stages of the cycle—executive
preparation, legislative consideration, execution, and audit—are considered in turn. The four phases recur, so at any time an operating
agency will be in different phases of different budget years. Suppose an
agency is on a July 1 to June 30 fiscal year, and the present date is May
1984. That agency would be in the execution phase of fiscal year 1984. It
would likely be in the legislative phase of the fiscal year 1985, in the
preparation phase of fiscal 1986, and in audit phase for fiscal 1983 and
prior years. Thus, the budget cycle is both continuous and overlapping,
as illustrated in Figure 2–3. The federal fiscal year begins in October;
many local governments have fiscal years beginning in January; all
state governments except Alabama, Michigan, New York, and Texas
start fiscal years in July. The fiscal year in Alabama and Michigan coin-

---

[5] A parliamentary government would not fit this cycle, for instance, because there is no
real separation between executive and legislative roles—the legislative leader is the chief
executive.

FIGURE 2-3
Phases of a budget cycle

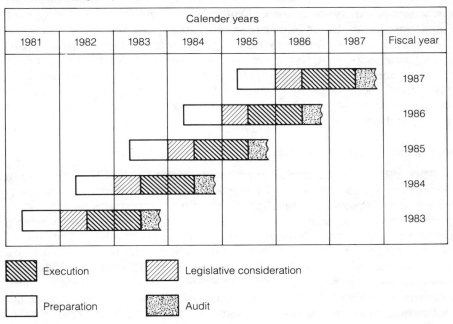

cides with the federal, but New York has an April start and Texas has a September start.

Executive preparation

Several separate and distinct steps constitute the phase of executive preparation. At the start of the preparation phase, the chief executive transmits general directions for agency request preparation. These instructions (sometimes labeled the "call for estimates") include a timetable for submissions, instructions for developing requests, and some overall priority direction to spending agencies. They may also provide forecasts of input price increases, service population trends, and so on, but not necessarily. Agencies develop an estimate of the cost of providing services it plans to deliver during the upcoming spending period and a narrative justification for the requests. These reflect the large number of program decisions that the agency has made. As Douglas Lee points out, a "budget, after all, is only an accounting of the financial cost of many political and social decisions.'"[6] The budget agency of the chief executive gathers the requests made by the operating agencies and consolidates these requests. The office reviews budget requests for consistency with the policies of the chief executive, for reasonableness of cost and logical content of the budget, and for total consistency with spending directions. Often there will be administrative hearings for reconciliations of the agency request and budget office adjustments. Finally, the executive budget document is transmitted to the legislature for its consideration. Law often establishes the date of transmission to the legislature.

Legislative consideration

After the executive has submitted the budget to the legislature, the legislature typically splits that budget into as many parts as appropriation bills will be finally passed and submits those parts to legislative subcommittees. A recent tally of the states shows that 25 usually have a single budget bill and 25 usually have multiple budget bills. Those multiples range from 2 to 450.[7] This consideration usually begins with the lower house of a bicameral legislature. In subcommittee hearings, agencies defend their requests in the budget document, often calling attention to differences between their initial request and what appears in the budget. After the lower house has approved the appropriation, the upper house goes through a similar hearing process. When both houses have approved appropriations, a conference committee from the two houses prepares a unified version for final passage by both houses and approval by the chief executive.

At the federal level, the president's options are to approve or veto the entire appropriation. Some governors have item veto powers; they can veto certain parts of an appropriation bill and approve the remainder. Some observers feel that the item veto provides a useful final screening of projects which political clout, not vitality of the project, has inserted in the appropriation bill. Others are skeptical about such power because of its possible use for executive vendettas against selected groups or agencies.

Appropriations are normally *annual* and agency funds revert to the general treasury for reallocation if not spent during the budget year. Other appropriation forms are, however, used. *Permanent* appropriations continue indefinitely without current legislative action. To add

---

[6] L. Douglas Lee, "How Congress Handles the Budget," *The Wharton Magazine,* 4 (Winter 1980): 29.

[7] James H. Bowhay and Virginia D. Thrall, *State Legislative Appropriations Process* (Chicago: Midwestern Office, Council of State Governments, 1975), p. 81.

greater certainty to public capital markets, interest on the federal debt is such an appropriation. *No year* appropriations provide specific amounts of money until the money is exhausted, without restriction placed on the year of use. Some space project appropriations have been handled on that basis. *Multiyear* appropriations provide funds for a particular activity for several years at once, specifying both the fiscal year and the amount for that year. General revenue sharing has been established on that basis. Finally, *advance* appropriation provides agencies with funds for fiscal years in the future. This structure is seldom used, although it can facilitate planning and has been strongly argued for use in defense system procurement. All appropriation types but annual reduce the ability of legislative and executive branches to realign fiscal policy when economic or social conditions change while increasing the ability of agencies to develop long-range program plans. The trade is not an easy one, but responsibility and accountability chains probably weigh the balance toward annual appropriation.

Two other methods of providing agency funds, in addition to these normal appropriations, should be mentioned. A *continuing resolution* allows agencies to function when a new fiscal year begins before agency appropriations have been made. The resolution—simply an agreement between both legislative houses—authorizes the agencies to continue operations at their prior year level, with no expansions. Without such approval, the agency could not spend and would not be able to provide services. The Congressional budget process establishes a timetable for appropriations which would eliminate the need for continuing resolutions—all appropriations bills must be passed before seven days after Labor Day. That deadline has not always been met, so federal continuing resolutions continue in use.[8] A second special form of providing funds is the *supplemental appropriation,* an appropriation of funds for spending during the current budget year. (Requests are normally for future budget years.) Thus, the budget request for fiscal 1985 which is considered during fiscal 1984 may well contain a request for funds for additional money for fiscal 1984. The request would ordinarily result because events have caused some agencies to spend more than anticipated during planning and consideration of that budget. The request is for appropriation in addition to funds previously approved by the legislature. Because of forecasting problems, most budgets will have requests for supplemental appropriation, but large supplements raise questions about the capability of those initially preparing and considering the budget.

---

[8] States occasionally end legislative sessions with neither appropriations nor continuing resolutions passed. Until a special session is held the state cannot operate.

Execution

During execution, agencies carry out their approved budgets: appropriations are spent and services are delivered. The approved budget becomes an important device to monitor spending activity. While there are other important managerial concerns, spending must proceed in a manner consistent with the appropriation laws. Law typically forbids—often with criminal sanctions—agencies from spending more money than has been appropriated.[9] Spending less than the appropriation, while a possible sign of efficient operation, may well mean that anticipated services have not been delivered or that agency budget requests were needlessly high. Finance officers must thus continuously monitor the relationship between actual expenditures and planned-approved expenditures (the appropriation) during the fiscal year.[10]

AUDIT AND EVALUATION

An audit is an "examination of records, facilities, systems, and other evidence to discover or verify desired information. Internal audits are those performed by professionals employed by the entity being audited; external audits are performed by outside professionals who are independent of the entity".[11] Information will be documented on the basis of a sample of transactions and other activities of the entity—a judgment about purchasing practices, for instance, will be made from a review of a sample of transactions, not from examination of all invoices. Post-expenditure audits determine compliance with appropriations and report findings to the legislature (or to a judicial body if laws have been violated).[12] At the federal level, the General Accounting Office supervises audits of agencies, although the actual auditing is done by agency personnel. States frequently have elected auditors or independent agencies which audit state agencies and local governments. Local governments sometimes have audits done by independent accounting firms as well as by governmental bodies, although some such governments have not frequently had independent audits.[13]

[9] The Anti-Deficiency Act of 1906 is the governing federal law; similar laws apply at state and local levels.

[10] The Office of Management and Budget handles that monitoring at the federal level.

[11] Peter F. Rousmaniere, *Local Government Auditing—a Manual for Public Officials* (New York: Council on Municipal Performance, 1980), p. 83.

[12] A pre-audit within an agency prior to expenditure ascertains the legality or appropriateness of making payment. Such an analysis often occurs, for instance, prior to the delivery of payroll checks.

[13] Federal general revenue sharing has required since 1976 an audit at least once in three years for general-purpose governments receiving such money.

Audits take different forms, depending on their orientation as determined by the expected use of that budget. The first, a *financial audit*, checks financial records to determine whether the funds were spent legally, whether receipts were properly recorded and controlled, and whether financial records and statements are complete and reliable. This audit concentrates on establishing compliance with appropriation law and on determining whether financial reports prepared by the operating agency are accurate and reliable. The financial audit still must determine, however, whether or not there has been theft by government employees or their confederates, although this part of the task will be minor for modern governments because of internal control methods.

A second type of audit is a *management,* or *operations, audit.* This audit focuses on efficiency of operation, including utilization and control of resources. The stress is on managerial aspects, including such concerns as duplication of effort, utilization of resources, and mismanagement of equipment, supplies, stocks, etc. The audit is more concerned with waste of government resources than on the theft aspects of a financial audit.

Program audits, a third approach, examine the extent to which desired results are being achieved and whether there might be lower cost alternatives to reach the desired results. An important focus of the program audit is whether objectives of the program are being met.

The fourth variety, a *performance audit,* assesses the total operations of an agency, including compliance, management, and program audits. Sunset reviews are one opportunity for such audits. Sunset legislation establishes "a set schedule for legislative review of programs and agencies and an automatic termination of those programs and agencies unless affirmative legislative action is taken to reauthorize them. Thus, the 'sun sets' on agencies and programs."[14] States with such legislation typically include a performance audit as part of the preparation for action on agencies or programs eligible for termination.

A simple example may illustrate the focus of each audit. Consider a state highway department's appropriation to purchase road salt for snow and ice removal. A financial audit would consider whether the agency had an appropriation for salt purchased, whether salt purchased was actually delivered, whether approved practices were followed in selecting a supplier, and whether agency reports showed the correct expenditure on salt. A management audit would consider whether the salt inventory is adequately protected from the environment, whether the inventory is adequate or excessive, and whether other methods of

---

[14] Advisory Commission on Intergovernmental Relations, "Sunset Legislation and Zero-Based Budgeting," *Information Bulletin no. 76–5* (December 1976), p. 1.

selecting a supplier would cause cost to be lower. A program audit would consider whether the prevailing level of winter highway clearing is an appropriate use of community resources and whether approaches other than spreading salt would be less costly to the community. Finally, a performance audit would examine all operations of the highway department.

When all audit work is completed, the budget cycle is complete for that fiscal year.

The federal cycle

The general budget cycle may be illustrated by a brief review of federal budget timing. Because the federal government is a continuing institution, its budget cycle operates across several calendar years. The flow of events confuses neophytes, but the pieces are arranged on the four-phase logic previously outlined. An abbreviated federal timetable appears in Figure 2–4; more complete detail appears as Appendix B at the end of the book.

FIGURE 2–4
Federal budget timetable: Fiscal 1985 dates

Action to be taken	Date
OMB instructions for budget estimates (executive preparation)	June 1983 (approximate)
Agency submits budget estimates	September–October 1983
Current Service Budget to Congress	November 10, 1983
President's budget message to Congress (legislative consideration)	15 days after Congress meets (January 1984)
Congress passes first budget resolution	May 15, 1984
Congress passes all appropriation bills	7 days after Labor Day (September 1984)
Congress passes second budget resolution	September 15, 1984
Fiscal year begins (execution)	October 1, 1984
Fiscal year ends (audit)	September 30, 1985

Three organizations constitute the primary professional budgeting establishment for the United States government and play a major role in the federal budget cycle. These are the two units formed by the Budget and Accounting Act of 1921 and the Congressional Budget Office (authorized by the Congressional Budget and Impoundment Act of 1974). They work with agency budget staff and appropriation committee staff to produce the budgets, appropriations, and expenditures of the federal government. The Office of Management and Budget (OMB) is a part of the Executive Office of the President. (It initially was part of the Treasury Department, but became part of the newly established Executive Office in 1939.) The president appoints its director, and its staff is expected to carry out the policies of the president. The Office develops the executive budget by consolidating agency requests for appropriations within the guidelines provided by the president. Initial agency requests are usually reduced by OMB; an administrative process within OMB considers protests of these reductions before transmission of the budget to Congress. After congressional appropriation, OMB meters the flow of spending to ensure that agencies do not spend more than the amount appropriated. Most states and many local governments have budget agencies which function like OMB, although not all have the skilled staff required for review and analysis of requests.[15]

The General Accounting Office (GAO) is the congressional agency which holds accountable the operations of federal departments and agencies. In most instances, it supervises the accounting done by others and emphasizes investigations to improve the effectiveness of government. Much of the audit detail is, in fact, done by inspector generals appointed for *internal* audit of agencies. The head of GAO, the comptroller general, is appointed by the president with consent of the Senate for a single 15-year term; the comptroller general is almost unremovable.[16] Much of the current emphasis of GAO work is on evaluation of government programs, sometimes at the request of a single member of Congress, sometimes at the request of a committee. Some states have similar agencies working for their legislatures, but many have elected state auditors. Skills and emphases differ dramatically, but many limit their work to accounting for funds.

The third federal organization is the Congressional Budget Office (CBO), a unit established to provide Congress with staff having expertise similar to that of OMB. Before CBO, there appeared to be an imbalance: the President had a permanent, professional budget staff with well-honed abilities and continuing knowledge about the mechanics

---

[15] Complete views of the agency appear in Percival Flack Brundage, *The Bureau of the Budget* (New York: Praeger Publishers, 1970) and Larry Berman, *The Office of Management and Budget and the Presidency, 1921–1979* (Princeton, N.J.: Princeton University Press, 1979). Brundage was Budget Director for President Eisenhower, after a career with a national accounting firm.

[16] Two major recent studies provide a detailed view of the GAO. Frederick C. Mosher in *The GAO: The Quest for Accountability in American Government* (Boulder, Colo.: Westview Press, 1979) traces the development of the GAO to the end of the 1970s and Erasmus H. Kloman, ed., *Cases in Accountability: The Work of the GAO* (Boulder, Colo.: Westview Press, 1979) collects several cases which illustrate the kind of audits or evaluations done by the GAO.

and content of the budget; Congress had only appropriation committee staff, none of whom maintained a view of the budget as a whole. Legislation in 1974 provided the CBO, a professional director, and a professional staff. That supplied Congress with an independent source of budget information and expertise, although there remains doubt whether Congress can truly have a single slate of priorities in light of the many interests of its individual members.

In the first phase, executive preparation and submission, the Office of Management and Budget collects agency estimates of expenditures for the fiscal year and consolidates these requests. The overall requests are compared with presidential program objectives, expenditure ceilings set by the president, Department of Treasury revenue estimates, and economic forecasts from the Council of Economic Advisers and the Federal Reserve System. The economic estimates—the rate of inflation, the level of unemployment, the level of gross national product—are especially important for the federal budget because many budget totals are sensitive to the economy. In other words, Congress has passed laws which provide expenditures that depend on the level of economic activity: unemployment assistance depends on the level of unemployed workers qualifying for assistance, food stamp assistance depends on the number of eligibles and prices of food, etc. Furthermore, federal revenues are particularly sensitive to economic activity. As a result, the forecast of economic activity used to prepare the budget can substantially alter the spending and revenue plans the budget encompasses.

The OMB transmits broad policy decisions back to the agencies for final expenditure estimates. Any remaining excess requests by agencies are defended before OMB hearing examiners. Transmission of the final document—the president's budget message—occurs 15 days after Congress meets in a new session (about mid-January). This document presents the president's program plans, with price tags attached, for the upcoming fiscal year. For a fiscal year beginning on October 1, 1984, for instance, the message would be delivered in mid-January 1984; first work on this budget began in the spring of 1983.

The period between delivery of the budget message and the end of its fiscal year is long. Not only can there be economic and social surprises to upset plans, but Congress may not agree with the presidential agenda. Nevertheless, differences between presidential plans and actual spending have been surprisingly small in relative terms. Table 2–1 traces those differences from 1971 to 1980: the median difference is only 2.15 percent of the initial request. There are, of course, greater differences in individual programs than appear in these aggregates.

Present budget legislation requires an earlier budget message to Congress. The Current Services Budget is delivered to Congress on

TABLE 2–1
Initial administration budgets and actual federal spending, 1971–1981

Fiscal year	Original budget ($ billions)	Actual spending ($ billions)	Percent difference
1971	$200.8	$211.4	5.0
1972	229.2	232.0	1.2
1973	246.3	247.1	0.3
1974	270.2	269.6	−0.2
1975	305.6	326.2	6.3
1976	351.2	366.4	4.1
1977	394.2	402.7	2.1
1978	440.9	450.8	2.2
1979	501.6	493.7	−1.6
1980	531.6	579.6	8.3
1981	615.8	n.a.	—
Mean difference			2.8
Median difference			2.15

n.a. = not available.
Source: "Budget Triumph, But No Time to Relax," *The Morgan Guaranty Survey,* July 1981.

November 10, prior to the Budget Message (or President's budget request). The Current Services Budget estimates what the cost would be to continue current programs at their current level without additions or deletions. If this report has any use, it would be to help gauge the effects of price change on public spending and to help sort out program expansions from program continuations. It is not a request for money, and its usefulness or role have not been proven.

The second phase of the cycle, legislative review and authorization, has been revised significantly since 1974. Before the 1974 Congressional Budget and Impoundment Act, the federal budget was considered only as split into the several appropriation bills; Congress did not consider the budget as a whole. The budget was fragmented back to general administrative department chunks, with each chunk considered by a separate appropriation committee. That procedure might give greater scrutiny to individual department requests, but it certainly did not permit the overall comparison of revenues, expenditures, and accompanying surplus or deficit. More importantly, that practice did not permit consideration of government-wide priorities—transportation versus agriculture versus defense, etc.—that effective budget formulation requires.

The new process, used initially for the 1977 budget, produced a dual flow through Congress: while the appropriations committees work as before, separate budget committees consider federal spending as a whole. Figure 2–5 diagrams that dual path. The budget committees

FIGURE 2-5
Budget reconciliation process

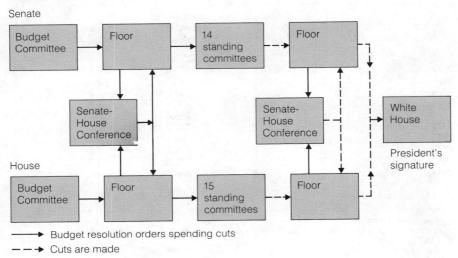

Senate

House

→ Budget resolution orders spending cuts
- - → Cuts are made

Source: *The Wall Street Journal,* June 9, 1981. Reprinted by permission of *The Wall Street Journal* © Dow Jones & Company, Inc., 1975. All rights reserved.

produce a budget resolution which sets ceilings for total taxes and expenditure, a debt or surplus target, and broad spending priorities among major activities. The First Concurrent Resolution is approved by both houses of Congress in May, before appropriation consideration begins in earnest. Congress can change ceilings in a second resolution passed shortly before the start of a new fiscal year, but Congress is not supposed to adjourn before reconciliation of appropriation totals and ceilings. Congress violated that requirement for the 1981 budget. The congressional budget process permits Congress to develop its own spending priorities, particularly with the assistance of the Congressional Budget Office established by the act, and to consider the appropriate macroeconomic impact for its spending actions. Without this element, the process emphasizes presidential priorities; the element allows a congressional view, an important part in the American system of separation of powers. Many state and local governments have but a single appropriation bill, not the dozen or so that this federal government has, so there is less significance in the distinction between budget consideration and appropriation consideration.

The end points of the fiscal year presumably set the bounds for execution, the third stage of the process. This is the period in which appropriated moneys are spent and public services are provided. The fact that money is appropriated for a purpose, however, does not automatically and immediately lead to public expenditure. To prevent agencies from exhausting funds before the end of the fiscal year and to use expenditure timing for macroeconomic purpose, the OMB divides total money to agencies into sums for distribution over the year (apportionments). Current law makes it difficult for the president to direct OMB to delay scheduled expenditure (deferral), and even more difficult to cancel expenditure of funds appropriated (rescission). Congress can reject deferrals by disapproving them; either house of Congress may reject a recission.

The audit phase of the federal cycle, supervised by the General Accounting Office, formally begins at the end of the fiscal year. Some audit functions do, however, continue through the fiscal year as agencies themselves work to prevent illegal and irregular transactions by various approval stages. In an important sense, the audit phase ensures that everything else in the budget process matters: unless the decisions made elsewhere in the process get carried through, the process is irrelevant. The audit phase determines whether those directions were followed. The General Accounting Office reports to the House and Senate Committees on Government Operations.

BUDGETS AND POLITICAL STRATEGIES

The incrementalist view maintains that budgeting is heavily, if not exclusively, a process of political strategy. It rejects the public service delivery orientation of models from public finance economics and rejects budgeting techniques that attempt to make the process more rational. Budgeting, appropriating, and spending is a process of strategies and role playing. As Aaron Wildavsky diagnoses the process,

> *Budgeting is incremental.* The largest determining factor of the size and content of this year's budget is last year's budget. Most of the budget is a product of previous decisions. . . . The budget may be conceived of as an iceberg with by far the largest part below the surface, outside the control of anyone. Many items in the budget are standard and are simply reenacted every year unless there is a special reason to challenge them.[17]

Budget making and appropriating becomes a process of percentage monetary adjustments to existing programs, that is, the application of rule-of-thumb percentage increases to the budget base of agencies, the base being the prior year budget. Analysis during budget construction

---

[17] Aaron Wildavsky, *The Politics of the Budgetary Process,* 3d ed. (Boston: Little, Brown, 1979), p. 13. Treatment here of roles and strategies relies heavily on work by him.

is not a mechanism for consideration of basic policy choices. Agencies and legislatures use strategies within the context of anticipated roles. Budgets are built from percentage increments to the historic budget base in accord with some notion of fair shares to each agency.

Roles

Service delivery choices in the budget process involve several different roles, each with different approaches and biases. Participants in the budget process recognize and expect those approaches in the budget process, being aware of the errors, incentives, and organizational blindspots inherent in each. The major orientations of attitude are those of operating agencies, the office of the chief executive, and the position of the legislator. All participants in the budget process seek to provide service to the public without waste. Each, however, works from different perspectives, resulting in differences of incentives and different definitions of that objective in practice. A full understanding of the budget process obviously requires recognition of those roles.

Operating agencies. Operating agencies are the units which spend money for the delivery of government services. These agencies focus on the clientele they serve. It is unreasonable to expect an agency to be concerned with services provided by other agencies or to be interested in relative priorities among services of agencies. The agency probably will not be much concerned with comparisons of the cost of service with the value of that service. They recognize the value of the services they provide to their clients and will ordinarily try to increase those services, regardless of overall budget conditions of the government. There will be a virtually limitless expanse of service opportunities, many of which will go unfunded simply because other uses of public resources yield a greater social return. Agencies, however, seldom recognize those competing uses and complain about their lack of resources. Large agencies will have both operating people who have little direct contact with the budget and budget people who have little direct contact with service delivery. Both groups of people, however, can be expected to have essentially the same point of view and clientele orientation.

Chief executive. The Office of the Chief Executive, whether it be president, governor, mayor, or whatever, has budget specialists acting on its behalf. The agencies will have different names (federal: Office of Management and Budgeting; state: state budget agencies, etc.), but their function and role are the same regardless of name and level. Analysts in that agency will operate with the priorities of the chief executive, not their own, and will have the constraint of available revenue in mind. The analysts will cut requests in line with the executive priorities until total spending fits within that constraint. Reductions will be typically for items not adequately justified, items which are not closely related to achieving the objective of the agency, and items not consistent with the priorities of the chief executive. While agencies have a clientele orientation, the chief executive (selected by the entire population) must balance the interests of the total population. Thus, priorities for an individual agency should not be expected to coincide with those of the chief executive, because specific client group priorities seldom match those of the general public. The interests of corn belt farmers, for instance, are not the same as those of the general population. The chief executive's priorities will dominate in the reductions done by these budget analysts.

Legislature. The priorities of elected representatives can be expected to follow those of their constituencies. They will be concerned with programs and projects serving the people who elect them. It is not reasonable to expect them to consistently take an overall view of agencies or of programs of agencies. Their focus will be on a specific subset of the population, as is the case for operating agencies. Their subset, however, will be regionally oriented rather than specific client group oriented. Most electoral regions will, of course, contain numerous client groups.

Strategies

Wildavsky has identified agency strategies employed within the roles pursued in the budget process on the basis of an analysis of the United States Congress.[18] Many of these strategies—"links between intentions and perceptions of budget officials and the political system that imposes restraints and creates opportunities for them"[19]—are transferrable to other governments. Two agency strategies are *ubiquitous.* The first is cultivation of an active clientele for help in dealing both with the legislature and with the chief executive. The clientele may be those directly served (as with farmers in particular programs provided by the Department of Agriculture) or those selling services to the particular agency (as with highway contractors doing business with a state department of highways). Agencies unable to identify and cultivate such clientele will find budget hearings difficult, as active support may be difficult to identify and mobilize.

---

[18] Ibid., chap. 3.
[19] Ibid., p. 63.

A second ubiquitous strategy is the development of confidence of other government officials. Agency administrators must avoid being surprised in hearings or by requests for information. Officials must show results in the reports they make and must tailor the complexity of their message to their audience. If results themselves are not directly available, proxies from procedure and processes are substituted. Confidence is critical because in the budget process many elements of defense must derive from the judgments of the administrators, not on hard evidence. If confidence has been developed those judgments will be trusted; if not, those judgments will be suspect.

Another group of strategies—*contingent* strategies—depend on the budget circumstances. The crucial circumstance is what is being proposed with respect to the agency's programs from the prior year (its base). In defense of its base from cuts, an agency may: (1) suggest that the politically popular program be cut, as with reduction in athletic and band programs when school districts face fiscal problems; (2) argue that the program is an all-or-nothing choice: any reduction would make the program impossible, so it might as well be eliminated; (3) take advantage of a strong clientele on individual projects within the program by listing those projects separately to prevent across-the-board reductions; or (4) force the representative to choose what programs ought to be cut rather than attempting the difficult choices within the agency.

In an effort to increase the agency base (increase the scope of existing programs), the agency may (1) argue that the program is really nothing new but is simply a continuation of existing effort; (2) round all cost estimates upward: agencies round at different levels, ranging from $100 million to $10, but any agency can make at least small expansions by rounding; or (3) maintain an expenditure category dollar amount, but move the duties elsewhere, using released funds to increase the scope of a particular program.

Efforts to expand the agency base require different tactics. Among them are the following: (1) the agency may practice "foot-in-the-door finance" by starting small and gradually expanding through the base-increasing process; (2) the program may start on a "temporary" basis, with interim extensions until it is made permanent; (3) the program may be sold on the basis of it "paying for itself," and thus has no net budget impact; and (4) the activity may be sold on the basis of a crisis (energy, environment, etc.), preferably advertised using some catchy name for the ensuing programs. Base expansion is generally difficult because of the lack of developed clienteles. Base expansion should continue to be difficult because of the difficulty of cutting back or eliminating a program once it is started.

The uses of incrementalism

Few developments in society occur without warning, without build-ing gradually over the years. In that environment, agencies reasonably prepare their budgets in an incremental fashion: what better guide can there be toward the next year than the recent past, even in a rational world? The forecasting models of rational analysts are based on recent history, so building from the recent past cannot be tagged as an attri-bute of rationalism or incrementalism. It is simply a logic tool to use in budget construction. Similarly, the nature of roles and strategies in the budget process contributes important insights into incentives motivat-ing budget behavior.

It is not clear, however, that appropriations follow the pattern of small adjustments implicit in the incrementalist view.[20] Bailey and O'Connor examined the pattern of budget results from one year to the next for agencies in the federal government (appropriations and expen-ditures), in the state of Virginia (expenditures), and in Colombia (expen-ditures). They computed for each agency of the government the change in expenditure (or appropriation) from one year to the next over the time period studied. Table 2–2 reports the distribution of those changes. The striking result of the analysis is the large number of changes well above 10 percent—and in periods not characterized by substantial inflation in the United States. (Comparable Colombian

TABLE 2–2
Distribution of annual percentage changes in expenditure or appropriation by agencies*

	Incremental (change from 0 to 10 percent)	Intermediate (11 to 30 percent)	Nonincremental (31 percent and above)
Congressional appropriation (12-year period, pre-1960?)	52.5%	34.2%	15.2%
Federal expenditures (1961–71)	49.1	32.1	19.8
Colombian central government expenditures:			
actual (1961–71)	22.7	34.5	42.8
Adjusted for inflation	43.9	25.9	30.2
Virginia expenditures (1967–70)	34.7	52.1	13.1

* John J. Bailey and Robert J. O'Connor, "Operationalizing Incrementalism: Measuring the Muddles," *Public Administration Review,* 35 (January/February 1975): 60–66. Reprinted with permission from Public Administration Review © 1975 by The American Society for Public Administra-tion, 1225 Connecticut Avenue, N.W., Washington, D.C. All rights reserved.

---

[20] In a generic sense, any change—large or small—is an increment. The change is limited to small ones simply to give the view meaning.

results are those adjusted for inflation.) Agencies were in fact capable of major increases in their operations. In more recent times, inflation has caught up with the United States, and substantial annual changes could be expected for that reason alone. The deflator for state and local government purchases—an index of the prices that these governments pay—rose at an annual compound rate of 7.97 percent from 1972 through 1980. That makes it easier for governments to cut into the service base of any agency: increases less than that rate of growth will reduce the real spending power of the agency.

Conclusion

Budgets serve as the choice mechanism for allocation of public resources. The flow of budget decisions from plan to expenditure is accomplished in a four-phase cycle involving legislative and executive branches of government. The phases: executive preparation, legislative preparation, execution, and audit. While budgets are constructed and approved in a political environment, it is not clear that appropriations are the simple product of adding a small increment to the prior year appropriation. There is at least some room for attempts at rational choice in budget structures.

APPENDIX: ILLUSTRATION OF OBJECT-OF-EXPENDITURE CLASSIFICATION

An agency would be required to classify its budget request into the following resource classes. It would, of course, use only the classes in which it intended to make purchases.

Expenditure classifications:
1. Personal services.
    1.1   Head of department.
    1.2   Classified positions.
    1.3   Unclassified positions (temporary).
    1.4   Overtime, shift differentials.
    1.5   Vacation, sick relief.
2. Contractual services.
    2.1   Freight, express, deliveries.
    2.2   Travel.
    2.3   Telephone, telegraph.
    2.4   Repairs.
    2.5   Subscriptions and dues.
    2.6   Printing, binding, advertising.

    2.7   Postage and postal supplies.
    2.8   Water, heat, light, power.
    2.9   Professional and other fees (consultants, physicians, lawyers, etc.).
    2.10   Other contractual services.
3. Supplies.
    3.1   Food.
    3.2   Fuel.
    3.3   Feed and veterinary supplies.
    3.4   Office.
    3.5   Household, laundry, janitorial.
    3.6   Medical.
    3.7   Educational, playground, recreational.
    3.8   Motor vehicle supplies.
    3.9   Agricultural supplies.
    3.10   Clothing and dry goods.
    3.11   Maintenance supplies.
    3.12   Data processing supplies.
    3.13   Other supplies.
4. Rents and insurance.
    4.1   Rents—privately owned properties.
    4.2   Rents—publicly owned properties.
    4.3   Rents—data processing equipment.
    4.4   Rents—other equipment.
    4.5   Rents—other.
    4.6   Insurance.
5. Equipment.
    5.1   Office equipment.
    5.2   Medical equipment.
    5.3   Household equipment.
    5.4   Motor vehicles and equipment.
    5.5   Agricultural equipment and livestock.
    5.6   Aircraft equipment.
    5.7   Educational, playground, recreational.
    5.8   Data processing equipment.
    5.9   Library books.
6. Land and buildings.
    6.1   Purchase lands.
    6.2   Buildings.
    6.3   Nonstructural improvements.
7. Employee benefits.
    7.1   State retirement.
    7.2   Police-fire retirement.

7.3   Social security.
7.4   Workers' compensation.
7.5   Health insurance.
8.   Contingencies.

A CASE FOR DISCUSSION

Agencies without a specific clientele face special problems in defending their budget requests against budget cutters. A classic illustration of agency strategy appears in the following case, reproduced in entirety from *The Wall Street Journal.*

Consider these questions:

1.   What budget strategies did NASA use in defense of ERTS?
2.   At what stage of the budget cycle were the reductions made?
3.   How might other agencies use similar approaches? For instance, suggest explicitly how a state university might adopt those strategies in dealing with a legislature.

How Backers of a Technology Satellite Induced Ford to Overrule His Advisers, Provide Money

BY ARLEN J. LARGE
Staff Reporter of THE WALL STREET JOURNAL

WASHINGTON—Frank Moss is an ERTS nut, in a world of people who aren't.

So he considers it his duty to spread the gospel about his pet project. It helps that he is a U.S. Senator from Utah and chairman of the Senate Space Committee.

Daniel Evans may not be a nut on the subject, but he is an ERTS fan. As governor of the state of Washington,

he wrote Sen. Moss an unspontaneous letter saying that the "Earth Resources Technology Satellite has provided valuable information to both the agriculture and forestry industries and to the state of Washington."

Gerald Ford may not even be an ERTS fan, but he is a friend. Not long ago, he overruled his White House advisers and put $11 million in the new budget to start work on a third ERTS satellite, which will be launched in the fall of 1977.

So some very heavy politicians have been rallying around this little-known and unglamorous project of the National Aeronautics and Space Administration. The backstage tugging over the money for the third satellite is the kind of thing that goes on all over town during preparation of a new budget, and it provides a good case study of how budget winners win.

The loser was the President's Office of Management and Budget, which for months had urged that the third satellite be deferred to some future budget. Roy Ash, the just-departed OMB director who was overruled by Mr. Ford, observed with sarcasm that "one must congratulate NASA for its notable job of mobilizing outside opinion" on behalf of the new satellite.

The Show-Biz Problem

However, it would be hard to pin the whole mobilizing effort on the space bureaucrats at NASA. There's something called "the ERTS community"—geographers, foresters, pollution fighters and land-use planners—that lobbied heavily for the new satellite. For its part, NASA has tried to tackle the show-biz problem caused by the satellite's grating, uncommunicative name. The agency is trying to get people to call it Landsat, but even space officials sometimes forget, and the names are used interchangeably.

The first satellite in the series was shot into polar orbit in 1972. It still is there but is running down. The second went up last Jan. 22 with similar equipment for looking at the earth in four wavelengths of light and sending images back to ground stations for analysis by computers. Computer-processed pictures are sold by the Interior Department at Sioux Falls,

S.D., to anyone who wants to use them to count crops, spot oil, see insect-chewed forests, trace earthquake-producing faults, and do a lot of other things.

All this really turns Sen. Moss on, making him a self-admitted "virtual zealot" for these satellites. "ERTS was the first thing I could see where you have a very distinct and obvious applications return," he says. "It's a great example of the benefits coming out of the space program." People who appreciate the down-to-earth value of the ERTS pictures, he says, are more likely to embrace the space agency's flightier doings, such as the exploration of Mars.

The satellite launched last month is expected to work for two years. Congress last year authorized a third ERTS to take its place in 1977. NASA was more than willing to start building it, and so, of course, was General Electric Co., the main contractor for the first two. Plans were made to upgrade the new model with a heat-measuring sensor.

Mr. Ash's OMB, the government-wide spending monitor, demurred. A third satellite shouldn't go up, budget officials argued, until NASA succeeded in developing cameras with sharper vision. Without that, ERTS satellites would never be useful in making good crop-production forecasts, forest surveys, or pollution maps.

The space agency intends to double the sharpness of vision of one of the cameras on the third satellite. The other equipment, officials contend, sees sharply enough on the second and third satellites to undertake a large-scale survey of U.S. wheat production. And with a little practice, space officials think that they will get a better notion of the size of each year's Soviet wheat crop, thus giving a more accurate forewarning of export market demand.

NASA and its allies argued all last year that a third satellite should be on duty in 1977 to take over when the second one dies; otherwise, there would be a gap in the data that would discourage picture buyers in "the ERTS community."

The trick was to bring this argument to OMB's attention in an impressive way. An important part of the lobbying blitz was orchestrated on Capitol Hill by Sen. Moss and his ally, Arizona's Sen. Barry Goldwater.

Letters to the States

Hoping to show that the ERTS community had plenty of political muscle, Sen. Moss wrote every governor, asking if state agencies had made use of ERTS and whether the federal government should sell the pictures on a permanent basis.

The Senator got replies from 25 governors, plus some top officials in other states. Vermont's Thomas Salmon said ERTS pictures will be used to trace pollution in Lake Champlain. In California, said then Gov. Ronald Reagan, ERTS has helped outline land-use patterns. Missouri's Christopher Bond said the pictures have been used to spot flood-prone areas. Only Delaware's Sherman Tribbitt replied bluntly that the pictures didn't prove useful.

One by one, Sen. Moss dribbled the gubernatorial letters into the Congressional Record in the closing months of last year. "It was like the drop-of-water technique, day by day," he says.

Besides that, Sen. Moss waved letters of support from the Society of Photographic Scientists and Engineers, the American Society of Photogrammetry, the Association of American Geographers, the American Forestry Association, and various distinguished professors. Meanwhile, on the scientific-seminar circuit, General Electric's people were forever turning up with ERTS displays. Daniel Fink, general manager of GE's space division, preached the need to keep those space photos coming in.

Nevertheless, OMB last December turned down NASA's request to put money for the third satellite, called Landsat-C, into the budget being prepared for the new Congress. Word spread along the ERTS community's grapevine. OMB got letters from the National Academy of Science and the National Academy of Engineering, both quasi-government bodies. Letters came from important scientists.

Appealing the Decision

The budget keepers still said no. Under the rules, an agency can go over OMB's head and appeal directly to the President So ERTS was kicked around at a meeting between Mr. Ford, Mr. Ash, and James Fletcher, the NASA boss. "It was not a confrontation," Mr. Fletcher insists.

He says his agency kept explaining to OMB that the third satellite didn't represent an "operational" earth-scanning system but would remain an experimental instrument. Then in early

January the remaining differences between the two agencies were reduced to an "issue paper" that went to Mr. Ford. The satellite money was approved.

Mr. Ash appeared to see a connection between NASA's victory and a praise-filled article on ERTS in the February issue of Fortune magazine. The article portrayed OMB as the villain in trying to block the third satellite, concluding: "To cripple or kill this program, after the millions of words spewed out about the coming 'fallout' from space research, would certainly be foolhardy."

NASA had indeed been eager for Fortune to do the article. "It was Fletcher who put this bug in my bonnet about a year ago," recalls Robert Lubar, the magazine's managing editor. John Donnelly, the agency's assistant administrator for public affairs, also remembers writing Mr. Lubar about the ERTS project. "I tried to plant the seed of an idea for a story I thought was of quite legitimate interest to businessmen," he says. Editor Lubar says that he doesn't remember seeing that letter and that the decision to have the article written was his. Anyway, he says, the February Fortune didn't hit the streets until the last week in January, after Mr. Ford had made his decision.

Budget methods and practices

Many tasks in the budget cycle can be learned only by dealing nose to nose against, and elbow to elbow with, other participants. There are some methods and perspectives important to understand, however, before that first crunch. This chapter provides an initial introduction to some methods and activities in each phase of the budget cycle.

PREPARATION OF AGENCY BUDGETS

A budget request includes both the estimated cost of planned activities and a written justification of those activities. Both elements are critical for successful operation of any government because they provide the "how much" and "what it does" information needed for public decisions. The estimates may be developed and organized through one or more of the following approaches. First, the cost may be grouped by the organization (branch, section, division, etc.) incurring the cost. The estimates originate in the offices where the costs occur. The costs thus follow the organization chart. For example, if a city has organizational units called the mayor's office, the comptroller's office, and departments of streets, of public safety, of public works, and of recreation, cost estimates would be prepared for each of those six units on the organization chart. Second, they may be grouped by program, purpose, or budget activity. What is the cost of cleaning streets, controlling traffic, collecting garbage, and so on? Sometimes the organization breakdown will coincide with these program breakdowns, but often organization costs are attributable to several different programs. Third, the cost may be broken down by object class, that is, by the nature of goods and services to be purchased. Agencies will use the uniform object classification required and provided by the budget office of that particular government. An example of such an object classification appeared in Chapter 2.

The foundation of any budget, regardless of eventual focus on performance or program accomplishment, is the object class estimates. This is the basis for estimates of requirements for organization program or budget activity. Ideally, the agency would determine what it intends to do, determine what resources are needed to get it done, estimate the price of those resources, and multiply price by number of input units to get a total cost of the request. Budget routines do in fact implicitly use this process.

Elements of cost estimation

Costs occur as agencies acquire resources (personnel, materials, and facilities) to provide public services. Somewhat different estimating techniques apply to each class, with a particular distinction between personnel and nonpersonnel costs.

Compensation of personnel. Personal services usually are the largest single cost element in budget requests of government agencies. The problem is to determine the kind and amount of personal services needed and to apply prevailing wage rates to compute the total cost. A standard procedure works from personnel data on individuals in each pay step, adjusted for anticipated movements to the next pay step in the budget year. Thus, if there are 50 people in the Tax Auditor I category with five years experience this year, there likely will be 50 people in the Tax Auditor I category with six years experience next year. The budget estimate for them would be 50 times the annual pay of a Tax Auditor I with six years experience. The request must be supplemented by lapses that reduce total cost: turnover (retirements, quits, and terminations) with replacement at lower pay grades or with personnel not replaced, delays in filling vacant positions, and so on. Such lapses may be estimated from experience on position turnover. Requests for new personnel ordinarily would be based on changes in expected workload, including new programs.

Associated with ordinary compensation are substantial costs for personnel benefits (pensions, insurance, uniform allowances, social security, etc.). These benefits are usually a separate object class but may be considered for estimation purposes in association with compensation itself. Most such benefits are computed by application of formulas established by law or labor contract that relate the benefit to work force size or to total compensation of the labor force. For instance, state law may require city government payment into a pension fund equal to 20 percent of wages and salaries paid. Such computations, once requirements of the law are worked out, are simple.

Nonpersonnel costs. Other object costs may be more difficult to estimate for the request than are personnel costs. They are often computed using estimating ratios, as adjusted by recent experience. Much information for the request can be located in prior year budget materials. Five estimation techniques are frequently used in these computations: volume times unit price, workload times average unit cost, work force ratios, ratios to another object class, and adjustment to prior year cost.

First is the volume-times-unit-price method, an attractive approach when a particular quantity and single average price is applicable to a relatively high ticket price object class. Items such as typewriters or automobiles may be estimated in that fashion. The second method is workload multiplied by the average unit cost of providing the service, a method usually used to estimate fairly homogeneous categories making up a large part of a cost in an object class. The unit cost is taken from recent cost experience adjusted for inflation and/or productivity changes. For instance, food expenses for a training class could be estimated by such a method (300 trainee days at $20 per trainee day, for a request of $6,000). Third, some categories of cost, particularly small categories of miscellaneous costs, may be estimated by relating them to the work force. For example, office supply expenses for a district office could be related to the size of the staff stationed there. Fourth, when there is some relationship between certain categories and other resources used in the production process, that expense group may be estimated by use of ratios to that nonpersonnel object class. As an example, a parts inventory for motor vehicles may be linked to the number of vehicles in the motor fleet. The final method, best suited for small, heterogeneous cost categories, makes estimates by adjustments to prior year lump sums. Prior cost is adjusted to reflect anticipated changes in qualities or quantities in the budget year. This method may be necessary when other means are not feasible or economical, but it lacks the precision of other techniques.

No formula or ratio can be automatically applied without hazard. Cost ratios and other relationships may change if operating methods are altered, if prices of inputs change, or if production technologies change. All of these change in a dynamic economy, often with great impact on operating cost.

Budget estimates must be carefully prepared because the quality of the presentation shapes the impressions that budget analysts develop about agencies. Analysts are less likely to trust the judgments of budget officers who prepare sloppy budget requests. Several simple errors are particularly frequent, although they ought never occur. First, budgets may not coincide with current budget instructions, budget guidelines, and forms. Budgets may be developed using the prior year budget as a guide, but the submission must coincide with current regulations. Failure to follow instructions produces needless embarrassment. Second, budget submissions may lack required supplemental documents or the documents may not be properly identified. Budget examiners seldom give the benefit of doubt to budgets with missing material. And finally, cost estimate detail columns may not add to totals carried forward in the presentation. Continuous cross-checking must be maintained to preserve the internal consistency of the budget request.

Budget justification

Program status reports, requests for supplemental funding, supporting explanation for increased staff, budget increases, and so on, require justification of any planned agency action. Well-developed justifications are the important key to attainment of agency budget objectives. There are several general and specific guidelines for the effective writing of budget justifications, beyond the standard rules of English prose. The justifications must pass the general test of clarity and preciseness. The justification must avoid jargon and uncommon abbreviations, because the justification's purpose is to communicate to individuals less familiar with the details of the proposed activity than are personnel in the operating agency. Neither budget agency examiners or legislators are likely to approve poorly described projects. The justification must be factual and must provide documented sources. And the justification must go through ordinary review and revision to produce a polished presentation.

In terms of structure, the justification will address the current situation, the additional needs, and the expected results from honoring the request. One section describes the current program situation in terms of measurable workloads, staffing, funding, or productivity trends. It will briefly and specifically inform the budget examiner of existing conditions, without extraneous detail which might misdirect the examiner's attention. Another section of the justification will describe the additional needs. It must specifically identify additional funds, personnel, and materials needed for the budget activity at issue. The reason for the need must be explicitly developed. Common reasons include (1) mandates from higher levels of government, the courts, or legislative requirements; (2) improvement of methods of operation; (3) increased workload; (4) higher prices of resources to be purchased; and (5) development of new programs. The third section describes expected results from the proposal and tries to convince the budget office and the legislature of the need for the proposed activity. It will describe the results that will occur if the requested resources are or are not provided. Because the reviewer will want to know whether partial funding will help, whether critical program objectives will be endangered without funding, whether workload can be backlogged to get around the problem, and what the implications of the request will be for future requests, answers to those questions should be available and defensible. The justification should make a solid case for a realistic increase. There is no reason to spread a justification thin to defend a large increase when a solid case for a smaller increase is possible.

Phantom balance

Governments may find it politically convenient or legally necessary to produce a balanced operating budget when reasonably produced figures would show a deficit.[1] Governments have developed a number of pragmatic devices to produce such an artificial balance; a frequently encountered handful include: high revenue estimates, shifting requests among budgets, changed revenue or expenditure timing, low requests for high priorities, and unlikely assumptions. Because of their use by governments in trouble, the strategies are worth some attention.

Any budget must be constructed with estimates of revenue for the upcoming fiscal year. Phantom budget balance can therefore be developed through use of artificially high revenue estimates for that year. Such estimates can be produced then by assuming artificially high economic activity (state and federal taxes, as well as many local nonproperty taxes, are sensitive to the level of economic activity), unrealistically diligent administration of the tax, or by presuming that the linkage between revenue collections and economic activity has changed in an improved fashion. Local property taxes ordinarily could not be overestimated, as rates are set on the basis of assessed value on a prior

---

[1] An operating budget would include the expenditures to be made for services delivered within the year; the resources purchased from the operating budget would largely be used up within the year.

valuation date. (More about this in a later chapter.) Thus, the property tax base is not estimated, but is actual. The estimated revenue can be manipulated, however, by assuming unrealistically low delinquency (or noncollection) levels: if 90 percent of the levy historically has been actually collected, a budget boost is possible by assuming 95 percent collection. During the late 1970s, New York City got such boosts toward budget balance by presuming 100 percent collection, a completely unrealistic basis for budgeting. Similar inflation of revenue estimates can be produced by making unrealistic assumptions about the process of intergovernmental assistance from either federal or state sources. A similar unsustainable revenue boost can be produced by sale of property or other assets held by the government—a "one-time revenue crutch."[2]

A second device involves manipulation among budgets. State and local governments often have capital budgets in addition to and separate from operating budgets. Capital budgets finance purchase of assets with long useful life (as discussed in Chapter 5) and often have no requirement for balance, because such long-life assets may logically be financed on a pay-as-you-use basis through the issuance of debt. Some governments have shifted activities which would ordinarily be included in the operating budget to the capital budget to produce the desired balance in the operating budget. For instance, services of the city planning department have a long lifetime, so why not finance them through the capital budget, even though the expenditure flow is continuous? The shift can destroy the logic of the capital budget and, more importantly, can endanger the capability to finance the government's capital infrastructure.

Third, single-year deficits may be managed by accelerated collection of revenue to create a cash "bubble" in the year of acceleration. The advantage is one-shot, as the process effectively borrows revenue from the next year to accentuate any revenue gap in that next year. The "bubble" can be duplicated in forthcoming fiscal years only by accelerating collections even more, an unlikely possibility. Two examples show how acceleration works. In 1969, Illinois state expenditures seemed destined to exceed revenue. The problem was reduced by acceleration of sales tax collections. Retailers had been required to pay sales tax collections to the state at the end of the month following the month of collection: December collections would be due at the end of January. The accelerated schedule required them to remit collections by the end of the business month: December collections were due at the

---

[2] Karl Nollenberger, "It's More Than Balancing the Budget," *Public Management* (April 1980), p. 3.

end of December. That change of schedule created a year with 13 months of sales tax collections: December 1968 (remitted in January 1969) through December 1969 (remitted at the end of December 1969).[3] A second example comes from the Philadelphia property tax. Businesses willing to pay estimated 1978 taxes along with their 1977 taxes were given a special discount on their 1978 tax bill, a method of obtaining greater 1977 revenue by reducing the flow available in 1978.[4] Both accelerations create a revenue bubble for the problem year by altering future collection flows.

The balance problem may also be concealed by manipulating when expenditures occur. One approach loads the cost of multiyear programs in later fiscal years rather than in a sequence consistent with normal project development flow. The low request in the current budget year may help achieve balance in that year; the result, however, may well be greater problems in achieving balance in further budget years. A somewhat different method of expenditure manipulation, particularly within a fiscal year, uses delayed payment for purchases made toward the end of a fiscal year until the next fiscal year (and the next year's appropriations). The technique conceals a short-term operating deficit and amounts to short-term borrowing from suppliers across the two fiscal years.[5] It obviously reduces funds available for the next year. Unless the imbalance is corrected, similar problems will result in following years and the operating deficit carry-over will expand with time.

A fourth device is delivery of a balanced executive budget which omits some activities which political pressures will prevent the legislature from excluding. The executive can thus claim a balanced budget, but the hard choices have not been made, and appropriations actually made will likely produce a deficit. An artificially balanced budget may even be passed, relying on supplemental appropriation in the next year

---

[3] Illinois accelerated sales tax collections in 1969 and corporate income, retail sales, and individual income withholdings in 1976. Robert M. Whitler, "Accelerated Tax Collection in Illinois," *Revenue Administration, 1977,* Proceedings of the 45th Annual Meeting of the National Association of Tax Administrators, pp. 55– 58.

[4] Estimated 1978 property taxes were to be borrowed in May 1977 to ease a city revenue problem without going to banks for financing. ("Early Taxpayers Can Get a Break in Philadelphia," *Louisville Courier-Journal,* April 3, 1977.)

[5] For example, the city of Chicago in 1980 delayed payments to vendors who regularly did business with the city to avoid bank loans in a cash crisis. The problem emerged because property tax bills were not mailed as scheduled because of a judicial challenge of a homestead exemption program. The city had short-term borrowing authority but feared it was insufficient to cover the shortage. ("City May Delay Payment to Suppliers," *Chicago Tribune,* August 19, 1980.) Because the taxes were actually levied, there is no borrowing across fiscal years in this instance; the strategy is simply one of cash flow management.

to provide required funds.[6] Such proceedings may go largely unnoticed, because emphasis traditionally focuses on the budget presentation and consideration, not on what actually happens during the budget year. In a similar fashion, the imbalance may be handled in some budget years by shifting expenditures normally planned for the early part of that budget year into a supplemental request for the current year.

A final mechanism exploits the nature of a budget as a combination of a plan and a forecast. Budget results can be managed by use of unlikely environmental assumptions concerning, for instance, state assumption of local welfare responsibilities, major new intergovernmental assistance programs, artificially low employment or inflation conditions, or other conditions which favorably influence expenditures or revenue. Those assumptions may allow a balanced budget presentation with no real potential that those conditions will actually occur. If deficits can readily be accommodated in capital markets, such manipulations may scarcely be noticed.

REVIEW OF BUDGETS

Agency requests are reviewed by a central budget office before inclusion in the government budget and by legislative committees after inclusion in the budget. Two features are common to both reviews: the reviewer is expected to reduce some items in the proposal and the reviewer will be less informed about agency operations than are those who prepared the budget. Those features dominate budget review.

Meltsner has examined budget operations in Oakland, California, in some detail, finding patterns in the way budget analysts review budgets:

> Inexperience in itself forces upon the budget analyst the use of a set of
> .rules of thumb. The analyst first looks at last year's appropriations to
> identify any significant changes. It is the changes or incremental requests
> which get his attention. Without going into detail, here is an outline of the
> rules of cutting:
>
> 1. Cut all increases in personnel.
> 2. Cut all equipment items which appear to be luxuries.
> 3. Use precedent—cut items which have been cut before.
> 4. Recommend repair and renovation rather than replacement of
>   facilities.

---

[6] Regular appropriations are passed before the start of a budget year. Those appropriations may prove inadequate because of unforseen events. Supplemental appropriations provide additional funds within a current budget year.

5. Recommend study as a means of deferring major costs.
6. Cut all nonitem operating costs by a fixed percentage (such as 10 percent).
7. Do not cut when safety or health of staff or public is obviously involved.
8. Cut departments with "bad" reputations.
9. When in doubt ask another analyst what to do.
10. Identify dubious items for the manager's attention.

The analyst, by looking for enough items to cut, proceeds until the budget is balanced within the existing revenue constraint.[7]

Beyond those rules of thumb, is there anything that a budget analyst—always less knowledgeable about the program under review than those who run the program, always looking for budget reductions—can do? There are some points that must be considered in each instance. First, the reviewer must verify the arithmetic used to produce program requests. Overambitious rounding and errors seem to increase requests more often than they reduce them. Second, reviewers should check linkages between justifications and dollar requests. Is there reason to believe that the request will have the desired result or will things stay about the same, regardless of the money requested? Requests in the latter category are good candidates for elimination, regardless of budget conditions. Third, are there changes in the agency program or changed directions in existing programs? Are these changes consistent with legislative (and executive) intent? Fourth, are there omissions from the budget requests? Some years ago, a major university constructed a large center for performing and creative arts, but neglected to request money to cover utilities (electricity, and so on) needed for its operation. That created significant budget problems during the first year, as major reductions had to be imposed on other university activities to cover that utility bill. Finally, the analyst must use all resources available for analysis, particularly the prior year budget and actual expenditure, the current year budget and reported expenditure to date, and the proposed budget. A comparison of these documents can indicate potential problem areas and areas in which reductions may be made without special trouble. The analyst should establish the cause of any deviations from trends apparent in those comparisons.

MANAGING BUDGET EXECUTION

An approved budget becomes an important managerial tool, both to guide agency operations according to plan and to ensure that expendi-

---

[7] Arnold J. Meltsner, *The Politics of City Revenue* (Berkeley: University of California Press, 1971), p. 178.

ture does not exceed appropriation. Ordinary budgets are approved for an entire fiscal year; execution of the budget occurs on a day-to-day, week-to-week, month-to-month basis. How can the budget be a useful device for control of this execution activity? Well-functioning fiscal systems divide the total budget appropriation to operating units for the year into quarterly (or monthly) allotments on agreement with the central budget office. Suppose the department of streets and storm sewers has an appropriation of $4 million for the fiscal year from January 1 to December 31 and relatively constant expenditure rates are anticipated during the year. An allotment plan adopted by the department and the city budget office could then be as follows:

	Allotment to quarter	Cumulative allotments
January 1	$1,000,000	1,000,000
April 1	1,000,000	2,000,000
July 1	1,000,000	3,000,000
October 1	1,000,000	4,000,000
Total	$4,000,000	

A comparison of actual expenditure at each quarter end with the allotment provides an early warning for control of department activity to prevent overspending or unnecessary underprovision of service. If reports of spending plus commitments to spend (encumbrances) through the end of June exceed $2 million, activity (spending) curtailment is needed; if the total is less than $2 million, the activity may be accelerated.[8]

Service delivery and, hence, spending profiles for many agencies will not spread equally through the year. A typical outdoor swimming pool in the northern United States will be in service during the summer months only, so its operating expenditures will concentrate in these months; equal quarterly allotments would not be useful for control and management. Activities that produce uneven expenditure flows during the year (seasonal needs, major capital equipment acquisitions, opening or closing of new facilities, etc.) require uneven allotments. The schedule must be both consistent with the approved budget and activity flow expectations if it is to be usable for control and management.

Comparisons of the allotments and expenditures to date can suggest (1) areas in which expenditure may have to be curtailed, (2) areas in

---

[8] The comparison between expenditure plan and spending activity must include both payments made and contractual commitments made that will involve payment later. These latter totals have different titles in different political jurisdictions (encumbrances and obligations are two) but, regardless of title, they reduce the available spending authority and must be included in the comparison against the expenditure plan.

which surpluses may be available for use against deficits in other areas, (3) patterns that may be helpful in preparation of future budgets, and (4) the possible need to request a supplemental appropriation (funds beyond those initially appropriated for the fiscal year). Some spending faster than allotment may simply be accelerated acquisition, an unexpected transfer between quarters. Other spending may imply spending above the approved appropriation. These latter overruns require spending unit action, generally according to budget office direction. Both agencies and finance officers can thus maintain better control of budget execution with these periodic allotment-to-expenditure comparisons. While the objective of execution is delivery of services to the public, funds must not be spent in a fashion contrary to the appropriation.

AUDIT AND EVALUATION

Many audits will be conducted using a prescribed checklist of steps to establish uniformity in the conduct of a class of audits by several different auditors. Much of the audit will focus on controls built into the systems of the agency. If the system operates satisfactorily the audit agency need not be concerned with tracing the body of individual transactions because the system will produce substantial compliance. Accounting controls prevent fraud and waste and ensure the accuracy of operating data and financial reports; administrative controls improve efficiency of operations, ensure compliance with applicable laws, and promote adherence to stated policies (including legislation). The audit determines whether those control systems work. In their audit, examiners look for errors and abuses such as those listed in Table 3–1.

Regardless of their relative importance, theft from government receives extensive publicity when discovered. Thus, it is worthwhile to review some of the methods that have historically been used to steal from government: phantom resources, procurement fixing, honest graft, straightforward theft, shoddy materials, and kickbacks.

1. Ghosting. Theft through phantom resources—receiving payment for resources not actually delivered—can take several different forms. One method, the ghost employee, involves placing on an agency payroll individuals who do no work for that agency. The person receives pay but provides no service. A second method is payment for supplies or services which are not actually delivered. Invoices sent by the firm show delivery, but the agency never receives the supplies or services. Closely related is double payment for supplies or services. The services are performed once, but invoices show delivery of two shipments. Each method causes government to pay for resources not delivered and each artificially increases the cost of public service.

TABLE 3–1
Some errors or abuses sought by auditors*

Year-end accounting manipulations that push revenues and expenditures from one year to the next.

Unrecorded liabilities: commitments to vendors that are suppressed by withholding written agreements and purchase orders from the paperwork system.

Overestimation of revenues, to keep down tax rates.

Failure to reserve adequately for nonpayment of taxes.

Miscalculation of utility, hospital, and other service bills.

Unauthorized transfer of funds between appropriation accounts.

Recording of grant receipts in the wrong funds.

Use of a commingled cash account to disguise use of restricted funds for unauthorized purposes.

Failure to observe legal requirements for review and approval of budgets.

Failure to compile and submit financial reports to state and federal agencies punctually.

Improper computation of state aid claims.

* Peter F. Rousmaniere, *Local Government Auditing—A Manual for Public Officials* (New York, N.Y.: Council on Municipal Performance, 1980), p. 10.

2. Bid rigging. The procurement fix involves the rigging of bids on supply contracts. Suppose a section of highway is to be repaved. Potential suppliers would establish beforehand the bid winner and the winning price; other firms would submit noncompetitive bids for show alone. Firms would cooperate in the collusion because their turn to win would come on another project. The collusion increases the profits of the firms and increases the cost of government. Government employees may or may not profit from the procurement fix, depending on the arrangements of the bid rigging.

3. Honest graft. Honest graft uses advance information to produce private profit for the individual employee. The reminiscences of George Washington Plunkitt, Tammany Hall leader of the early 20th century, describe the process:

There's an honest graft, and I'm an example of how it works. I might sum up the whole thing by sayin': 'I seen my opportunities and I took 'em.'

Just let me explain by example. My party's in power in the city, and it's goin' to undertake a lot of public improvements. Well, I'm tipped off, say, that they're going to lay out a new park at a certain place.

I see my opportunity and I take it. I go to that place and I buy up all the land I can in the neighborhood. Then the board of this or that makes its plan public, and there is a rush to get my land, which nobody cared particular for before.

Ain't it perfectly honest to charge a good price and make a profit on my investment and foresight? Of course, it is. Well, that's honest graft.[9]

That profit measures the extent to which the honest grafter, through use of inside information, steals from the public by forcing excess payment for a resource. Honest graft may likewise involve acquisition or formation of companies to do business with a government. Bid specifications may then be written so that company would be the only one qualified. Prices for that commodity or service would be artificially increased for the enrichment of the government employee.

4. **Diversion.** Public assets or the service of employees may be stolen for private use. Office supplies, equipment, gasoline, and so on are as usable for private purposes as for government activities. Public employees may be diverted to private uses, including construction or maintenance projects on property owned by government officials. Employees are sometimes used as workers in political campaigns while on government time—a special illegal advantage of incumbency. These activities involve straightforward stealing as individuals use assets owned by government without payment.

5. **Shoddy material.** Because low quality supplies and material can generally be delivered at lower cost than can higher quality supplies and material, government contract specifications require delivery of one quality of material. A contractor who provides lower than specified quality ("shoddy material") can thus profit at public expense.

6. **Kickbacks.** Public officials who have power to select who receives contracts to do business with governments, what banks receive public deposits, and who works for government agencies may profit by arranging for artificially high contract awards or artificial wage payments with a portion of that payment kicked back to the government official. The favored individual or firm receives higher than the appropriate price for the contracted service, so is able to profit even after making the payment to the contracting agent.

SOME SPECIAL PROBLEMS OF PUBLIC EMPLOYEE COMPENSATION

Governments ordinarily acquire resources by purchase on the open market. Occasionally they use powers of condemnation or draft to acquire them, but this practice generally conflicts with prevailing views of freedom and property ownership. The resources are acquired not because of their individual attributes, but because they can be used to

---

[9] Recorded by William L. Riordon, *Plunkett of Tammany Hall* (New York: E. P. Dutton, 1963), pp. 3–4.

provide desired services to the general public. A very large percentage of the total cost of providing those services does in fact consist of wage and salary payment to individuals. Table 3–2 indicates the share of direct wage and salary payments in total expenditure by governments

TABLE 3–2
Relative expenditure on salaries and wages, 1976–1977

	Salaries and wages as percent of direct expenditure	Salaries and wages as percent of current operating expenditure
Federal	18.6%	47.0%
State	27.4	46.6
Local:	46.6	60.4
Cities	39.8	54.5
School districts	63.4	70.6

Source: Census of Governments, 1977, vol. 4, Compendium of Government Finances (Washington: U.S. Government Printing Office, 1979), p. 26.

in 1976–77. The percentage for the federal government is much lower than for the other levels presented there because the federal government does much spending by contract. The contracted service is produced by private employees receiving salaries from private employers, but the resources are being produced for federal provision. Compensation to those employees, however, is established by the private firms for whom they work. The percentage for local government is much higher—60 percent of current operating expenditure for wages and salaries—and even higher for school districts independent of other local governments. Those data clearly demonstrate that much of the cost of modern government will be determined by the compensation paid to employees.

Wages and salaries

A reasonable objective of an employee compensation program is to ensure delivery of public service at least cost to the taxpayer. The key question is whether the government can obtain and retain employees with desired skills, balancing the interests of taxpayers/service recipients against the interests of public employees. If employees are overpaid, the taxpayer pays too much for services provided; if employees are underpaid, the taxpayer receives artificial subsidization at the expense of those employees, and government must bear the disruption and cost of high employee turnover. Neither situation is healthy for the survival of the community, and both artificially increase the full cost of government.

With that background, it is reasonable to question how the appropriate wage rates might be established. Although some salaries continue to be set by law passed by higher units of government or by tradition, a large number of governments now establish payment through classification and wage comparability studies or through collective bargaining with employee unions. Both structures will be considered here because they have somewhat different implications for finance officers.

Position comparability studies seek to establish what the attributes are of a particular government position so that those attributes may be matched to similar private sector positions. The private sector salary presumably has been determined through the working of market forces and measures the value of the contribution of that employee to the economy. If a position in the public sector is paid an amount equivalent to that of a position with similar characteristics in the private sector, the recipient of that salary is presumed to be neither overpaid nor underpaid, but will be compensated at the fair market rate. Of course, there are some special data requirements for the system to operate, but these can usually be fulfilled with some effort.

There are, however, problems with the logic of salary comparability. First, some public sector positions have no business equivalents in the relevant market area. It is difficult, for instance, to establish a comparable position to fire fighter (duty hours, danger, special skills, etc.) in most localities—and any positions actually found may be occupied by off-duty fire fighters, a circumstance not likely to produce reasonable full-time pay equivalents. That would not be a problem for secretaries, data processing personnel, and other general-skill personnel found working for government, but it is a problem not easily solved for other positions.

Second, government is the predominant employer of numerous employment skills in several labor markets. Actions resulting from comparability studies will bring compensating private employer reactions which then feed through comparability, in a continuing cycle. In that circumstance, private local markets simply are not especially helpful and private markets in other areas do not provide usable guidance because regional peculiarities can influence prevailing wages. (Some areas are generally desirable to live in and others are not, according to the reactions of individual families.)

Third, wage comparisons are complicated by differences in employment stability and by differences in fringe benefits provided public and private employees. Despite well-publicized problems of employee layoffs by several large cities, public employment tends to be more stable than employment in business. Business employment depends on product and service sales, which fluctuate with general economic conditions. When the economy slumps, employees are laid off. That employment instability does not occur with public employment—the work force remains stable during economic decline. Because of the difference in employment stability, positions paying the same rate will, over time, yield the public employee greater income than is received by the private employee. Just as work stability varies between private and public employment, so too does the extent of employer-financed fringe benefits.[10] Unless care is taken to adjust compensation levels for fringe benefits, true comparability will not be attained. While adjustments for fringe benefits are frequently made—with uneven success—there is no satisfactory present adjustment for stability differences.

Finally, public and private employees typically work with dramatically different capital endowments. Thus, secretaries in private business often work with word processing equipment which enables them to produce perfect copy very quickly and in multiples. Secretaries in many local governments continue to use nonelectric typewriters. As a result, output per day differs dramatically between the two secretaries (regardless of how skilled the secretaries are, in fact). If the two secretaries are paid comparable rates, the cost of public service is artificially high—to the detriment of citizen/taxpayers. It is not clear what adjustments could appropriately be made to allow properly for those productivity differences.

Such pay classification is attractive for budget makers because it makes budget estimation relatively simple, particularly in comparison to the uncertainty produced by salaries established through collective bargaining (some of those uncertainties will be discussed shortly). The budget officer determines the personnel classification of individuals to be handling the workload during the budget year, determines the salary for each classification, and multiplies the number of people in the classification by the salary of that classification to obtain the budget requirement. Many units will structure their compensation schedules so that personnel receive automatic increments with each year on the job. That situation is handled by adding one year to the experience of those currently working and using that experience factor in the schedules. There is thus a permanence of structure that is convenient in classified schedules.

The second method of public sector salary establishment is through collective bargaining with employee unions. Salaries are determined by

---

[10] Roy W. Bahl and Bernard Jump, "The Budgetary Implications of Rising Employee Retirement System Costs," *National Tax Journal,* 27 (September 1974): 479–90.

bargaining skills and relative power; comparisons with private employers are not directly relevant. A former budget director of the City of New York reports that public sector union militancy

> has made the job of the budget director more difficult and more complex. More accurately, it has made the job, at least in the City of New York, almost impossible. In smaller and simpler governments, the diagnosis is not likely to be that dismal.[11]

His reasons for that extreme observation hinge around the reduced ability of the budget director to manage the budget within a collective bargaining environment. That is because (1) the municipal labor relations director and the union leaders are comfortable with each other and not with questions of budgets and resource constraints, (2) salary changes for one employee group create disruptions in historic relationships with other groups (sanitation with police or fire fighters, for instance) which bring demands for more changes; (3) work rules prevent changes to introduce new technologies or otherwise improve productivity; and (4) unsettled union contracts make budget preparation and approval uncertain, because salaries, a major component of total expenditure remain undetermined.

The relationship between the budget process and the collective bargaining process is interesting because of the importance of spending on employee wages and salaries relative to total spending. Derber and colleagues point out: "Collective bargaining introduces considerations that may not be entirely compatible with traditional budget-making practices."[12] The budget process presumably establishes the size of the government and the allocation of finances among various activities; bargaining establishes labor cost of the government. Participants in a budget process occurring before bargaining will have to guess the outcome of that bargaining to use in the personnel cost lines of the budget, but the adopted budget will establish the personnel cost ceiling for bargaining. Bargaining them becomes only a process for dividing the funds approved in the budget. On the other hand, bargaining before budgeting will determine a large fraction of the total budget. In sum, a failure to integrate the two processes reduces the significance of whichever process occurs last.

There are some ways that governments have devised to accommodate the failure to synchronize budgeting and bargaining. They all in-

---

[11] Frederick O'R. Hayes, "Collective Bargaining and the Budget Director," in *Public Workers and Public Unions,* ed. Sam Zagoria (Englewood Cliffs N.J., Prentice-Hall, 1972), p. 89.

[12] Milton Derber et al., "Bargaining and Budget Making in Illinois Public Institutions," *Industrial and Labor Relations Review,* 27 (October 1973): p. 49.

volve adding flexibility to one process or the other. Bargaining can be made flexible by providing for retroactive pay or supplemental negotiation if it occurs before budget passage. Budgets can be made more flexible through transfer of funds between accounts or supplemental appropriations. If they are not conducted simultaneously, it is critical that the process occurring first have some provision for revision after the other has occurred. Otherwise, participants in the second process will claim—and with some justification—that their hands have been tied by the other process.

Public sector bargaining grows, even as bargaining covers a continually smaller fraction of private employment. Several analysts argue that public sector bargaining is not desirable:

> In private sector bargaining two responsible parties meet with power to represent themselves. But when public service unions demand collective bargaining rights and ultimate arbitration, they do not contemplate dealing with taxpayers, who, responsibly, are saddled with paying the bills. Instead, the public service union hopes to wrangle it out with other public employees who in many cases happen to be dependent on union votes and union money. Market considerations are far away, and mayors are just other hired hands.[13]

The problem is described as the Hanslowe effect, "a neat mutual back-scratching mechanism, whereby public employee representatives and politicians reinforce the other's interest and domain."[14] In that circumstance, the personnel cost share will expand, with little the public can do. The crunch ultimately comes when service cost encounters limits imposed by referenda. What happens then is not clear, but public service delivery will undoubtedly suffer during the transition.

Retirement programs

Public employee retirement programs—the delayed, but often lucrative, portion of employee compensation—typically include two elements: social security coverage financed through a federal trust fund and a retirement plan provided by the employer. Payroll taxes on employer and employee finance the social security system; payments by the employer and, usually, by the employee finance the latter. State and local governments can, however, choose to be excluded from the social security system, a choice not available to private employers. There are

---

[13] John Chamberlain, "When Cops and Teachers Strike," *The Wall Street Journal,* October 22, 1975, p. 16.

[14] Kurt L. Hanslowe, *The Emerging Law of Labor Relations in Public Employment,* 1967, p. 268.

several separate retirement systems for federal government employees. Those for civil service and the military are the two largest. A number of governments remain outside the system and, in the past few years, a handful have left the system, feeling that equivalent or better coverage could be provided employees at lower cost.

Social security

There are fundamental differences between social security for public employees and public employee pension systems, even though both are payments made by government to a government employee. Most significant is the fact that the pension is part of an employer–employee exchange; it is a contractual or insurance relationship involving an agreement about delayed compensation. Social security is a relationship between government and a claimant on that government; it is not an employer–employee relationship and, possibly unfortunately, there is no delayed compensation agreement involved. With that system, the federal government supports politically determined benefits with politically determined taxes—there is no employer–employee contractual agreement involved.

Taxes on payrolls finance social security benefits—half legally from the employer, half legally from the employee. Many analysts believe that a much larger share, possibly all, of that burden actually rests on the employee as employers adjust rates of wages or other compensation to allow for the payroll tax owed. If the tax is shifted to the employee, the two parts combined would currently equal a flat rate of over 12 percent on wages and salaries, by far the largest tax burden on many people. Receipts from the tax go to the Social Security Trust Fund, a special fund the federal government uses for social insurance transactions. Any money in the fund is invested in U.S. government securities to provide financing for general government activities. When individuals become eligible for social security assistance, money from the fund (contributions and interest earned) or from payroll taxes paid by those in the current work force cover the expenditure. Levels of benefits and eligibility for them are legislatively determined, although regular benefits are normally based on earnings during the last 10 years worked before retirement. After retirement, benefits can increase by legislative decision.

For many years, there were relatively large numbers of people in the workforce contributing to the fund and relatively few people receiving benefits from it (the system only began in the mid-1930s). As a result, the trust fund grew in size as inflow substantially exceeded outflow. In recent years, more eligible people have retired and, at the same time, retirees have been living longer. Fund accumulation has reversed and payroll tax rates have increased substantially to cover promised payments. Unfortunately, the payroll tax is significantly regressive (it is a flat rate tax, it covers only wage and salary income, and it does not apply to income above specified limits) and legislators are reluctant to use it more heavily. Congress continued liberalization of benefits, including the addition of automatic benefit increases tied to the consumer price index. Unfortunately, the rate of increase of payrolls seldom keeps pace with the consumer price index, so the outflow accelerated with inflation. While social security benefits are not in jeopardy, the system will require substantial alteration in the next few years. Likely options are (1) regular assistance from general federal taxes, either by direct payment to the fund or by shifting some medical care support programs from social security to general finance, or (2) a change in the tax used to support the fund, either to a new base (such as value added) or to a tax more like the ordinary income taxes.

Pensions

The other piece of retirement compensation, public employee pensions, are in worse condition than the social security system and responsibility for repair rests primarily with state and local government. Public employee pension funds have not accumulated sufficient reserves during employee work careers to cover the benefits to which they will be entitled through their retirement. Thus, the government will have to pay from its current revenue in later years part of the compensation promised in earlier years. For example, in fiscal 1990, the government would pay the wages and salaries of the 1990 work force and the 1990 pension payments to all prior employees whose work in earlier years entitled them to pensions.

For many years, governments and employees seemed content with this financing approach. There appeared to be little danger of missed payments to employees, because governments do not go out of business or get acquired by conglomerates, the dangers faced by private employees. Payments can easily be made by raising taxes on the future tax base. Jump aptly summarizes the traditional view of state and local employee pensions:

> The pension, along with a degree of job security not generally associated with employment in the private sector, was assumed to be a fair offset for lower wages in public sector jobs. Commonly, public pension administration encountered few problems that required more than perfunctory attention from governments' top elected and professional officials. Each year, legislatures appropriated whatever was needed to cover the year's share

of pension costs. In some jurisdictions, appropriations simply equalled the actual benefits to be paid during the year; in other instances, appropriations reflected at least nominally the actuarial cost of benefits accrued during the year by active employees. As long as work force size, benefit levels, and the number of retirees did not grow too rapidly and the jurisdiction's financial condition remained stable, the fiscal implications of the pensions did not appear to be significant.[15]

That easy approach to pensions was shattered in the 1970s. Expenditures for employee retirement suddenly increased, absolutely and relative to current personnel cost, as many employees started drawing lucrative pensions. State and local governments began encountering impressive resistance to tax increases, including new constitutional restrictions against rate increases, and some governments teetered on the brink of default on contractual obligations in the midst of fiscal crisis. Credit rating firms, bond underwriters, and investors all became wary of lending to governments with sizable long-term obligations, such as pension liabilities, that could endanger repayment of debt. And, possibly most important, investigators discovered an important incentive problem with traditional pension finance: elected officials could seek public employee support with generous pension promises now, knowing that when the payments were made, those officials would not be part of the governing team required to raise those funds. From those influences came a major effort to switch public pension finance from the traditional pay-as-you-go basis to an actuarial funding basis.

Actuarial funding is "a procedure where the estimated cost—the actuarial present value—of pension benefits accruing to active employees is systematically paid by the employer into a fund (perhaps with a share paid in by the employee as well). In turn, the retirement fund makes payments to retirees and invests surplus funds."[16] Thus, the anticipated future cost of pension payments to an employee will be handled while the employee is working. Pension payments on retirement will come from money set aside during the years of employment plus interest on that accumulation. Funding will be on the basis of estimates computed on several assumptions: whether and when the employee will retire, when the retired employee will die, the progression of employee salary, and the rate of interest earned on invested pension funds. None of those

---

[15] Bernard Jump, Jr., "Public Employment, Collective Bargaining, and Employee Wages and Pensions," in *State and Local Government Finance and Financial Management: A Compendium of Current Research,* ed. John E. Petersen et al., (Washington, D.C.: Government Finance Research Center, Municipal Finance Officers Association, 1978), p. 78.

[16] Bernard Jump, Jr., *State and Local Employee Pension Plans: Watching for Problems* (Columbus, Ohio: Academy for Contemporary Problems, 1976), p. 9.

factors will be known; all must be reviewed and revised on a reasonable schedule if funding is to be meaningful.

When pension funds accumulate, they become attractive and lucrative items for abuse.[17] First, some governments have used employee pension funds as guaranteed markets for their debt. This debt yields an artificially low rate of return because interest on state and local debt is excluded from federal taxation—a benefit of no value to the public employee pension fund because it is not subject to federal tax. Second, pension fund management is sometimes restrained to local firms in an effort to assist those firms, even though they lack the expertise or scale for high quality, low cost management. Both actions cause pension participants to lose potential return. Whether these actions are questionable depends on the role of pensions: are they compensation for work rendered or are they gratuities given past employees? If the former, those actions clearly represent mismanagement as they sacrifice net earnings of funds owned by pension participants. If the latter, the funds may be regarded as fair game for any public purpose because they belong to the host government. Governments and employees may well have different answers to the role of pensions, although logic is stronger for the compensation and employee ownership view.

Conclusion

Budget skills combine techniques which can be taught and cunning which develops with experience. The start for all budgets must be a sound understanding of what the agency request intends to accomplish. Without that foundation, no amount of tricks can help much. As in many government operations, the great problem is information—those who have that information and are able to communicate it will have greater than average success. Beyond that, there are few general truths.

A CASE FOR DISCUSSION

Budgeting would be easier if rules could be established to eliminate the need for human decisions and if incentives could be established which would induce individuals to behave in a desirable fashion. Those rules and incentives are, however, difficult to invent for public agencies. If they were simple to create, they would have been enacted years ago.

The following case, excerpted from *The Wall Street Journal,* illustrates what can happen when a desirable goal is approached by a broad, general rule.

---

[17] Louis M. Kohlmeier, *Conflicts of Interest: State and Local Pension Fund Asset Management* (New York: Twentieth Century Fund, 1976).

Consider these questions:

1. What orientation toward budgeting does the approach applied by Senator Sasser represent?
2. What is the Senator's objective? Is it worthwhile?
3. How might the desired effect be achieved without the unexpected results of the approach used here?

Federal Travel Cuts Can Take a Big Slice Out of Unrelated Pies

BY BROOKS JACKSON
Staff Reporter of THE WALL STREET JOURNAL

WASHINGTON—To some people, the skies appear dark with federal employees flying about unnecessarily. "There are probably more than 20,000 government employees in the air at any one time," Sen. James Sasser once declared. "I think 18,000 would be sufficient."

Sen. Sasser, a Tennessee Democrat, played a lead role in persuading Congress to slash $500 million from last year's federal travel and transportation budget. Then he asserted the action had saved that much in "unnecessary travel."

Ronald Reagan no doubt was similarly concerned about needless travel when he signed an executive order, within 48 hours of becoming President, aimed at cutting $300 million from the year's $3.7 billion travel budget.

Yet the evidence is that last year's cuts went well beyond frivolous government travel, into such things as law

enforcement, military training, and safety inspections in factories and mines.

OMB's Study

The cut did help prompt the White House Office of Management and Budget to look for more ways to save money in government travel. And in sampling travel vouchers for the first time, the OMB found to its amazement that there really are an average of 20,000 one-way commercial flights each day by civilian and military federal employees.

But OMB also found that only about 14.5 percent of government travel is for speeches, conferences and meetings—the sort of travel most often criticized as excessive. Most goes for operations, training, or relocation.

As a result of last year's travel cut, law enforcement by federal park rangers literally came to a standstill for three months on the Natchez Trace Parkway, which winds through federal parklands in Tennessee, Mississippi, and a corner of Alabama. On the parkway, and at many other national parks as well, government trucks and cars are leased and therefore show up as "travel" under federal accounting procedures.

So to meet their share of the travel reduction, Natchez park rangers ceased patrolling and responded only to emergency calls. "We didn't chase any violators," recalls David L. Tomlinson, chief ranger. "People were really hotfooting it there for a while."

Increase in Road Deaths

Ranger Tomlinson says fatalities on the road doubled from five in 1979 to 10 last year, and vandalism increased at remote campsites. Collections of litter and garbage, using the leased vehicle, were cut to one day a week from five, and road repairs were deferred.

At the Defense Department, which accounts for roughly 70 percent of federal travel money, military training was affected. Some maneuvers were scrubbed for lack of funds to get troops to the scene, and summer reserve training was especially hard hit. "For the reserve forces it very nearly amounted to a training disaster," asserts the Association of the U.S. Army. "Units had funds to pay for special schooling, but no money to get students to the training."

Operations were curtailed at some agencies whose employees must travel to accomplish their jobs. The Occupational Safety and Health Administration cut the number of job-safety inspections from about 60,000 in 1979 to 50,000 in 1980. For several months, OSHA couldn't send any inspectors to its special training academy in Illinois.

Mine-safety inspections also were reduced. The federal Mine Safety and Health Administration got rid of 200 leased vehicles from its fleet of 1,700. Officials began taking appeals of fines over the telephone, rather than meeting personally with mine operators. The agency also cut back its on-the-scene technical help to mine operators.

Sometimes the cut actually cost taxpayers money. At Shenandoah National Park in Virginia, for example, patrols weren't curtailed, because the park owns its own cars, which are thus charged to "operations" and not to travel. But the travel cut left the park without enough money to pay lodging and carfare for sending six rangers to Roanoke, Va., for a five-day course in fighting forest fires.

So the park asked the rangers to commute each day, 150 miles each way, in park-owned cars. The resulting overtime pay showed up as salary, not travel. "We had to pay more and use our own cars to do the same job," said Bill Loftis, assistant park administrator. "We can't believe this is what Congress had in mind."

Indeed, congressional concern about federal travel, typically is directed at bureaucrats the Congressmen view as living it up at public expense as they travel to needless conferences and meetings. "I find two or three people from the same department at a small meeting in Anchorage or Fairbanks," said Alaska's Republican Sen. Ted Stevens during consideration of last year's cut. "Of course, a lot of it depends on whether it is the fishing season or not."

*   *   *   *   *

A Deceptive Cut

What did the cut accomplish? "I think you can make a good case that it did in fact save $500 million," Sen. Sasser insists. Yet the government actually spent more for travel last year than it had budgeted before the cut.

Sen. Sasser says the supplemental appropriations were needed because of such unexpected events as the big increase in oil prices and U.S. military operations in the Persian Gulf following seizure of American hostages in Iran and the Soviet invasion of Afghanistan. But Pentagon officials say the supplemental appropriations included enough extra money to wipe out much of the "saving" from Sen. Sasser's cut.

Without the extra money, military officials say, shipments of arms and ammunition to Europe and the Mideast would have been curtailed. More than half the $500 million "saving" was scheduled to come not from the $3 billion budgeted for travel, but from the $5 billion budgeted for costs of shipping such things as military equipment and the household goods of transferred federal employees.

The lesson many federal budget officials draw from all this is that meat-ax cuts in travel don't save much money but do make it harder for the government to do its job. "It's the kind of mentality that makes you eliminate one helicopter from a rescue mission to Iran," says one civil servant at the OMB.

Recommended Approach

Wayne Granquist, who headed the OMB's management-improvement efforts in the Carter administration, says that cutting the size of federal programs is the only way to achieve savings in overhead costs of the size claimed by Sen. Sasser and predicted by President Reagan. "Politicians are saying you can save huge sums by cutting out things that nobody thinks are important," such as travel, says Mr. Granquist. "That isn't true. There's no free lunch."

Nonetheless, some travel economies are possible. Indeed, the government says it saved $5.4 million in the last half of 1980 through a new program of bargaining for airline discounts. A new round of discounted fares is expected to yield savings of $12 million in the first six months of this year. The OMB estimates savings from discounts could eventually reach $72 million a year if promoted vigorously.

Another suggested way to save money would be through *looser* regulation of travel. Detailed accountings and audits of travel expenses add $400 million a year to costs associated with travel, the General Accounting Office estimates. Millions could be saved through fewer audits.

It remains to be seen whether savings of $300 million a year, as President Reagan has ordered, are possible without hurting basic government and military operations again.

4

Selected budget
reform techniques

Budget processes can help allocate government resources, control agency operations, and manage service delivery. Unfortunately, prevailing practices often impede the full use of budgeting for planning and analysis to guide public choices. Traditional budgets historically emphasize control of fund use and have not been appropriately structured for resource allocation decisions. That emphasis exists largely because public budgeting emerged in a period when the concern was, purely and simply, prevention of theft. Hence, budgets focused on control of input purchase and little else. Modern governments have moved beyond that stage. Governments do provide valued services, so keeping a lid on their actions is not sufficient: budgets no longer are simply devices for restraining thieves. Decision makers must control waste and make allocation choices, so governments need budget structures that permit planning and management for efficiency.

BUDGETS AS A TOOL FOR
DECISION MAKING

Traditional budgets embody several impediments to public management and planning. These include the administrative department basis for budget requests and appropriation, the short-period concept for costs in budget considerations, the focus on agency inputs rather than products or outputs, and the absence of comparison of project costs with project benefits. The federal government also has problems with uncontrollability, the problem of spending outside the annual appropriation process. Each will be considered, for most reform techniques seek to reduce one or more of these barriers.

First, public decisions require meaningful measurement of the total cost of achieving a desired objective. Traditional budget processes do not provide that information. Budgets are proposed and appropriations are made on an administrative department basis, not on the basis of what departments actually intend to achieve. Such categorizations blur the allocation process and impede consideration of alternatives, the essence of resource allocation. Categories of administration—Defense, Justice, Public Works, etc.—are too broad for judgment about the appropriate relative amounts for spending. Further, the agency titles include activity conglomerations that are often more related to the work of other agencies than to each other. One observer suggests that in many instances the work of the agency has little or nothing to do with what its title sounds like. In short, intelligent resource allocation decisions are unlikely to emerge from budget considerations based on administrative departments. Budgets and appropriations which go through organization charts complicate identification of the cost of achieving a particular objective because most agencies have multiple outputs. Weiss notes the "fallacy of appellation . . . the rhetorical act of obscuring the distinction between the name of a budget category and the actual phenomenon generally associated with that name".[1]

Second, traditional budgets are developed and considered on a single-year basis without development of cost profiles over time. Budgets usually cover a single year of agency operation[2]—an appropriate period for control purposes—even though many activities proposed by an agency have significant future cost implications. The single-year cost often is little more than a program down payment with many installments ahead. Reasonable decision making requires that total cost of a project be examined, not just the single-year project cost. Because such data are seldom a part of the budget process, budget choices must be made without appropriate information.

Third, reasonable choice requires that alternative methods of reaching a desired objective be compared. Agencies traditionally build budgets from existing input combinations. The agencies lock them-

---

[1] Edmond H. Weiss, "The Fallacy of Appellation in Government Budgeting," *Public Administration Review,* 34 (July/August 1974), p. 377.

[2] Some governments have biennial budgets, but these are essentially single-year budgets times two. Only by accident will the complete cost of a project be captured in a biennial budget.

selves into "normal" operating techniques and alternative methods don't get considered. An important cause is the general focus on what public agencies *buy* (inputs) to the near exclusion of what the agencies *provide* (services or outputs). Ordinary reviews emphasize changes in the objects of expenditure, that is, the personnel to be hired (or fired) and their pay grades, changes in the pay of current staff, and the supplies and equipment to be purchased. An input orientation produces the following logic: if the price of gasoline increases by 25 percent, agency operation requires an increase in the appropriation for those purchases of 25 percent. Otherwise, the agency must cut back its services. That logic implies that the objective of the agency is the purchase of given amounts of specific inputs. A budget process should induce consideration of alternative production strategies to economize on the use of resources which have become relatively more expensive. Seldom is there but a single way to provide a service, and budget processes need to consider alternatives, especially when the price of some inputs has increased dramatically. The reviewers too infrequently consider the public services to be provided with these inputs or the alternative combinations of inputs which could produce those services. A simple analogue to traditional budgeting would be a baker who purchases flour, milk, sugar, etc., without considering the number of cakes, cookies, breads, and so on to be sold, or the alternate recipes for their production. These physical input requirements get selected before any cost estimation and without reference either to alternative production methods or to the programs sacrificed if a particular choice is made.[3]

Fourth, meaningful public decisions must weigh the cost of programs relative to their worth. The line-item costs in traditional budgets are financial, out-of-pocket costs. They exclude social costs not directly paid; they reflect financial transactions, not the value of opportunities not chosen; and they do not distinguish between sunk and incremental costs of actions. Thus, the cost data presented may not be entirely appropriate for making decisions, but budget costs do get reported. Worth of programs delivered, however, seldom is reported or formally considered. That comparison, vital to intelligent resource allocation, is not a regular component of budget processes. Unless some point of the budget process regularly compares total benefits of a program to its cost, poor public decisions are likely. Public decisions based on pro-

---

[3] Niskanen, Tullock, and others point out that government agency administrators have individual incentives to spend as much as possible (conduct any project at the highest feasible cost). (Gordon Tullock, *The Politics of Bureaucracy* [Washington, D.C.: Public Affairs Press, 1965] and William A. Niskanen, Jr., *Bureaucracy and Representative Government* [Chicago: Aldine Publishing, 1971].)

gram cost—either high or low—will not consistently lead to a wise use of scarce resources, just as would consideration solely of project worth to the exclusion of cost. A society with scarcity must require consideration of worth against cost, if only in the sense of considering how society would be poorer in the absence of the service. Regardless of whether worth is easily measurable, no choices are possibly solely on a cost basis.

Finally, governments have trouble controlling expenditure from one year to the next in response to changed priorities or to needs for macroeconomic stabilization. At the federal level, a large percentage of total expenditure is legally *uncontrollable* in the short run.[4] This absence of control differs from the legislative problems of changing politically popular programs and the difficulty of intervening in an incremental process; this uncontrollability emerges because some spending occurs outside the annual appropriation process. There are several sources of relative uncontrollability. First, much federal spending results from "entitlements" to individuals, as with the food stamp program. An individual who meets the established eligibility requirements receives the defined financial assistance—appropriation must follow the actual expenditure. Congress appropriates an initial amount with the understanding that supplemental appropriation will be made as those funds are exhausted. Second, social service grants to states add to the uncontrollability. If the state spends, federal expenditure must compensate the state for that expenditure.[5] The federal expenditure is thus determined by state action. Third, interest on public debt (and public agency debt) is a contractual obligation permanently appropriated and not annually controllable. Finally, obligations carried from prior years can be controlled only with great difficulty, as actual expenditure may occur well after the year of appropriation. Deobligation is both difficult and expensive; rescission is particularly difficult since the 1974 legislation.

Another variety of contractual obligation generates similar expenditure outside the normal appropriation process. Here, a substantive committee bypasses appropriation committees by authorizing an agency to enter into contracts or spend the proceeds of agency borrowing. The contractual obligations have to be met, so spending occurs without normal appropriation scrutiny. This procedure, called "backdoor spending," emerged in the period when the substantive committees had a dramatically different political viewpoint than did the

[4] The concept of relative controllability comes from Murray L. Weidenbaum, "On the Effectiveness of Congressional Control of the Public Purse," *National Tax Journal,* 18 (December 1965): 370–74.

[5] Martha Derthick, *Uncontrollable Spending for Social Service Grants* (Washington, D.C.: Brookings Institution, 1975).

appropriations committees. Backdoor spending was seen as a way of getting action on socially important policies, even though it seriously bent control processes in public expenditure. This spending is outside the scope of ordinary budget summaries.

Table 4–1 shows the pattern of uncontrollable budget outlays from 1971 to 1981. The percentage relatively uncontrollable has drifted upward from 66 percent in 1971 to 77 percent in 1981, heavily driven by payments to individuals. That category more than tripled over that decade. Of course, the problem of uncontrollability introduces short-term rigidity into federal expenditure, but no federal expenditure is beyond the ultimate control of Congress and the President. Those institutions can change entitlement formulas, can alter grant systems, can reduce debt levels, and can deobligate funds. The point is that those actions are difficult in any single year, not that Congress and the President have no options available. What has been enacted can be changed. Uncontrollability cannot be a legitimate reason for inaction. Uncontrollability, however, can limit quick changes in direction and strong countercyclical policy; it clearly suggests the need for multiyear budget planning. Neither the legislature nor the administration should be permitted the political luxury of hiding behind uncontrollability in rough times.

Reform philosophy.   Budget reforms typically seek systems which deliver the right information at the right time to decision makers or which erect an incentive structure directing individuals in agencies to work toward the social interests. Many new budget reform techniques are consistent with the classical principles for appraising budgets.[6]

1. *Comprehensiveness.* The budget should include all receipts and outlays of the government. The single process would thus include all activities of the government.
2. *Unity.* All spending and revenue collecting parts should be related to each other. Consistent evaluation criteria should be applied to any expenditure, regardless of the part of the government in which it is located.
3. *Exclusiveness.* Only financial matters should be in the budget. (Modern analysts recognize, however, that almost every governmental action has financial implications.)
4. *Specification.* The budget should be executed as it is enacted. There should not be cavalier changes made during the budget year.
5. *Annuality.* The budget should be prepared every year for the next year of agency existence.
6. *Accuracy.* Forecasts should be as reasonable as possible.

---

[6] S. Kenneth Howard, *Changing State Budgeting* (Lexington, Ky.: Council of State Governments, 1973), pp. 5–8.

TABLE 4–1
Controllability of federal budgets outlays, 1971–1981 ($ billions)

	1971	1973	1975	1977	1979	1980 (esti- mated)	1981 (esti- mated)
Relatively uncontrollable under present law:							
Open-ended programs and fixed costs							
Payments for individuals:*	77.6	99.8	149.2	190.7	224.9	261.9	298.5
Net interest	14.8	17.3	23.2	29.9	42.6	51.8	54.8
General revenue sharing	—	6.6	6.1	6.8	6.8	6.9	6.9
Farm price supports	2.8	3.6	.6	3.5	3.7	3.1	3.7
Other	4.9	6.1	7.8	8.3	8.0	10.6	8.3
Total, open-ended and fixed costs	100.2	133.4	186.9	239.1	286.1	334.2	370.2
Outlays from prior year contracts and obligations	40.2	39.6	50.7	55.3	80.0	94.5	101.4
Total, relatively uncontrollable	140.4	173.1	237.6	294.4	366.1	428.7	471.6
Total, relatively controllable	73.7	76.9	92.6	112.9	132.8	140.8	150.3
Total budget outlays†	211.4	247.1	326.2	402.7	493.7	563.6	615.8
Percent relatively uncontrollable	66.4%	70.0%	72.8%	73.1%	74.2%	76.1%	76.6%

* Includes social security and railroad retirement, federal employees retirement and insurance, unemployment assistance, medical care, assistance to students, housing assistance, food and nutrition assistance, public assistance, etc.
† Includes undistributed employer share of employee retirement not separately reported.
Source: *The Budget of the United States Government, Fiscal Year 1981*, pp. 598–99

7. *Clarity.* The budget should describe what is proposed in under-standable fashion.
8. *Publicity.* The budget in a representative democracy ought not be secret.

The particular budget reform systems considered here are performance budgets, program budgets, and zero-base budgets. Most particular budget reform systems mix elements of these systems.

PERFORMANCE BUDGETS

Performance budgets emphasize agency performance objectives and accomplishments, not the purchase of resources used by the agency. Budgets present the cost of performing measured accomplishment units during the budget year. The budget process then has the dual role of providing funds and establishing performance objectives. Perfor-mance budgeting dates to the mid-1910s in New York City; similar ef-forts continue in state and local governments to the present. Such budgets emphasize activities to be completed (audits performed, miles of streets swept, gallons of water treated, etc.) and the total expenditure needed for that activity. Figure 4–1 shows a simple performance for-

FIGURE 4–1
Performance classification

			Department	Number of units	Total cost
Function	01.	Provision of streets and roads			
Program	.1	Street construction	Bureau of streets		$x
	.2	Street lighting	Bureau of streets		$x
	.3	Traffic control	Police department		$x
	.4	Street maintenance	Bureau of streets		$x
Performance	.41	Streets cleaned		y miles	$x
	.42	Resurfacing		y miles	$x
	.43	Inspections		Number	$x
	.44	Bridge reconstruction		Number	$x
	.45	Storm sewer repair		y miles	$x
Objects of		a. Personal services			$x
expenditure		b. Material and equipment			$x
		c. Other expense			$x

Source: Jesse Burkhead, *Government Budgeting* (New York: John Wiley & Sons, 1956), p. 149.

mat. Classification of requests follows the activities of the agency, not the inputs it purchases nor the services it provides. The presentation links cost with activities, to permit unit cost comparisons across agen-cies and over time within agencies to emphasize improvements in operating efficiency.

The performance structure has some special implications. First, the budget becomes a powerful analytic tool for management responsibility and accountability. Budgeting must be a central management responsibility because activity levels and their costs are specifically presented in a document which will guide agency operation. Operating supervisors can no longer permit separate budget personnel to prepare budget requests because those budget requests now become detailed operating plans for the budget year.[7] Second, legislatures have to change their review and appropriations from the traditional line items to agency activities. The legislature may feel uncomfortable considering something other than objects of expenditures, particularly where there is no apparent linkage to revenue and budget balancing. Finally, a performance budget can make a management by objectives program easier to operate. The objectives would be the performance measures (activities) appearing in the budget. Performance and budget attainment can thus be monitored through the fiscal year.

The performance budget hinges on the quality of the measures. Some performance measures may be misleading or irrelevant: audit quality, for instance, may be more important than audit volume. The number of audits could well be the performance measure, however, simply because it is more easily quantified. Furthermore, the performance budget does not ask whether the performance being measured is the service the public actually wants. And, of course, there is no necessary consideration of alternative ways of doing a particular task. The drive to lower unit cost of performance should induce development of improved methods, not sacrifice of unit quality, but the technique is not geared to handle that problem.

Curiously enough, advocates of performance budgeting come from two ends of the political spectrum. Some public officials see performance budgets as a way to justify their contribution to the community and possibly to expand their budgets. Others see performance budgets as a tool to expose waste of money and, hence, as a guide to expenditure reduction and tax cuts. The performance budget structure does not question whether objectives are appropriate or whether a service is worth its cost of production. Performance budgets consider whether activity is being done at low cost; it does not consider whether the activity is worth doing.

PROGRAM BUDGETS

The program budget format organizes proposed expenditure according to output or contribution to governmental objectives. Programs are

---

[7] Traditional budgets are operating plans as well, except they do not contain identifiable operating objectives. That addition provides the new constraint on the agency.

constructed on the basis of contribution to those objectives. Their focus is neither on what governments buy nor on activities in which the government is engaged, but on, as nearly as can be defined, the outputs of government. This budget places together programs which contribute to a similar objective so that competition for funds occurs among real alternatives. In an ordinary budget, agencies or departments compete for funds, as do programs within agencies or departments, so similar programs may receive different treatment simply because different agencies house them. In a program budget, similar approaches for handling a public problem will compete with each other, not with dissimilar programs housed in an administrative agency.

Program budgeting defines the goals of an agency and classifies organization activities contributing to each goal. Grouping is by end product, regardless of the administrative organization functions, to focus competition for resources among objectives and alternative programs for achieving objectives. The program structure identifies agency products; it does not focus on the inputs used by the agency. Figure 4–2 illustrates a program structure produced for the city of In-

FIGURE 4–2
Functional classification of expenditures for general government, city of Indianapolis, 1979

Function	Amount ($ 000s)	Percent of total
Protection of people and property	$ 56,176.2	21.4%
Community cultural and recreation	13,227.0	5.0
Community development and welfare	24,893.1	9.5
Transportation and related services	27,237.3	10.4
Environmental services	26,435.7	10.1
Executive/legislative affairs of government	932.0	0.4
Administrative services	6,283.1	2.4
Total current expenditures	$155,184.4	59.2
Debt service	22,505.7	8.6
Capital outlay	84,334.2	32.2
Total expenditures	$262,024.3	100.0%

Source: *Annual Report of the City of Indianapolis,* December 31, 1979.

dianapolis. Notice that the format classifies by service provided to the public. It does not classify by individual department (several services would in fact be provided in more than one department), it does not classify by input purchased, and it does not classify by departmental activity. The structure seeks a product orientation.[8] The two house-

[8] For full program classification, the capital outlay component needs to be allocated to services provided.

keeping functions—executive/legislative affairs and administrative services—are normal in program classifications; those functions provide unallocable assistance in the provision of the other services.

The approach of program budgeting may be illustrated by indicating how a particular item of expenditure might be classified under three alternative budget structures. Suppose that the item in question is the salary of an instructor employed by a high school operated in a state prison. With a traditional budget, that salary would appear as a part of the personal service line of the budget of the state department of corrections. It would thus compete for funds, in the first instance, within the priorities of that department. Money received could well depend on how the governor and legislature viewed the overall prison system. If that budget were to be classified according to performance, that expenditure would appear as part of the cost of achieving a target number of instruction hours by that department. Again, competition for resources would be with other activities of that department. A program structure, however, could well classify that expenditure as a part of a human development program, separating it from its link to incarceration and causing it to be considered with training and education activities. The salary expenditure is the same dollar amount, but the different budget classifications cause it to be treated differently to accommodate different purposes of the budget. The manner of classification undoubtedly would influence the questions asked about the expenditure and, possibly, the size of its appropriation.

Program budgeting requires careful definition of programs. That exercise in taxonomy is the essence of such budgets. While a good understanding of government operations is vital for program classification, some logical criteria for program design provided by Arthur Smithies a number of years ago remain generally helpful:

1. Design programs so that they "permit comparison of alternative methods of pursuing an imperfectly defined policy objective".[9] If there are competing ways of reducing some social problem, make certain they end up in the same program. That breakdown can clarify issues for analysis.
2. Programs must include complementary components which cannot function separately. Thus, health programs require doctors, nurses, physical facilities, etc., in appropriate proportions—and those elements must all be in the program.
3. When one part of a government serves several others, separate

---

[9] Arthur Smithies, "Conceptual Framework for the Program Budget," in *Program Budgeting,* 2d ed., ed. David Novick, (New York: Holt, Rinehart & Winston, 1969), p. 42.

supporting service programs may be needed. Thus, central electronic data processing, personnel administration, etc., may permit
operating economies not possible if each agency handles them
separately. These activities can be handled as programs, even
though their outputs are not governmental objectives. (Recall the
administrative services function in the Indianapolis example.)
4. Governments may have to have overlapping program structures to
    direct progress toward achievement of objectives. Many revenue
    departments, for instance, have structures arranged both function-
    ally and geographically. That approach appears when both regional
    and national (or statewide) objectives are important.
5. Finally, some activities involving research, development, or long-
    term investment may be considered as separate subprograms be-
    cause of the long time span over which the expenditure takes effect.
    That is because of the uncertainties which preclude reasonably reli-
    able estimates of resource requirements beyond relatively short
    portions of their life.

It can be presumed that all government activities seek to improve the
general welfare. The goal of programming is to identify the components
of that broad objective so that choices can be made among those components and among alternative approaches to their achievement.

Program construction is the identifying feature, but program budgets
often have other elements accompanying them. First, budget time hori-
zons expand beyond an annual appropriation to the lifetime of the program. While appropriation remains annual, decision makers are presented the total cost of the program considered, not simply a down
payment. Second, steps in preparation induce agencies to consider alternate operating methods and to propose only those which require
least cost to achieve the desired results. Because agency administrators
traditionally have incentives toward larger budgets for prestige or ad-
vancement, such steps are difficult to enforce. Finally, program budgets
often include some benefit–cost analysis of the resource use of programs proposed.[10] Programming brings together costs for achieving
particular objectives, so an important piece of the data needed for such
analysis is provided.

All these elements appeared in the federal planning programming
budgeting system (PPBS) experiment, applied initially to the Department of Defense in 1961, expanded to other federal agencies in 1965,
and officially terminated in 1971. Elements of that system remain in
budget frameworks of many federal agencies and of many state and

---

[10] Benefit–cost analysis is discussed in Chapter 5.

local governments.[11] In fact, many of the important elements of zero-base budgeting were included in the old PPB structure.[12]

Program budgets create one important complication for large organizations. Without accompanying reorganization of administrative agencies to match programs, budgets in program form must have an accompanying "crosswalk" to translate program costs to administrative unit appropriations. Without an easy, quick, and understandable crosswalk, the program format yields numbers which are not usable by budget decision makers and choices will continue to be made in the familiar setting of the traditional budget. That problem heavily contributed to the demise of federal PPBS.

Even where used, program budgets cannot cure all budgetary illnesses. Three problems merit special attention. First, many public activities contribute to more than one public objective and the best programatic classification for them is not always apparent. Whatever choice is made will emphasize one set of policy choices at the expense of another set. Thus, federal expenditures on military academies might be attributed to higher education elements or to defense objectives. The placement of that expenditure will establish the analysis which it faces, so it must depend on the most important issues it currently raises. It should be apparent that any long-maintained program structure will produce the bureaucratic blindness associated with continued examination of the same issues from the same approach. Furthermore, difficult interrelationships among public programs remain. Thus, highway transportation activities may influence urban redevelopment or complicate environmental protection. These interrelationships can baffle any budget navigator.

Second, cost estimates for programs may be less meaningful for public decisions than imagined. There is no scientifically defensible method for allocating the substantial joint costs appearing in agencies. Because most units work with several programs, many resources used by the agency are shared and not clearly attributable to a single program. Furthermore, public decisions require concern for social implications—not simply money out of pocket—while program budgets still focus on agency cost alone. Thus, the program cost data are unlikely to be directly usable for guiding choices.

Finally, program budgets may have little impact on decisions. Legislatures, lobbyists, and governmental departments have experience with the traditional budget format. All are familiar with that construction and

[11] See Allen Shick, *Budget Innovation in the States* (Washington, D.C.: Brookings Institution, 1971) for a review of state use of program and performance structures.

[12] The federal zero-base budget process does, however, involve line managers more and central budget staff less than did the planning programming budget.

have developed general guides for analysis of that format. New presentations require new guides and extra effort by all. Unless the major participants in the budget process actually want the improved presentation, it will be ignored in favor of the format to which they are accustomed.

ZERO-BASE BUDGET

A zero-base budget (ZBB) system annually challenges and requires defense of all agency programs. The system does not presume that an agency will receive at least its prior year's appropriation level. (It is not clear, however, that any budget system formally makes that presumption.) At least in theory, the budget must be defended in its entirety, just as if it were the start of a new program. Zero-base budgeting seeks to make government more flexible, to eliminate low-yield programs, to improve government effectiveness by forcing administrators to consider the total program annually, and to ease shifts of government spending in response to changed service demands. In sum, ZBB attempts to prevent a budget process focused only on program increases.

The Office of Management and Budget reported the following objectives of zero-base budgeting:

Involve all managers at all levels in the budget process.

Justify the resource requirements for existing activities as well as for new activities.

Focus the justification on the evaluation of discrete programs or activities of each decision unit.

Establish, for all managerial levels in an agency, objectives against which accomplishments can be identified and measured.

Assess alternative methods of accomplishing objectives.

Analyze the probable effects of different budget amounts or performance levels on the achievement of objectives.

Provide a credible rationale for reallocating resources, especially from old activities to new activities.[13]

The systems used by different governments have individual peculiarities, but many include elements of the system adopted by the federal government and diagrammed in Figure 4–3. In the first stage, unit managers prepare decision packages, which are alternatives for performing a particular function with different amounts of money. The

---

[13] Office of Management and Budget, "Zero Base Budgeting," Bulletin no. 77–9, April 19, 1977.

FIGURE 4–3
The flow of zero-base budgets

package includes funding levels and increments, a description of the activity, compilation of resource requirements, description of the short-term objective of the package, and a statement of its impact on major objectives of the agency. It also describes the implications of not providing funds for the package. Because of the requirements for preparing the package, the unit manager must be engaged in analysis of objectives, operational planning, consideration of alternatives, and cost estimation.

As the chart shows, unit managers submit their ranked decision packages to agency heads. Agency heads consolidate the packages received from the various unit managers, rank the packages, and transmit the packages ahead in the hierarchy. The packages flow through successive consolidation and ranking to the departmental level. The final consolidation and ranking produces the budget request transmitted to the Office of Management and Budget for eventual inclusion in the presidential budget. Each program element will have survived a number of rankings if it ends up in the request.

The process has numerous potential strengths. It will develop much operating data—workloads, performance measures, etc.—for use in management and should induce consideration of alternative delivery devices. Furthermore, it will require formal consideration of priorities throughout the organization. This feature is reportedly one element of the system retained by the Reagan administration. Finally, it forces thought about the objectives of agency activities. Along with the benefits, there are, however, substantial problems. First, package development generates massive volumes of paper. Administrators must be serious about the system if they choose to inflict it on agencies, because, even under the best of circumstances, some of that paper will not be serious. Several programs cannot realistically be considered candidates for zeroing out, some packages will never be realistically considered for funding, and some production alternatives may be less than serious alternatives. Many capable administrators simply won't take the ZBB system seriously. Second, performance information may be contrived and not especially germane to the operation of an agency. Measured performance may be accurate, but the performance measured may be trivial to agency purpose. Third, many spending activities won't be amenable to zero-base treatment. Several such categories are mandates on the state and local level, activities controlled by earmarking, contractual relations (debt and pension), or formula entitlements. Unfortunately, these account for a sizable proportion of total spending (as was shown in Table 4–1). Finally, the ZBB process does not compare service worth with service cost. Systems seldom identify whose priorities are to be used in ranking, even though unit manager priorities will quite possibly differ from the social priorities. Most analysts of ZBB doubt that it has had much impact. Shick says zero-base budgeting "changed the terminology of budgeting, but little more."[14] Zero-base budgeting probably directs too much attention to the routine details of the budget process and away from the tough questions of that process—the questions of program objectives and social value. Zero-base budgeting is not a magic solution to government decision making. Whether it contributes to or hinders the decision process is uncertain, but some key elements have survived a presidential transition. The Carter administration introduced federal ZBB, and the Reagan administration ended the name, but decision units, variable funding level documentation, and priority rankings remain. As with PPB, the name died, but useful practices continue in the budget system.[15]

---

[14] Allen Shick, "The Road from ZBB," *Public Administration Review,* 38 (March/April 1978): 178.

[15] Some of the logic of ZBB likewise appears in "decremental budgeting," an approach to greater flexibility through imposing request reduction constraints on managers. See Jerry McCaffery, "Revenue Budgeting: Dade County Tries a Decremental Approach," *Public Administration Review,* 41 (January 1981): 179–89.

Conclusion

Performance budgets, program budgets, and zero-based budgets all try to increase the rationality of budget choices. None provide the complete solution to the budget problem—it is wrong to expect any system to provide decisions which must be made by people. Each system, however, tries to organize information in a fashion allowing decision makers to make those choices in a reasonable fashion. All arrange information in a more usable way than do traditional budgets and, in varying degrees, seek to increase the flexibility of action open to decision makers. People will continue to make budget decisions, and that is appropriate; useful organization of information and erection of reasonable organizational incentives are the role of budget systems. Each of the structures described here can represent significant improvements over the traditional, line-item, administrative unit structure—if executive, bureaucratic, and legislative branches choose to use them. Reluctance to participate on the part of any group can doom any structure.

A CASE FOR DISCUSSION

Zero-base budgeting emerged as the budget fashion of the latter years of the 1970s. The following article appeared in *The Wall Street Journal,* just as that system was adopted for federal budget preparation.

Consider these questions:

1. Why did Professor Anthony (a member of the Harvard Business School faculty) view ZBB as a fraud?
2. In this application, could a fraud still serve a useful purpose?

Zero-Base Budgeting Is a Fraud

BY ROBERT N. ANTHONY

Zero-base budgeting is supposed to be a new way of preparing annual budgets, which contrasts with the current way, which is called incremental budgeting. Incremental budgeting, it is

correctly said, takes a certain level of expenses as a starting point and focuses on the proposed increment above that level.

By contrast, if the word "zero" means anything, it signifies that the budgeting process starts at zero and that the agency preparing the budget request must justify every dollar that it requests.

There is only one recorded attempt to take such an approach to budgeting in a government organization of any size. In 1971, the governor of Georgia hired a consultant to install such a system. He did so because of an article the consultant had written for *Harvard Business Review.*

A casual reader of that article could easily get the impression that the author had successfully installed a zero-base budgeting system in a large industrial company. A more careful reader would learn that the author had installed a system in certain staff and research units of that company, comprising an unspecified fraction, but less than 25 percent of the company's annual expenditures, and that the judgment that the system was a great success was entirely the author's and based on a single year's experience.

Anyway, the consultant started to work for the state of Georgia. He was well-intentioned and probably sincere in his belief that it is possible to prepare and analyze a budget from scratch. This belief did not last long. Well before the end of the first budget cycle, it was agreed that expenditures equal to approximately 80 percent of the current level of spending would be given only a cursory examination and that attention would be focused on the increment.

Thus, even before one go around of the new system, the "zero" bench mark was replaced by 80 percent. Moreover, amounts above this floor were in fact "increments" despite the claim that the process is the opposite of incremental budgeting. Eighty percent is a long way from zero and increments above 80 percent are just as much increments as increments above some other base. To put it bluntly, the name zero-base budgeting is a fraud.

Facts Don't Support

The facts don't even support the glowing reports about what happened with respect to the amounts above the 80 percent. In 1974, 13 heads of Georgia departments were interviewed, and only two went so far as to say that zero-base budgeting "may" have led to a reallocation of resources. (The whole idea of budgeting is to allocate resources.) None of 32 budgets analysts reported that the system involved a "large" shifting of financial resources, and only 7 said it caused "some" shifting: 21 said there was no apparent shifting, and four were uncertain.

People experienced in budgeting know that zero-base budgeting won't work. Basically, the idea is that the entire annual budget request is to be broken down in "decision packages." These packages are to be ranked in order of priority, and budget decisions are made for each package according to the justification contained therein and its relative priority ranking. There are several things wong with this approach.

Most important is that large numbers of decision packages are unmanageable. In Georgia, there were 11,000 of them. If the governor set aside four hours every day for two months he could spend about a minute on each decision package, not enough time to read it let alone analyze the merits. If he delegated the job to others, the whole idea of comparing priorities is compromised.

In the Defense Department, whose budget is 30 times as large as Georgia's, top management makes budget judgments on a few hundred items, certainly not as many as a thousand.

Even if the numbers of decision packages were reduced to a manageable size, it is not possible to make a thorough analysis during the time available in the annual budget process. In a good control system, basic decisions are made during the programming process, which precedes the budget process. And the annual budget process is essentially one of fine tuning the financial plan required to implement these decisions during the budget year; there is not time to do anything else.

In zero-base budgeting, there is no mention of a programming process. The assumption evidently is that program decisions are made concurrently with budget decisions. This simply can't be done in an organization of any size; there isn't time.

Experience also shows that the idea of ranking decision packages according to priority doesn't work. Such rankings have been attempted from time to time in government agencies, as far back as 1960. They have been abandoned. Honest agency heads will admit that program priority is influenced by the amount of funds likely to be available, rather than the other way around. If they are less than honest, they will deliberately structure priorities so that essential or politically popular decision packages are given low priority, knowing they will probably be approved and that their approval will automatically constitute approval of packages listed as having a higher priority. Only quite naive people would not expect this to happen.

The budget process is not primarily a ranking process. It is primarily the fine tuning of an approved program. The worth of programs can't be determined by reading words on a two-page form. Judgments about new programs are based on discussions with people involved, in which words on paper play some but not a dominant part. The budget analyst has a whole set of techniques for squeezing water out of budget requests for continuing programs; reading "decision packages" is not one of them.

Compared with the antiquated budget process which Georgia had at the time, zero-base budgeting was probably an improvement—almost any change would have been. Compared with the procedures that already are used in the federal government, it has nothing of substance to offer. The new parts are not good, and the good parts are not new.

Nevertheless, zero-base budgeting is rapidly becoming a highly prestigious term. I think there is a way of capitalizing on this prestige so as to give impetus to improvements in the budget process that really need to be made.

First, by a slight change in wording, the push behind the phrase might be transferred to a process called "zero-base review." This is an extremely valuable part of the control process. It is used by some agencies, but it is not widely used in a systematic way. It should be made systematic and extended throughout the government.

Time Consuming and Traumatic

In a zero-base review, outside experts go into an agency, or some part of it, and carefully examine its reason for being, its methods of operation and its costs. It is a time consuming and traumatic process, so it cannot conceivably be conducted annually. Instead, each agency should be examined about once every five years. It is by far the best way of controlling ongoing programs, just as benefit/cost analysis is the best way of making decisions on proposed new programs.

Next, the "decision packages" discussed so glibly could be used to give renewed emphasis to program budgeting, in contrast to the old-fashioned line item budgeting that persists in some agencies. Decision packages actually are what are called program elements in a program budget system. Budgeting by programs was a central part of what was called the PPB system, installed by Robert S. McNamara and Charles Hitch in the Defense Department in the early 1960s.

In 1965, an effort was made to extend this system to the entire government, but the extension was made without adequate preparation. Partly for this reason, and partly because it was developed in a Democratic admin-

istration, PPB was officially killed by the Republicans in 1969. [sic]

The basic idea of program budgeting remains sound, however. Indeed, in many agencies the basic idea continues to be used under other labels. The zero-base budgeting rhetoric could well be used to push for the complete installation of program budgeting throughout the government.

Third, the emphasis on stating measurable results in the budget proposal, which is implied in the form used to describe the decision packages, is a good one even though there is nothing new about it except the label. Under the term "management by objectives," this idea has been common in industry and in certain parts of the government for years. Zero-base budgeting could be used to strengthen it, particularly to focus more serious attention on the development of better output measures.

So, even though zero-base budgeting is a fraud, and even though the good parts of it are not new, experienced budget people should not let the phrase make them nauseous. They should disregard the rhetoric and latch onto the term as a way of accomplishing what really needs to be accomplished anyway.

5

Capital budgeting and project evaluation

Capital expenditures purchase assets that are expected to provide services for several years. More technically, "a capital expenditure can be defined as an outlay that produces benefits . . . in periods beyond the current accounting period."[1] Examples include buildings, bridges, motor vehicles, computers, and the like. Their impact extends well beyond the fiscal year in which the asset is acquired, so special care is appropriate in decisions about them. Furthermore, the price tag on these items tends to be high. For those reasons, many governments prepare and maintain a capital budget separate from the current service expenditures in an operating budget. The distinct capital budget focuses decisions, facilitates financial planning, and regularizes the provision of such projects.

Capital budgeting by state and local government requires integration of physical and financial planning. That combination has not always been found in the provision of government capital assets:

> During one phase of development of municipalities, there was a tendency to consider the capital improvement program as the exclusive domain of the Public Works Department. It was assumed that since capital improve-

---

[1] Maynard Comiez, *A Capital Budget Statement for the U.S. Government* (Washington, D.C.: Brookings Institution, 1966), p. 4.

ments were largely in the nature of construction projects, the planning was of an engineering nature. After all the planning was complete, then a price tag could be established and proper plans made for the obtaining of funds necessary to carry out the program.[2]

That simple engineering approach seems terribly primitive today as urban mobility and socioeconomic change can render facilities obsolete in a handful of years, as the strings of intergovernmental assistance complicate many financial arrangements, and as governments operate near their legal or economic debt limits. Thus, the designers of a facility must integrate their plans with the social, economic, and financial environment. In fact, that environment will usually be of greater consequence to the capital expenditure profile than the construction plans. The capital budget process establishes the formal mechanism for consideration and adoption of construction plans within prevailing constraints. This chapter describes government capital budgets and introduces cost—benefit analysis, a powerful tool which can help guide capital budget and other public decisions.

Why have separate capital budgets?

A budget process is a complex set of mechanisms in which decision makers select individual projects for funding while simultaneously trying to keep total expenditures within a revenue constraint. Maintaining two different budgets certainly seems to increase complexity of an already complex process. For capital budgets to be defensible, they must make a substantial contribution to improved fiscal choice. At state and local levels, that contribution is substantial.

First, separate consideration can improve both the efficiency and equity of provision and finance of nonrecurrent projects with long-term service flows. These projects will serve, for good or bad, the citizenry for many years beyond the year of purchase. Separate consideration in a budget where deficits may be financed rather than balanced[3] provides important opportunities to improve equity between generations and between local citizenry pools. If a local government project with a 30-year service life is constructed and paid for this year, all the costs will be borne by those paying taxes to that government this year—no construc-

---

[2] Morris C. Matson, "Capital Budgeting—Fiscal and Physical Planning," *Governmental Finance,* 5 (August 1976): p. 42.

[3] In other words, the spending program in a capital budget can be covered either by revenue raised currently (taxes, charges, grants, etc.) or by borrowing on the promise to repay from future revenues. Thus, the budget is financed (the money is raised from current revenue or debt sources), not balanced (total expenditures equals current revenue). Operating budgets typically must be balanced; capital budgets, financed.

tion cost will be paid during the rest of the life of the project. Anyone entering the area's taxpaying pool after the construction year (by moving into the area or by growing up) will receive project services without appropriate contribution. Thus, handling high-price, long-life projects through a debt-financed capital budget has strong equity advantages. Furthermore, the use of capital budgets can improve decision efficiency as well. In a single budget, there may well be a bias against big-ticket items. Separate consideration can avoid that bias and improve the chances for more reasonable response to service demand.[4] Dual budgets—a balanced operating budget and a financed capital budget— thus can make important improvements in the equity and efficiency of provision of projects producing long-term service flow.

Second, capital budgets can stabilize tax rates when individual capital projects are large relative to the tax base of the host government. If a city with a tax base of $150 million decided to construct a reservoir for water supply that would cost $15 million, it would undoubtedly be dissuaded if it were required to collect in one year sufficient revenue for construction—the cost would be 10 percent of the total city tax base, hardly leaving enough for police and fire protection, street operation, and so on. The reservoir may have a service life of 50 years, however. It is reasonable, then, to divide the construction cost over the service life, thus reducing the burden on the tax base each year and, accordingly, preventing the dramatic fluctuation in tax rates which would result from financing the project in the construction year. The case for a regular capital budget process is strong whenever projects are likely to be large enough to significantly influence tax rates.[5]

Third, the special reviews of capital budgeting are appropriate because of the permanence of capital projects—mistakes will be around for many years. Howard illustrates the problem:

> If a new state office building is built today, it will stay there for a long time. Everybody may know by next year that it is in the wrong place, but not much can be done about moving it then. Perhaps it is disrupting the development of a downtown business district; perhaps it is affecting

---

[4] In a related vein, Moak and Hillhouse suggest that governments having financial trouble may find that identifiable capital projects are more easily postponed than are expenditures for operating agencies. A capital budget separately considered can improve the chances for preservation of those projects when the operating budget is under great pressure. Lennox L. Moak and Albert M. Hillhouse, *Concepts and Practices in Local Government Finance.* (Chicago: Municipal Finance Officers Association, 1975)), p. 98.

[5] Projects in a capital budget need not automatically be debt-financed. As will be discussed in the debt administration chapter, capital projects that *recur* can and should economically be financed from current revenue.

traffic flows and parking facilities in a most undesirable way; or perhaps its location makes it psychologically, if not geographically, far removed from certain segments of the population. Whatever these effects may be, they are real, and they will endure awhile. They should be anticipated to the fullest extent possible *before* the project is undertaken.[6]

The capital budget reviews will not prevent all mistakes, but they can provide as much opportunity as possible for reduction of costly errors. On the positive side, those reviews and associated planning processes can produce the orderly provision of public capital facilities to accommodate economic development. Thus, the capital budget process serves to reduce errors both of commission and omission in public infrastructure construction.

Finally, capital budgets are valuable tools for management of limited fiscal resources, particularly in light of the special care required to plan activities which necessitate long-term drains on those resources. Items in this budget tend to be "lumpy." A capital budget provides a mechanism to smooth out peaks and valleys, to regularize construction activity in an effort to avoid local bottlenecks that can delay projects and inflate their cost, to avoid bunching up of debt issues with unfortunate effects on interest cost, to avoid excessive drains on the tax base when projects must be paid for, and to balance spending with the resources available within political, economic, and legal tax and debt limits. Thus, the capital budget is an important resource management tool for governments operating within fiscal limits.

The reasons supporting a separate capital budget are strongest for local and state governments. They are less strong at the federal level. First, the federal government is charged with economic stabilization responsibilities which, according to many proponents of fiscal policy, require periods of net federal deficit and net federal surplus to induce appropriate macroeconomic stimulus. Dual budgets—one balanced, one not—would unnecessarily hinder federal stabilization efforts. Second, the federal government is so large that no single project can influence tax rates. Third, the federal government does not need the careful planning of project financing inherent in capital budgeting to preserve its debt rating. It has, after all, the ultimate power of printing money to cover deficits. And finally, skeptics say that another budget would simply provide federal bureaucrats, already insulated from public scrutiny by existing spending and personnel mechanisms, with another way to conceal fiscal conditions. Thus, the gains from capital budgeting at

---

[6] S. Kenneth Howard, *Changing State Budgeting.* (Lexington, Ky.: Council of State Governments, 1973), p. 241.

lower government levels, particularly local, cannot be translated to a similar federal case.[7]

Capital budgeting promises a significant contribution to the fiscal operation of state and local government:

> The capital budget . . . provides a vehicle for financial planning and for the regulation of local tax rates. It thus contributes to financial solvency, and at the same time assures that over a period of years needed improvements will be constructed.[8]

A capital budget process

Governments apply capital budgeting processes in many different ways, using various terms, steps, and staging of those steps. The process described here amalgamates several processes for illustration; most operating systems can easily be identified with this outline. In broad strokes, capital budgeting processes are concerned with (1) the selection of capital projects from the multitude of possible alternatives, (2) the timing of expenditure for projects selected, and (3) the impact on total government finances of various plans which might be used to finance that spending. The steps outlined here encompass both physical planning and financial emphasis.

A capital budget process involves both planning and financial officers; Figure 5–1 provides a rough view of the flow and relationships in the process. The initial stage in the process is the preparation of a capital improvement program, a listing of capital expenditure projects appropriate for the next six years or so. That list is proposed by government agencies and sometimes private organizations as well; each project includes justifying narrative along with cost data. These project proposals are screened by a city planning department or a similar body to evaluate costs, to locate interrelationships, and to establish initial priorities. This screening is particularly concerned with scheduling: projects should be timed to avoid waste (the sewers should be put in before the streets are resurfaced), predetermined program emphases should be implemented, and postponable projects should be identified.[9] Part of

---

[7] As an aside, it should be pointed out that governments work with capital budgets as a device for managing their capital assets. Contrary to the practice of businesses, governments do not use depreciation accounting, nor do they need to. Businesses depreciate so that they can estimate what their profit (or loss) is in any particular year. Governments do not sell products, so they simply cannot produce such estimates. Their capital management task involves deciding whether particular projects are worth undertaking or continuing; there is no need for annual cost judgments. More discussion of this point appears in Jesse Burkhead, *Government Budgeting* (New York: John Wiley & Sons, 1963), p. 205.

[8] Ibid., p. 185.

[9] Moak and Hillhouse, *Concepts and Practices,* pp. 104–5.

FIGURE 5–1

Capital improvement program			
Projects ($000s)			
Year	Fire station	Library	Sewer expansion	Park
19X0...	185	0	15	15
19X1...	10	0	20	0
19X2...	0	20	30	0
19X3...	0	100	50	0
19X4...	0	0	75	0
19X5...	0	0	40	0

Capital budget	
Projects for 19X0	($000s)
Fire station	185
Sewer expansion.	15
Park	15

Operating budget	
	($000s)
Personnel costs.	640
Supplies and equipment	140
Other	20
	800

Capital expenditures	Operating expenditures
$215,000	$800,000

Total expenditures
$1,015,000

this priority review may be linked to a community master plan—a long-term (10- to 25-year), broad-gauge estimate of community growth encompassing estimated needs for public improvements and controls on private use of property. (Because long-term forecasts of social, demographic, and economic behavior are so bad, however, that plan ought not be taken too seriously as a guide to action.) The final capital improvement program will thus have a segment scheduled for each year of its span. The capital budget proposal then includes the current year's work from the capital improvement program.

The second stage of the process coordinates a financial analysis of the government with the facility additions envisioned in the capital improvement program. This interrelationship is vital because of the long-term fiscal commitments that such facilities can involve: just as a poorly conceived structure can disrupt a city for many years, so too can a poorly conceived financing approach disrupt that city's fiscal condition. Finance officers must examine the present and anticipated revenue and expenditure profile to determine the financial cushion available for new projects. Particularly important are the status of existing debt issues (Will any issues be retired soon? Will funds be available to meet contractual debt service—principal and interest—payments? Are there needs for extra funds for early bond retirement?), the estimated growth profile of the tax base, and the potential for new revenue sources. This fiscal profile, year by year, can be then related to the priority list of projects, again scheduled by years. In this analysis, fiscal officers usually consider the financing alternatives available for specific projects (special assessments for sidewalks, user charges for water utilities, state or federal aid for highways, etc.) and further reports will have sources attached to projects.[10] From those considerations, the project list is revised in preparation for its insertion into the annual budget process. The financial analysis may permit the project schedule to remain intact, but it may well require changes based on financial conditions. In the latter instance, budget officers must devise priorities for funding, often in consultation with the chief executive (mayor or governor). One set has been used in Wisconsin:

1. Hazard to safety.
2. To fully utilize present facilities.
3. For present program expansion.
4. For future program expansion.[11]

Other projects may be evaluated with cost—benefit analysis, as described later in this chapter. Ordinarily, some choices must get made even before the projects are proposed for legislative approval.

Capital items, thus, typically are reviewed for inclusion in the capital improvement program (CIP) and then for inclusion in the capital budget before they are proposed for legislative review and approval. Because capital items often have implications for many future years, it is appropriate that they receive that special scrutiny in the decision process. Furthermore, the CIP review is typically by planners, not budgeting personnel, so the two reviews won't focus on the same questions. In addition, the CIP may have been prepared some years before and economic

---

[10] Furthermore, the fiscal officers make choices about the financing policy selected for each project: borrowing (general obligation or revenue bond), use of capital reserve funds (special funds accumulated over time for future capital spending), or pay as you go. These choices are examined in the debt administration chapter.

[11] Howard, *Changing State Budgeting*, p. 257. The system does bias against new programs.

or demographic conditions may not match those forecast earlier by planners. The process thus provides a timely review of the project.

Finally, the surviving projects envisioned in the capital improvement program become the capital budget section of the annual budget. The projects will be reviewed by the legislature and sometimes are substantially modified. When projects are approved, provision must also be made in the operating budget for operation and maintenance of the facility when it is complete: the new civic arena won't do much good if the operating budget has no money for its interior lighting. The capital portion of the budget document usually provides a distribution of projects by function and agency, shows prior and estimated future cost of the project (initial appropriations may well have been annual—each year's construction plan requires a new appropriation), and summarizes sources of financing (type of debt, aid, etc.). The capital improvement program thus feeds the capital budget on an annual basis: next year's segment of the capital plan becomes the capital budget proposal for next year, subject to revisions produced by environmental conditions and the legislative process.

Total expenditures by the government include both the operating expenditures from the operating budget and capital purchases from the capital budget. The former expenditures will normally be financed by current revenue (taxes, grants, charges, etc. collected in the current year). Part of the capital budget will likely be handled on a current basis as well. The balance of capital project cost, however, will undoubtedly be debt-financed, so revenue to liquidate that debt will be raised in later years. Thus, the revenue to be generated in any budget year will equal the operating budget plus a capital project component. The latter equals capital items purchased without debt plus the debt service requirements (interest and repayment of principal) on borrowing for capital items purchased in prior years. Those debt costs would ideally approximate a depreciation charge for capital assets that have been acquired in the past; serial bonds (bonds in a single project issue which are to be paid off at various dates through the life of the project) are a rough approximation of that cost distribution.

Problems in capital budgeting

As is always the case with mechanisms to assist in making public decisions, there are problems in the application of capital budgeting. First, the capital improvement—capital budget process presumes a continuous cycle of reappraisal and revaluation of project proposals. That is necessary because the world changes, bringing substantial changes in the need for public projects. Unfortunately, many processes regard pri-

orities, once established, to be unchangeable, even in the face of different project cost and different project demand. As Howard points out:
"Too often cost fluctuations do not generate a reassessment of priority
rankings; original rankings are retained *despite* the fluctuations."[12]
Thus, many state highway construction plans are based on traffic patterns assuming 50 cent per gallon gasoline—they need to be revised. In
a related manner, the time a project has spent in the priority queue
sometimes establishes its priority rank: all old project proposals have
higher rankings than any new ones. That approach makes no sense,
because time alone does not improve the viability of a project which
was marginal when it was first proposed. Furthermore, items entering
the priority queue some years ago may have outlived their usefulness
by the time they reach the funding point. Again, the problem can be
resolved by maintaining reviews of projects in the capital improvement
program.

Second, there can be questions about what projects or programs
belong in the capital budget because, in the strictest sense, more than
capital assets provide future benefit flows. Planning and zoning departments, educational institutions, training programs, and so on all
provide benefits which extend beyond the year in which the service
expenditure is made. Most generally, however, these activities would
properly be excluded from the capital budget because spending for
them is *recurrent:* it is not the single-year spending situation, the kind
that needs special capital treatment. Further, most processes will establish dollar-size limits for capital budget treatment: a $500 typewriter,
useful life of eight years, would be part of the operating budget,
whereas an $8,500 automobile, useful life of four years, would be in the
capital budget. Dollar limits will differ, but some limit will usually be
encountered. Such arbitrary rules are a common factor in any decision
process.

Third, availability of funds can distort the priority ranks. As Howard
observes: "Despite the fact that how a project is financed does not
change the need for it, there is a strong tendency for differences in the
availability of capital outlay funds to skew priority decisions."[13] The
appropriate approach in establishing final priorities should involve a
general comparison of the cost of the project with the return to the
community from the project—the source of money doesn't fit in that
comparison. Some projects can get favored, however, because earmarked funds are available (a special tax creates a fund pool which can
be spent only on one class of project); because they produce revenue
which can be pledged to repayment of revenue bonds without direct tax

---

[12] Ibid., p. 256.
[13] Ibid.

burden or need to satisfy restrictions placed on general debt; or because federal or state assistance is available for particular projects. The purpose of many grants is to bend local priorities, so that influence is excusable. The other influences, however, are inappropriate and show why most analysts oppose such fiscal constraints.

Fourth, capital budgeting can bias toward acquisition of items by borrowing. Borrowing may not always be desirable, as with items which are acquired on a regular flow basis. Furthermore, during inflation the bias can add to macroeconomic pressures if state and local governments all operate in about the same fashion. Thoughtful fiscal analysis, however, should prevent that bias—if political pressure can be withstood.

Finally, there is the standard problem in all public decisions. That is the problem of establishing priorities in the capital improvement program. How do items get put into the capital improvement program, and which ones finally enter the capital budget? Benefit–cost analysis, to be examined next, gives some assistance, but as with ordinary items, there are no final answers.

BENEFIT–COST ANALYSIS

The constant problem in public program choice is the judgment whether a particular program is worth its cost, because society cannot afford to waste its scarce resources. Benefit–cost analysis provides a way of organizing information about a program under consideration so that priorities may be reasonably established. A private firm considering a major project, say, the purchase of a new delivery truck to replace an older and smaller one, compares the anticipated increase in revenue from the new truck with the anticipated increase in cost, after making adjustments for the time the costs and revenues are received (see the coverage of discounting in Appendix A). If the revenue exceeds cost, the purchase of the truck is a wise use of the firm's scarce resources; if not, the purchase is unwise.

Benefit–cost analysis is the governmental analogue to that process described for the firm: governments can and have used it for assistance in making decisions as diverse as decisions on word processing equipment acquisition, vehicle fleet modernization, water resource development, communicable disease control programs, development of a supersonic transport plane, and license plate reflectorization. It has also been applied to evaluate the worth of numerous governmental regulations.[14] For capital budget purposes, however, its application is much

---

[14] James C. Miller III and Bruce Yandle, *Benefit–Cost Analyses of Social Regulation* (Washington, D.C.: American Enterprise Institute, 1979).

like that of private firm choice: the analysis estimates whether the gain to society (benefit) from the project is greater than the social sacrifice (cost) required to produce the project. If so, the project is worthwhile; if not then the project is not worthwhile. Worthwhile projects improve the total economic affluence of society because they direct resources where their use provides a greater return than would any known alternate use.

Skeptics point out that political bargaining characterizes the public decision process; it is not an exercise in rational consideration by non-political administrators.[15] So what service can benefit–cost analysis provide in that environment? First, the analysis informs that bargaining—because it can augment the political influence of underrepresented potential beneficiaries or identify the position of cost bearers. A display of costs and benefits makes it more difficult for the unrepresented to be ignored in political bargaining. In some instances, it can be a valuable weapon in the "it pays for itself" budget strategy. Second, economic efficiency—the guiding force of benefit–cost analysis—is but one of several public goals. Even though a decision is not based primarily on those grounds, the potential gains sacrificed in the selection of a particular public policy is important information. And finally, benefit–cost analysis forces public decisions to focus on the value of competing alternatives. Valuation and the accompanying process of establishing priorities are the keys to sound decision making, so benefit–cost analysis directs attention to vital questions.

Elements in benefit–cost analysis

Five steps make up formal benefit–cost analysis: categorization of project objectives; estimation of the project impact on objectives; estimation of project costs; discounting of cost and benefit flows at an appropriate discount rate; and summarization of findings in a fashion usable for choices. Their exact content varies according to the type of project considered; the following discussion focuses on common elements and their application in selected situations.

Project objectives

The project analysis should identify the benefits the project will produce. What desirable results will happen because of the project? The

---

[15] Federal water resource projects have one of the longest histories of cost–benefit applications. Even here, Schenker and Bunamo indicate that these projects are strongly influenced by purely political factors when examined across regions in the United States. [Eric Schenker and Michael Bunamo, "A Study of the Corps of Engineers' Regional Pattern of Investments," *Southern Economic Journal,* 39 (April 1973): 548–58.]

relationship between the project and the objective must be traceable to establish a sound foundation for the analysis. Some examples: a rapid transit system could increase travel speed (saving time, a valuable commodity), reduce accident costs, and reduce vehicle operating cost. A water project might reduce flood damage, provide water for residential and other use, and improve effluent dilution conditions for water quality management. A new fire station may reduce operating costs of an older facility and reduce prospective fire loss in a service area. A word processing system may reduce labor and material costs and filing expenses.

The benefit–cost logic is not limited to complex projects, but can be particularly useful in more narrow public management decisions about alternative methods of accomplishing a particular task. Among the applications are repair–replace and lease–purchase decisions, fuel conversion, modernization choices, EDP equipment acquisitions, and so on. In these decisions, the objective is simply to perform a task at least cost, often when one option involves a capital expenditure and others do not.

Benefit estimation and valuation

A Senate guide to water project evaluation defines benefits as "increases or gains, net of associated or induced costs, in the value of goods and services which result from conditions with the project, as compared with conditions without the project."[16] The same logic applies to any project. Thus, the analyst must estimate for the life of the project both physical changes from the project and the value of these changes. No standard method applies for all projects: techniques used to estimate benefits of a personnel training project would not be the same as those used in water projects. Regardless of the project, however, the decision must be made from information that is *estimated,* not factual, because facts in economic or social relationships can only be historical. Present decisions cannot change what has already happened. One observer points out: "No amount of sophistication is going to allay the fact that all your knowledge is about the past and all your decisions are about the future."[17] The analysis must proceed with best estimates; it cannot be paralyzed by a lack of complete information because complete information only is available when it is too late to make a decision.

An initial step estimates the physical size of the change that can be

---

[16] *Policies, Standards and Procedures in the Formulation, Evaluation and Review of Plans for Use in Development of Water and Related Land Resources,* 87th Cong., 2d sess., Senate document 97, approved May 1962.

[17] J. H. Wilson, quoted in *MBA Magazine,* November 1975.

expected from the project. Sometimes a controlled experiment on a sample can estimate probable effects before resources are committed to the entire program. For instance, the state of Virginia estimated the likely benefits of reflectorized motor vehicle license plates by comparing accident frequency among a random sample of cars equipped with these plates with frequency in the remainder of the population.[18] The controlled experiment results could be used to estimate accident reduction from reflectorized plates for the entire state.

Controlled experiments are, however, seldom possible. More often, models developed from the social, physical, or engineering sciences are used to estimate that change. For water resource projects, hydrological models can yield estimates of influences of reservoirs, canals, channelization, etc. on water flows and levels. From that information can be derived the effects on navigation, probability of flooding, water supply, and so on. Gravity models from economic analysis and marketing can indicate likely drawing power of various public facilities. Trip generation models can suggest traffic flows from transportation facility changes. Any model allows the analyst to apply experience from other environments to predict the results of projects under consideration, so that these changes can be valued: they are the key to linking government inputs to government outputs. Hovey strongly presents the importance of models:

> To analyze any program . . . requires a model, which describes the relationship between what we put into the activity (inputs) and what we expect to get out of it (outputs). Good models explain what exact relationships are, not just that a relationship exists. . . . To require that the model be made explicit is one of the greatest potential contributions of systematic analysis to government. An explicit model can be studied, criticized, evaluated, and improved. Too often, decisions are made without explicit models. The result can never be better than if the model is explicit, it can frequently be worse.[19]

When the project impact has been estimated, the worth of that impact must then be estimated. Such valuation permits comparison of project cost to project returns to establish whether the undertaking increases the net well-being of the region. Money values are used, not because of any glorification of money, simply because exchange values provide a standard yardstick to compare how individuals value the project with how they value the resources used by that project. For exam-

---

[18] Charles B. Stoke, *Reflectorized License Plates: Do They Reduce Nighttime Rear-End Collisions?* (Charlottesville: Virginia Highway Research Council, 1974). Drivers were not told and could not control the type of plates they received.

[19] Harold A. Hovey, *The Planning-Programming-Budgeting Approach to Government Decision-Making* (New York: Praeger Publishers, 1968), p. 23.

ple, one million tons of concrete applied to highway construction may prolong by one year the useful life of 5,000 automobiles: resources of one type are used to save resources of another. Will the community be better off with that use of its scarce resources? A direct comparison is impossible because units being measured (cars and concrete) aren't the same. Our only meaningful alternative is to estimate the value individuals place on cars and concrete: how much general purchasing power individuals are willing to give up to acquire each. Those purchasing power units provide the measuring standard.

The particular valuation approach chosen depends on the project, but the task is always easiest when values can be connected to a private market. For instance, river navigation projects may reduce shipper costs: the estimated difference between cost of river shipment and that of the cheapest available alternative can indicate project value of increased volume of shipping. The value of employment training projects can be estimated from differences in anticipated pre- and post-project incomes of trainees, allowing for differences in employment prospects.[20] Many capital expenditure items purchased by governments may reduce operating cost, the primary benefits in those instances.

For some projects, however, project outputs are not linked to goods or services sold in private markets: the output is desired for its own sake (relaxation in a city park), not because it contributes to another production process.[21] When the product or service is of this type, or when prices of marketed commodities change as a result of the project, a different approach is used. That is the estimation of consumer's surplus—the difference between the maximum price consumers would willingly pay for given amounts of a commodity and the price that the market demands for the commodity (which would be zero for public services provided at no direct charge). The underlying logic of the consumer surplus approach is relatively simple, although its application is anything but simple: points along an individual's demand curve for a product or service represent the value that the person places on particular amounts of the product in question. The individual would voluntarily exchange any amount up to the level on the demand curve rather than not have the product. He will not pay more, so the price on the curve represents the individual's valuation of the product. Refer to Figure 5–2, a representation of an individual's demand for visits to a park: for ten visits to the park, the maximum that individual would pay is $5. If

---

[20] Joe N. Nay et al., *Benefits and Costs of Manpower Training Programs: A Synthesis of Previous Studies with Reservations and Recommendations* (Washington, D.C.: Urban Institute, 1973).

[21] Economists distinguish these as final products and intermediate products. See Richard A. Musgrave, "Cost–Benefit Analysis and the Theory of Public Finance," *Journal of Economic Literature,* 7 (September 1969).

FIGURE 5–2
Individual demand for a park

Price

the price actually charged is above $5, the individual would visit fewer times (if at all); if the price is below $5, the individual receives a consumer surplus—he receives the service at less than the price he would have willingly paid. Consumer surplus then equals the difference between the maximum price the individual would have paid less the price he actually pays multiplied by the number of units purchased. If the price were zero (the park has no admission charge), the total consumer surplus here would equal $90, computed by: ($10 × 5) + ($5 × 5) + ($2 × 5) + ($1 × 5). That is the entire area under the demand curve for the service.

Public services are seldom sold, so how is it possible to consider quantities demanded as a function of price? The demand curves are constructed by recognizing that implicit prices have to be paid to use most free services. Thus, individuals must pay transportation cost to use even a free facility—they bear the cost of getting from where they live to where the facility is. This cost is the implicit price; analysis of user patterns allows estimation of a demand curve. Use (quantity demanded) usually is greater by those who are closest to the facility (travel cost, or implicit price, is lower), following the configuration of a conventional demand curve.[22] The approach is not without its problems, but it really is the only feasible technique for that class of public services.

---

[22] An interesting application of the technique to estimate benefits from visits to historical sites using the consumer surplus approach is Richard J. Cirre, *Estimating User Benefits from Historic Sites and Museums* (Ithaca, N.Y.: Program in Urban and Regional Studies, Cornell University, 1977).

Estimation of project costs

An estimate of the resource cost of the project includes construction cost and operating cost for the life of the project. Obviously these estimates require the close cooperation of engineers and accountants skilled in costing, particularly if heavy public works facilities are involved. The analyst must recognize, however, that the important cost for society is the opportunity cost of the resources used in the project. That complication can produce three types of adjustments to cost estimates based initially on resource purchase prices. First, ordinary project cost estimates include only private or internal costs. Many public projects, however, can create undesirable effects on others, or negative externalities. Examples include the damage done to surrounding properties by pollutants produced by a municipal incinerator or the traffic delays created when streets are blocked by construction of a government office building. These are costs inflicted upon parties outside the market transaction, but they are just as real as wages or payments for construction materials. These adjustments are made using the same indirect methods applied in benefit estimation—these impacts are, logically, negative social benefits.

Second, adjustments are appropriate if the project uses completely unemployed resources or resources for which there is no alternative use. If such is the case, there is nothing sacrificed in consuming those resources in the project being considered. Thus, the actual social opportunity cost of the resource to the project is zero, not the financial cost involved in paying the resource's owner. For that reason, it can be sensible to undertake programs in areas with massive unemployment when that program ordinarily would not be economically justifiable: putting the idle resources to work adds a desired product without the loss of any other product.

Finally, many public projects use property already owned by the government. Property acquisition brings no out-of-pocket cost; when sites for a new highway, incinerator, etc., are being compared, the site using public property has lowest financial cost. The real social cost of that site for the proposed project is the site's value in its existing (or other possible) use because that is what the community loses if the site is selected for the new use. There is no justification for valuing already-owned properties at zero.

Selection of a discount rate

The costs and benefits of most public projects, particularly those proposed in a capital budget, do not occur in any single year. More often than not, an initial capital expenditure is made in one year and both operating cost and program returns accrue over a long project life. The flow must be discounted to its present-value equivalent (that process is discussed in Appendix A). The general present-value formula applies:

$$PV = \sum_{i=1}^{n} \frac{Vi}{(1+r)^n}$$

where PV is the present-value equivalent of the flow of funds, Vi is the current dollar amount received in year i, and r is the discount rate appropriate for the project in question.

The choice of discount rate has an important impact on the present value of a project. Suppose a project has construction cost of $10,000 and no operating cost. Its benefits of $1,500 per year start at the end of the first year and continue for nine years. The project ends with no salvage values. Table 5–1 summarizes the project data and computes

TABLE 5–1
The impact of discount rates on project present values

Year	Cost outlay	Benefit received	Present value of benefits, alternative discount rates		
			8 percent	10 percent	15 percent
1.............	$10,000	$1,500	1,389	1,364	1,304
2.............	—	1,500	1,286	1,240	1,134
3.............	—	1,500	1,191	1,127	986
4.............	—	1,500	1,103	1,025	858
5.............	—	1,500	1,021	931	746
6.............	—	1,500	945	847	648
7.............	—	1,500	875	770	564
8.............	—	1,500	810	700	490
9.............	—	1,500	750	636	426
10.............	—	1,500	695	578	371
Present value total..........	$10,000		10,065	9,218	7,527

present values, using different discount rates. An 8 percent discount rate shows the project to produce a return slightly greater than its cost, a 10 percent discount rate shows the project to be slightly more costly than its value, and a 15 percent rate shows the project to have substantially higher cost than its value. The discount rate selected clearly influences the economic evaluation of the project.

There is, however, no single discount rate which is immediately obvious as *the* appropriate rate for analysis—market imperfections and differences in risk cause a broad spectrum of interest rates in the economy. Several candidates have, however, been proposed for such use. Two important candidates proposed for such use are the cost of borrowed funds to the government (the interest rate the government must pay) and the opportunity cost of displaced private activity (the return that private resources could earn). There are conditions under which either may be appropriate.

The cost of borrowed money provides the closest analogue to private project analysis—it is an interest rate which, presumably, must be paid by a borrower. Because most public programs are financed at least ultimately by tax revenues, use of the rate at which a government can borrow would not direct resources to their best-yield uses because absence of default risk on (federal) government debt makes that rate abnormally low. Allocation using that rate would pull resources away from higher-yielding private activities to prospectively lower-yield public use. For state and local government decisions, the borrowing rate would be particularly misleading because the exclusion of this interest from the federal income tax allows these governments to borrow at much below the appropriate market rate.[23] Public authorities which generate their revenue from sales of product or service might use that rate, as that does estimate the market attitude toward the prospects of the enterprise, but even here the interest exclusion from income taxes complicates the analysis. The borrowing rate is generally not a good test for a social discount rate.

The return which could have been achieved in displaced private spending is generally more appropriate for the logic of benefit–cost analysis, an analysis aimed at increasing the welfare of the community. It is a rate which the analyst must estimate—there is no defined interest rate being paid. Baumol lucidly expresses the essential argument:

> If the resources in question produce a rate of return in the private sector which society evaluates at r percent, then the resources should be transferred to the public project if that project yields a return greater than r percent. They should be left in private hands if their potential earnings in the proposed government investment is less than r percent.[24]

The problem is to estimate what the rate of return would have been on these displaced resources, because that is the opportunity cost a

---

[23] An individual in the 30 percent federal tax bracket would receive the same after-tax rate of return on a taxed corporate bond yielding 15 percent or an untaxed municipal bond yielding 10.5 percent.

[24] William J. Baumol, "On the Discount Rate for Public Projects," in *Public Expenditures and Policy Analysis,* ed. Robert H. Haveman and Julius Margolis (Chicago: Markham Publishing, 1970), p. 274.

public project must exceed if it is not to misallocate resources of the community. In general, this rate can be estimated according to the formula:

$$P = k_1 r_1 + k_2 r_2 + \ldots + k_n r_n$$

where P = rate of return on displaced resources (the project discount rate), r = return on investment in a particular private sector, k = fraction of project cost extracted from a particular sector (usually the percentage of total taxes collected from it), and n = the number of private sectors with displaced resources. This weighted average provides a workable estimate of the private opportunity cost of the displaced resources and the resulting discount rate is applied to the estimated benefit and cost flows.

Decision criteria

The final stage in project analysis applies a decision criteria to the discounted cost and return flows to summarize the economic case for the project. The summarization can be either to identify whether a project is economically justifiable or to establish rankings among projects to be fitted into a limited budget. Two criteria often used are the benefit–cost ratio (the present value of benefits divided by the present value of costs) and the net present value of the project (the present value of benefits less the present value of costs). If the ratio exceeds 1 or if the net present value is positive, the project passes the test of economic efficiency: resource use for the project will increase economic well-being because alternative uses of those resources will produce a lower return for the community. Application of the criteria will ignore politics, desires for wealth redistribution, regional problems, and other side concerns, but it will capture the economics of the project.

Two additional measures sometimes proposed should be mentioned briefly. These are the internal rate of return and the payback period. The payback-period method divides the estimated net annual flow of project returns into the capital cost of the project to obtain the number of years it would take to fully recover (pay back) the capital cost. Thus, if the net annual return from a project with a capital cost of $8,000 is $2,000, the payback period is four years. The shorter the period, the more attractive the project. This measure is defective because it ignores the time profile of returns (proceeds available only late in project life are valued equal to earlier returns) and proceeds after the payback point. For example, consider the following projects:

| Project | Capital cost | Annual net benefits (end of year) | | | Payback period |
		Year 1	Year 2	Year 3	
A	10,000	10,000			1 year
B	10,000	9,000	1,100		1 + years
C	10,000	3,000	4,000	7,000	3 + years

By payback-period reasoning, the project ranks would be A, B, C: if a discount rate of 10 percent were appropriate, the net present value of A = −909; of B = −909; and of C = +1,292. Payback periods are simply not reliable as a project guide. The internal rate-of-return method "is to find a rate of interest that will make the present value of the cash proceeds expected from an investment equal to the present value of the cash outlays required by the investment."[25] That return rate is compared with the discount rate: the project passes the economic efficiency test if its rate of return is higher than the discount rate. The present-value methods are "simpler, safer, easier, and more direct"[26] because of the adaptability of multiple discount rates during investment life, the problem of multiple internal rates of return which can emerge in computation, and the need for additional tests to determine the validity of a computed rate of return. If conditions are right, however, internal rate of return will give the same results as present-value computations.

Project analysis may require not just an evaluation of the economics of a number of projects but also selection of particular projects from several alternatives. Two ranking indexes are available: rank by ratios of benefit to cost or by net present value.[27] Project rankings are often the same with either criteria, but sometimes—especially when project sizes are substantially different—the ranks are substantially different. Which ranking should apply: that produced by net present values or the ratio of benefit to cost?

Table 5–2 presents the discounted cost and benefit data for two capital projects. If $500 is to be budgeted, should project X or project Z be undertaken? Project Z has a higher net present value while project X has the higher benefit/cost ratio. Each criterion supposes particular facts about the projects. Ranking by the ratio assumes that either project

[25] Harold Bierman, Jr., and Seymour Smidt, *The Capital Budgeting Decision* (New York: Macmillan, 1975), p. 28.

[26] Ibid., p. 57.

[27] The ratio of excess benefit to cost (benefit minus cost divided by cost) provides no additional information, as project ranks are the same as with the benefit–cost ratio: $B/C = [(B − C)/C] + 1$.

TABLE 5–2
Projects with ranking criteria conflict

Project	Cost	Benefit	Net present value	Benefit/cost ratio
Z	$500	$600	$100	1.20
X	150	200	50	1.33

can be increased in any proportion without changing the return relationships. In the present comparison, ranking by ratio presumes that
project X can be expanded $3\frac{1}{3}$ times its present size at the same
benefit–cost payoff to obtain a project costing $500 with benefits of
$667, yielding a net present value of $167. That expansion must be
technically and economically possible if ratios are the guide to the decision. Ranking by net present value presumes that the alternate investment streams are of the size indicated, without the possibility of increase or decrease with returns constant.

In many situations, of course, neither presumption is met entirely.
When such is the case, the decision must rely on comparison of present
value of benefits from the use of available funds in feasible combinations of all project sizes. If the concern is with indication of economically
feasible projects, not with allocations within a fixed budget, either
method will be proved satisfactory: if net present value is positive, the
benefit–cost ratio will be greater than 1. Conflict emerges only with
rankings.

Some special problems

Multiple objectives. Benefit–cost analysis provides information
about the economic impact of projects. Overall economic impacts may
not, however, be the sole or even the most important objective of some
programs, particularly those concerned with redistribution of income in
society. If redistribution is important, benefits received by some groups
in society will be more important than benefits received by others. Market values will not measure this objective, so benefit values would need
explicit adjustment to encompass redistribution concerns.

Normal benefit–cost analysis accepts all portions of the economy as
equal; gaining and losing groups are not considered. It accepts the
"hypothetical compensation" criterion of theoretical welfare economics: a public decision will be regarded as sound if those gaining from a
public action receive sufficient benefits to compensate any losses, with
some surplus gain remaining.[28] The principle ignores distribution of

---

[28] J. G. Head, "The Welfare Foundations of Public Finance Theory," *Rivista di diritto finanziario e scienza della finanze,* 24 (September 1965): 379–428.

gains and losses across society and can be defended by these arguments: (1) that changes resulting to income distributions can be viewed as negligible,[29] (2) that public investment is not a proper tool for redistributional change because other fiscal policies are superior and can easily correct for any investment-related maldistribution; or (3) that many projects over time will have benefits randomly distributed, causing the overall effect to "average out" at no redistributional change. On these views, distribution effects may be ignored with some theoretical justification. The view has been growing, however, that such treatment assumes away too many issues.

Two general techniques have emerged to deal with this distributional concern. Some analysts have allowed for distribution effects by weighting benefits by a measure of the societal importance of the recipient. Values received by meritorious groups (those society wants to help) count more than values received by others. Selection of weights is obviously a problem. Weisbrod has applied weights implied in past public project decisions that have not followed strict benefit–cost ranks.[30] This approach does not, however, attack the problem of how the distribution ought to be changed, but would weight analysis in the historical pattern. Besides, the pattern may measure clout of congressional delegates, not social goals. Krutilla and Eckstein approach the problem by using marginal rates of federal taxation as weights, presuming that these rates roughly measure the importance of redistribution to society.[31] The technique does focus directly on income distribution, but it, too, has political pressure problems. Furthermore, it ignores the difference between statutory rules (those in tax law) and effective rates (those applicable after loopholes). Other approaches would apply specific weights supplied by the analyst. All bend the general rule that the analyst be an impartial observer in the analytic process. Decision makers may not recognize (or accept) the value system assumed by the analyst.

An alternative, the display technique favored by McKean,[32] would supplement general cost and benefit totals with a tabulation of how costs and benefits are divided among the population. Many distributions could be important: income, age, race, sex, geographic area, etc.

---

[29] Otto Eckstein, *Water Resource Development* (Cambridge, Mass.: Harvard University Press, 1958), pp. 36–37.

[30] Burton A. Weisbrod, "Income Redistribution Effects and Benefit–Cost Analysis," in *Problems in Public Expenditure Analysis,* ed. Samuel B. Chase (Washington, D.C.: Brookings Institution, 1968).

[31] John V. Krutilla and Otto Eckstein, *Multiple-Purpose River Development* (Baltimore: Johns Hopkins Press, 1958).

[32] Roland McKean suggests the importance of indicating in exhibits the impact of projects on the distribution of wealth, and demonstrates its use in water resource project evaluation: *Efficiency in Government through Systems Analysis* (New York: John Wiley & Sons, 1958), pp. 131–33, 208, 242.

By providing such a display, the analyst need not weight the social importance of groups. Decision makers could supply their own weights to each recipient group as desired. The number and type of displays provided would not likely be the same for all projects. If the goal of analysis is to provide information for decision makers and consumers and not to yield conclusive, social-maximizing decisions, such displays seem a prerequisite.

Valuing life-saving projects. A sticky problem occurs when public projects seek to reduce the loss of human life, as with transportation safety, cancer research, nutrition education, or fire protection. Decisions can save or endanger lives: life or death can rest on government allocation of resources to particular resources. Those decisions are distasteful, but they have been and will continue to be made. The important question is not whether a value has been placed on the saving of human life. The real question is whether decision makers know what they are assuming. Any set of decisions that denies resources to activities which have a life-saving element have implicitly placed a value on life: they imply that the value is less than the cost of the rejected activity. Is that implicit value reasonable?[33]

A number of methods, none flawless but some better than others, have been proposed to value life saving. Historically, the first was average life insurance face values outstanding, under the logic that this was a value on loss of life that individuals placed on themselves. The obvious problems are that individuals buy life insurance for varied motives, including some—for example, forced saving—which have nothing to do with death potential, and that individual holdings vary substantially by family characteristics. These influences render insurance values generally inappropriate for this use.

A second technique, the earnings loss method, views the human as something equivalent to a machine. Thus, the value of a life saved is estimated at the present value of lifetime earnings less subsistence cost through the work career of the individual. That, it is alleged, equals the contribution of the individual to the economy and is the value of a life saved. There are questions both about what earning pattern to use and about whether that narrow production view truly gauges the social worth of an individual; this approach is seldom used in benefit–cost analysis today.[34] However, the judicial system does use this approach in

[33] A questionnaire to 435 adult Americans asked the question "How much, in dollars, is the average human life worth?" The average response was $28,000. (Leonard C. Lewin, "Ethical Aptitude Test," *Harper's,* 253 [October 1976]: 21.) The methods examined here have substantially stronger logical basis than this.

[34] A close variant is reportedly used in military pilot safety decisions: the value used is the cost of training a replacement. Safety feature costs are balanced against that value estimate.

wrongful death cases: one element in awards to families is estimated net lifetime earnings of the individual killed.

The third technique uses evidence generated by labor market response to higher risk of death across occupations. A number of occupations (logging, off-shore drilling, etc.) have greater risk of death than other occupations with similar skills. The wage premiums necessary to recruit workers to that work provides an estimate of the value of life in the labor market. Thus, life-saving values emerge directly from the choices of individuals. There are some logical questions about the method—for one, the values may be artificially low because those jobs apparently appeal to individuals whose attitudes toward risk are different from those of others (they may actually enjoy extreme danger)—but it apparently gives the soundest estimates generally available.[35]

Government decisions do generate implicit values for life saving. That valuation cannot be avoided. Benefit–cost analysis must ensure that these valuations are conscious and consistent. It can hope for little else.

A final note on benefit–cost analysis

Benefit–cost analysis can supply decision makers valuable information about government activities. The analysis can estimate whether a particular project improves the efficiency of resource allocation. Supplemental displays, where relevant, can indicate its distributional impact across income classes, regions, races, sexes, etc., depending on the classifications deemed relevant.

The relationships and variables in the computations are estimates based on assumptions made by the analyst. Those making project choices must know what those assumptions are and how the analysis would differ with other reasonable assumptions. At minimum, the public decision maker must comprehend the structure of benefit–cost analysis to safeguard against delusion by self-interested parties.

Public choices are political. No computerized, sterile analysis can substitute. Benefit–cost analysis is, however, an invaluable information tool and merits expansion as such, in spite of its possible weaknesses and potential misuses. As John Krutilla has observed:

> Since the alternative is not to retire to inactivity but, rather, to reach decisions in the absence of analysis, we may take some comfort from the belief that thinking systematically about problems and basing decisions

---

[35] W. K. Viscusi, "Wealth Effects and Earnings Premiums for Job Hazards," *Review of Economics and Statistics,* 60 (August 1978): 408–16.

on such analysis are likely to produce consequences superior to those that would result from purely random behavior.[36]

CASES FOR DISCUSSION

A. The federal government has no formal capital budget and, as discussed earlier, may well not need one. Federal agencies do, however, have substantial capital assets and do need some systematic method for managing that capital. The following selection examines capital investment in four federal agencies—the U.S. Postal Service, the General Services Administration, the Veterans Administration, and the Corps of Engineers. Although dramatically different in services rendered, all have significant capital investment.

The material is excerpted from a General Accounting Office report.* Not only is it a useful case study of capital acquisition practices in four federal agencies, but it also nicely illustrates the work done by the GAO.

Consider these questions:

1. Do the agencies use capital budgeting as described in the chapter? Explain.
2. What agency does the best job of managing its capital investments? Why?
3. How do funding mechanisms influence the process? Should they?

General Accounting Office Report

The U.S. Postal Service, the General Services Administration, the Veterans Administration, and the Corps of Engineers (civil works) invest directly in capital assets, which means they acquire and manage federally owned physical capital. Organizations (whether they are federal, state, or local governments or private industry) possess certain elements that determine the success of their capital investment process. The elements that can enhance or hamper successful capital budgeting in the four agencies discussed in this chapter are shown in Table 1.

Of the four federal agencies discussed in this chapter, we believe that

* Source: U.S. General Accounting Office, "Federal Capital Budgeting: A Collection of Haphazard Practices" (PAD-81-19, February 26, 1981).

[36] John Krutilla, "Welfare Aspects of Benefit–Cost Analysis," *Journal of Political Economy,* July 1961, p. 234.

TABLE 1

Element	Does element enhance capital investment program?			
	USPS	GSA	VA	CORPS
Agency management attitude enhances long-term capital investment	yes	no	yes	yes
Agency prepares long-term capital investment plan	yes	no	yes	yes[1]
Congressional authorization process encourages planning for capital acquisition	yes[2]	no	yes	no
Agency has sufficient funds to execute capital program	yes	no	yes[3]	yes[3]
Agency controls and monitors capital project execution	yes	yes	yes	yes
Agency uses economic analyses to justify projects	yes	yes[4]	yes[5]	yes
Agency performs postcompletion study to determine if project accomplished its objectives	yes	no	yes	no

[1] Corps annually prepares a five-year investment program that identifies projects likely to be started during the next five years, given probable funding constraints. The corps has the capability of formulating a range of alternative five-year investment programs responsive to alternative funding levels.
[2] The Congress has granted the Postal Service broad authority over capital investments. The authorizing committees do not participate in the selection of projects.
[3] Subject to appropriated amounts.
[4] Analysis focuses on identifying the least costly way of meeting a need.
[5] Analysis focuses on demographics and identifying the least costly way of meeting a need.

the Postal Service is the closest to what we have defined as a successful organization; however, we are not advocating that its flexibility (off-budget status and freedom from congressional authorization of capital projects) be extended to the other federal agencies. The Postal Service is unique among the agencies we examined in that it operates like a business, selling well-defined services to the public. We cite it as an organization with a capital budgeting process that has many desirable planning, budgeting, and control features that could be readily adapted by other federal agencies.

Although the Postal Service has many good capital budgeting features, it operates under a cloud of criticism because of capital investment decisions made before the effective date of the Postal Reorganization Act of 1970 and before its current capital investment system was established.[1] Today, the Postal Service's capital investment process seems sound, but we are planning to review some of USPS'

[1] U.S. General Accounting Office, "Grim Outlook for the United States Postal Service's National Bulk Mail System" (GGD-78-59, May 16, 1978).

more recent investments and will report our findings to the Congress.

Postal Service management recognizes that capital assets are important to productivity. USPS is an independent, off-budget agency and is not required to seek congressional authorization for individual projects. This independence makes it relatively free of the Congress as a source of funds for its operating and capital investment programs. USPS does not have to compete with other federal programs for capital investment funds. The Postal Service prepares five-year capital investment plans and performs extensive economic and cost analyses before it funds capital investment projects. Once capital programs are under way, USPS tightly monitors and controls them for cost and time of completion. After a project is completed, a postaudit analysis is done to find out if proposed results were achieved and to identify any trends that need management attention or action.

In contrast to the Postal Service, GSA is subject to strong congressional control. It must first obtain authorization committee approval for each project over $500,000 before it can request funds from congressional appropriations committees. While this requirement does not specifically restrict GSA planning, it does not encourage it either. GSA's funds are generated from user charges that finance lease payments, purchase contract payments, operations, repairs and alterations, program management, and new construction. Because of legal obligations (lease and purchase contract payments) and other priorities, new con-

struction is the last budget item to receive funds, and the remaining funds are not sufficient to execute a successful capital investment program. Because funds are insufficient, and to keep the budget down, the executive branch has preferred to meet capital building needs by continuing GSA's leasing program. These factors do not encourage capital planning. The result is that GSA management does not have a long-term capital investment program at the moment. However, the agency is now developing a management planning system that sets forth long-range policies for public buildings acquisition, leasing, and major repair. The system is scheduled to be fully operational in early 1981. GSA says it is trying very hard to plan effectively for the future.

MANAGERS HAVE DIFFERENT VIEWS OF CAPITAL INVESTMENTS

In successful organizations, managers recognize and understand the long-term effects of capital investment. We found that managers in the four federal agencies had different views of capital investment. Postal Service officials place a very high priority on acquiring and maintaining physical capital. Corps officials told us that they consider capital investment and operations and maintenance decisions separately. VA places highest priority on operations, which are to provide medical services to veterans, and a lower priority on nonrecurring maintenance. GSA, on the other hand, for years has been preoccupied with meeting its capital investment needs by leasing and rehabilitating existing space rather than constructing new federal buildings.

U.S. Postal Service

Postal Service management wants to keep costs low and increase productivity. Officials believe they can accomplish this only by mechanizing and improving their physical capital. Through its 11-member Board of Governors, USPS can make independent decisions about capital investment, and since the Congress has granted it borrowing authority (up to $1.5 billion annually to finance capital acquisition), USPS management has sufficient funds to invest in needed capital assets.

Since 1972, the Postal Service has committed over $4 billion to capital investment, an average of about $532 million per year over the last eight years. This is considerably higher than the average of about $200 million per year for the six years (1966 to 1971) before the Postal Service became an independent agency. (In constant 1972 dollars, these averages would be, respectively, about $438 million and $233 million.)

Corps of Engineers

Since the 1960s the Corps has planned and budgeted capital investments and operations and maintenance separately. The Congress appropriates these items separately, too; thus, funds cannot be transferred from one account to the other. Traditional budget practice has been to prepare separate justifications for capital investments and operations and mainte-

nance, and to handle priorities separately as well. Corps officials said that the Congress generally specifies funding increases or decreases by category, and only if there were an unspecified, across-the-board, appropriation increase or decrease, would there be any choosing of priorities between capital and operations and maintenance.

Veterans Administration

Like the Corps of Engineers, VA's capital and operations and maintenance are planned, budgeted, and funded separately. Priorities within each account are handled separately and funds cannot be transferred from one account to the other.

To protect its priorities, VA sets a high priority on operations essential to its mission, which is to provide medical care to veterans, and a lower priority on nonrecurring maintenance. VA officials said they understand the long-term effects of capital investments and strive to balance construction projects by selecting those compatible with their mission.

General Services Administration

For years GSA has met its capital investment building needs primarily by leasing rather than by constructing new federal buildings. From 1968 to 1979 federally owned space decreased about 23 million square feet (from 160.4 million to 137.4 million), while leased space increased by 45.1 million square feet (from 48.2 million to 93.3 million). GSA continues to rely on leasing, despite the concerns of the House and Senate Committees on Appropriations and Public Works about the increasing amount and cost of leased space. The Committees have advocated direct federal construction as the most economical way to provide space for federal agencies. GSA said it would prefer to meet more space needs by new construction, but budgetary constraints have limited its ability to do so.

We have reported that from the standpoint of the budget for the Federal Buildings Fund, the best way to finance space is to build new buildings.[2] This means large initial cash outlays for construction, but over the long term less of the Fund's resources would be used and a larger budget surplus would result. A study of eight buildings showed that under the purchase-contract method it would take 27 years to recover their costs. Had these buildings been new construction, their costs would have been recovered in 14 years. Leasing buildings provides a positive cash flow from the start, but over the entire building life direct federal construction provides a larger positive cash flow than either leasing or purchase contracting.

For years GSA's management has not been committed to an aggressive capital investment program for several reasons: its current authorization process does not encourage long-range capital planning, it does not have enough funds to implement an effective capital program, and recently it has received adverse publicity about fraud and mismanagement. In addition, during the last five years the top management of GSA's Public Buildings Service has changed six times and the agency has been criticized by the Congress and the media about kickbacks to GSA employees from contractors.

GSA recognizes the shortcomings of its capital investment plan. It is currently developing a management planning system that delineates long-range policies for physical capital. According to GSA, the system proposes to closely link planning and budgeting and to provide information on facility planning, prospectus review, resources availability, and assessment of accomplishments against planned targets.

LONG-RANGE PLANNING IS NECESSARY FOR EFFECTIVE CAPITAL INVESTMENT PLANNING

A successful capital investment program depends heavily on long-range planning.[3] Every organization that we identified as successful prepares long-range plans, usually for a five-year period. These organizations understand the many advantages of gauging future trends and developments. They know that long-range planning:

> Encourages early review of priorities and capital investment objectives.

---

[2] U.S. General Accounting Office, "Costs and Budgetary Impact of the General Services Administration's Purchase Contract Program" (LCD-80-7, October 17, 1979).

[3] Part of OMB Circular A-109, issued in 1976, directs federal agencies that acquire major systems to (1) relate capital investment needs to agency mission and goals, and communicate this relationship to the Congress early in the planning cycle and (2) identify and explore alternative concepts through early contractual competition and continue competition as long as economically feasible.

Serves as a vehicle for coordinating projects and fostering short-term planning.

Helps determine future funding requirements.

Informs other agencies and the executive and legislative branches of its capital investment needs in relation to its mission.

U.S. Postal Services

The Postal Service prepares a five-year capital investment plan which, when approved by its Board of Governors, becomes the financial plan for the budget year. The plan is developed "bottom-up" by the field offices and undergoes various reviews by headquarters. Priorities are then set in the plan for the projects to be undertaken.

Each regional office is sent an approved financial plan based on the approved capital investment plan. The regions then implement their plan within the established dollar limits. Before funds are committed, the requesting regional office must prepare a cost analysis for each procurement over $2,000 and a full economic analysis for each project over $30,000.

Veterans Administration

The VA prepares a five-year medical facility construction plan, which is also developed from the bottom up. The plan lists all construction projects that exceed $2 million by year, categories of construction, and location. Public Law 96-22, Section 5007, requires the VA to submit its plan to the congressional authorizing committees for approval.

VA's 1980–84 plan contains 16 different categories of construction such as boiler plants, general projects, medical facility improvements, replacement and modernization, and safety and fire. The plan also includes a list of 10 hospitals most in need of construction, replacement, or major modernization.

Corps of Engineers

Each year the Corps prepares a five-year investment program that lists the projects available for initiation during that five-year period, given the probable funding constraints. The selection of individual projects is based on national and regional needs within the region's allocated share of the total probable funding level. The five-year investment program does not set individual project priorities but does list, by region, the status of a project's availability for initiation.

Annual recommendations for new starts are made from categories in the five-year plan that have a high priority. Right now, the Corps is emphasizing projects that satisfy the need for hydroelectric power, urban flood control, municipal and industrial water supply, and commercial navigation.

General Services Administration

Right now GSA does not prepare any long-range capital investment plans. Officials said they used to prepare them, but since there have been so few funds for new construction in recent years they feel it is a waste of time to prepare long-range plans for construction projects. However, GSA is currently working on a five-year plan for housing its federal customers. This plan is expected to be ready for use for the 1983 budget cycle.

The lack of capital plans by GSA has

recently come to the attention of the Senate Environment and Public Works Committee. Committee members introduced S. 2080, which passed the Senate on June 20, 1980. Among other things, the bill requires GSA to prepare and submit to the Congress each year a program for construction, renovation, and acquisition, along with a five-year plan for accommodating the public building needs of federal agencies.

The Committee has also expressed concern about the piece-meal authorization of individual projects throughout the year. Right now the committee approves or disapproves individual projects without the benefit of knowing the relative priority of projects, or how a particular project fits in the building program. In testimony before the Committee in January 1980, GAO said that S.2080 is an improvement over the current authorization and planning procedure. We also discussed the need for long-range plans in our report "Foresighted Planning and Budgeting Needed for Public Buildings Program," (PAD-80-95, September 9, 1980). GSA acknowledges that it now has no cohesive, prioritized plan for all construction projects. However, such a plan is in the development stage and would be required by S. 2080.

THE CONGRESSIONAL AUTHORIZATION PROCESS CAN ADVERSELY AFFECT FEDERAL GOVERNMENT PLANNING

Today the Congress must authorize many projects individually before they can be funded. We think that planning and executing capital investment programs can be more effective if the authorization process focused more on an agency's mission and related capital investment needs. Authorizing legislation is the basic substantive legislation that sets up or continues the legal operation of a federal agency or program. Such legislation sanctions a particular type of obligation or expenditure. It is a prerequisite for the subsequent appropriation of funds to carry out a program. The four agencies we studied have diverse requirements for congressional authorization of individual projects, ranging from no control, as in the case of the Postal Service, to almost absolute control, as in the cases of the Corps of Engineers and the General Services Administration.

Each agency has general legislative authority to acquire, operate, and maintain certain types of physical capital. For GSA, VA, and the Corps, the Congress determines (by authorizing individual projects) the location, scope, and timing of capital investments. These requirements are designed to maintain congressional authorization control (in addition to the appropriation control) of individual projects. In practice, however, such requirements, though not necessarily by design or desire, can sometimes lessen congressional control, or at least divert attention from the agency's mission. Without benefit of adequate long-range plans, these requirements force committees and the agencies to make decisions about projects without knowledge of overall needs or priorities in relation to authorized missions.

Only the Postal Service is not required to have individual projects authorized by the Congress. Since it became an independent agency in 1971, the Postal Service prepares five-year

TABLE 2
Requirements for congressional authorization of individual capital investment projects

U.S. Postal Service............................	No approval required
General Services Administration...............	All projects over $500,000
Veterans Administration.......................	All projects over $2 million
Corps of Engineers	All projects over $2 million*

*Some projects have lower authorization levels.

capital plans. It has also averaged two to three times more capital investment than it did as a cabinet department under more direct congressional control. In contrast, GSA, which has the strongest congressional authorization requirements, has no long-range capital plans. It has averaged significantly less than USPS in capital investment because of lack of funds in recent years. VA has authorization requirements similar to GSA's, but unlike GSA, its authorizing legislation requires that five-year plans be developed and forwarded to the authorizing committees.

U.S. Postal Service

When the Post Office Department was changed to an independent agency by the Postal Reorganization Act of 1970, it was given general authority to construct, operate, lease, and maintain buildings, facilities, equipment, and other improvements without further authorization from the Congress. Since it has become an independent agency, investment in capital assets has increased dramatically.

Veterans Administration

Only recently has the Veterans Administration been required to seek authorization of individual medical facilities before requesting appropriations for their acquisition. From 1931 to 1979, the authority to establish VA hospitals and health care facilities rested solely with the president, subject to the appropriation of funds by the Congress. The location and need for facilities was determined by the Administrator of Veterans Affairs, subject to presidential approval. The only restraint put on the VA by the Congress was the funds made available in the annual appropriation acts.

This procedure was changed in 1979 by the Veterans' Health Care Amendments of 1979 (P.L. 96-22, June 13, 1979). Title III of this Act provides that no appropriation to construct, alter, or acquire a medical facility costing over $2 million can be made unless it is first approved by a resolution of the Committees on Veterans' Affairs of the House and the Senate. These provisions also apply to leased facilities with an annual rental of more than $500,000. The VA must now submit a prospectus to both committees showing a detailed description of the project, its location, its general costs, and the cost of the equipment to operate it.

The Act also requires that VA submit to the committees a five-year plan for constructing, replacing, or altering facilities; a list of 10 hospitals most in need of construction, replacement, or major modernization; and general plans (costs, location) for each project in the five-year plan.

General Services Administration

Section 7 of the Public Buildings Act of 1959, as amended, says that no appropriation in excess of $500,000 shall be made to construct, alter, purchase, or acquire any building to be used as a public building until it has been approved by the Committees on Public Works of the Senate and House of Representatives. This section also applies to leases with an average annual rental exceeding $500,000.

The GSA Administrator submits case-by-case prospectuses to the Committees since there is no legal requirement to submit an annual or multiyear plan. The prospectus authorization by each of the Committees is a separate action and is not subject to the committee conference process. Thus, GSA's proposed projects are submitted to the Public Works Committees without regard to available appropriations and without explanation of relative priorities. Senator Moynihan, in a statement in the December 5, 1979, Congressional Record on S. 2080, said that:

> Other than a pro forma declaration asserting the importance of each to the efficient functioning of the Government, we have no idea of the relative priorities among the proposals, nor do I believe that the GSA itself has any notion of the priorities. We can—and do—authorize projects without knowing whether there will

later be an appropriation sufficient to undertake them. Some authorized projects languish unfunded for years, and some are never carried out at all.

Senator Stafford, then ranking minority member of the Environment and Public Works Committee stated that "the prospectus process may no longer be adequate or appropriate." He added: "the current prospectus process leads to piecemeal approvals without program review or oversight of the policies, and procedures inherent in project proposals."

GSA officials told us that even though they cannot get funds from the appropriations committees until the authorizing committees approve their prospectuses, 40 or 50 prospectuses are pending approval. We have reported that the authorizing committees may take several months to well over a year to approve some alteration and major repair prospectuses.[4] For example, GSA asked for $180 million for FY 1980 alterations and major repairs, but the appropriations committees reduced the request to slightly less than $146 million because several proposed projects had not yet been authorized. According to GSA officials, delays in prospectus approvals have hampered their plans for funding projects. GSA said it is trying to limit its budget requests to only those projects previously approved, but the agency points

---

[4] U.S. General Accounting Office, "Repairs and Alterations of Public Buildings by General Services Administration—Better Congressional Oversight and Control Is Possible" (LCD-78-335, March 21, 1979).

out that often it is forced to add projects for which prospectuses have not been approved because of critical repair work and the space needs of other federal agencies.

Corps of Engineers

The Corps of Engineers has the most complex and lengthy authorization process of the four agencies studied. The conception, authorization, and construction of a Corps flood control project travels through several phases of congressional authorization. In 1978, we reported that of 77 flood control projects studied, an average of 26 years had elapsed since initial authorization and start of construction.[5] Planning and design consumed 12 years of this 26-year period; reviews and the appropriations process took most of the remaining time.

Authorization of Corps projects is at the sole discretion of the Congress. There are three basic phases—study, design, and construction—and Congress must authorize the study and construction phases. Public Works Committees authorize the conduct of studies, usually after local interests make their desires known through their elected representatives. Congress must then appropriate funds for the study. After the study is completed, the Secretary of the Army (after review by the administration) makes a recommendation to the Public Works Committees. If the project is vi-

able and funds are available for planning, preliminary planning is done. Before detailed plans can be completed and construction permitted, the Congress must pass substantive legislation authorizing the construction. However, some projects under $2 million can be initiated by the Secretary of the Army without Congress' authorization, if they meet statutory dollar limits.

FUNDING METHODS INFLUENCE CAPITAL INVESTMENT

The source and type of funds, and an agency's ability to control its funds can hinder or facilitate the acquisition of capital assets. Funding methods affect priorities and the extent to which agencies are able to execute a viable capital investment program.

GSA and generally VA construction projects are fully funded. Postal Service projects are funded incrementally from operating receipts and/or borrowing, and Corps projects are incrementally funded by congressional appropriation. Full funding means that all of the estimated costs of a project are appropriated in the first year. Incremental funding is the appropriation of funds yearly for the estimated costs of the project for that year. As a matter of budget policy, we favor the full funding concept. However, not considering lease commitments for all future years clearly understates leasing costs and diverts decisions away from construction and acquisition to constantly escalating leases which are justified on the next year's cost only.

VA and Corps projects are funded from general fund appropriations. Their

_____

[5] U.S. General Accounting Office, "Corps of Engineers Flood Control Projects Could Be Completed Faster through Legislative and Managerial Changes" (CED-78-179, September 22, 1978).

funds are placed in accounts to be used exclusively for specific capital construction projects and/or acquisition projects. GSA and the Postal Service, on the other hand, are funded through revolving funds set up by the Congress—the Federal Buildings Fund and the Postal Service Fund. These two Funds are similar in that receipts from them finance expenditures, which in turn generate receipts. There are, however, important differences in the way the revenues are collected and the Funds are controlled.

Activities of the Postal Service are financed by congressional appropriations and by receipts from (1) mail and services revenue, (2) reimbursements from federal and nonfederal sources, (3) interest on investments, and (4) proceeds from borrowing. These receipts are deposited into the Postal Service Fund and are used to pay for operating expenses, retirement of obligations, investments in capital assets, and investment in obligations and securities as determined by USPS. The Postal Service has a distinct advantage over GSA because it does not have to compete with other federal programs for capital investment funds and it can borrow up to $10 billion. A net increase of up to $2 billion in any one year can be used for either capital investment (no more than $1.5 billion) or operating expenses (no more than $500 million). The borrowing authority of the Postal Service greatly increases its flexibility to finance operations and capital investment.

The Federal Buildings Fund, authorized in 1972 and begun in 1975, obtains receipts from rates charged to federal agencies occupying GSA-controlled space. According to law these rates are to approximate commercial charges for comparable space and services. Collections are deposited into the Federal Buildings Fund and used, subject to annual appropriation act limitations, to finance GSA's real property operations, which consist of six program categories: (1) new construction, (2) alterations and major repair, (3) purchase contract payments, (4) lease payments, (5) real property operations (utilities, cleaning, etc.), and (6) program direction and centralized services. GSA is also reimbursed from federal agencies for space and improvements that are in excess of those covered by the standard level user charge.

New construction is a low priority in GSA's real property operations. GSA officials told us that new construction gets what funds remain after other program needs are met. Since the Federal Buildings Fund began operating in FY 1975, it has not generated enough money for new construction. Only $386 million was available in FY 1975 through 1980, an average of $64 million a year. In addition, because of language in the appropriations acts from 1975 through 1979, about $2.4 million in excess Fund receipts related to the new construction program were deposited in the Treasury as miscellaneous receipts.[6] Beginning with the 1979 appropriation act, the language was changed to provide that the excess receipts remain in the Fund.

---

[6] A total of $13 million for the entire Fund were deposited in the Treasury.

GSA's current annual average of $64 million for construction projects contrasts sharply with the $115 million annual average during the years (1959–71) before the Fund was established. Even then, GSA considered the $115 million inadequate. In 1971 GSA had a backlog of 63 projects, with estimated construction costs of $750 million, that had been authorized but not funded. GSA pointed out during hearings on the 1972 purchase-contract legislation that with annual appropriations averaging only $115 million, it would take at least 10 years to eliminate the backlog of construction already approved but unfunded by the Congress.

To reduce that backlog, the Public Buildings Amendments of 1972 (P.L. 92-313) was passed to give GSA a three-year stop-gap authority to enter into purchase-contract agreements to construct the unfunded projects. Since then, GSA has arranged for the construction and financing of 23 projects for which it makes semiannual payments to contractors for interest, real estate taxes, and amortization of principal. At the end of the contract period, title to the buildings vests with the Government.

GSA also used a dual method for constructing and financing 45 building projects. Construction contracting under the dual method was made the same as under direct federal construction, but the projects were financed by the sale of participation certificates and by borrowing from the Federal Financing Bank.

Today GSA is again faced with a backlog of projects of about $737 million. The Senate Environment and Public Works Committee recognized that direct construction funds from the Federal Buildings Fund will not put a dent in this backlog over the next several years. The Committee reported out a bill (S. 2080) that passed the Senate on June 20, 1980, authorizing GSA to borrow construction funds from the Treasury and to repay the Treasury from user charges.

In October 1979,[7] we recommended to the Congress that any new financing authority for GSA be limited to direct loans from the Treasury or the Federal Financing Bank. In January 1980 testimony before the Senate Environment and Public Works Committee, we concluded that federal construction is the best alternative for acquiring space and that borrowing money for direct federal construction is the most practical current alternative due to the limited funds generated from the Federal Buildings Fund.

---

[7] U.S. General Accounting Office, "Cost and Budgetary Impact of the General Services Administration's Purchase Contract Program" (LCD-80-7, October 17, 1979).

B.   Air travel to England through Heathrow or Gatwick, the airports serving London, can be complicated and slow. Projections done in the 1960s indicated that those airports would be unable to handle future traffic loads. A commission was established to recommend sites for a third London airport. (The concern was *where* to locate the airport, not whether the airport was needed. Thus, the effort was a cost-effectiveness analysis, not a benefit–cost analysis.) The case presented here, reproduced from *The Wall Street Journal,* provides an interesting illustration of the problems created in valuing public losses and gains.

Consider these questions:

1. What problems do you see with valuation according to fire insurance values?
2. What is wrong with the antiquarian's approach?
3. Can you propose an alternate approach?

As a postscript, a third London airport has not been built, and none is currently under serious consideration.

Fight Over an Old Church Raises a Tough Question

By a WALL STREET JOURNAL *Staff Reporter*

What's in a number? It seems inevitable that corporations will try to assign numerical values to elusive social values, but in so doing they may run a risk of absurdity.

Professor C. West Churchman, professor of business administration at the University of California, gives an example from the search for a site to build a third airport to serve London. One spot under serious consideration would have required demolishing the 12th Century Norman church of St. Michael's in the village of Stewkley.

It was disclosed that a cost–benefit analysis had calculated in monetary terms just what would be lost by tearing down St. Michael's. The calculations had used the face value of the fire insurance of the church—the equivalent of a few thousand dollars.

When the calculation was made public, an outraged antiquarian wrote to the *London Times* to urge another, perhaps no less plausible, method of calculation: Take the original cost of St. Michael's (perhaps 100 pounds sterling or about $240), and assume the property grew in value at a rate of 10 percent a year for 800 years. That would put the value of St. Michael's at roughly one decillion pounds. A decillion is a one followed by 33 zeroes.

St. Michael's was spared after a public outcry arose. But to Professor Churchman it was striking how glibly either side could pin a numerical value on the church. "Only a modicum of plausibility is needed to convince people that the numbers represent reality," he says. "I don't think the need is for more numbers at all. The need is for justifying the numbers"—for some rationale that "tells us what difference the numbers make."

1. The relative size of government has been an important concern for public policy in the past decade. Size and growth questions have been important at the state and local level, as demonstrated by the several state referenda to limit state and/or local expenditure, and at the federal level, as illustrated by the major disputes during 1981 over the size of the budget. Some evidence for those discussions can be drawn from data on trends of spending activity, using information from the Department of Commerce's *Survey of Current Business* (monthly), the Census Bureau's *Governmental Finances* (annual), and the Advisory Commission on Intergovernmental Relations' *Significant Features of Fiscal Federalism* (biennial). From those sources, prepare answers to these questions about the size of government in the United States.

   a. Has the public sector grown relative to the private sector? How does the size of the federal government compare with that of state and local government? (Some benchmarks for comparison are the percentage of gross national product or personal income accounted for by the sectors.)

   b. Which sectors have been fastest growing? Compare growth of the public sector in your state with that of its neighbors and of the nation. Why might a comparison based on expenditure growth differ from one based on employment?

   c. Which functions account for the greatest share of federal, state, and local government expenditure? Does the pattern differ much among states?

   d. What is the relative significance of local government compared to state government expenditure in your state? (Make the comparison first counting state aid to local government as state expenditure. Then, omit that portion from state expenditure.) How does your state compare with its neighbors and the nation?

2. Identify these key elements of your state budget process:
   a. Does your state have an annual or biennial budget?
   b. What units direct the preparation of the executive budget? (Not all states have an executive budget.)
   c. How many appropriation bills are usually passed?
   d. How much object-of-expenditure detail appears in these bills?

3. McKinley, a municipality in the central United States, has 217 employees, 41 of them in the fire department. The fiscal year begins July 1. McKinley has the following salary schedule in the fire department.

Classification	Number of persons in classification	Rate of compensation
Fire chief	1	$28,150
Assistant chief	1	22,900
Assistant chief	1	20,600
Lieutenant	1	17,524
Lieutenant	2	16,584
Fire fighter	3	16,224
Fire fighter	5	15,844
Fire fighter	6	15,524
Fire fighter	11	15,004
Fire fighter	6	14,524
Fire fighter	2	14,224
Account clerk-typist (part-time)	2	6,000

The following information about other compensation cost may be useful:

a. The city pays a share of the cost of hospitalization and disability insurance for each full-time employee, an amount equal to $875 per person. The insurance rate will increase by 15 percent on January 1 of next year.

b. The city is part of the federal social security system. The present rate paid by the city is 6.65 percent on salaries up to $29,700.

c. Each full-time employee receives a clothing allowance of $700 per year.

d. Pensions for current employees are financed from state tobacco tax revenues with no local contribution. Employees hired in the next fiscal year and later are part of a new pension system: the city must contribute 20 percent of the salary of these employees to a retirement fund. These employees must also contribute 6 percent of their salaries to the fund.

Compute the following:

(1) The current cost to the city of labor for the fire department.

(2) The total cost of labor to the fire department next year, assuming no new employees and no salary increases.

(3) If salaries increase by 10 percent, the percentage increase of labor cost next year over the current labor cost.

(4) The cost to the city of hiring one additional firefighter next year at the lowest salary in the existing salary schedule.

4. A midwestern city has contracted with a solid-waste collection and disposal firm for service the five years from January 1, 19X7, to December 31, 19Y1. Selected provisions of the contract state:

THE BIDDER HEREBY PROPOSES to furnish all required materials, supplies, solid waste disposal facilities and equipment; to provide and perform all necessary labor and supervision; and to perform all work stipulated in, required by, and in accordance with, the proposed contract documents and the specifications, and other documents referred to therein (as altered, amended, or modified by addenda), in the manner and time prescribed, and to accept in full payment sums determined by the bid plus the following unit price plus or minus any special payments and adjustments provided in the Specifications.

Proposition 1

For the complete performance of all the terms, conditions, and provisions of Proposition 1, as per Specifications, namely:

A five (5) year contract providing for total solid waste (including garbage, rubbish, and household rubbish) collection and disposal on a weekly schedule from:

a. Curb or alley location for each household unit.
b. Proper storage area for apartment complexes.
c. Approved curb location for mobile home courts.

Also, daily collection (five days per week) and disposal of garbage from commercial food service establishments, all in accordance with regulations described herein.

Total base amount per year $1,598,888.33, subject to adjustments provided in the Specifications.

Proposition 2

Adjustments in the contract price for the providing of collection and disposal of solid waste caused by changes in the total number of residences or commercial food service establishments and active fire stations referred to herein, resulting from annexation, deannexation, new construction, or demolition.

Per collection unit change $34.89

The contract also contains an escalator clause to handle changes in the cost of doing business. The clause states:

The compensation payable to the Contractor for the second and subsequent years of the term hereof shall be adjusted upward or downward to reflect changes in the cost of doing business as measured by fluctuations in the Consumer's Price Index, published by the U.S. Department of Labor, Bureau of Labor Statistics, for "All Items" in the "U.S. City Average" category. At the start of the second year and every year thereafter, the compensation to the Contractor shall be increased or decreased in a percentage amount equal to ¼ of the net percentage change in the said Consumer Price Index computed as follows: Beginning with the first month of the second year, the net change shall be the difference between the said Consumer's Price Index during the month immediately prior to the beginning of the first contract year and the last month of said year, and said percentage change shall be computed annually in like manner for each subsequent year of the contract.

In addition to the above, the following evaluation will be made:

Ten (10) days after the beginning of the second and each subsequent contract year, a determination shall be made of the then existing status of the wage scale of regular drivers and laborers of the City Street Department. For each 1 percent of average rate change over or under the rate prevailing at bid time, the Contractor's yearly compensation shall be adjusted up or down by ¾ of 1 percent of his total bid, effective at the beginning of each succeeding contract year. The wage rate at the time of bidding for fully qualified men with over 15 months' experience in the City Street Department of the Ctiy, is $5.01 per hour for drivers and $4.74 per hour for laborers.

Additional information

a. The consumer price index (1967 = 100) has behaved in the following fashion in recent years:

19X5:		19X7:	
December	166.3		
19X6:			
January	166.7	January	175.3
February	167.1	February	177.1
March	167.5	March	178.2
April	168.2	April	179.6
May	169.2	May	180.6
June	170.1	June	181.8
July	171.1	July	182.6
August	171.9	August	183.3
September	172.6	September	184.0
October	173.3	October	184.5
November	173.8	November	185.4
December	174.3	December	186.1

Annual:	
19X4	147.7
19X5	161.2
19X6	170.5
19X7	186.1

b. The street department signed a two-year contract for 19X8–X9 with an 8 percent wage increase.

c. The national pattern of wages and salaries per full-time equivalent state–local government employee (noneducation) has been:

19X3	$ 9,170
19X4	9,822
19X5	10,517
19X6	11,126

Questions

a. Compute the payment to the contractor for 19X8 if 278 units are annexed and 13 are demolished.

b. The city is proposing to annex an area with 45 collection units. What is the garbage collection charge for this area likely to be in 19X9, 19Y0, and 19Y1?

5. From records maintained over several years, the local water utility finds that its monthly purchases of raw water from the state water authority follow these patterns:

Gallons (000s)		Gallons (000s)	
January	35,000	July	125,000
February	35,000	August	100,000
March	50,000	September	85,000
April	65,000	October	60,000
May	68,000	November	50,000
June	100,000	December	40,000

Presume that the city pays a flat rate per thousand gallons of water purchased and that the fiscal year begins on July 1. Payment is made in the month after use. Prepare quarterly allotments for $2,000,000 appropriated for water purchase.

6. The following presents an appropriation, allotment, and status report for an agency. Indicate the status (overspent, underspent, on target) for each category and suggest appropriate managerial actions.

	Total appropriation Jan. 1 to Dec. 31	Quarterly allotments				Status to July 1	
		I	II	III	IV	Spent	Encumbered
Travel	$50,000	$10,000	$14,000	$16,000	$10,000	$23,000	$ —
Office supplies	32,000	8,000	8,000	8,000	8,000	17,000	2,000
Postage	64,000	16,000	16,000	16,000	16,000	35,000	—
Rent	24,000	6,000	6,000	6,000	6,000	12,000	—
Utilities	96,000	24,000	24,000	24,000	24,000	50,000	—
Capital equipment	14,000	0	5,000	9,000	0	4,000	3,000

7. The following sections are narrative from the 1973–74—1974–75 budget request for the South Carolina Department of Social Services. They are part of a nicely prepared and presented line-item budget which requests funds for organizational units.

Goals

In our opinion there are only two reasonable goals for any governmentally supported welfare or social service agency—these are (1) to assist the citizenry in achieving through self-sufficiency a living standard which eliminates the need for public support and (2) for the needs for societal services to be met within society and the family unit without the public provision thereof.

Means of achieving these goals

These are generational goals. It is not feasible this year or this decade to achieve "self-sufficiency" for aged, blind, or disabled adults or dependent children who have insufficient income to provide the basic necessities of life. Further, as technological changes occur the demand for unskilled labor decreases. It becomes increasingly difficult for an illiterate or semieducated person to obtain employment paying wages sufficient to enable him/her to support the family. But the basic sexual drive remains, and children are born into families or to women who probably did not want them and have no means to support them. Many children born into these situations have no one to enunciate the expectations of society or to show them an acceptable way of life. Many of them see no books, papers, or pencils until school. There is little or no home training or "push" for achievement in school. And the cycle repeats itself.

It seems to us that the means of achieving the stated goals are as follows—

(1) Social and moral guidance—This must come through churches, civic groups, and other interested parties. It can only be effective when it comes through peer groups—outside forces can encourage and guide but cannot force acceptance.

(2) Family planning—To assure that no unwanted child is conceived. We are of the opinion that family limitation is a personal matter, but we also believe that most persons will gladly accept assistance in this regard and few have any desire to bring additional children into a deprived setting.

(3) Adequate nutrition and medical care to the prospective mother to assure, insofar as possible, a mentally and physically healthy baby.

(4) Adequate "preschool" training for socially deprived children to enable them to enter school on a level comparable to that of other children. We support the Department of Education's continuing emphasis on kindergartens, but we also believe that this preschool training should be for the "whole" child and thereby be comprehensive in social services to enable both the child and his family to integrate into society.

(5) Adequate and enforced educational opportunities and standards. Illiterate high school graduates may end up on welfare rolls. Many

children should be directed to vocational opportunities which do not require a high level of academic achievement.

(6) Adequate scale of living and housing distributed so that "pockets" of persons living on welfare do not form, thereby giving people a sense of belonging to society and a desire to contribute thereto, and thus eliminating the "welfare" mentality, if indeed such exists.

(7) Adequate medical care so that physical deficiencies and disease can be early detected and treated, thereby contributing a healthy individual to society and maintaining him therein.

(8) Adequate varied job opportunities so that the individual can be productive.

(9) Adequate industrial safeguards, highway standards, and public safety enforcement, to reduce the occurrence of accidental disability.

(10) Adequate employer pensions and health insurance plans to provide for an adequate living standard upon retirement and medical care treatment during and after retirement.

Objectives

Many of the objectives of the department have been stated in the "means" section. Also, over many of the means this department has no control. The following list of objectives are those which we feel are more urgent in alleviating current conditions and assisting in moving toward the stated goals.

(1) Provision of adequate means of living to those persons in South Carolina unable to provide such for themselves.

(2) Provision of "protective services" to those adults and children who are unable to fend for themselves. Neglect of older and disabled adults, abuse and neglect of children should not be tolerated. Our social service program is geared toward these persons now but much additional work needs to be done.

(3) Provision of adequate medical care to these persons.

(4) Provision of family planning services to those individuals willing to accept such services.

(5) Provision of comprehensive social services in a fashion which will prevent dependency and/or encourage persons to become self-sufficient. Such services include but are not limited to early childhood development (including day care), emergency homemaking assistance, transportation, adoptions, counseling, foster care, assistance in obtaining information or aid from other groups, locating suitable housing, developing community aid resources, self-support services, etc.

(6) Provision of prenatal medical care to unwed mothers.

Measures of success in meeting these objectives

(1) Provision of adequate means of living.

A. Adults—Effective January 1, 1974, the categorical aid (welfare payment) program for the aged, totally and permanently disabled, and blind will be transferred, along with major funding responsibility, to the social security administration under a new program entitled "supplemental security income (SSI)." The assistance payments which will be made under this program are nationwide in application. These payments are set at a maximum of $130.00 for an individual and $195.00 for a couple.

These payments, while inadequate, are far better than the present payments made by this agency. It is estimated by the social security administration that approximately 50,000 additional persons will be covered under this program. For this reason we are not requesting funding to supplement payments made by SSI. We must, however, under the legislation, provide certain mandatory supplements to this program in the areas of nursing services and boarding home payments. This will be discussed later.

B. Children—The General Assembly provided funds for a 10 percent increase in payment levels for FY 73–74. This increase was badly needed; however, we will pay only 50 percent of the budget deficit for dependent children and their mothers. An example of items included in the budget is rent which is budgeted at $44.00 per family per month—of which we pay a maximum of 50 percent ($22.00). We submit that this payment level is not sufficient to allow any individual or family unit to live within our society. There will be little upward mobility of persons coming from this environment. As a matter of interest there is no valid welfare payment in this state made to, or on behalf of, an able-bodied male under the age of 65. They are not covered under our operational plans. Food stamps may be purchased by such an individual, but only upon registration with Employment Security Commission for employment. Our long-range goal is—that bonus value of food stamps plus our payment level equal the poverty level in South Carolina.

We are requesting for FY 74–75 funds to raise the payment level to the maximum for federal matching purposes—approximately 75 percent of the budget deficit.

(2) Protective services to adults and children—there are service units in each county office dedicated to providing at least a minimum of these services to children. There are, however, children who are unwanted, abused, and neglected because of a lack of adequate care arrangements, lack of proper legal attention, and lack of legal ability to take action. Further, most people will not report instances of child abuse. A child in South Carolina is effectively a chattel—to be treated as the owner sees fit. There must be a revulsion by society and adequate legal authority granted to eliminate the "bat-

tered child syndrome." Additionally there must be adequate provision for emergency placement of abused, unwanted, or neglected children until adequate long-term care be arranged or the family situation resolved. The case of the neglected (and often abused) older adult is becoming more prevalent. With our present mobile society and our peculiar youth orientation, in-home care for the aged parent is becoming a thing of the past. "Grandma" or "Grandpa" is in the way. Many of our older citizens become the living dead, eking out only a marginal existence. Many are placed as long-term terminal residents of substandard, unlicensed, unofficial boarding or nursing homes where they may be treated as animals if the attendants so desire. We owe the people who made this country great more than this.

There are social service units in each county office working with these problems. We license and enforce boarding and foster home standards. We have initiated a bedside audit of persons in nursing homes and an examination of patients' records to ascertain the proper level of care and to monitor the care they receive. We are not this year requesting major additional funds for this program—we believe adequate staff is available to enable continuation of implementation.

(3) Provision of adequate medical care—under the present state medicaid plan medical care is available only to welfare recipients. During fiscal years 73, 74, and 75 services are being expanded (by virtue of federal directive) to include health, screening diagnosis, and treatment of all children receiving aid under the financial assistance program. Many of these services were not provided under the state plan. This program is estimated to cost an additional $6 million annually. We are requesting in the budget for FY 74–75 funds to implement a categorically related medically indigent program. Because of our low AFDC payment level, such a program would be on a "spend-down" basis and would be available only after a disabled, blind, or aged adult or mother with dependent children had spent for medical costs funds sufficient to reduce their income to the AFDC payment level. This coverage would not be available to what is normally termed the "working poor." Coverage for other low-income families can only be provided with fully state funds.

(4) Provision of family planning services—we have a contract with the Board of Health to provide these services to former, current, or potential welfare recipients. For this purpose we receive 90 percent federal matching funds. Adequate family planning services are necessary to prevent a continued increase in welfare rolls. We provide all interested persons with a referral to the Board of Health and pay the Board of Health for the provision of this service.

(5) Provision of comprehensive social services—there is a social service unit within each county department of social services charged

with the responsibilities outlined in this objective. The services provided by this staff are those which assist the individual in daily living, adoptions, foster care, licensing, etc. For certain "hard" services—such as day care and clinical service for family planning we must rely on other agencies to provide either the service or the "state" share of the funds. We have not requested major funding increases in this area. We have entered into contracts with many state and local agencies to use their funds to match federal funds for the provision of social services. The total amount of these contracts cannot exceed the federal allocation and it appears that the usable amount for this program will not exceed $20 million. We will be better able to judge our position as to social service delivery upon the final determination by HEW as to what these funds can be used to provide.

We have not shown in the budget the full impact of the possibilities of these contracts. Federal regulations and approvals are at this time far too nebulous for us to draw any conclusion as to what will finally be determined. If regulations are approved by HEW which enable us to generate an appreciable amount of these social services funds, the funds must be used to expand services. They may not revert to the general fund of the state. Nor may state funding decrease as a result of these funds.

(6) Provision of prenatal medical care to unwed mothers—the General Assembly provided funds in this year's appropriation to enable us to provide an AFDC award and medical assistance to the unwed woman who is pregnant with her first child. We deplore such a situation but know that adequate medical care and nutrition will increase the probability of delivery of a mentally and physically healthy child. On behalf of the child let me express appreciation for this program. We believe you have resolved this problem if the AFDC award is raised to an adequate level.

Conclusion

We have discussed the goals, means, and objectives of the department. It is important to emphasize that this is our plan of action as best we have been able to formulate it to date.

From this information, prepare a program budget classification for the Department.

8. An important piece of zero-base budgeting is the identification of agency decision units. Decision units should have measurable accomplishments and represent a level where policy decisions can be made. They may or may not coincide with the present budget structure. While instructions for construction of such units varies by governments selecting the ZBB technique, the federal Office of Management and Budget Bulletin 77-9 provides a general guide:

The program or organizational entity for which budgets are prepared and for which a manager makes significant decisions on the amount of spending and the quality of work to be performed.

The OMB provides further guidance in the selection of decision units:

Agencies should ensure that the basic decision units selected are not so low in the structure as to result in excessive paperwork and review. On the other hand the units selected should not be so high as to mask important considerations and prevent meaningful review of the work being performed.

Use those criteria in questions which relate to a state department of taxation. Divisions of that department follow:

(1) The *administrative division* provides direction and administrative supporting services including personnel, research and statistics, purchasing, legal counseling, and collection enforcement.
(2) The *income tax division* administers income tax laws as they relate to individuals, corporations, fiduciaries, and partnerships, including withholding tax.
(3) The *property tax division* assists in programs of reassessment and equalization of real property valuations in counties requesting assistance. It also assesses real and personal property of all manufacturers and public utilities and all personal property held by commercial establishments.
(4) The *sales and use tax division* administers the sales and use tax law.
(5) The *data processing division* processes all returns, deposits all receipts, maintains account files, and performs mathematical checks on all returns.

Some additional detail about the department:

Division	Employees	Budget	State revenue collected
Administrative	90	$1,526,692	—
Income tax	155	1,842,647	$592,657,202
Property tax	34	467,140	—*
Sales and use tax	156	1,761,465	471,555,323
Data processing	75	799,475	—

*The property tax is levied only at the local level.

a. Would each of the five divisions be a decision unit? Why or why not? If not, would the decision units be larger or smaller than a division? Indicate what some decision units would be.
b. Should the costs of the administrative division be prorated to the other divisions or kept separate in preparing decision package costs? Why or

why not? If prorated, what basis could be used that is sensible for the purposes of the budget?

9. Roachdale has a population of 22,000 more or less. Several of its important features appear on the map. The city eagerly awaits the full operation of the Intercontinental Widget Plant early in 19X3. While the plant has few employees now, it will have a work force of around 900. The plant has caused a shift in city population to the south. Many people are moving to the Wonder Hills subdivision (45 percent developed now), although a good number are located along SR 4 outside of town.

The data presented here, along with departmental project proposals, should be used to prepare a capital improvement program for the years 19X0 to 19X4 and a capital budget for 19X0. Financial conditions suggest that the city will be unable to pay more than $900,000 for capital investment in any year, so one part of the exercise requires that priority criteria be established if all requests cannot be included in the budget.

The city has two special capital asset problems. First, the main sanitary sewer at Westside Elementary School near the Red River has suffered structural failure and must be replaced. Second, the SR 4 bridge over Red River is unsafe. The bridge replacement will take two years. During the first year, traffic will have to be detoured. The state will pay 90 percent of the bridge costs.

Projects proposed:

These projects have been proposed by city department heads.

Streets, roads, and bridges

(1) SR 4 bridge replacement—19X0, $350,000; 19X1, $250,000 (costs are totals).
(2) Street upgrading, Wonder Hills subdivision—19X0, $600,000; 19X1, $50,000; 19X2, $20,000.
(3) Street sign replacement—19X0 to 19X9, $18,000 per year (high visibility, break-away signs).

Parks and Recreation

(1) Bowen Park pool—19X0, $300,000 (construction of new above-ground aluminum pool).
(2) Winslow Park Recreation complex—19X1, $25,000; 19X2, $125,000; 19X3, $300,000; 19X4, $300,000; 19X5, $85,000 (pool, ice skating rink, baseball diamonds).

Library

Air condition building—19X0, $45,000; 19X1, $20,000.

Water and sewer

(1) Water line upgrading, Wonder Hills—19X2, $725,000.
(2) Storm sewer installation, Wonder Hills—19X3, $850,000.
(3) Sanitary sewer replacement (structural failure)—19X0, $150,000.

Fire department

(1) New fire substation—19X3, $450,000; 19X4, $65,000.
(2) Fire equipment.
    a. Pumper (main station)—19X0, $25,000
    b. Pumper, hook and ladder (substation)—19X0, $130,000.

10. What problems appear in the following statements involving benefit–cost analysis?

    a. A federal public power project uses a discount rate of 12.5 percent, the after-tax rate of return for electric utilities in the area.
    b. Evaluation of a new municipal fire station uses a discount rate equal to the rate at which the city can borrow long-term funds.
    c. Evaluation of a new four-lane highway to replace an older two-lane highway shows saved travel time for truckers and for private vehicles, the value of increased gasoline sales, and increased profits of trucking firms.
    d. A cost–benefit analysis of removal of architectural barriers for the handicapped from commercial buildings produced these benefit estimates for 202,000 square foot shopping center:

Economic benefit during 50-year useful life of center (1975– 2024) = $4,537,700 cumulative gross revenues from leasable area.

(This increase in gross revenue per year attributable to new accessibility to handicapped persons is calculated by multiplying gross revenues per year by the ratio of handicapped to nonhandicapped persons in the area. The estimate is based on gross revenue per leasable area experienced nationally in 1969, brought forward to 1975 by the rate of consumer price index increase, and extended through the 50-year life of the building according to the compounded rate of growth in sales revenue experienced by community shopping centers, 1966 to 1969. A 7 percent discount rate is employed.)

e. The Big Walnut Creek reservoir proposed for central Indiana has been estimated to cost $92.4 million (land acquisition and preparation, dam construction, etc.). A 1972 Task Force report indicated that total annual benefits from the reservoir would exceed total annualized costs by $2.9 million. A committee of area farmers, using 1973 production figures, calculated that 16,000 acres of cropland, pasture, and woodland in the "reservoir area" would net $3.4 million annually. An opponent of the dam declared: "This is a beautiful area. It should be preserved— especially if farmland is producing more than reservoir benefits."

PART TWO

Revenue sources, structure, and administration

6

Taxation: Evaluation criteria

Governments in the United States collect most of their own-source general revenue from taxes on income, sales, or property. Own-source general revenue excludes revenue from intergovernmental aid and revenue earmarked (or reserved) for a specific use (motor fuel taxes for highway uses only, for example). The first exclusion makes revenue own-source; the second, general. Table 6–1 shows the very small role that charges and miscellaneous revenue plays in government finance. The bottom portion of the table shows revenue from payroll taxes that are reserved for special purposes. The federal payroll tax for social security is the second largest revenue producer among all sources at all levels; it is exceeded only by the federal individual income tax.

The table reflects a distinct separation of revenue sources by level of government. The federal government relies predominantly on income taxes, both individual and corporate, for revenue and raises more money from those taxes than state and local governments raise from all taxes combined. Federal dominance in income taxation is still greater because of the payroll tax for social security which, for individuals receiving only wage and salary income, is a second federal income tax. State governments apply income taxes as well (44 states taxed individual income and 46 taxed corporate net income in 1979), but their aggregate collections do not approach that of the federal government. A number of states, however, do receive more revenue from income taxes

TABLE 6-1
General revenue received by federal, state, and local governments, from own sources, 1978- 1979 ($ millions)

	All	Federal	State	Local
General revenue, own-source	640,543	372,428	150,906	117,209
Taxes	524,446	318,932	124,908	80,606
Property	64,944	-0-	2,490	62,453
Individual income	254,773	217,841	32,622	4,309
Corporation income	77,805	65,677	12,128	-0-
Customs duties	7,688	7,688	-0-	-0-
General sales and gross receipts	46,559	-0-	39,505	7,053
Selective sales and gross receipts	46,715	19,026	24,163	3,526
Other taxes	25,963	8,700	13,999	3,264
Charges and miscellaneous general revenue	116,096	53,496	25,998	36,603
Special revenue, payroll taxes: Unemployment compensation contributions	12,660	194	12,391	75
Old age, survivors, disability, and health insurance contributions	120,522	120,522	-0-	-0-
Total special revenue	133,182	120,716	12,391	75

Source: Bureau of the Census, *Governmental Finances in 1978--1979* (GF-79, no. 5) Washington, D.C.: U.S. Government Printing Office, 1980.

than from any other source. State income taxes often copy the federal tax; the state tax return copies data directly from the federal return. A number of cities levy local income taxes, but the overall revenue from them is inconsequential and, in many cases, the taxes are simply taxes on employee payrolls, not taxes on income from all sources.

Sales taxes in their several forms are the largest single source of state revenue, and states are the largest overall users of that source. All states receive revenue from sales or gross receipts taxes and only five (Delaware, New Hampshire, Montana, Oregon, and Alaska) do not use a general sales tax. Many local governments levy general sales taxes as well; they are second only to the property tax as a tax revenue source to localities. While the sales tax shows no sign of eclipsing the property tax in local importance, there are some communities in which it is the major tax revenue producer. Contrary to the local income tax which is typically locally administered, local sales taxes are usually administered by the state government in conjunction with the state tax. The U.S. Constitution prohibits the states from levying customs duties (selective excises on imported items) and of total federal revenue such taxes yield only a minor proportion.

The property tax remains the major own-source revenue producer for local governments. Despite continued popular and academic attacks on the tax, it remains the predominant local tax, possibly because it is the only major tax generally within the means of independent local administration. State property taxes continue their decline—a path which began during the Great Depression, when widespread property tax delinquency and declining property values, combined with a growing demand for state spending, produced a switch to other sources, particularly the sales tax. The U.S. Constitution effectively prohibits a federal property tax as a consequence of the requirement for direct tax apportionment:

> Representatives and direct Taxes shall be apportioned among the several States which may be included within this Union, according to their respective numbers . . . (Article I, Sec. 2 [3])

A state with 1/20 of the national population, by that provision, would have to pay 1/20 of the tax. To produce that apportionment, a federal property tax would require high tax rates in poor states and low rates in wealthy states. Any state-by-state difference in federal tax rates would be politically impractical—as the writers of the Constitution surely knew.

These are the taxes which will be analyzed in the next chapters. The remaining sections of this chapter will provide a framework for evaluation of taxes in general. The following three chapters will outline the structure of the major taxes and will examine the process of administering these taxes.

CRITERIA

Taxes are the normal source of revenues used to provide public services. When public goods are financed, the involuntary nature of the tax is essential. Otherwise, rational actions of nonpayers—who could fully enjoy the public good provided without financial payment—would keep the system from producing expected revenue. Regardless of other attributes, a tax may be distinguished from other ways of raising revenue by its compulsory nature: if a potential taxpayer possesses the tax base, the tax is paid without regard to utilization of services provided by the taxing unit. Absence of voluntarism distinguishes taxes from the user charges—recreation admissions, tolls, etc.—that many governmental units collect. The tax is neither a price for service received nor a voluntary contribution. (Governments do not rely on "fair share" contributions because of the susceptibility of fairness to widely different individual definition.)

Ability to pay or benefits received

Given that a specific amount of money is to be raised by a tax system, how ought the revenue burden be distributed? Two general standards are available: (1) burden allocated according to the benefits from the public service and (2) burdens distributed according to taxpayer capability to bear the burden. Choice of approach must finally be partly philosophic and partly pragmatic.

The logic of the benefit-received approach is an appealing adjunct to the exchange economy for private goods. In a quasi-market arrangement, individuals would pay for a public service if and only if they are judged to benefit from the public service. If the individual benefits, he pays; if he doesn't benefit, he doesn't pay. There are neither the dangerous over-supplies of public services that can result when individuals receive a service at artificially lowered cost nor the equally dangerous underprovision that can emerge when individuals perceive a payment greater than the value of services expected to be received. Services to be received and payment to be made are determined in a quid pro quo exchange. A taxpayer receiving 1 percent of the benefits of a public service would pay 1 percent of the cost of providing that service; there will be no cross-subsidization among taxpayers.

Problems prevent wholesale application of the benefit-received approach, as even the staunchest supporter of a social contract version of government recognizes. For one thing, pure public goods, by their very nature, produce benefits for the general community. No individually apportionable unit of service can be unambiguously bought by the citizen, so there is no divisible exchange in the public good transaction. Furthermore, modern governments are typically involved in redistribution—the provision of services directly aimed at transfer of affluence from one group to another. In this circumstance the benefit approach fails: the objective of the action is subsidization, not exchange. When circumstances of measurement and redistribution do not prohibit, however, the benefit base has strong logical support.

The ability-to-pay approach eschews the market exchange philosophy. The argument is, in simplest form, that appropriability (and its absence) make public services and market goods different by nature. The decision to provide public services can be considered separately from the choice of financial burden distribution, so the distribution may be set according to concepts of fairness or equity. Unfortunately, scientific tools do not provide the analytic references to establish fairness measures. If individual satisfaction levels could be measured and compared among individuals, tax systems might be designed to yield revenues for public use at least satisfaction loss to society. There remains no calibration method, so the hope of scientific burden distribution seems beyond reach. Distribution is a matter of political opinion, not science.

Application of the ability approach has two decision elements: selection of an ability measure and choice of the manner in which tax payments should vary with that measure. The appropriateness of alternative ability measures varies with the economic circumstances of development. In an agrarian society—possibly 18th-century American— usable measures of ability might be property ownership, particularly land, buildings, carriages, and cattle. Present-day conceptions lean toward current income—the corporate form of business and development of debt forms make gross property values an unreliable measure of ability. While most public discussion about ability to pay concentrates on income as the appropriate measure, a more comprehensive measure would encompass net wealth as well (possibly on an annuity basis), because both income and wealth figure into the real affluence of an individual.[1] The major danger in the ability-to-pay approach is the problem of clearly tying down taxable capacity. Legislative deliberations about the distribution of tax burden too often hinges on the principle: "Don't tax you, don't tax me, tax that other guy behind the tree—but tax the eyeballs off him."[2]

The second choice is the extent to which households with different abilities ought to pay different taxes. Suppose current income has been selected as the appropriate measure of ability to pay. A household with $20,000 income presumably should pay more tax than a household with $10,000 income. Should the payment by the higher income household be twice that of the other, somewhat more than twice, or somewhat less than twice? This decision determines the extent to which affluence is redistributed through the tax system, and is an important element of social policy. It is, however, significant only for the ability-to-pay approach; it is not a major factor for a benefit-base approach.

Equity in taxation—horizontal and vertical

Consideration of equity of the distribution of tax payments from households has both horizontal and vertical components. The former considers equal treatment of taxpayers who have equal capability to pay taxes: if two taxpaying units are equivalent in all relevant aspects,

---

[1] Some observers have argued for taxation primarily on consumption, as consumption represents a withdrawal of resources from social use. Ignoring some definitional problems, one must still handle the fact that investment likewise involves resource utilization. For a defense of the consumption view, see Nicholas Kaldor, *The Expenditure Tax* (London: George Allen and Unwin, 1958).

[2] Senator Russell Long quoted in *People & Taxes,* May 1976.

but one unit pays significantly greater tax, the tax structure lacks horizontal equity. Such a condition may emerge when taxes vary by individual taste and preference, as with taxes levied on commodities that are used by a narrow segment of the population. It may also occur when tax administration is haphazard or capricious. An obvious problem here is defining equivalence of taxing unit condition: the behavior that creates the failure of horizontal equity may be regarded as evidence of elevated taxpaying capability. In sum, the concept of horizontal equity may have problems in application, but the principle is strong. Equal treatment, after all, is a principle derived from the equal protection requirements of the U.S. Constitution.

Vertical equity concerns the proper relationship between the relative tax burdens paid by individuals with *different* capability to pay taxes. The comparison is between unequals and the question is the appropriate different treatments to be afforded them. No scientific guides indicate what *the* proper differentiation might be, but most would argue that those with more capacity ought to pay more taxes. This simple observation, however, provides little guidance for tax policy. What needs to be determined further is whether the tax structure should be proportional, progressive, or regressive. Table 6–2 illustrates the three distributions.

TABLE 6–2
Proportionality, progressivity, and regressivity

Taxpaying unit income (annual)	Proportional structure		Progressive structure		Regressive structure	
	Tax paid	Effective rate	Tax paid	Effective rate	Tax paid	Effective rate
$ 1,000	$ 10	1%	$ 10	1%	$10	1 %
5,000	50	1	100	2	20	0.4
10,000	100	1	300	3	30	0.3
15,000	150	1	600	4	40	0.27
20,000	200	1	1,000	5	50	0.25

The vertical equity concept gauges the relationship between income and effective rates. A structure is *regressive* if effective rates are lower in high ability groups than in low, *progressive* if effective rates are higher in high ability groups than low, and *proportional* if effective rates are the same in all groups. Effective rate behavior distinguishes the structures. All equity comparisons use the effective rate (tax paid divided by the relevant affluence measure, usually income) not the statutory or nominal rate (the rate legally defined as applicable to the tax base). Effective and statutory rates are not the same because tax bases are not the same as affluence measures. Thus, a nominal 4 percent tax on consumption would equal an effective 2 percent tax on income if half of the income is consumed. Much tax analysis concerns the relationship between tax bases and affluence measures.

Table 6–2 also illustrates measures which cannot reliably indicate whether a structure is progressive or regressive. For instance, a comparison of total tax paid by high- and low-income groups will not produce meaningful information about vertical equity. For each structure here, tax paid rises with income, despite the dramatic differences in relative burden. That measure does not provide an appropriate comparison. Neither will a comparison of the proportion of total taxes paid by an income group with that group's proportion of the total population. If holding of the tax base per taxpaying unit is unequal among income groups (as it certainly must be), proportional or regressive taxes will cause high-income groups to pay a disproportionately high share of taxes and low-income groups, a low share. Thus, effective rate comparisons or their logical equivalents are the only reliable guide to vertical equity of a structure.

Because vertical equity is so significant for decisions about taxes levied on the ability-to-pay principle, analysts often must estimate whether a particular new tax or a revision in an old tax will be progressive, regressive, or proportional. There are some standard approaches to presenting such information, although none is completely satisfactory. Fiscal administrators should understand the approaches, which all follow the same general pattern in application.

Preparing measures of vertical equity

The initial stage in the analysis is identification of data on taxpaying units which contains, by unit or by typical unit within affluence classes, information on all economic behavior needed to construct (1) the level of income (or whatever measure of taxpaying capacity is seen as appropriate) and (2) the tax base being considered for each taxpaying unit. Widely used sources include Bureau of Labor Statistics, *Survey of Consumer Expenditures;* U.S. Internal Revenue Service, *Statistics of Income;* and special data files which have been constructed for tax analysis by many states and the U.S. Treasury.

The second step estimates, from that data base, the tax which would be paid by each taxpaying unit in the data file. With a sales tax, for instance, each identifiable consumption category which would be taxed is added for each taxpaying unit to estimate the individual tax base. That base multiplied by the sales tax rate yields the sales-tax-paid estimate.

156

Thus, when this construction is completed, tax-paid and ability-to-pay estimates will be available for each observed taxpaying unit.

Finally, vertical equity conditions are summarized, following one of three general methods. First, a table or chart may display the effective rate for each ability-to-pay class. Table 6–3 is such a display, a very

TABLE 6–3
Comparison of effective rates of federal, state, and local taxes, by adjusted family income bracket, 1970

Adjusted family income ($ 000s)	Effective rate
0–3	31.4%
3–5	24.4
5–10	25.2
10–15	26.3
15–20	26.3
20–25	26.1
25–30	26.2
30–50	26.5
50–100	29.3
100–500	30.3
500–1000	36.7
1000 and over	32.9

Source: Benjamin A. Okner, "Total U.S. Taxes and Their Effect on the Distribution of Family Income in 1966 and 1970," in Henry J. Aaron and Michael J. Boskin, editors, *The Economics of Taxation,* Tables 1 and 2, pp. 72 and 74, copyright © 1980 by The Brookings Institution.

effective and complete presentation of the data. Sometimes, however, the data need to be collapsed into a quick index for comparison, a need not met by tabular detail. The second method computes a progressivity/regressivity index by dividing the effective tax rate in the highest income class by the effective rate in the lowest income class. Regressive structures have an index below 1.0; progressive structures, above 1.0; and proportional structures, equal to 1.0. Thus the 1.05 index (32.9 divided by 31.4) computed from Table 6–3 indicates that the structure is mildly progressive. Other problems, however, often overwhelm the ease of summarization. For one thing, the index ignores patterns of effective rates in all income classes but the highest and lowest. An index computed for the structure charted in Figure 6–1 would indicate a regressive structure, even though the tax is progressive for most groups. Furthermore, the index is computed from data for only a small portion of the population: most taxpayers are in neither the highest nor the lowest group. Thus, it ignores the structural conditions applicable to the

FIGURE 6–1
**Effective rates of a hypothetical tax, by adjusted family
income**

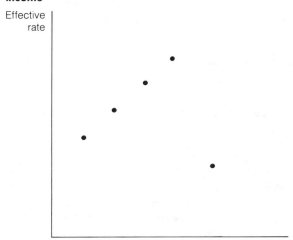

Family income class

bulk of the population. The third approach attempts to summarize the
pattern of effective rates in all classes in a single index. This index,
pioneered by David Davies, computes the index by running a simple
regression equation for the taxpaying unit data by income groups:

$$w \ln \overline{T} = \ln a + b\,(w \ln \overline{Y}) + \ln e$$

where $\overline{T}$ = the mean tax base for each ability class, $\overline{Y}$ = the mean affluence level (probably income) for each ability class, w = the share of the
total population in the ability class, b = the regressivity index, a = the
intercept, and e = a random error term.[3] If b is greater than one, the tax

---

[3] David G. Davies, "Progressiveness of a Sales Tax in Relation to Various Income
Bases," *American Economic Review*, 50 (December 1960). Population weights were added
by Jeffrey M. Schaeffer, "Clothing Exemptions and Sales Tax Regressivity," *American
Economic Review* 59 (September 1969). Concerning the notation used in the equation:
"The logarithm of a positive number p to the *base a* (>1) is defined as the index of that
power of a which equals p. In symbols:

$$\text{If } p = a^q, \text{ then } q = \log_a p."$$

(R. G. D. Allen, *Mathematical Analysis for Economists* (London: Macmillan & Co., 1964, p.
213). Logarithms can be computed for any base, but common logarithms (base 10) and
natural logarithms (base 2.71828 or "*e*") are most frequent in fiscal analysis. Typically, but
not always, "log" designates common and "ln" designates natural (most pocket cal-

is progressive; if less than one, regressive; if equal to one, proportional. The index identifies whether tax paid increases more or less rapidly than does income from class to class. If it does, effective rates must be increasing. Thus, the regression approach seeks the average relationship between income and effective rates to summarize from all income classes.

Progressive rate structures will redistribute affluence within society. At one time, public finance economists sought scientific support for this structure through reference to diminishing marginal utility of income: those with higher affluence gain less satisfaction from income (increments to affluence) than do those with less affluence. Thus, total utility loss to society from taxation to obtain a given revenue would be minimized by applying higher tax rates to those with greater affluence. The argument of diminishing marginal utility of income has not been provable, at least partly because it may be wrong, so progression remains unscientific.[4] There continues, however, a general feeling that tax systems should redistribute, although the evidence in Table 6-3 shows that the systems in practice are not strongly progressive.

Estimates of vertical equity will not be made simply from the rates specified by tax law. Two conditions cause trouble: shifting of tax burdens and the statutory base/affluence measure relationship. Accounting and/or surveys can compute the distribution of payments to the government by income class (the impact of a tax). This distribution will not necessarily show whose real income (or purchasing power) is lower because of the tax because both businesses and individuals make economic responses to imposition of a tax. Those feeling the initial impact of the tax may respond in such a way that a portion of the real burden of the tax is borne by others. For example, the payroll tax to finance social security has two components, one paid by the employer and one paid by the employee. Some economists argue that both components reduce the real income of the employee: the payroll tax paid by the employer represents wages, salaries, and fringe benefits that would have been paid to employees in the absence of the tax. Hence, the real bur-

---

culators follow that convention). Examples:

$$2 \quad = \log 100 \text{ since } 10^2 = 100$$
$$3.163 = \log 1455.5 \text{ since } 10^{3.163} = 1455.5$$
$$4.605 = \ln 100 \text{ since } e^{4.605} = 100$$

Logarithms will be used in the analysis of revenue adequacy (elasticities) and in revenue forecasting later in the text.

[4] See Walter J. Blum and Harry Kalven, Jr., *The Uneasy Case for Progressive Taxation* (Chicago: University of Chicago Press, 1953).

TABLE 6–4
Tax incidence assumptions used to compute the effective rates shown in Table 6–3

Tax, and basis of allocation
Individual income tax
to taxpayers
Sales and excise tax
to consumption of taxed commodities
Corporation income tax
half to property income in general
half to consumption
Property tax on land
to landowners
Property tax on improvements
to shelter and consumption
Payroll tax on employees
to employee compensation
Payroll tax on employers
half to employee compensation
half to consumption

Source: Benjamin A. Okner, "Total U.S. Taxes and Their Effect on the Distribution of Family Income in 1966 and 1970," in Henry J. Aaron and Michael J. Boskin, editors, *The Economics of Taxation,* Tables 1 and 2, pp. 72 and 74, copyright © 1980 by The Brookings Institution.

den, or incidence, is on the employee. As a general principle, laws define tax impacts but market forces (preventing or permitting shifting) define incidence. The shifting process is not simple to sort out, but is necessary to determine the vertical equity of a tax. Table 6–4 illustrates this by presenting the shifting assumptions used to prepare Table 6–3.

The second complication in measuring vertical equity emerges because taxes are levied against convenient handles, not measures of taxpaying capacity. As an example, most states have taxes on the sale of consumption goods, with constant tax rates. The rate does not vary between consumer and levels of consumption, so the tax appears proportional by statute. Vertical equity, however, hinges on other considerations. Consumption studies show that the percent of income (a normal measure of true capacity) consumed on items in the sales tax base declines as income is greater, so the effective tax rate declines as income is higher. Suppose a state applies a 5 percent sales tax to many purchases of items by consumers. Two families which are generally representative of similar units in the state have the following characteristics.

	Family A	Family B
Income	$5,500	$22,000
Family size	3	4
Purchase of taxed items	4,300	12,000
Sales tax paid	215 (4,300 × 5%)	600 (12,000 × 5%)
Effective rate	3.9% (215/5,500)	2.7% (600/22,000)

The statutory (legal or nominal) rate paid by each family is five percent. However, the effective tax rate on income is 3.9 percent for Family A and 2.7 percent for Family B. (Full shifting of the tax to the purchaser is assumed.) The difference emerges because of the different percentages of income spent on taxable items by the two families. In this example, the effective rate falls as income is higher, so the tax has a regressive burden—even though the statutory rate is constant and even though the higher-income family pays more than twice as much sales tax than does the lower-income family. Thus, the rate which was proportional by statute is regressive in effect. But what if consumption or even consumption of items identified for consumption in the tax base is really seen as the appropriate measure of taxpaying capacity?[5] Conclusions about the tax change, with resulting disagreement among both expert and amateur policy observers.

Business and individual shares

Analysts occasionally estimate the relative share of taxes paid by businesses and individuals, especially at the state and local level of government, as a guide to tax policy. Business taxes are usually defined to include taxes on business property, corporate net income taxes, business gross receipt taxes, corporate franchise taxes, miscellaneous business and occupation taxes, licenses, severance taxes, document and stock transfer taxes, and the like. Taxes on individuals include property taxes on residences and personal property, individual income taxes, retail sales taxes, and selective excise taxes. Special classification problems arise with taxes on agricultural property (what portion of a farmer's property tax bill is individual and what portion is business?), with taxes on unincorporated business income (the business is taxed through the individual income tax system), and with sales tax paid on business purchases, but those complexities can usually be resolved by allocations based on a sample of taxpayers.

---

[5] If that truly is the appropriate capacity measure, it ought to be the standard applied for consideration of other taxes as well.

There is, however, some question about the usefulness of these share measurements. The final incidence of any tax is on individuals, regardless of its initial impact. A business may respond in three ways to a tax levied on it: the business may increase its prices to reflect the tax, the business may reduce the price it pays to owners of resources it purchases, or the business may return a lower profit to its owners. What actually occurs depends on the form of the tax and on the market conditions the firm faces, but it can be expected to respond in whatever fashion will leave it with greatest profit after tax.[6] With each possibility, however, the business tax reduces the real income of individuals, either by causing customers to pay higher prices, by causing workers or other resource owners to receive lower income for what they sell to the firm, or by leaving owners of the business with lower profit from the business. The business/individual tax share question is usually less significant for tax policy than the patterns of individual tax burdens after business response (tax shifting) has occurred. The business is merely a conduit between the tax-collecting government and the burden-bearing individual.

State and local governments are interested in relative business/individual shares, however, for reasons other than fairness of the burden distribution. In many instances, the individuals ultimately bearing the burden of business taxes live out of state.[7] A higher business share thus means that a greater amount of the cost of state and local government will be exported to nonresidents. That exporting is politically attractive, even if the extent of exporting attempted may not always be logically justified. While those businesses do receive services provided by the host community, the appropriate amount of payment is always subject to dispute between businesses and the government. Furthermore, states must take care that out-of-state businesses are not treated more harshly than are domestic businesses because differential treatment would violate the commerce clause of the U.S. Constitution.[8]

The capability to use taxes with initial impact on business as a means of exporting the cost of government to nonresidents does, however, have an important limitation. That is the concern that the taxes will

---

[6] The responses are carefully analyzed in Richard A. Musgrave, *The Theory of Public Finance* (New York: McGraw-Hill, 1959), chap. 13.

[7] Note that certain individual taxes may be substantially exported in special circumstances: residential property taxes in second-home communities, lodging taxes in tourist areas, etc.

[8] "The Congress shall have Power . . . to regulate Commerce with foreign Nations and among the several States and with the Indian Tribes . . . " (Article 1, Sec. 8[3]). Differential treatment by a state involves a power reserved to Congress.

adversely affect the competitive positions of business in the state. As John Bowman observes:

> if firms in states A and B compete in the same market, and state A raises all its revenue from industry (100 percent business share) while state B raises none of its revenue from industry (zero business share), it may well be that state taxation will place the firms in state A at a competitive disadvantage[9]

Share data must be tempered with evaluation of the overall level of taxes in the competitive states (all of a very low absolute tax would have less influence on competitive position than a moderate share of a very high absolute tax), but the concern with competitive balance does influence the quest for cost exporting. Thus, states frequently trade exporting for competitive balance in policy deliberations because relative shares, in addition to vertical and horizontal equity, make up part of the fairness criterion for them.

Adequacy

A tax levied for revenue is worthwhile only if it can generate meaningful revenue at socially acceptable rates. Some taxes may be levied for reasons other than revenue—punatively high rates to stop an undesirable activity or taxes applied simply to keep track of a particular activity—but revenue is the prime objective of most taxes. One aspect of adequacy—absolute adequacy or the capacity of the source to fund the functions of the levying unit—can best be understood using an analytic device called the Laffer curve.[10] This curve, illustrated in Figure 6–2, relates revenue collected from a specific tax base and tax rates applied to that base (all other influences held constant) and shows that a given amount of revenue, R_z, can be collected at two tax rates, one high (t_a) and one low (t_b). Thus, no revenue will be collected from a particular tax base if no tax is applied to that tax base or if a rate is applied which is so high that the taxed activity ceases to exist. There is for each tax base a rate (t_1) which produces the maximum possible revenue from the base (R_1); efforts to obtain more than that amount will be futile, as higher

---

[9] John H. Bowman, "What is the Business Share of Taxes?" *Bulletin of Business Research,* 47 (January 1972): 3.

[10] The Laffer curve, after Arthur Laffer, as described by one of its early and strong proponents, Jude Wanniski, hinges on shifts of economic activity between the money economy and the barter economy: when tax rates on transactions in the former reach some level, transactions switch to the latter, where they are difficult or impossible to trace and tax (Wanniski, "Taxes, Revenues, and the 'Laffer Curve'," *The Public Interest,* Winter 1978, pp. 3–16.) Wanniski also maintains that U.S. tax rates certainly are on the upper half of the function. That presumption has not been demonstrated; further, the relationship can hinge on more than evasion.

FIGURE 6–2
Illustration of Laffer (or rate-revenue) curve

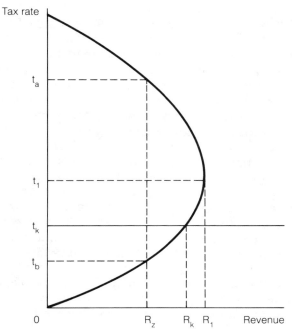

rates will discourage the taxed activity sufficiently to cause revenue collections to decline. Studies of the relationship between tax rates and revenues, at least for major state taxes, show that states are on the lower portion of the curve.[11] That is, a tax rate increase of 1 percent produces a collection increase of something less than 1 percent, but it is an increase. It is quite likely that some selective excises (cigarette or liquor taxes) may be on the upper portion in some areas, but the only portion discovered to date is that which slopes upward.

The problem of absolute adequacy is more substantial when state restrictions interfere with local actions. For instance, a state legislature may establish a special district to provide services financed only from a single excise tax base or may impose restrictive property tax rate ceilings on local governments. These circumstances may be illustrated again in Figure 6–2. The legally limited rate would be t_k, producing revenue level R_k for the taxing unit. If revenue needs of the special

---

[11] Gerald E. Auten and Edward H. Robb, "A General Model for State Tax Revenue Analysis," *National Tax Journal,* 29 (December 1976): 422–35.

district or local government exceed R_k, then the modern absolute adequacy problem exists and there is little that decision makers for the affected unit can do, except scrimp and seek other revenues.

Adequacy also considers revenue patterns across both cyclical (short-run) and secular (long-run) time dimensions. Efforts to manage the national economy have not eliminated economic fluctuations, particularly in states and smaller economic regions, some of which suffer from episodes of unemployment approaching depression levels. Governmental functions continue during depressed economic activity and may even grow because of social tensions in these periods. A revenue source with good cyclical adequacy will not fall dramatically with declining economic activity, but will remain reasonably stable. Such stability is vital for state and local governments, because they lack the borrowing flexibility and money creating powers that allow the federal government to accommodate deficits. In general, taxes on corporate profits will be particularly unstable because of the volatility of that base. Some states historically were reluctant to rely on that source for that reason. Property taxes have great stability, except for delinquency problems in deep depression. General sales taxes and individual income taxes lie somewhere between the extremes.

Revenue stability, however, is a problem for governments when economic growth continues with little interruption. Demand for many government services increases more rapidly than the increase in economic activity. The demand pattern can be examined using the income elasticity of service expenditure, a measure which estimates the percentage increase in expenditure resulting from a 1 percent increase in income. Those services for which expenditure increases more rapidly than does income have an income elasticity greater than one: an increase in income of 1 percent generates an increase in government spending greater than 1 percent. Governments lacking revenue sources with similar growth characteristics face the prospect of increased debt, increased tax rates (or new taxes), or unmet demand for government services. Each of these options is politically unpleasant, so there is a general preference for responsive taxes, those whose revenue increases more rapidly than does income (the income elasticity exceeds one). Table 6–5 reports income elasticities by individual tax bases as found in several recent tax studies.[12] Overall, the income tax bases show greatest responsiveness (caused both by rate graduation and sensitivity

---

[12] These elasticities are typically computed from a time series regression of the form $\ln B = a + b \ln Y$ where B is the tax base analyzed, Y is the measure of economic activity, and b is the income elasticity of the tax. Other influences on the base—for instance, statutory tax rate changes—may also be included as independent variables.

TABLE 6–5
Compilation of selected tax income elasticities as found in various
tax studies

	Median	High	Low
Personal income tax (9 studies)	1.75	2.4	1.3
Corporate income tax (9 studies)	1.1	1.44	0.72
General property tax (12 studies)	0.87	1.41	0.34
General sales tax (10 studies)	1.0	1.27	0.80
Motor fuels tax (10 studies)	0.73	0.80	0.43
Tobacco tax (8 studies)	0.26	0.54	0.00

Source: Compiled from ACIR (Advisory Commission on Intergovernmental Relations), *Significant Features of Fiscal Federalism, 1976–1977,* vol. 2, *Revenue and
Debt,* p. 254.

of the base), while motor fuel and tobacco taxes—taxes generally
applied on a specific (volume or unit) basis, rather than on a value
(volume times price) basis—have the least responsiveness. The general
sales tax is in an intermediate position. The property tax elasticity estimates are probably artificially high, as some studies reported do not
separate out the revenue effects of increased property tax rates, so the
elasticity result is not purely the outcome of automatic base growth.[13]
Because responsive taxes may not be stable, the appropriate choice for
adequacy over time will depend on whether problems of growth or
problems of decline are most likely and whether the government has
access to debt markets and the ability to raise rates during periods of
economic decline.

Collectability

A tax must be collectable at reasonable cost to society. Resources
used in the collection of revenue provide no net service to society: the
revenue, not its collection, is valuable. In general, taxes and tax provisions ought to be designed to keep total collection cost as low as is
feasible within the constraint of satisfactory equity. Unfortunately, there
is frequently an equity-collectability trade-off. For instance, taxes on
payrolls represent the income tax format with least collection cost: collection is made by employers (there are far fewer of them to keep track
of than there are employees), the problem of checking on interest and

---

[13] A study which extracts out both rate changes and general reassessments of property
found a property tax base elasticity of 0.27 in one state (Indiana). This measure is more
comparable to those reported for sales and income taxes bases because it extracts all
statutory and administrative sources of base change. (John L. Mikesell, "Property Tax
Assessment Practice and Income Elasticities," *Public Finance Quarterly,* 6 (January 1978):
61.

dividend income is avoided, and special questions about rents and capital gains do not arise. Unfortunately, self-employed individuals and those with interest, dividend, rental, and capital gain income tend to be more affluent than those receiving only payroll income. Thus, the tax which is simple to administer has equity problems. As a rule, collection complexity with broad-based taxes (property, sales, and income) results from attempts to improve the equity of the particular tax. That is the critical trade. Narrow-base taxes—particularly selective excises—often simply cannot be collected at low cost and are good candidates for elimination in tight economic times: the resources used in their collection can be more profitably used in administration of other taxes. A more detailed analysis of the tax collection process, along with collection costs, appears in Chapter 9.

Economic effects

A final criterion used in evaluation of taxes is the extent to which the tax distorts economic activity. There are philosophic differences in the interpretation of such distortions. Some argue that a tax should be neutral in its effect: market systems can be trusted to function well without intervention, so the most that one should expect from a tax is that it disturbs such functioning as little as possible. Others argue that a tax should have favorable economic effects: the outcome from market operations can be improved by using taxes to alter private behavior in some desired fashion. Regardless of view about the appropriateness of such distortion, it is clear that taxes do influence economic behavior and that influences differ among taxes. Most would agree that taxes ought not harm economic welfare, even if they ought not be used to stimulate desired behavior.

Efficiency effects—the economic dislocations induced by taxes— seldom will be the primary influence on selection of financing mechanisms. As McKie observes, "Failure of efficiency is not a slogan that brings men cheering into the street."[14] The imposition of taxes, however, can have important effects on economic activity. Whenever a tax wedge produces a difference in the return which can be gained between two or more competing economic activities, individuals and businesses can be expected to respond toward the alternative leaving a greater after-tax return. That wedge can influence many different choices:

1. Work versus leisure. High taxes on extra income earned may induce workers to choose more leisure time instead of more hours worked with much of the proceeds taken by government.

---

[14] James W. McKie, "Organization and Efficiency," *Southern Economic Journal,* 38 (April 1972): 451.

2. Business operations. A state property tax on business inventory held on a particular date can induce firms to ship inventory out of state on that date for return later.
3. Consumption choice. High tax rates on cigarettes and liquor in some states induce their residents to purchase those items from nearby states with lower taxes and lower prices.
4. Personal management. Because travel expense to professional conventions can be subtracted from income subject to the federal individual income tax, such conventions frequently are held in resort locations. Those attending can thus combine vacation and business while reducing their tax obligation.
5. Productive investment. High-income entities may direct investible funds to municipal bonds, the interest on which is tax-free, rather than to the purchase of productive capital equipment, the return on which would be taxed.

It would seem reasonable to favor taxes which do not discourage employment or economic growth or encourage inflation more than the minimum needed to extract resources for government operation. Undesirable distortions should be minimized.[15]

Conclusion

The number of handles available to governments seem almost without end. In general, the many possible handles eventually translate into taxes on incomes, taxes on ownership and ownership exchange, and taxes on purchase or sales. Taxes require an involuntary payment; they are not collected for services received on a normal exchange basis. Because of separation of service receipt and payment, it is possible to evaluate taxes on the basis of planning criteria. Those criteria are equity (vertical and horizontal), adequacy, collectability, and economic effects.

A CASE FOR DISCUSSION

The Governor of Pennsylvania created a commission in 1979 to review the structure of state and local taxes in that state. After considerable research by professionals recruited from universities around the state, the commission released its final report in 1981.

---

[15] Some taxes intend distortions. For instance, the Canadian federal government applies a $100 tax on automobile air conditioners—an extra inducement to convince automobile purchasers to skip an accessory which reduces fuel economy in that climate.

The following selections from the report outline the goals of a tax system, as viewed by the Commission.

Consider these questions:

1. Does the Commission see an appropriate balance between income, sales, and property taxes?
2. Is the Commission concerned with vertical and horizontal equity?
3. Do the criteria used by the Commission match those described in the chapter? Where are there differences? What might cause those differences?
4. How does your state compare on the burden measures reported in the table?

Overall Considerations: Goals for Pennsylvania's Tax System

The objective of this Commission has been to examine the totality of the Pennsylvania Tax System. While total tax revenue collected and the number of taxes levied have grown significantly over the last 100 years, the tendency has been to meet the revenue needs of the moment with ad hoc taxes. As a result, the system has too many taxes which lack a clear rationale. The system lacks a clear set of objectives and fails to display a set of criteria which are met by the various taxes.

In this *Report,* we will specify objectives for the tax system and attempt to develop a system that will meet these objectives. In addition, we will articulate the criteria that individual taxes should meet in order to be used as part of the system. Our long-run objective is to establish a model tax system for state and local governments

Source: Selections from Section I of the *Final Report of the Pennsylvania Tax Commission* (March 1981).

with the hope that such an accomplishment will influence tax policy throughout the country.

A. Goals

It is common to state goals to achieve unanimous approval by reducing the content within them. That is not our desire. The goals we state are to be used as standards that will aid in the reform of the system. We also recommend that these goals be utilized in any future examination of the tax system.

1. Simplicity

In order for a tax to be accepted, the individual paying the tax must understand it. As the complexity of a tax increases, understanding decreases and, as a result, resistance to the tax increases. The Federal Individual Income Tax is an excellent example of this proposition. As Congress has tried to influence taxpayer behavior with respect to certain economic and social objectives, it has created a myriad of provisions that define income, taxpayers, and tax rates, and provided many exceptions from the general rules. The Pennsylvania Personal Income Tax, on the other hand, has been kept simple and is much better understood. Simplicity of structure is important in the long run in a democratic society to maintain positive attitudes by the electorate toward government.

2. Certainty

The tax system should be stable, predictable, and relatively permanent so that the taxpayer, whether an individual or a corporation, can determine his tax bill at any time. This characteristic also serves the Commonwealth since budgeting is facilitated when revenue estimates are accurate. Uncertainty leads to different opinions as to taxpayer liability and such differences lead to litigation. In turn, litigation increases the cost of collection and also increases hostility toward government. For individuals and businesses considering the decision to move to Pennsylvania, or to stay in Pennsylvania, certainty can be an important ingredient in the final decision, and thus indirectly affect Pennsylvania's potential for economic growth. When state and local taxes are uncertain or ambiguous in application, individuals and firms may find other states more attractive.

3. Equity

The tax system and the individual taxes must be viewed as fair and equitable if taxpayers are to comply voluntarily with it. Attempts to evade and avoid the payment of taxes increase when the system is perceived to be inequitable. A system that is fair is one in which all persons (or firms) with the same economic situation are treated equally. Also, a system that is fair is one in which all persons or firms in different economic situations contribute resources through the tax system in a manner that the electorate finds consistent with its social values. Balanced against the need to redistribute income to achieve social justice must be a concern for the impact such sacrifices have on various segments of society. As we will show later, the property tax, as currently assessed in Pennsylvania, does not meet the equity standard. The large amount of subjective judgment involved in property appraisal leads to differential taxes for taxpayers with property of equal market value in the same jurisdiction. As the lack of equity becomes apparent in a tax, taxpayers become disillusioned with their government.

4. Economy of Administration

Different taxes may require different collection systems and costs. In general, a tax system should contain taxes that can be collected as inexpensively as possible. When the cost of collection, including costs to the taxpayer, is a high percentage of the revenue (3 percent or more), the desirability of the tax must be questioned.

5. Impact of Taxes on Economic Efficiency

From the standpoint of resource allocation, the goal of economic efficiency is central. The objective of neutrality, which enhances economic efficiency, is to avoid distortions of economic choices which can be induced by taxes. When price and output decisions by firms or the decision to work or not to work by individuals are modified as a result of a tax, the tax is not economically efficient. For example, a specific sales or excise tax can have the effect of a price increase. As a result, for those products being taxed, there will be a reduction in demand for the commodity. Consumers will make new sets of decisions with respect to their expenditures as a result of the changes in price due to the sales tax. In this sense, then, such a specific sales tax is not economically efficient because it affects economic decisions. Similarly, relatively high rates of taxation on personal income can dissuade individuals from working, and relatively high rates of taxation on the wealth of business can discourage necessary capital accumulation by business. A tax system should be neutral with respect to the allocation of resources.

6. Revenue Adequacy

The Commission is committed to the principle that the overall burden of state and local taxes should not increase over time as a percent of personal income. As a corollary, it believes that public expenditures should be financed with a system of taxation that meets these needs with a minimum of change from year to year. To the extent that tax receipts at given tax rates fail to grow in relation to economic growth, legislators are forced constantly at the state and local level to revise tax rates and in turn cause uncertainty about the future course of tax policy. This revenue adequacy, generally determined by the level of growth elasticity, is most problematical at the local level where such taxes as the property tax and various per capita taxes grow much more slowly than the economy.

7. Efficiency and Effectiveness of Tax Expenditures

Despite a preference for neutrality, it is sometimes necessary to use the tax system to achieve social goals. The use of the tax system to subsidize or support various types of activities is usually referred to as tax expenditure policy. The Commission recognizes the utility of tax expenditures, especially in light of the efficiency of tax expenditures in establishing automatic incentives which affect individuals or businesses with a minimum of governmental interference. When the General Assembly appropriates public funds through tax expenditures, however, the same caution should be applied which is customarily employed in making direct appropriations from the public treasury. Tax expenditures should be clearly tied to socially desirable new activities and should not subsidize activities which would occur regardless of tax expenditures. Such tax expenditures should be made for a fixed period of time, following which a detailed evaluation of the efficiency and effectiveness of the tax expenditure should be carefully conducted prior to continuing authorization for the tax expenditure. All too often millions of dollars of potential public funds are lost because of ineffective tax expenditures which continue far beyond their initial rationale.

B. Implications of Goals

There are certain important inferences that can be drawn from the goals discussed above for the type of tax system we recommend for Pennsylvania. It should be clear that we cannot develop a tax system in which each tax meets each goal. Moreover, Pennsylvania already has a tax system in place which must be taken into account in making recommendations for change. We do not propose to eliminate every tax in existence and develop an entirely new system. Many taxes that do not meet all the goals are functioning effectively and meet certain goals successfully. They compensate for their weakness vis-a-vis other goals. Thus, the sales tax, as applied in Pennsylvania, has much to recommend it even though it may not meet the economic efficiency criterion. On the other hand, taxes which do not achieve any of these goals are candidates for elimination in the view of the Commission. Resultant revenue losses must be made up by greater reliance on taxes that are successful in achieving these goals.

It is also clear that the more broadly based the tax is, the better it is. By broadly based, we mean that the tax base permits few exemptions in the definition of income or in the definition of taxpayer and does not easily permit avoidance. Pennsylvania's personal income tax is a good example. Broadly based taxes are generally simple to understand and calculate and are also

stable and predictable. Such broadly based taxes are often viewed as most fair by taxpayers.

*   *   *   *   *

Looking at the total system in terms of these goals, it seems reasonable to question the differential taxation Pennsylvania imposes on various industries. In particular, the banking and insurance industries are both exempt from the Corporate Net Income Tax (CNI). Other taxes have been devised to tax the firms in those industries. Uniform taxation for business as a whole on the basis of net income would increase the fairness of the system, contribute to simplification, and result in lower costs.

We believe application of these goals can be effective in ensuring that Pennsylvania improves its tax system over time, eliminates the tendency to pass new taxes on an ad hoc basis to meet pressing revenue problems of the moment, and adequately finances government. Any proposed new taxes should be analyzed in relation to these goals to see how well they meet the goals before being admitted to the system.

C. Criteria for a Tax

One of the striking features of Pennsylvania's current system of taxation is the tremendous range of taxes that compose the system. The justification for many of the taxes comes from the necessity of meeting a particular revenue deficiency at a point in time rather than from a well-defined criterion. We have attempted to solve this problem by emphasizing the importance of goals that should be met by the various taxes. Nothing has yet been said, however, about the basic criteria justifying particular taxes.

The literature on public finance is replete with discussions on the criteria justifying a particular tax. The two basic criteria are the ability to pay and the benefit received. Thus, an income tax is justified on the basis of ability to pay. The federal income tax with its progressive features is justified by that criterion, as is an income tax, such as Pennsylvania's, that uses proportional taxation. On the other hand, property taxes and gasoline taxes are justified on the benefits-received criterion. Property owners receive police and fire protection, rubbish collection, and other services of local governments; it is widely believed that the benefits of many municipal services are in proportion to the property they serve. The gasoline tax is paid by automobile owners and the revenue is channelled into road maintenance and improvement. Again, the benefit criterion justifies the tax. We propose to justify every tax in the system that we propose on the basis of one of these two criteria. Where the tax cannot meet one of these two criteria, it will be rejected as a candidate for the system.

* * * * *

D. Characteristics of the System

It can be argued that the ideal tax structure would be one in which there was a single tax, and that tax would be on income. The income tax could meet the goals that we have established and could be justified on the ability-to-pay criterion. Since income, broadly defined, is the ultimate objective of the economic system, a good argument could be made for such a tax system.

However, even if one accepted that argument intellectually, it does not make sense operationally. The interdependence among states is an important factor to be taken into account when developing a tax system. The ease with which capital and human resources can move to other states means that states must have tax systems that are roughly comparable both in types of taxes in the system and in the level of rates applied by each tax. Obviously, no two systems are exactly the same, but there will be difficulties if one state attempts to establish a radically different system. Thus, we conclude that one characteristic of the system is that it must be a portfolio of taxes rather than a single tax system.

A second characteristic relates to the social justice or the distributive effects of a tax. At the federal level, the personal income tax and gift and estate taxes are strongly progressive and materially affect the distribution of income and wealth. The federal system attempts to reduce the inequality in income both by applying a progressive tax rate structure to income and wealth and by using transfer payments. Because of the mobility of human and physical resources, and in view of the Commonwealth's constitutional impediments to progressivity, the Commission believes that major income redistribution across all income classes through the tax system must be obtained at the federal level.

However, the Commission also believes that the state should seek to achieve through its tax system certain distributional objectives which are consistent with the constitutional framework. Within the current constitutional framework, this means that the tax system should seek to alleviate tax burdens on the poor, elderly, and infirm, and as such, should seek progressivity in the tax system for these groups of persons. Also, in viewing the state's role in achieving progressivity, the Commission believes that both state and local taxes, to the extent possible, should be taken into account.

There are, in addition, other objectives of the system that we want the system to achieve. We want a tax system that is consistent with economic development in the state. There is increasing evidence that the tax structure is not the crucial factor in determining the location of new business. Many other factors, such as the labor climate and other intangible factors relating to the physical and economic conditions of the area, seem to be more important to the location decision than the tax system. Nevertheless, it is still important to make certain that the tax system keeps Pennsylvania competitive with its neighboring states.

E. Assumptions and Additional Considerations in the Report

1. Overall Tax Burden

In reviewing Pennsylvania's current tax system, certain assumptions about the overall revenue needs of the Commonwealth and the constitutional framework had to be made. The Governor charged the Commission to devise tax reform proposals which do not increase the level of overall taxation. To implement this, the Commission presents in this *Report* a set of recommendations which do not increase or decrease materially the percent of total Pennsylvania personal income dedicated to the public sector. Only in this manner can proper attention be focused on the effective rate of taxation. *real tax you're paying*

The effective tax rate measures taxes as a percent of an indicator of resources available to pay taxes, usually personal income. These rates measure the true "burden" of taxes on the economy, in contrast to nominal or statutory rates which may fail to be responsive to economic activity. For example, the Commission finds that the flat cent-per-gallon motor fuel tax is really a tax with a decreasing effective rate despite a fixed nominal rate, because the price of motor fuel has risen so much over the past few years. Moreover, higher fuel prices and more fuel-efficient vehicles have meant that total motor fuel taxes have not kept pace with the increasing cost of road repair. Therefore, the Commission recommends changes in the structure of motor fuels taxes which will increase nominal tax rates, but which will not lead to any long-term growth in the size of the public sector. In the short run, Motor License Fund revenues will increase to finance the needed restoration of our roads and bridges.

Table 1 shows the pattern of overall effective tax rates in Pennsylvania, U.S. average, and several other major states. While per capita taxes have risen since 1968–69, the effective tax

TABLE 1
State and local tax burden: 1968–1979 in Pennsylvania and other states

State and local taxes as a percent of personal income

Year	Pennsyl-vania	U.S. average	Cali-fornia	Illinois	Michi-gan	New Jersey	New York	Ohio
1968–69	9.992%	11.220%	11.341%	9.411%	11.688%	10.349%	14.049%	8.839%
1969–70	10.963	11.658	13.480	11.428	11.547	10.576	14.260	9.107
1970–71	11.394	11.887	13.733	11.467	12.237	11.000	14.538	9.253
1971–72	12.710	12.694	14.942	12.118	12.976	11.617	15.788	10.071
1972–73	12.994	12.947	14.909	11.911	12.960	12.042	16.952	10.436
1973–74	12.247	12.358	14.010	12.002	12.308	11.639	16.552	9.790
1974–75	11.675	12.284	14.591	11.728	11.665	11.591	16.653	9.694
1975–76	11.540	12.472	14.892	11.418	12.064	11.826	17.329	10.017
1976–77	11.880	12.805	15.493	11.726	13.039	12.606	17.683	10.004
1977–78	12.254	12.753	15.799	11.803	12.668	12.419	17.188	9.933
1978–79	11.887	12.031	12.042	11.261	12.395	12.095	16.697	9.768

Per capita state and local taxes

Year	Pennsyl-vania	U.S. average	Cali-fornia	Illinois	Michi-gan	New Jersey	New York	Ohio
1968–69	$339.52	$379.94	$ 539.99	$ 372.80	$ 428.26	$ 406.06	$ 575.51	$305.77
1969–70	401.40	427.14	559.33	486.78	455.54	447.25	652.32	343.24
1970–71	444.37	460.47	603.22	513.48	491.33	498.55	688.60	363.87
1971–72	525.93	522.49	687.11	575.19	569.36	554.25	788.68	418.76
1972–73	581.34	577.08	738.84	613.03	635.11	630.51	893.61	475.42
1973–74	614.95	618.39	762.25	699.03	679.15	683.19	952.29	496.70
1974–75	636.43	663.77	868.62	730.27	681.77	725.48	1025.09	533.82
1975–76	683.91	730.52	964.20	769.42	749.04	792.83	1139.94	585.79
1976–77	770.01	813.01	1088.92	860.29	878.17	931.45	1252.22	640.74
1977–78	861.77	888.00	1227.47	916.99	958.84	993.06	1308.28	700.52
1978–79	921.47	933.93	1379.80	1003.75	1049.32	1060.37	1372.71	768.55

Source: U.S. Bureau of the Census, Governmental Finances, 1968–79, Series GF-78 Washington, D.C., (U.S. Government Printing Office).

rate in Pennsylvania has generally been below the U.S. average, below that of New York, about the same as New Jersey, and somewhat higher than Ohio. The Commission has sought to keep the overall effective rate of taxation at about 11.9 percent of personal income in connection with its recommendations.

2. Balance of Taxes between Business and Personal Sectors, Capital and Labor

In testimony before the Commission, reference was made repeatedly to the importance of maintaining a balance between business and personal taxes. The 1968 Tax Study and Revision Commission recommended that 70 percent of taxes be derived from personal taxation and 30 percent from business; these figures were cited before this Commission by public witnesses and representatives of industry and organized labor. This Commission believes its recommendations have not materially altered the current balance; in main, recommendations have substituted personal income taxes for occupation taxes and business income taxes for other types of business taxes.

While the Commission has observed the importance of this dichotomy, it also believes that such distinctions can be somewhat mechanical and misleading for a number of reasons. First, the Commission believes that the issue of balance is more properly the issue of the taxation of labor income vis-a-vis the taxation of income from capital. Business per se does not pay tax, but does so on behalf of the individuals who own the firm or its capital. By the same token, the local property tax, while collected from individuals is, in fact a tax on the ownership of capital. The local wage tax is, on the other hand, clearly a tax on labor income. Second, in trying to ascertain what the "balance" of taxation is between labor and capital income, it is importunt to examine the actual incidence of the tax as contrasted with the nominal impact of the tax. Thus, while the utilities literally write a check to the Department of Revenue for the gross-receipts tax, it is clear that consumers pay the tax through higher prices that include the tax. Unfortunately, the limitations of time and resources prevented the Commission from performing such incidence analysis and from measuring the current balance of taxes on labor and capital under current law and under its recommendations. The Commission believes that this is an important topic for future analysis.

With regard to overall revenue needs, the Commission assumed that the current expenditures financed by the Personal and Corporate Net Income taxes would be continued although their rates are scheduled to decline in 1982 from 2.2 percent to 2.0 percent and 10.5 percent to 9.5 percent, respectively. Thus, the Commission has assumed that the current personal and corporate tax rates would be continued.

3. Tax Reform in Pennsylvania versus Tax Reform in Other States

In reviewing the history of effective Pennsylvania tax rates, the Commission feels an obligation to caution the public and the General Assembly that tax reform in Pennsylvania has a different meaning than the term has generally been given in other states in recent years. Nationally, state and local governments have been experiencing overall budget surpluses of better than $20 billion as reflected in the U.S. Department of Commerce's national income accounts. These surpluses arise because of the inflation dividends generated by progressive income taxes, or because of the fortuitous location of certain energy resources.

Higher wages and prices have placed taxpayers into higher tax brackets despite relatively stable real personal income. As a result, in other states a type of tax reform has been possible in which across-the-board rate reductions were achieved. Because the Uniformity Clause of Pennsylvania's Constitution prohibits progressive nominal tax rates, Pennsylvania has not experienced the budget surpluses of other states. Because of Pennsylvania's tax structure, Pennsylvania cannot approach tax reform with a tax-reduction perspective, but must use a balanced budget approach. Any tax reductions in one area must be counterbalanced by revenue generating proposals in some other area. The Commission has sought to achieve this balance in its recommendations.

7

Major tax structures: Income and consumption taxes

Because governments rely on taxes as the ultimate source of funds to buy resources for use in service delivery, an understanding of the structure of taxes is important. While structures differ among the states and localities and the federal taxes do not remain unchanged over time, there is a logic and a language used to define tax bases and the manner in which rates are applied to the chosen base. Furthermore, there are common issues of tax design that arise wherever a particular base is considered. For those reasons, the following two chapters examine the general nature of the three predominant tax bases: income, consumption, and property. Taxes on income and consumption typically apply to current transaction values; property taxes apply to the value of holdings, not transactions. Because of that important distinction, income and consumption taxes will be examined separately from property taxes. Property taxes are considered in Chapter 8.

One important point to be emphasized at the outset: all taxes labeled "income" (or sales or property) do not operate in the same fashion, and statements about the elasticity, progressivity, or other properties of a particular tax must carefully define what the structure of the tax actually is. Thus, the federal individual income tax has a generally progressive burden distribution; many local income taxes have a generally regressive or proportional burden pattern because of their limited coverage of income, and the way they apply rates to that income. It would be incorrect to observe that income taxes have progressive burden distributions. Some do, some do not: it depends on the structure of the particular tax.

INCOME TAXATION

Governments apply taxes to the income of individuals and/or corporations.[1] Unincorporated business (partnership, proprietorship) income will ordinarily be taxed by the individual income tax. Because individual income taxes yield so much more revenue than do corporate income taxes, most of the consideration here will focus on the former. Many of the structural elements of individual taxation also apply to the corporate form as well; many other corporate tax questions are too arcane for coverage here. One important issue to which there may be no answer will be considered: how should corporate income taxes be related to the income tax of individual corporate stockholders? Otherwise, the coverage will emphasize the individual tax.

Some background

Before the Civil War the federal government relied on excises (customs duties, liquor taxes, etc.) to finance its limited activities. War was too expensive to finance with that revenue, so the federal government enacted a low-rate (three percent of income above $800) income tax in 1861. The tax reached a rate and revenue peak in 1865 and expired in 1872 after making a significant contribution to war finance. There remained an important question, however. Article I, Sec. 9 [4] of the U.S. Constitution stated: "No Capitation, or other direct, Tax shall be laid, unless in Proportion to the Census or Enumeration herein before directed to be taken." Thus, whether an individual income tax is a direct tax is especially important.[2] If the tax were direct, the tax would have to be divided among the states according to population and each state's share then raised from its population according to their income. A state with lower per capita income would have to apply higher income tax rates than would a state with higher per capita income. Because the writers of the Constitution surely understood political forces and the ire of the Congressional delegations from the prospectively higher tax rate

---

[1] A corporation is an entity created by a government (state or federal) which grants it legal powers, rights, privileges, and liabilities of an individual, separate and distinct from those held by the individuals who own the entity. Each owner has a liability equal only to his investment in the corporation.

[2] Corporate income taxes were never regarded as direct taxes on individuals and, thus, were never subject to apportionment. The federal corporate income tax began some years before the modern individual income tax.

states, one must conclude that they really did not want direct taxes! The U.S. Supreme Court held in *Springer* v. *United States* (1880) that the income tax was, for purposes of the Constitution, indirect and hence valid. The tax was not then in force, so the ruling had minimal importance.

In 1894, the federal government again enacted an individual income tax, this time in a package with reduced tariffs (taxes on imported items). The tax had a low rate affecting only a small portion of the population (2 percent on income above $4,000), but it was challenged on constitutional grounds. This time, the U.S. Supreme Court, in *Pollock* v. *Farmers' Loan and Trust* (1895), ruled that the income tax was direct and, hence, subject to the apportionment requirement. The case left the federal government with no broad-based revenue source and without a means of financing the increased international role the nation was taking in the early part of the 20th century. This problem was resolved by the 16th Amendment (1913): "The Congress shall have power to lay and collect taxes on incomes, from whatever source derived, without apportionment among the several States, and without regard to any census or enumeration." That provided the financial base for defense and an expanded federal role in domestic affairs.

Many regard an income tax as a fair source of revenue because of the nature of the base and the method of its administration—and it certainly is productive. Why is the income tax a satisfactory source? First, income is an important measure of capacity to bear the burden of financing government. Economic well-being is largely determined by current income. An exception is the person with substantial wealth and minimal current income, so a better measure would include current income and net wealth converted into an income equivalent. Such logic does not appear in tax codes, however. If only one base is to be used, for most people income is a reliable affluence measure. Second, the income tax can be made to take account of individual taxpayer conditions. Any tax not based on individual filing will not easily be adjusted to such conditions: a package of cigarettes is taxed regardless of the economic status of the purchaser. Adjustments that can be made in income taxes allow the distribution of burdens in a fashion judged equitable. Third, the size of the income base permits significant revenue at socially acceptable rates and growth of that base keeps pace with general economic activity. Governments with income taxes need not seek rate increases as often or apply such high nominal rates as those with narrower bases. And, finally, the resource distortion with the general income tax may be less than with narrower taxes.[3]

---

[3] Income taxes may distort work and investment decisions made by individuals and businesses. Thus, the resource distortion basis for general income taxation is unclear at best.

Individual income taxation

The following sections describe the logical construction of the federal individual tax. Many states link their tax to this tax. For instance, some use adjusted gross income or taxable income as the computation point for their tax. Some even define their tax as a specified percentage of federal liability. For that reason, an understanding of this system is thus important for all governments. (Local governments tend to avoid links to the federal income tax—their income taxes generally are completely independent.) Figure 7–1 provides a schematic overview of the federal

FIGURE 7–1
Elements of U.S. individual income tax structure

Total income
less

Adjustments
equals

Adjusted gross income.
Subtract

Zero bracket amount or (excess) itemized deductions
equals

Tax table income (taxable income).
Apply

Tax tables, which include personal exemptions and rate structure
to obtain

Tax.
Subtract

Credits
to obtain

Tax liability.
Subtract

Withholding
to obtain

Tax refund or tax due.

structure. That schematic represents the pattern of the federal individual return forms shown in Figure 7–2 and Figure 7–3. The itemized deduction form (schedule A in Figure 7–3) was used by less than 30 percent of taxpayers in 1978, but those filers produced almost 65 percent of all individual income tax revenue.[4] They represent the heart of

---

[4] Internal Revenue Service Preliminary Report, *Statistics of Income—1978, Individual Income Tax Returns* (Washington, D.C.: U.S. Government Printing Office, 1980).

the federal revenue system and, because many states base their income tax on the federal system, they are vital at that level as well.

Problems of income tax structure: Defining income. Tax statutes do not define income, but rather list the types of transactions which produce income for tax purposes. Items on the list include wages, salaries, interest, stock dividends, royalties, etc. There is no general definition for use in cases of doubt. (Instructors usually receive a copy of this book at no charge: would that be income for them?) Many analysts favor the Haig-Simons income definition as a standard. The version proposed by Simons defines personal income for tax purposes as "the algebraic sum of (1) the market value of rights exercised in consumption and (2) the change in the value of the store of property rights between the beginning and end of the period in question."[5] In other words, income equals consumption plus any increase in net wealth during the year.

This definition can yield results that differ from application of the existing tax law, as three examples illustrate. Suppose Mr. Smith owns shares of a corporate stock that increase in value by $10,000 during the year, but he does not sell the stock during the year. The Haig-Simons concept views that as income—it is an increase in Smith's net wealth which adds to his total potential command over the economy's resources. The existing tax system would not tax that gain; the system taxes such gains only as they are realized, i.e., when the higher value stock is actually sold. Second, suppose Ms. Jones lives in a home that she owns. She thus consumes the services provided by that structure. These services are part of Jones' consumption and would be part of Haig-Simons income. The current tax system taxes no imputed incomes, thus providing a significant incentive for use of assets to produce noncash flows of return to the owner. Finally, suppose Mr. White's great aunt gives him $10,000. That clearly will increase his net wealth (or permit increased consumption) so would be part of Haig-Simons income. Because that transaction occurred without any work by White, however, the current system does not regard that as part of income. It would be taxable under the gift tax, but White's aunt's economic circumstances, not his, would determine tax liability.[6] Tax structures avoid general definitions of income, particularly Haig-Simons. They avoid tax-

---

[5] Henry C. Simons, *Personal Income Taxation: The Definition of Income as a Problem of Fiscal Policy* (Chicago: University of Chicago Press, 1938), p. 50. A similar concept appears in Robert M. Haig, "The Concept of Income—Economic and Legal Aspects," in *The Federal Income Tax,* ed. R. Haig (New York: Columbia University Press, 1921), p. 7.

[6] That means the tax on the gift to White (who has an annual income of $3,000) is the same as the tax on her similar gift to his brother (who has an annual income of $60,000). Same aunt, same gift, same tax—regardless of recipient's economic status.

FIGURE 7–2

Form **1040** Department of the Treasury—Internal Revenue Service
U.S. Individual Income Tax Return **1980**

For Privacy Act Notice, see Instructions | For the year January 1–December 31, 1980, or other tax year beginning ____ 1980 ending ____ 19

Use IRS label. Other-wise, please print or type.	Your first name and initial (if joint return, also give spouse's name and initial) Last name Your social security number
	Present home address (Number and street, including apartment number, or rural route) Spouse's social security no.
	City, town, post office, State and ZIP code Your occupation ▶ Spouse's occupation ▶

Presidential Election Campaign Fund

Do you want $1 to go to this fund? . . . .   Yes ▨ No

If joint return, does your spouse want $1 to go to this fund? . . .   Yes ▨ No

Note: Checking "Yes" will not increase your tax or reduce your refund.

Requested by Census Bureau for Revenue Sharing

A Where do you live? (actual location of residence)? (See page 2 of Instructions.) State: City, village, borough, etc.

B Do you live within the legal limits of a city, village, etc.? ☐ Yes ☐ No

C In what county do you live?

D In what township do you live?

Filing Status

Check only one box.

1 ☐ Single
2 ☐ Married filing joint return (even if only one had income)
3 ☐ Married filing separate return. Enter spouse's social security no. above and full name here ▶ _____
4 ☐ Head of household. (See page 6 of Instructions.) If qualifying person is your unmarried child, enter child's name ▶ _____
5 ☐ Qualifying widow(er) with dependent child (Year spouse died ▶ 19___). (See page 6 of Instructions.)

For IRS use only

Exemptions

Always check the box labeled Yourself
Check other boxes if they apply.

6a ☐ Yourself   ☐ 65 or over   ☐ Blind   } Enter number of boxes checked on 6a and b ▶
b ☐ Spouse   ☐ 65 or over   ☐ Blind
c First names of your dependent children who lived with you ▶ _____   } Enter number of children listed on 6c ▶

d Other dependents: (1) Name	(2) Relationship	(3) Number of months lived in your home	(4) Did dependent have income of $1,000 or more?	(5) Did you provide more than one-half of dependent's support?

Enter number of other dependents ▶

Add numbers entered in boxes above ▶

7 Total number of exemptions claimed . . . .

Income

Please attach Copy B of your Forms W–2 here.

If you do not have a W–2, see page 5 of Instructions.

Please attach check or money order here.

8	Wages, salaries, tips, etc.	8
9	Interest income (attach Schedule B if over $400)	9
10a	Dividends (attach Schedule B if over $400)_____, 10b Exclusion _____	
c	Subtract line 10b from line 10a	10c
11	Refunds of State and local income taxes (do not enter an amount unless you deducted those taxes in an earlier year—see page 9 of Instructions)	11
12	Alimony received	12
13	Business income or (loss) (attach Schedule C)	13
14	Capital gain or (loss) (attach Schedule D)	14
15	40% of capital gain distributions not reported on line 14 (See page 9 of Instructions) .	15
16	Supplemental gains or (losses) (attach Form 4797)	16
17	Fully taxable pensions and annuities not reported on line 18	17
18	Pensions, annuities, rents, royalties, partnerships, etc. (attach Schedule E) . . .	18
19	Farm income or (loss) (attach Schedule F)	19
20a	Unemployment compensation (insurance). Total received _____	20b
b	Taxable amount, if any, from worksheet on page 10 of Instructions	
21	Other income (state nature and source—see page 10 of Instructions) ▶ _____	21
22	**Total income.** Add amounts in column for lines 8 through 21 . . . . ▶	22

Adjustments to Income

(See Instructions on page 10)

23	Moving expense (attach Form 3903 or 3903F) . .	23
24	Employee business expenses (attach Form 2106) . .	24
25	Payments to an IRA (enter code from page 10 ____) .	25
26	Payments to a Keogh (H.R. 10) retirement plan . . .	26
27	Interest penalty on early withdrawal of savings . . .	27
28	Alimony paid	28
29	Disability income exclusion (attach Form 2440) . . .	29
30	**Total adjustments.** Add lines 23 through 29 . . . . ▶	30

Adjusted Gross Income

31 **Adjusted gross income.** Subtract line 30 from line 22. If this line is less than $10,000, see "Earned Income Credit" (line 57) on pages 13 and 14 of Instructions. If you want IRS to figure your tax, see page 3 of Instructions . . . . ▶ | 31

☆U.S.GPO:1980-0-313-414   EI#430814328

Form **1040** (1980)

FIGURE 7–2 (continued)

Form 1040 (1980)   Page 2

Tax Computation (See Instructions on page 11)	32 Amount from line 31 (adjusted gross income)	32	
	33 If you do not itemize deductions, enter zero . . . . }	33	
	If you itemize, complete Schedule A (Form 1040) and enter the amount from Schedule A, line 41 . . .		
	Caution: If you have unearned income and can be claimed as a dependent on your parent's return, check here ▶ ☐ and see page 11 of the Instructions. Also see page 11 of the Instructions if: • You are married filing a separate return and your spouse itemizes deductions, OR • You file Form 4563, OR • You are a dual-status alien.		
	34 Subtract line 33 from line 32. Use the amount on line 34 to find your tax from the Tax Tables, or to figure your tax on Schedule TC, Part I . . . . Use Schedule TC, Part I, and the Tax Rate Schedules ONLY if: • Line 34 is more than $20,000 ($40,000 if you checked Filing Status Box 2 or 5), OR • You have more exemptions than are shown in the Tax Table for your filing status, OR • You use Schedule G or Form 4726 to figure your tax. Otherwise, you MUST use the Tax Tables to find your tax.	34	
	35 Tax. Enter tax here and check if from ☐ Tax Tables or ☐ Schedule TC	35	
	36 Additional taxes. (See page 12 of Instructions.) Enter here and check if from ☐ Form 4970, } ☐ Form 4972, ☐ Form 5544, ☐ Form 5405, or ☐ Section 72(m)(5) penalty tax . . .	36	
	37 **Total.** Add lines 35 and 36 . . . . ▶	37	
Credits (See Instructions on page 12)	38 Credit for contributions to candidates for public office . . .	38	
	39 Credit for the elderly (attach Schedules R&RP)	39	
	40 Credit for child and dependent care expenses (attach Form 2441) .	40	
	41 Investment credit (attach Form 3468)	41	
	42 Foreign tax credit (attach Form 1116)	42	
	43 Work incentive (WIN) credit (attach Form 4874)	43	
	44 Jobs credit (attach Form 5884)	44	
	45 Residential energy credits (attach Form 5695)	45	
	46 **Total credits.** Add lines 38 through 45		46
	47 **Balance.** Subtract line 46 from line 37 and enter difference (but not less than zero) . ▶	47	
Other Taxes (Including Advance EIC Payments)	48 Self-employment tax (attach Schedule SE)	48	
	49a Minimum tax. Attach Form 4625 and check here ▶ ☐	49a	
	49b Alternative minimum tax. Attach Form 6251 and check here ▶ ☐	49b	
	50 Tax from recomputing prior-year investment credit (attach Form 4255)	50	
	51a Social security (FICA) tax on tip income not reported to employer (attach Form 4137) . .	51a	
	51b Uncollected employee FICA and RRTA tax on tips (from Form W-2)	51b	
	52 Tax on an IRA (attach Form 5329)	52	
	53 Advance earned income credit (EIC) payments received (from Form W-2)	53	
	54 **Balance.** Add lines 47 through 53 . . . . ▶	54	
Payments Attach Forms W-2, W-2G, and W-2P to front.	55 Total Federal income tax withheld	55	
	56 1980 estimated tax payments and amount applied from 1979 return . .	56	
	57 Earned income credit. If line 32 is under $10,000, see pages 13 and 14 of Instructions.	57	
	58 Amount paid with Form 4868	58	
	59 Excess FICA and RRTA tax withheld (two or more employers)	59	
	60 Credit for Federal tax on special fuels and oils (attach Form 4136 or 4136-T)	60	
	61 Regulated Investment Company credit (attach Form 2439)	61	
	62 **Total.** Add lines 55 through 61 . . . . ▶	62	
Refund or Balance Due	63 If line 62 is larger than line 54, enter amount OVERPAID . . . . ▶	63	
	64 Amount of line 63 to be REFUNDED TO YOU . . . . ▶	64	
	65 Amount of line 63 to be applied to your 1981 estimated tax . . . ▶	65	
	66 If line 54 is larger than line 62, enter BALANCE DUE. Attach check or money order for full amount payable to "Internal Revenue Service." Write your social security number on check or money order . . ▶ (Check ▶ ☐ if Form 2210 (2210F) is attached. See page 15 of Instructions.) ▶ $	66	
Please Sign Here	Under penalties of perjury, I declare that I have examined this return, including accompanying schedules and statements, and to the best of my knowledge and belief, it is true, correct, and complete. Declaration of preparer (other than taxpayer) is based on all information of which preparer has any knowledge		
	Your signature Date ▶ Spouse's signature (if filing jointly, BOTH must sign even if only one had income)		
Paid Preparer's Use Only	Preparer's signature ▶ and date	Check if self-employed ▶ ☐	Preparer's social security no.
	Firm's name (or yours, if self-employed) and address	E.I. No. ▶ ZIP code ▶	

184

FIGURE 7-3

Schedules A&B—Itemized Deductions AND Interest and Dividend Income

(Form 1040)

Department of the Treasury
Internal Revenue Service

▶ Attach to Form 1040. ▶ See Instructions for Schedules A and B (Form 1040).

1980

08

Name(s) as shown on Form 1040

Your social security number

Schedule A—Itemized Deductions (Schedule B is on back)

Medical and Dental Expenses (not paid or reimbursed by insurance or otherwise) *(See page 16 of Instructions.)*

1 One-half (but not more than $150) of Insurance premiums you paid for medical care. (Be sure to include in line 10 below.) . ▶

2 Medicine and drugs .

3 Enter 1% of Form 1040, line 31 . . .

4 Subtract line 3 from line 2. If line 3 is more than line 2, enter zero . . . .

5 Balance of insurance premiums for medical care not entered on line 1 . . . .

6 Other medical and dental expenses:

a Doctors, dentists, nurses, etc. . . .

b Hospitals . . . .

c Other (itemize—include hearing aids, dentures, eyeglasses, transportation, etc.) ▶

7 Total (add lines 4 through 6c) . . . .

8 Enter 3% of Form 1040, line 31 . . .

9 Subtract line 8 from line 7. If line 8 is more than line 7, enter zero . . . .

10 Total medical and dental expenses (add lines 1 and 9). Enter here and on line 33 . ▶

Taxes *(See page 17 of Instructions.)*

Note: Gasoline taxes are no longer deductible.

11 State and local income . . . . . .

12 Real estate . . . .

13 General sales (see sales tax tables) . .

14 Personal property . . . .

15 Other (itemize) ▶

16 Total taxes (add lines 11 through 15). Enter here and on line 34 . . . ▶

Interest Expense *(See page 17 of Instructions.)*

17 Home mortgage . . . .

18 Credit and charge cards . . . . . .

19 Other (itemize) ▶

20 Total interest expense (add lines 17 through 19). Enter here and on line 35 ▶

Contributions *(See page 17 of Instructions.)*

21 a Cash contributions for which you have receipts or cancelled checks . . . .

b Other cash contributions (show to whom you gave and how much you gave) ▶

22 Other than cash (see page 17 of Instructions for required statement) . . . .

23 Carryover from prior years . . . . .

24 Total contributions (add lines 21a through 23). Enter here and on line 36 . . ▶

Casualty or Theft Loss(es) *(See page 18 of Instructions.)*

25 Loss before insurance reimbursement .

26 Insurance reimbursement . . . . .

27 Subtract line 26 from line 25. If line 26 is more than line 25, enter zero . . .

28 Enter $100 or amount from line 27, whichever is smaller . . . .

29 Total casualty or theft loss(es) (subtract line 28 from line 27). Enter here and on line 37 . ▶

Miscellaneous Deductions *(See page 18 of Instructions.)*

30 Union dues . . . .

31 Other (itemize) ▶

32 Total miscellaneous deductions (add lines 30 and 31). Enter here and on line 38 ▶

Summary of Itemized Deductions *(See page 19 of Instructions.)* **A**

33 Total medical and dental—from line 10 .

34 Total taxes—from line 16 . . . . .

35 Total interest—from line 20 . . . .

36 Total contributions—from line 24 . . .

37 Total casualty or theft loss(es)—from line 29 .

38 Total miscellaneous—from line 32 . .

39 Add lines 33 through 38 . . . . .

40 If you checked Form 1040, Filing Status box:
2 or 5, enter $3,400 . . . .⎫
1 or 4, enter $2,300 . . . .⎬
3, enter $1,700 . . . .⎭

41 Subtract line 40 from line 39. Enter here and on Form 1040, line 33. (If line 40 is more than line 39, see the Instructions for line 41 on page 19.) . . . . ▶

FIGURE 7 – 3 (*continued*)

Schedules A&B (Form 1040) 1980 | **Schedule B—Interest and Dividend Income** | Page **2**

Name(s) as shown on Form 1040 (Do not enter name and social security number if shown on other side) | Your social security number

Part I   Interest Income

1 If you received more than **$400** in interest, complete Part I and Part III. Please see page 8 of the instructions to find out what interest to report. Then answer the questions in Part III, below. If you received interest as a nominee for another, or you received or paid accrued interest on securities transferred between interest payment dates, please see page 19 of the instructions.

Name of payer	Amount

2 Total interest income. Enter here and on Form 1040, line 9 . . . .

Part II   Dividend Income

3 If you received more than **$400** in gross dividends (including capital gain distributions) and other distributions on stock, complete Part II and Part III. Please see page 9 of the instructions. Write (H), (W), or (J), for stock held by husband, wife, or jointly. Then answer the questions in Part III, below. If you received dividends as a nominee for another, please see page 19 of the instructions.

Name of payer	Amount

4 Total of line 3 . . . .
5 Capital gain distributions. Enter here and on line 13, Schedule D. See Note below . . .
6 Nontaxable distributions . . . . . .
7 Total (add lines 5 and 6) . . . . . .
8 Dividends before exclusion (subtract line 7 from line 4). Enter here and on Form 1040, line 10a . . . .

Note: *If you received capital gain distributions for the year and you do not need Schedule D to report any other gains or losses, do not file that schedule. Instead, enter 40% of your capital gain distributions on Form 1040, line 15.*

Part III   Foreign Accounts and Foreign Trusts

If you are required to list interest in Part I or dividends in Part II, OR if you had a foreign account or were a grantor of or a transferor to a foreign trust, you must answer both questions in Part III. Please see page 19 of the instructions.

	Yes	No
A At any time during the tax year, did you have an interest in or a signature or other authority over a bank account, securities account, or other financial account in a foreign country (see page 19 of instructions)?		
B Were you the grantor of, or transferor to, a foreign trust which existed during the current tax year, whether or not you have any beneficial interest in it? If "Yes," you may have to file Forms 3520, 3520–A, or 926.		

ation of accrued or imputed values with that policy. At the same time, however, the less broad income concept can distort individual choice and can create equity problems as it favors certain incomes over others. Furthermore, the broad base reduces the administrative problems of determining whether a particular income falls into the taxed or untaxed category. And finally, breadth permits the psychological (and possibly economic) advantage of low rates to produce a given yield.

Adjustments to income. The general philosophy of income taxation is that the tax should apply to net income. It ought not apply to gross receipts, as such a tax would apply to the cost of earning an income, as well as the income itself.[7] Those costs do not contribute to individual well-being, so they should be subtracted from income. That is the logic behind the adjustments.

Current federal law (which is copied by many states) allows adjustment for moving expenses, job-related education costs, and certain expenses of salesmen, for example. It is, however, difficult to distinguish between certain costs of earning personal income and ordinary consumption expenditures. There simply is no clear and logical line between the two. For example, commuting expenses apparently are a cost of earning an income: if one does not get to work, income is not earned. This expenditure, however, results from choice of residence (commuting expense can be reduced by choosing to live closer to the point of employment) and is thus a consumption choice. To change this approach would provide a further incentive to urban sprawl. Moving expenses to follow a changed place of employment, on the other hand, are considered a cost of earning income and are subtracted from income to obtain the tax base. The presumption is that such expenses are necessary for the job, not expenses from consumer choices. Of course, many people seek jobs elsewhere because they prefer different climate, different cultural activities, and so on—personal consumption choices, not costs of employment—but our tax system chooses to err in favor of enhancing labor mobility.

Similar considerations apply for other income adjustments. Advanced education is primarily a cost of earning income for many, while a consumption (noninvestment) expenditure for others. The problem is one of drawing a clear line; once the line is drawn, many people will soon rearrange their expenses to qualify for the adjustment. The line between job cost and consumption will remain indistinct. Choices must finally hinge on the question of what side the error is best made on.

---

[7] For ease of collection, numerous locally administered taxes apply to payrolls (wages and salaries) almost exclusively. Rental, income, dividends, interest, capital gains, etc., do not get included in the base and adjustments to estimate net income are not made. These taxes are classifiable as income taxes only by tradition.

Exclusions from income. Exclusions from income simply do not show up on the tax return (and do not appear on Figure 7–1), but appear to be income by popular or Haig-Simons concepts.[8] Among the exclusions are interest received on state and local government debt holdings, government transfer payments (food stamps, welfare, etc.), social security payments, gifts or inheritances, employer-paid insurance premiums and related fringe benefits, insurance settlements, retirement pay, and so on. Several exclusions seem reasonable, particularly those directed to low-income individuals: it is not sensible to assist individuals because of their poverty and then tax away part of that assistance. Some assistance categories, however, are not limited to the poor and eligible recipients may have sizable income from other sources. Thus, if one desires to apply tax according to net well-being, there is a case for including retirement pay, social security, and similar payments not conditioned on economic circumstance.

The exclusion of interest received on state and local government debt historically stems from principles of reciprocal immunity of governments. The federal government cannot destroy state or local governments (and vice versa). Because "the power to tax involves the power to destroy," the federal government does not tax instruments of state and local governments.[9] Nondiscriminatory taxation of such interest would likely not be ruled unconstitutional by present courts, but the exclusion continues as a valuable subsidy to state and local government—it allows these governments to borrow at interest rates substantially below current market rates. To demonstrate the influence of exclusion on these interest rates, suppose an individual pays 30 percent of any additional income as federal income tax (the 30 percent bracket). A tax-exempt municipal bond paying 10 percent yields the same after-tax income as would a taxable bond paying about 14 percent.[10] Thus, the state or local government borrower automatically receives an interest subsidy through the federal tax system and can borrow at artificially low rates. These bonds are a favorite avenue of tax avoidance for higher-income individuals and the value of interest subsidization to state or local government must be balanced against the damage done to the progressivity of the tax system by the exclusion. It remains largely because it is a federal subsidy received entirely at the

---

[8] Some federal tax preferences were subjected to a minimum tax in the Tax Reform Act of 1969, particularly some capital gains income, some depletion deductions, accelerated depreciation on real property, and stock options. But much remains excluded.

[9] *McCulloch* v. *Maryland* 4 Wheat. 316, L. Ed. 579 (1819) is the source of John Marshall's famous "power to tax" quote. The reciprocal immunity doctrine, however, is enunciated in *Collector* v. *Day* 11 Wall. 113 20 L. Ed. 122 (1871).

[10] The taxable bond at 14 percent would leave the investor 70 percent (100% − 30%) of its yield after tax. Thus, 14% × 70% = 9.8%.

control of state and local governments. Those governments are reluctant to surrender that subsidy for any other unknown structure and, accordingly, fight aggressively against any change.

Another category which can be troublesome is the exclusion of fringe benefits provided by employers as a portion of employee compensation. While benefits like office Christmas parties would be difficult to value, many others (insurance, etc.) would not because they are purchased on the open market. This exclusion can induce individuals with higher incomes to choose untaxed fringes instead of pay increases simply to avoid tax burdens, thus distorting both production and consumption decisions. Further, it may artificially increase production costs as in-kind payment seldom is valued as highly by individuals as are cash payments: the cash can be used for anything, the in-kind payment cannot. Taxation of fringe benefits, while sensible and probably practical, has made little headway because a fringe benefit costing $1,000 per worker will be valued differently by different recipients. Just as we are reluctant to impute values to services from owner-used assets, we are reluctant to value fringes. The policy, however, promises continued mischief.[11]

Personal Deductions.   Personal deductions adjust measured ability to pay the tax to individual taxpaying unit circumstances. They may improve both horizontal and vertical equity of the tax by allowing individuals with such deductions to subtract them from adjusted gross income and hence lower their tax base. There are three logical categories of deduction. First, uncontrollable forces can cause particular expenditures which reduce the taxpayer's capacity to bear the tax below that of units with similar income. The deduction for selected state and local taxes, for casualty losses, and for medical expenses fall into this category. In each instance, individuals—through little fault of their own—must bear these special expenses that more fortunate individuals do not incur. Thus, an adjustment to tax-bearing ability is permitted. Second, some expenditures are deductible because the federal government has decided that private spending in those areas is meritorious and ought to be encouraged by reducing the after-tax cost of those actions. Thus, charitable contributions and a portion of medical insurance premiums are directly deductible. Both of these types of expenditure are optional

---

[11] Similar exclusions from the general income measure apply to gifts and inheritances. The problem appears here because there is often little difference between maintaining dependents and providing gifts. If it is a true gift, there is a separate tax; if the transfer occurs on death there are inheritance taxes that apply. One of the difficult problems is the delineation of fellowships and assistantships received by university graduate students. The fellowship is regarded as a gift and not taxed if there is no work requirement; assistantships or internships require work, there is an exchange transaction, and the income tax does apply, unless the degree program requires such work.

(not like state taxes or medical bills), but the federal government seeks to encourage private spending in both areas—thus, the deduction. And third, special circumstances produced deductibility of interest payments (included partly to subsidize certain activities and partly to exclude business interest costs), professional expenses (dues, professional travel, special equipment, etc., deducted because of the business cost problem if not removed), and alimony payments.

Each was inserted for reasons which seemed to improve the equity of the system or encouraged desirable individual actions. Because each has greater tax impact on high-income individuals (a charitable deduction of $100 has an after-tax cost of $60 to an individual in the 40 percent bracket and a cost of $80 to someone in the 20 percent bracket), there is a special incentive for such individuals to arrange their affairs so that their expenses fit in these deductible categories. Thus, professional meetings are timed to double as vacations, property settlements in divorce are converted to alimony, and so on. As a result, these provisions can reduce the overall progression of the tax system.

Not all taxpayers, however, use the personal deduction. Since 1944 there has been an optional standard deduction—now called the zero bracket amount—that permits individuals to subtract from their adjusted gross income base a given percentage of that adjusted gross income base up to a maximum dollar amount. This deduction eliminates the need for recordkeeping of deductible expenses. (Tax revision in 1981 allows charitable deduction even if the zero bracket approach is taken.) The initial idea was to make the tax simpler for the many people who became taxpayers for the first time during World War II as effective rates for lower-income classes rose dramatically. The optional deduction for people not having high itemized deductions has some psychological advantage. When all have a general deduction, however, tax rates must be higher for everyone, diluting the relief for the deserving and the undeserving alike.

Personal exemptions. The personal exemptions—per capita subtractions from the tax base—increase the progressivity of the system because the flat number of dollars removed from taxable income has a greater relative effect for low-income individuals than for high-income people ($1,000 is 20 percent of $5,000, but only 5 percent of $20,000). In fact, a high personal exemption combined with flat income tax rates can cause overall rate progressivity in the system. Table 7–1 demonstrates that impact. The reason for personal exemption in most systems, however, is generally not to increase progressivity. Their role is to adjust for tax capacity across family sizes: on a given income—say, $10,000—a family of four has substantially less tax capacity than does a family of one. The personal exemption adjusts for these differences in arriving at

TABLE 7–1
Effective rate impact of flat rate income tax (10%) and large personal exemption ($1,500 per person) on families of three

	Before tax income	Exemption	Taxable income	Tax	Effective rate
Family A	20,000	4,500	15,000	1,500	7.50%
Family B	10,000	4,500	5,500	550	5.50
Family C	5,000	4,500	500	50	1.00

the taxable income level. Systems may not treat all exemptions the same—say, $1,000 for the first two and $800 for any additional—depending on revenue needs, family incentives seen as desirable, etc. The U.S. system uses equal exemptions, but not all other countries do. The personal exemption likewise excludes small-income families to cut collection costs generated by low-yield returns.

The present system of special exemptions for the blind and elderly have a special problem when integrated with rate graduation. If the exemption is $1,000, an individual who is blind and in the 14 percent

TABLE 7–2
Illustration of income tax rate graduation: 1980 federal individual income tax rate schedules for *single* taxpayers*

If taxable income is:		Income tax is:	
Not over $2,300		0	
Over	But not over		Of the amount over
$ 2,300	$ 3,400	14%	$ 2,300
3,400	4,400	$ 154 + 16	3,400
4,400	6,500	314 + 18	4,400
6,500	8,500	692 + 19	6,500
8,500	10,800	1,072 + 21	8,500
10,800 ←——————→	12,900	1,555 + 24	10,800
12,900	15,000	2,059 + 26	12,900
15,000	18,200	2,605 + 30	15,000
18,200	23,500	3,565 + 34	18,200
23,500	28,800	5,367 + 39	23,500
28,800	34,100	7,434 + 44	28,800
34,100	41,500	9,766 + 49	34,100
41,500	55,300	13,392 + 55	41,500
55,300	81,800	20,982 + 63	55,300
81,800	108,300	37,677 + 68	81,800
108,300	. . .	55,697 + 70	108,300

Example computation:
  Taxable income = $11,000
  Income tax = $1,555 + 24% ($200) = $1,555 + $48 = $1,603

* Tax reductions passed in 1981 reduced rates by 1.25 percent for 1981, by 10 percent for 1982, by 19 percent for 1983, and by 23 percent for 1984.

marginal tax bracket has a net tax saving from this blindness equal to $140. A blind individual in the 50 percent marginal tax bracket, however, receives a tax saving of $500. The higher the marginal rate bracket, the more valuable in tax saving is the reduction in taxable income produced by the exemption. Persons with no taxable income receive no assistance at all from an exemption. The logic of the exemption would seem better served if aid did not increase with income, as occurs with the present system. Credits, as will be discussed shortly, seem more appropriate to this problem.

Tax rates. Federal individual income tax rates increase in steps as income increases. At each step, the rate applicable to additional income is slightly higher than the rate on lower income. Table 7–2 illustrates that upward graduation. (A number of states use similar graduation.) The average rate—taxable income divided by tax liability—always lies below the marginal rate—the increase in tax liability resulting from one dollar extra income. With that structure, an individual always ends up with greater income after tax when more income has been earned. The individual will never have greater after-tax income by having less income. The percentage of income going to federal tax does increase as income rises, but the absolute income left over will not decline. Table 7–3 shows the history of federal rates and exemptions.

The statutory, or nominal, rates of course are not the same as the effective rates. Analysis of the income tax system usually is conducted by looking at the relationship between taxes paid and adjusted gross income, the federal tax system equivalent of net income. The statutory rates are eroded substantially by the operation of tax provisions removing individual income from the base (adjustments, deductions, exemptions, and exclusions) and forgiving tax owed (credits). These elements can be regarded as the work of tax loopholes or as the work of tax policy designed to correct inequities or to encourage socially desirable behavior. Table 7–4 illustrates what the nature of these differences has been in recent years.

Rate graduation brings the phenomenon called "bracket creep" during inflation. Suppose a family has an income of $13,000, pays $150 in income tax, and is in the 14 percent marginal tax bracket. In two years, its income has increased to, say, $15,600 (a 20 percent increase), but the cost of living has increased by 20 percent as well, so its real income has not changed. The family will, however, pay taxes on that higher money income—additional income will be taxed at increasing marginal rates through the brackets—even though its living standard has not really changed. Thus, it may now pay $195, an increase of tax liability of more than 20 percent because of the upward rate graduation. While this graduation historically has been viewed as an automatic stabilizer in the

TABLE 7-3
History of federal individual income tax exemptions and first and top bracket rates

| | Personal exemptions[a] | | | Tax rates | | | |
| | | | | First bracket | | Top bracket | |
Income year	Single persons	Married couples	Dependents	Rate (percentages)	Income up to	Rate (percentages)	Income over
1913–15	$3,000	$4,000	—	1	$20,000	7	$ 500,000
1916	3,000	4,000	—	2	20,000	15	2,000,000
1917	1,000	2,000	$200	2	2,000	67	2,000,000
1918	1,000	2,000	200	6	4,000	77	1,000,000
1919–20	1,000	2,000	200	4	4,000	73	1,000,000
1921	1,000	2,500[b]	400	4	4,000	73	1,000,000
1922	1,000	2,500[b]	400	4	4,000	56	200,000
1923	1,000	2,500[b]	400	3	4,000	56	200,000
1924	1,000	2,500	400	1 1/2[c]	4,000	46	500,000
1925–28	1,500	3,500	400	1 1/8[c]	4,000	25	100,000
1929	1,500	3,500	400	3/8[c]	4,000	24	100,000
1930–31	1,500	3,500	400	1 1/8[c]	4,000	25	100,000
1932–33	1,000	2,500	400	4	4,000	63	1,000,000
1934–35	1,000	2,500	400	4[d]	4,000	63	1,000,000
1936–39	1,000	2,500	400	4[d]	4,000	79	5,000,000
1940	800	2,000	400	4, 4[d]	4,000	81.1	5,000,000
1941	750	1,500	400	10[d]	2,000	81	5,000,000
1942–43[e]............	500	1,200	350	19[d]	2,000	88	200,000
1944–45[f]	500	1,000	500	23	2,000	94[g]	200,000
1946–47	500	1,000	500	19	2,000	86.45[g]	200,000
1948–49	600	1,200	600	16.6	2,000	82.13[g]	200,000
1950	600	1,200	600	17.4	2,000	91[g]	200,000
1951	600	1,200	600	20.4	2,000	91[g]	200,000
1952–53	600	1,200	600	22.2	2,000	92[g]	200,000
1954–63	600	1,200	600	20	2,000	91[g]	200,000
1964	600	1,200	600	16	500	77	200,000
1965–67	600	1,200	600	14	500	70	100,000
1968	600	1,200	600	14	500	75, 25[h]	100,000
1969	600	1,200	600	14	500	77[h]	100,000
1970	625	1,250	625	14	500	71, 75[h]	100,000
1971	650	1,300	650	14	500	70[i]	100,000
1972	700	1,400	700	14	500	70[i]	100,000
1973–1980[j]	750	1,500	750	14	500	70[i]	100,000

[a] Beginning in 1948, additional exemptions are allowed to taxpayers and their spouses on account of blindness and/or age over 65.
[b] If net income exceeded $5,000, married person's exemption was $2,000.
[c] After earned income credit equal to 25 percent of tax on earned income.
[d] Before earned income credit allowed as a deduction equal to 10 percent of earned net income.
[e] Exclusive of Victory tax.
[f] Exemptions shown were for surtax only. Normal tax exemption was $500 per tax return plus earned income of wife up to $500 on joint returns.
[g] Subject to the following maximum effective rate limitations:

TABLE 7 – 3 (*continued*)

Year	Maximum effective rate	Year	Maximum effective rate
1944– 45	90.0%	1951	87.2%
1946– 47	85.5	1952– 53	88.0
1948– 49	77.0	1954– 63	87.0
1950	87.0		

[h] Included surcharge of 7.5 percent in 1968, 10 percent in 1969, and 2.5 percent in 1970.

[i] Earned income subject to maximum marginal rates of 60 percent in 1971 and 50 percent beginning in 1972.

[j] Plus credits for each exemption for the 1976 tax year ($35 per exemption or 2% of taxable income, up to $180) and for the 1974 tax year ($30 rebate for each exemption). Other changes—increased standard deductions and the zero rate bracket—have not disturbed the basic rates and exemptions.

Source: Joseph A. Pechman, *Federal Tax Policy,* revised edition, Table A-1, p. 255, copyright © 1971 by The Brookings Institution.

economy, accelerating tax collections during inflation to provide a macroeconomic brake and slowing tax collections during recession to provide a macroeconomic stimulus without requiring legislative action, recent observers have suggested that this process has become excessive. One solution is indexation, a technique for automatically adjusting tax liabilities downward to allow for inflation which has moved individuals into higher tax brackets without increasing their real income. Nine states (Arizona, California, Colorado, Iowa, Minnesota, Oregon, Wisconsin, Montana, and South Carolina) have systems of indexation; indexation of the federal income tax will begin in 1985.

Credits. In recent years, the federal government has made increasing use of a powerful device to stimulate certain private activities deemed desirable. That is the tax credit, direct forgiveness of taxes owed when eligible activities are undertaken. Thus, spending of $100 on the encouraged activity can be substituted for $100 income tax owed. To the prescribed limit of the credit, spending on that activity has no after-tax cost to the individual. Partial credits reduce by the credit percentage the cost of the activity. Among the recently supported credit activities have been new home purchase, household energy saving installations, child care,[12] and political contributions. Because of their high power, credits are expensive to the government and often could effectively be replaced by direct government spending.

Corporate income taxation

The corporate income tax applies to the net earnings of a corporation. The tax lacks the personal exemptions, deductions, and credits for dependents found in the individual income tax, but it does allow for deductions of charitable contributions. Notice that the corporate income tax applies to total corporate profit including both earnings retained by

---

[12] Child care logically would be an adjustment, as it is a cost of earning income.

TABLE 7–4
Effect of various federal tax provisions on effective rate, 1969 act

Total income class (dollars)	Nominal tax rate	Reduction due to						Effective tax rate
		Personal exemptions	Deductions	Tax preference items	Capital gains	Maximum tax	Income splitting	
1,000–1,500	14.8	11.1	3.6	—	—	—	—	0
4,000–4,500	17.5	8.3	3.9	—	0.1	—	—	5.0
8,000–9,000	20.8	7.7	4.0	—	0.1	—	0.8	8.1
15,000–20,000	27.9	6.4	6.2	0.1	0.5	—	2.7	11.9
25,000–50,000	38.8	4.6	8.1	0.6	2.2	—	6.3	16.8
100,000–150,000	57.5	1.6	9.7	1.5	9.6	0.5	5.6	28.7
200,000–500,000	64.8	0.7	10.1	1.7	16.6	0.3	3.4	31.8
500,000–1,000,000	67.8	0.3	9.5	2.0	21.1	0.1	1.5	33.1
1,000,000 and over	69.3	0.1	8.4	3.1	23.0	—	0.5	34.0
All income classes	25.4	7.1	5.1	0.2	1.1	—	1.7	10.1

Source: Joseph A. Pechman, *Federal Tax Policy*, revised edition, Table C-11, pp. 298–99, copyright © 1971 by The Brookings Institution.

the firm and those paid in dividends to stockholders. The individual income tax treats dividends in the same fashion as it does other income except for the exclusion of $100 dividends. Above that level, dividend income is fully taxed. Several problems created by the corporate income tax directly result from the taxation of dividend income at both levels. The basic federal rate is 46 percent of income above $100,000, but it is 17 percent on the first $25,000 of income, 20 percent on the second $25,000, 30 percent on the third $25,000, and 40 percent on the fourth $25,000. The rate graduation does not result from concepts of ability to pay (the shareholders of large corporations may well have low incomes), but from a desire to reduce the drain on retained earnings of growing firms.

Only six states (Nevada, South Dakota, Texas, Washington, Wyoming, and Michigan) do not have corporate income taxes currently, but the state taxes do create some special problems. Foremost is the interstate complication created because corporations conduct business in more than one state. Some income may be clearly defined as originating from a single state but much can not be so identified. For instance, a particular corporation may have retail outlets in 45 states, warehouses in nine states, and factories in two states. How much of that firm's profit should be taxable in any one state? To handle this problem most states have adopted what is called the three factor, or Massachusetts formula, for allocation of multistate corporation profits. That formula computes the average percentage of total property, total payroll, and total sales in a particular state to define the percentage of total profit taxable by any one state. Thus, if state A has 50 percent of the firm's total property value, 25 percent of the firm's total payroll, and 60 percent of the firm's sales, it would apply its corporate tax rate to 45 percent ([50 + 25 + 60] ÷ 3) of the firm's total profit. Some states, however, do not use the Massachusetts formula and create measures especially favorable to their own corporations.[13] Because most states do not have sufficient audit staff to verify the factor computed by all corporations, they must accept the calculations of many corporate filers. This problem of profit allocation makes local corporate taxes impractical.

A major question in the structure and operation of the corporation income tax is whether the corporation income tax serves to reduce the real income of the stockholders of the corporation, whether it produces higher prices for the products of corporations, or whether it causes the real income of labor and other resources used by the corporation to be

---

[13] The U.S. Supreme Court, in a case involving Moorman Manufacturing Company, upheld the Iowa formula using only sales. ("New Flexibility on Busines Tax Granted States," *The Wall Street Journal,* June 16, 1978.)

lower. Neither theoretical nor empirical evidence is clear but certainly there is no support for complete or predominant shifting of the corporate income tax.

The corporate income tax is the third largest source of federal revenue and that revenue would be difficult to replace from other sources. However, there are problems with the corporate income tax that must be considered. First is the problem of equity. If the tax is not shifted, why should dividend income be taxed more heavily than other kinds of income? Furthermore, there is much variation of dividend income received among individuals in particular income classes, so the special tax on that income obviously violates the equal treatment of equals rule of appropriate tax burden distributions. Corporate income tax does, however, fill a gap: without it, the portion of corporate income not distributed would go untaxed. In addition, the corporate income tax probably increases the progressivity of the system because dividend income tends to be more concentrated amongst higher income groups. At the state level the corporate income tax is a way for the state to extract compensation for benefits that the state provides to corporations whose owners may be largely out of state. The major problem currently with the corporate income tax is, however, its effects on saving and real investment. The corporate income tax probably constitutes a double tax on dividends and thus reduces the rate of savings, with undesirable effects on capital formation. Those capital formation effects add to the productivity problems of the nation, so some change might be appropriate.

Many of the undesirable economic and equity effects would be reduced if individual income and corporate income taxes were integrated either partially or completely. Complete integration would logically treat the corporation in the same way as partnerships. The tax would not apply to corporate income at all but the owners of the corporation would be taxed according to their proportionate shares of dividends and retained earnings. That treatment would eliminate the traditional difficulties with the corporate income tax but it would create some additional sticky issues. Those issues are as follows:

1. The tax would apply to income not realized. Individuals would be taxed according to income received as dividends and on income that the corporation retains. There is some question whether this would encourage greater corporate payout of earnings and thus might even lower the rate of real investment.
2. Many holders of corporate stock are tax-exempt entities. Under this integrated structure those entities would not pay individual income tax on their dividends and retained earnings and there would

be no collection of tax at the corporate level either. How could that revenue loss be replaced?

3. Sizable amounts of United States stock is held by foreign entities. How would that income be treated? What country would be entitled to tax those U.S. dividends and retained earnings? And if it is a country other than the United States, how would that revenue loss be made up?

4. Corporations do not have single classes of stock. Corporations frequently have common stock, preferred stock, and possibly other varieties of equity ownership representations. How would corporate income be divided equitably among those various classes of stock?

The alternate approach is partial integration. Partial integration would provide relief only on the share of corporate earnings that are distributed as dividends, either by giving some special credit to dividend recipients to take account of the corporate income tax already paid on the flow or by applying the corporate income tax only to undistributed corporate profit. That relief would cut tax collections substantially and there is the fear that it would appear to be an unwarranted tax break for business. Those two factors have kept interest in such reform low, although there is a revival in connection with the slow growth rate of the American economy and the slow rate of capital formation which has worked to produce that slow growth. Although there is a problem it is not clear that the current environment is one which is likely to produce substantial reform.

CONSUMPTION TAXATION

While a number of states receive sizable revenue from income taxes, the federal government obtains only trivial sums from consumption taxes. Most state revenue in the United States (and a substantial amount of major city revenue) comes from taxes applied to consumption through either general sales or selective excise taxes. The difference between the two taxes hinges on the logic of coverage. A sales tax applies to all transactions at, say, the retail level except for those enumerated as exempt (food purchases, for example); excises apply only to those transactions which are enumerated. Sales taxes emerged from fractional rate general business receipts taxes in Mississippi and West Virginia during the early 1930s when state revenue sources (predominantly property taxes) were unable to finance the spending activity of the period. They gradually became the dominant state revenue source. By 1980, all states but five (Alaska, New Hampshire, Delaware, Oregon, and Montana) levied such taxes, using rates from 2 (Oklahoma) to 7½ (Connecticut) percent. The excises generally are limited to taxes on motor fuels and nuisance items (tobacco products, alcoholic beverages, etc.).

A consumption-based tax can be applied to sales by manufacturer, wholesaler, or retailer. Some are applied at more than one of these levels, as is the case with turnover (cascade) taxes and value-added taxes. Single-stage, retail-level taxes have strong logical support.[14] First, the tax paid by the customer likely will be received by the government. Ordinary multistage taxes and preretail taxes tend to pyramid: the tax gets included in merchant markups, causing the price of the product to increase by more than the tax. Thus, the customer pays more than the government receives. Second, multistage taxes strike with each transaction. Integrated firms (those which manufacture, wholesale, and retail, for instance) have fewer transactions and, hence, lower tax embedded in product cost. Single-stage application (particularly at retail) eliminates that effect. And third, retail application will cause no incentive for the production process to move to a stage of trade above the point taxed to reduce the base to which the tax applies. In general, the more of total product value produced after the point the tax is levied, the lower the tax will be. Retail application leaves no point for escape. The retail application does, however, require somewhat greater administrative effort as there are more retailers than there are manufacturers or wholesalers and, hence, more taxpayers to keep track of.

Excise taxation

Many state and local governments levy excise taxes on commodities or services, including such items as motor fuels, hotel and motel lodging, admissions, restaurant meals, alcoholic beverages, tobacco products, soft drinks, etc. The federal government also uses a few excise taxes (automobile accessories, motor fuel) although not nearly as many as before a major restructuring in 1965. With the exception of lodgings and restaurant taxes, the excises tend to be applied at the manufacturer or wholesaler level. This eases administration, but can produce pyramiding. With that same exception, the excises tend to be specific (per unit), not ad valorem (on exchange value). Again, this eases administration, but can cause relative revenue declines during periods of inflation as unit consumption does not keep pace. The taxes have logical antecedents which permit division into three groups: luxury, sumptuary, and benefit base. Each will be examined separately.

---

[14] The special circumstances of value-added taxes will be examined later.

Luxury excises.   These excises are applied for revenue to commodities the purchase of which presumably reflects extraordinary taxpaying ability. Effective rates on these excises may be high because purchase of the taxed item demonstrates taxpaying ability beyond ability to pay as measured by other measures. If the luxury excise produces substantial revenue, it may ease rate pressure on other taxes. Unfortunately it seldom does.

The objections to luxury excises are several. First, such taxes distort producer and consumer choices: because the tax establishes a difference between the resource cost ratios in production and the price ratios to which consumers respond, there will be unnecessary loss of economic welfare in the economic system.[15] Second, and pragmatically more important, the tax will distribute burdens on the basis of personal preferences for the taxed items, a potential equity violation. The tax will impose higher effective rates on people within an income class who have high taste for the taxed commodities or services. Further, low-income people will buy the taxed items, because there are few products with no low-income purchasers at all. Finally, there are administrative problems with these excises. Because retailers would have difficulty separating the sales of the taxed luxury items from other sales, these excises typically apply to the manufacturer or wholesaler level. They thus fall prey to the objections to nonretail levies. But another administrative problem emerges in the definition of the taxed commodity. For example, the old federal excises taxed jewelry. Are watches jewelry? A definition either way will create injustices. The several state soft-drink taxes produce similar trouble. Are powdered drinks, imitation orange juice, bottled chocolate milk, etc. to be taxed? In each case, a difficult administrative problem in interpreting and applying the tax may well be handled only by separate, brand name determinations, a process which needlessly clutters the tax department rule makers.

The case for luxury excises is weak at best. There are better devices for reaching tax capacity, especially when the excises produce little revenue relative to administrative cost. Efforts of revenue departments are better directed to taxes of greater fiscal significance.

Sumptuary excises.   Sumptuary excises attempt to discourage consumption of selected items. Because demand for these items usually is rather insensitive to price, consumption does not change much with the tax and significant revenue is generated. Seldom do legislatures propose truly prohibitive tax rates because they want revenue. These taxes include excises on liquor and tobacco and are among the oldest taxes in

---

[15] John A. Tatom, "The Welfare Cost of an Excise Tax," *Federal Reserve Bank of St. Louis Review,* 58 (November 1976): 14–15.

the United States. Generally increases in them produce minimal protest from consumers, although sellers complain about illegal (nontaxed) competition. Bootlegging is a continuing problem; the typical enforcement procedure uses stamps applied to units upon which tax has been paid at the manufacturer level. Sizable rate differences among states swamp control structures with evasion.[16]

Two substantial advantages favor the sumptuary excises. First, they produce relatively high revenue with little public protest. There remains the feeling that people consuming those goods may be somewhat shady, so there is little political advantage for people who seek to reduce or eliminate these taxes. Consumers are likewise reluctant to make any direct protest. And second, there may be substantial social cost involved in the use of some of these commodities. For instance, excessive liquor consumption can lead to drunken driving, accidents on highways, and substantial cost to society. The excise may extract compensation for these social costs.[17]

There are three primary objections to sumptuary excises. First, the demand for the products taxed is often highly price-inelastic, so the tax will not reduce use of the product much. It may divert consumption from desirable or beneficial activities to pay the tax. (The unbelievable example sometimes quoted: the drunkard who fails to buy milk for his children because of the tax he pays on liquor!) Second, the absolute burden of these taxes may be particularly heavy on low-income people and may even involve greater effective tax rates on lower-income than higher-income families. The tax is applied, after all, on the basis of personal preferences, so the teetotaling millionaire will pay less liquor tax than the whiskey-drinking working man. And finally, a problem results from the specific (not ad valorem) nature of these excises. While that construction is logical because any social cost involved would be related to the amount of consumption, not its value, it does discriminate against lower-priced brands and those who purchase them. If the tax is $10 per gallon on distilled spirits, the effective rate is much higher on liquor sold for $6 a fifth than on liquor sold for $10 a fifth. This is a special problem if users of the lower-priced brands come from low-income groups. Furthermore, the specific nature of the tax obscures the actual ratio of the tax to the net price, which frequently turns out to be high.

In sum, the sumptuary excises tax something that people are judged

---

[16] For a review of the problem, see Advisory Commission on Intergovernmental Relations, Cigarette Bootlegging: A State and Federal Responsibility, A-65, May 1977 (Washington, D.C.: ACIR).

[17] Tobacco taxes have sometimes been earmarked for cancer research, a grim linkage to an associated social cost.

to be better off without and, possibly, compensate society for problems created by that consumption. In spite of any logical problems with these justifications, revenue from these taxes is reasonably high (especially for states) and extracted with little protest. They are unlikely to be eliminated.

Benefit base excise. Benefit base excises, primarily motor fuels taxes, operate as a quasi price for a public good. Highway use involves consumption of motor fuel, so a tax on fuel purchase approximates a charge for the use of the highway. These taxes allocate cost to road users and are clearly more economical than the system of direct user charges (tolls) for streets, roads, and highways. The motor fuel tax thus operates as a surrogate for price. It does have difficulties in the truck-to-car relationship because differences in incremental costs of providing highways are difficult to calibrate and relate to motor fuel use. The tax typically applies at the wholesale level, thus reducing the number of firms subject to review for proper compliance.

There are the additional questions whether motor fuel tax revenues ought to be segregated for highway construction and maintenance only, whether these funds should be spent for any transportation (highway or mass), and whether motor fuel tax revenue should receive the same budget treatment as other revenue, with no earmarked direction to transportation. These questions are not yet answered, but if revenues from the gasoline tax do not go to transportation projects, then they are probably subject to the complaints made against luxury excises. They sacrifice their benefit base logic and must be evaluated on ability-to-pay grounds. On the other hand, if revenues from the gasoline tax go exclusively to highways, there is a substantial bias for highways in the total transportation systems.

The benefit base logic of highway or motor fuel taxes suggests that the tax should be specific because the number of units of motor fuel used is related to the use of the service. At the same time, however, the specific nature of the tax means that, in times of inflation, there will be significant pressures placed on the motor fuel tax fund. Costs of highway projects increase dramatically but the specific tax will not capture the effects of higher gasoline prices. Thus, there will be continuing need for rate increases to finance those activities. Some states have attempted to avert the need for legislated rate increases by tying the specific tax rate to the prevailing price of gasoline, so that as the price of gasoline is higher, the specific gasoline tax rate is higher. This strategy may not succeed over the long run—historically, the price of gasoline has not kept up with inflation, with the exception of a couple of recent episodes. Highway finance and motor fuel taxation continue as problem areas for all levels of government.

General sales taxes

General sales taxes in the United States are the largest single source of state tax revenues. They cover all transactions at a given level of exchange (usually retail, although some states extend coverage to wholesale or manufacturing as well) unless a particular transaction is explicitly excluded. Payment is typically made by the seller in a taxable transaction; returns like that in Figure 7–4 cover all such transactions for a specified period (quarter, month, or year). While impact is on the seller, incidence usually is on the purchaser.

More often than not, computation of sales tax owed by multiplying sales price times the tax rate will yield fractional cents: a selling price of $1.65 multiplied by a 5 percent tax rate yields a tax of 8¼ cents, an amount not collectible with current U.S. coinage. States and merchants handle that problem by use of bracket systems to define the tax to be collected in exact cents for any transaction. Sometimes the brackets coincide with conventional rounding or major fraction rules (round at the ½ cent). The Massachusetts 5 percent nominal rate brackets in Figure 7–5 represent that system. Other states use different rules: the Maryland 5 percent nominal rate brackets in the same figure increase to the next cent before the Massachusetts brackets do. Although both sales taxes have the same nominal rate, the brackets established in Maryland will generate greater collections at a given level of vendor sales. Tax on the $1.65 transaction would be eight cents in Massachusetts and nine cents in Maryland.

How the collections from the brackets at purchase translate into vendor liability to the tax department differs among the states. Some states define vendor liability to be the tax rate multiplied by total taxable sales, regardless of the amount the brackets produce from individual transactions. The vendor keeps (or makes up) any difference between what the brackets generate and liability (breakage). Major fraction brackets normally cause breakage to be small. Other states, like Maryland, require payment of collections produced by the brackets on individual transactions. Compliance is easier with the former, but revenue will be greater with the latter.

A number of states also discount sales tax owed by the vendor to compensate for the cost of complying with the tax. (Note line 24 of the Texas return.) Discounts can reach 5 percent of collections, but many states provide none. Cooperation of vendors is clearly necessary for successful operation of a sales tax, but discounts represent a high price to pay for that help. Furthermore, there is little reason to believe that compliance cost is closely related to sales volume: the discounts will cause some firms to profit handsomely while giving trivial assistance to

FIGURE 7-4

TAC Comptroller Fórm 2A95-01-100 (DO NOT STAPLE OR PAPER CLIP)
of Public (Rev. 6-79)
Accounts

PL 05 1. T Code ■ 03200

2. ■

TEXAS SALES AND USE TAX RETURN
STATE AND CITY

Page 1 of _____

3. Taxpayer Number
■

4. Filing Period

5.

6.

Taxpayer Name and Mailing Address

If name or address is incorrect as shown, mark out incorrect item and write in correct information.

If ownership changes, new owner must make application for Sales Tax Permit.

Corporation name change must first be filed with office of Secretary of State.

7.

If trade name or location is incorrect, write in the correct information

Report only whole dollar amounts. Round to nearest whole dollar.

8. Outlet No. 9. Trade name and location

10. Gross sales	11. Deductions	12. Taxable purchases	13. Amount subject to 4% State Sales tax	14. Amount subject to 1% tax for this city only
Minus .00	Plus .00	Equals .00	.00	.00

Outlet No. Trade name and location

Gross sales	Deductions	Taxable purchases	Amount subject to 4% State Sales tax	Amount subject to 1% tax for this city only
Minus .00	Plus .00	Equals .00	.00	.00

Outlet No. Trade name and location

Gross sales	Deductions	Taxable purchases	Amount subject to 4% State Sales tax	Amount subject to 1% tax for this city only
Minus .00	Plus .00	Equals .00	.00	.00

Outlet No. Trade name and location

Gross sales	Deductions	Taxable purchases	Amount subject to 4% State Sales tax	Amount subject to 1% tax for this city only
Minus .00	Plus .00	Equals .00	.00	.00

Write in white areas only.

15. PL 07 T Code ■ 03400 COMPUTATION OF TAX DUE

	Col. A STATE TAX ■ 02	Col. B CITY TAX ■ 04
16. Total amount subject to tax - all locations on this page	16A. .00	16B. .00
17. Total amount subject to tax - ALL supplement pages	17A. .00	17B. .00
18. TOTAL AMOUNT SUBJECT TO TAX (Item 16 plus Item 17)	18A. .00	18B. .00
19. Tax rates for calculating tax due	19A. .04 (4%)	19B. .01 (1%)
20. Total tax due (Multiply Item 18 by Item 19. Enter dollars and cents)	20A.	20B.
21. Subtract Prepayment Credit (Use correct amount)	21A.	21B.
If return is filed on time. STATE CITY	If return is filed late. STATE CITY	
22. Subtract prior overpayment by prepayment. (Deduct ONLY overpayments for which no refund claim has been submitted.)	22A.	22B.
23. Tax due after prepayment credit(s) (Item 20 minus Item 21 and Item 22) (If this is a credit, see instructions BEFORE completing return.)	23A.	23B.
24. Enter 1% of Item 23 IF return is filed and tax paid on or before due date.	24A.	24B.
25. Net tax due (Item 23 minus Item 24)	25A.	25B.
26. Subtract prior overpayments (Deduct only overpayments - for which you have received a notice, no refund claim has been filed or not deducted in Item 22.)	26A.	26B.
27. Tax due after prior overpayments (Item 25 minus Item 26)	27A.	27B.
28. Late filing penalty: (Minimum penalty - $1.00 for each tax.) 1-30 days late - 5% of Item 27 More than 30 days late - 10% of Item 27	28A.	28B.
29. Interest: 7% per annum on unpaid balance of Item 27 starting 61 days after due date.	29A.	29B.
30. TOTAL AMOUNT DUE AND PAYABLE (Item 27 plus Item 28 and Item 29)	30A.	30B.

TYPE OR PRINT.

Please read instructions.

31. Due date

32. Total payment (Item 30A plus 30B)

33. ■ 34. 35.

Pay TOTAL AMOUNT DUE in full for BOTH TAXES. An overpayment of one tax may not be applied against an underpayment of the other. Any overpayment of either tax will initiate refund procedures when this return is processed.

Remit total of Item 32 in one check payable to
STATE TREASURER

Mail to: BOB BULLOCK
COMPTROLLER OF PUBLIC ACCOUNTS
Capitol Station
Austin, Texas 78774

FIELD OFFICE
No.
Date
EO Name

I declare under penalties prescribed in TEX.TAX.-GEN.ANN. art. 1.12 (1969) that the information contained in this document and any attachments thereto is true and correct to the best of my knowledge and belief.

36. sign here ▶   Taxpayer or Duly Authorized Agent

Business Phone   Date

For Sales Tax assistance please contact your Texas State Comptroller's Local Field Office.
You may also call Area Code 512 475-2206 OR call toll free from anywhere in Texas at 1-800-252-5555.

FIGURE 7-5
Brackets for collection of 5 percent (nominal) sales taxes in Maryland and Massachusetts

Sales tax collected	Maryland bracket	Massachusetts bracket
0	0-19¢	0-9¢
1¢	20¢	10-29¢
2¢	21-40¢	30-49¢
3¢	41-60¢	50-69¢
4¢	61-80¢	70-89¢
5¢	81¢-$1.00; then 5¢ on each $1.00 plus 1¢ for each 20¢ or fraction thereof above $1.00	90¢-$1.09; same breaks continue

others. Because other major taxes do not attempt to compensate for compliance, sales taxes probably ought not either.

The typical U.S. sales tax applies to purchases by the final consumer of tangible personal property. Most do not extend to purchases of services, but do apply to numerous purchases made by business. These latter purchases are hardly consumption, but they constitute about 25 percent of many sales tax bases.[18] The tax will often exempt some commodity purchases, particularly food and drugs, to reduce the burden of the tax on low-income families. To protect in-state retailers, states apply use taxes which apply to items purchased out-of-state and brought into the state for consumption. That prevents purchasers from avoiding the high rate in their state by purchase in a low rate state. Use taxes cannot be effectively enforced on most items, but do work for major business purchases and for registered consumer items (motor vehicles).

Two special evaluation standards apply to sales tax structures beyond those important for all taxes. Those are uniformity and neutrality.[19] The first standard holds that the tax should produce a uniform tax on consumer expenditures. If the tax intends to do anything else, it ought not be a sales tax. Thus, the structure should ease shifting to ultimate consumers, it should apply at a uniform rate to all consumption expenditures unless there is reason otherwise, and it should apply to the amount actually paid by the consumer. Second, in order to avoid loss of economic efficiency the tax should not create competitive dis-

[18] Richard F. Fryman, "Sales taxation of producers' goods in Illinois," *National Tax Journal,* 22 (June 1969): 273-81.

[19] John F. Due, *Sales Taxation* (Urbana: University of Illinois Press, 1957), pp. 351-52.

turbances among types of distribution channels, methods of doing business, or forms of business organization. Choices ought not be distorted because of the tax. Structures as currently applied do not always conform to these standards, as the following design elements will illustrate.

Exclusion of producers' goods. Business purchases are a tempting target for addition to the tax base. The overall sales tax base is greater with their inclusion, so a given statutory tax rate produces more money. A large piece of the tax burden is hidden, because customers cannot detect the embedded influence of the sales tax on producers' goods in consumer prices. If producers' goods are not excluded, the tax will not be a uniform percentage of consumer expenditures (some consumption items require use of more producer goods than others), the tax will affect choices among methods of production (it makes capital more expensive), and it may delay the replacement of old equipment by increasing the after-tax price of new equipment. Further, the firm has an incentive to produce goods for its own use, rather than purchasing the goods, because the cost of production would not be subject to sales tax, as purchases would be. Thus, it is clear that logic suggests producer goods should be excluded from the tax.

States have developed two general rules for business purchase exemption: the component part/physical ingredient and the direct use rules.[20] The former rule regards an item as being resold and hence not taxable if it becomes a physical ingredient or component part of a good which itself is being sold (flour sold to a bakery, or gasoline tanks sold to a lawnmower manufacturer). If the good does not become a physical part of the product, then its sale is taxed as a retail sale. This rule predominates, probably because it gives a larger tax base, although it also is somewhat clearer to administer. The direct use rule exempts both physical ingredients and machinery and equipment used in the production process (a stamping machine that forms lawnmower gasoline tanks, or an oven in a bakery). This rule produces a smaller tax base, but the base comes closer to consumer expenditures. No existing sales tax, however, is limited exclusively to final consumption expenditure.

Coverage of services. Many state taxes include virtually no services sold to consumers; others provide only partial coverage of services. If services are not taxed, the tax does not cover consumption uniformly, as it applies only to tangible personal property purchases. Initial objections to taxing of services were that the tax on services is a tax on labor. Of course, labor constitutes much of the production cost of tangible

---

[20] Daniel C. Morgan, Jr., *Retail Sales Tax, An Appraisal of New Issues* (Madison: University of Wisconsin Press, 1964), chap. 2.

personal property, so the argument lacks merit. More important is the frequent absence of a clear line between the worker/client relationship and the worker/employer relationship, e.g., an accountant doing personal tax returns and an accountant working for a business firm. The latter, a producer good relationship, ought not be taxed. Furthermore, there are some services—medical, and possibly legal, for instance—which probably should not be taxed as a matter of social policy. Consumers purchasing these services have enough trouble as it is, without adding the sales tax to their bill. The pragmatic difficulty of taxing services is not surprising, even though the logical case is sound.

Commodity exemption. Sales taxes typically exempt some items of tangible property which are clearly consumption expenditure. The most frequently exempt are purchases of food for at-home consumption and prescription drugs. There is a logical reason for these exemptions based on the standard evaluation criteria for taxes. Purchases of these items make up a higher percentage of the income of low-income families than they do of high-income families. Thus, if these items remain in the tax base, the sales tax will be regressive. If they are excluded from the base, the tax will tend to be proportional. Hence, there is strong logical reason for excluding these items, even though their exclusion makes the sales tax more difficult to collect (stores selling both food and taxed items must maintain segregated accounting records and the state must establish what constitutes food, as well as audit more complex sales data) and the tax rate must be higher to yield a given amount of revenue on the smaller base (food constitutes around one third of a prospective sales tax base). A small group of states have extended commodity exemption to purchases of clothing under the apparent logic of freeing from tax a base of necessities. Unfortunately, clothing expenditures increase as a percentage of income as income is higher, so the exemption provides greater relative relief to the more affluent and adds to the regressivity of the tax.[21] There is no logical virtue to clothing exemption: it increases regressivity, complicates compliance and administration, and causes higher rates for given revenues.

Several states use the tax credit or rebate as an alternative to commodity exemption to control sales tax regressivity. Rather than provide exemption for all purchasers of selected commodities, the credit systems return to taxpayers at year's end a fixed sum, usually equal to estimated payment of sales tax on food purchases by individuals in the lowest income class. If the prevailing sales tax rate is 4 percent and per capita food purchases by individuals in the under $3,000 annual income

---

[21] J. M. Schaefer, "Clothing Exemptions and Sales Tax Regressivity," *American Economic Review,* 59 (September 1969): 596–99.

class is about $600, the amount returned would be $24. Return of $24 to all individuals—either by rebate application or as a credit on a state income tax return—would effectively eliminate the sales tax on food purchases by very low-income purchasers. It would not increase, however, as food consumption increases through the higher income classes. Thus, it concentrates assistance where assistance is most needed as well as eliminates the need for separate accounting for taxed and exempt items. Overall, it effectively reduces (or even eliminates) regressivity at lower cost than commodity exemption. It does require that individuals file returns with the state and does require cash payment to individuals, but these would seem small disadvantages relative to the other efficiencies of the device.

Value-added tax

A final form of consumption taxation is the value-added tax (VAT), a tax levied on the value added in each stage of the production/distribution process. It is simply an alternate way of collecting a tax on consumption expenditure; it does not tax a base different from consumption. While it is not used by the United States today, some have proposed it as a means of financing the social security system, as a way to stimulate saving and investment through reduced reliance on the income tax, as a way to stimulate U.S. exports, or, during the Nixon administration, as a replacement for the property tax in the finance of public schools. Twenty-four countries levied VAT in 1980. The group includes all nations of the European Economic Community—the EEC selected the VAT as the consumption tax to be used by all members as a means of tax harmonization.

The VAT is a multistage tax that produces a burden equivalent to that of a single-stage retail sales tax. In other words, tax will be a constant proportion of the retail price of the product; it will not vary according to the number of transactions in the production process, as is normally the case for multistage taxes. The reason for the lack of pyramiding is that the tax at each stage depends on value added at that stage, not the total transaction price at that stage. The mechanics of the tax are described in Figure 7–6, an illustration of the value-added tax applied in the making of a table, from tree to final sale. At each stage in exchange, the tax rate applies to the transaction price. All such tax paid on the product to that stage in the process is a credit, however, against tax owed to the government (the sale from sawmill to furniture maker carries a tax of $15—$150 × 10%—but $10 of that tax is simply a credit representing tax already paid in the exchange between logger and sawmill), so the net tax paid is really only on value added at that production stage.

FIGURE 7–6
Application of a value-added tax (10 percent rate)

	Purchase			Sale				VAT	
	Price paid for goods	VAT	Total	Value added	Price charged (price paid plus value added)	VAT collected	Total	Credit for VAT paid	To government
Logger chops wood, sells to sawmill	—	—	—	$100	$100	$10	$110	—	$10
Sawmill saws wood, sells to furniture maker	$100	$10	$110	$ 50	$150	$15	$165	$10	$ 5
Furniture maker builds table, sells to retailer	$150	$15	$165	$100	$250	$25	$275	$15	$10
Retailer sells to customer	$250	$25	$275	$ 50	$300	$30	$330	$25	$ 5
Customer's purchase				$300					$30

* Adapted from Comptroller General's Report to Congress, "The Valued Added Tax in the European Economic Community," ID-81-2, December 5, 1980.

If a consumption tax is desirable, why should the VAT form be chosen? There are two circumstances in which the VAT can be appropriate. First, the VAT is appropriate if tax evasion and lack of vendor cooperation is a problem. The VAT induces every purchaser to want a documented receipt from every vendor for taxes paid, because that receipt will be used to pay part of the tax he will owe when he makes a sale. He will pay the tax because the person purchasing the item will demand a tax receipt for credit purposes, and so on through the exchange channel. The self-enforcing nature of VAT thus makes it attractive when the tax compliance climate is not good. Second, nations sometimes choose to remove their domestic taxes from items which will be sold in international trade. The chain of tax documentation produced by VAT makes this extraction simple, although it does not extract any taxes except VAT. It is not clear that these circumstances currently apply in the United States, although they do exist in other countries to greater or lesser degree.

Conclusion

Taxes on income and consumption are at the heart of the federal and state revenue systems. While questions of structure persist for each base, there is no doubt concerning the serviceability of these taxes. Establishing the coverage of both taxes continues to be a problem for each, as interests attempt to obtain provisions which reduce their tax burden. The most difficult administrative problems are avoided, however, because the taxes do normally apply to transaction values, not a value synthesized by a public official. Both taxes are completely dependent on the taxpayer for voluntary compliance.

A CASE FOR DISCUSSION

Large amounts of total sales and use tax collections typically result from sales of automobiles. The sales tax in each transaction is often substantial, so gains from avoidance or evasion can also be large. As a result, states often devise special taxes to replace the ordinary sales tax on such purchases. The Kentucky automobile usage tax considered in the following excerpt from an article in the *Louisville Courier-Journal* is such a tax.

Consider the following questions:

1. How is the tax supposed to be computed? What variants do the dealers use? How are dealers alleged to profit?

210

2. Does the tax base coincide with the standards used in evaluation of sales taxes? Explain.
3. Can you propose a system better able to eliminate abuses?
4. Kentucky collected sales tax on the original sale of most cars sold by used-car dealers. Should there by any tax at all on their resale by used-car dealers? Explain.

Probe Finds Some Dealers Overcharging in Used-Car Sales Taxes

BY LARRY WERNER
Courier-Journal Staff Writer

A major investigation by the attorney general's Consumer Protection Division into Kentucky's retail automobile industry has uncovered instances of "substantial" overcharging of consumers on the sales tax for used cars.

The investigation, which could result in thousands of dollars in refunds for the state's used-car buyers, has angered the powerful Kentucky Automobile Dealers Association (KADA), which is claiming that the attorney general has embarked on a "fishing expedition" to harass legitimate businessmen.

To this, Atty. Gen. Ed W. Hancock replied: "If we are (fishing), we've got the right bait, I would say."

* * * * *

What the attorney general's investigators are looking for are deviations by the dealers from the method of charging sales tax set out in Kentucky Revised Statute 138.450, the state officials said.

According to that statute, the 5 percent state sales tax must be assessed on the "retail value given in the automotive reference manual prescribed by the Department of Revenue" after deducting "a trade-in allowance equal to the value of the vehicle taken in trade."

The "automotive reference manual prescribed by the Department of Revenue" is the "National Automobile Dealers Association (NADA) Official Used Car Guide."

The statute also says that the trade-in allowance, which is sworn to by the seller on the bill of sale, shall not exceed "the fair market value of the vehicle taken in trade." Although the law doesn't spell out what the "fair market value" of the trade-in is, an attorney general's opinion has defined it as "in the area of" the NADA book value.

The attorney general's investigation has been aimed at the practice of certain dealers' charging used-car buyers more sales tax than is remitted to county clerks for payment to the state. There are several ways in which this is done, according to Hancock and [Asst. Atty. Gen. Robert] Bullock.

One method of overcharging the sales tax is outlined by former Asst. Atty. Gen. David R. Vandeventer in a memo to KADA on the investigation.

In the memo he wrote asking KADA to cooperate in the investigation. Vandeventer states that the overcharging "can be done in a number of ways."

The memo continues:

"For example, by charging the consumer 5 percent of the lot sale price for a used car and remitting 5 percent of the NADA guide book if, as usual, the sale price exceeds the NADA guide price."

Hancock and Bullock explained that if a dealer charges 5 percent of the sales price to the consumer and then gives the county clerk only 5 percent of the lower NADA book value, the dealer is "pocketing" illegally obtained income.

In other cases, they said, dealers seemed to be simply charging the consumer a "lump sum" for sales tax regardless of the NADA book price of the car. When the bill of sale is registered with the county clerk, they said, the proper sales tax is calculated and paid.

For example, a dealer might be charging buyers a uniform $150 for sales tax. But if the NADA price on the car is $2,500, only 5 percent of that amount—or $125—is paid to the county clerk, resulting in a $25 bonus for the dealer.

Hancock and Bullock emphasized that this "lump-sum" method of charging sales tax also results in undercharges in cases where the actual amount of tax due exceeds the lump sum charged the buyer.

In other cases, Hancock said, the investigators have been unable to determine how dealers have arrived at the sales tax they have charged buyers.

"In some instances, there seems to have been no rhyme or reason to the basis for the tax charged," Hancock said. "You can't tie it into any computation."

Bullock and his staff have been visiting auto dealers and asking to see both purchase orders—which are filled out at the time the sale is made—and the bills of sale that are registered with the county clerks.

In many cases, Bullock said, the sales tax figure on the purchase order—which is the amount of tax the buyer paid to the dealer—exceeds 5 percent of the "total" price that is recorded on the bill of sale and on which the tax paid by the dealer is based.

Examples provided by the attorney general's office included:

1. A case in which the purchase order indicated that $93.40 was charged the consumer, but in which the bill of sale indicated only $70 was paid by the dealer to the county clerk.

2. A case in which the purchase order indicated that $75 sales tax was paid by the consumer, but in which the bill of sale indicated only $39.15 was paid by the dealer to the county clerk.

3. A case in which the purchase order indicated that $143.75 was charged the consumer for sales tax and other incidental fees, but in which the bill of sale indicated only $62.50 was paid by the dealer to the county clerk.

Hancock and Bullock suggested that consumers who have purchased used cars since June 16, 1972, check to see if they have been overcharged for sales tax.

They said this is done by checking the amount of sales tax listed on the purchase order. This should amount to 5 percent of "total" purchase price listed on the "motor vehicle bill of sale" that is sent to the purchaser by the county clerk.

The "total" listed on the bill of sale is equal to the "average retail as shown in NADA Book," less the trade-in value of the car. These figures are listed on the bill of sale in a section entitled "USED VEHICLES VALUATION OF MOTOR VEHICLE FOR COMPUTATION OF USAGE TAX."

Hancock said the Consumer Protection Division was alerted to the overcharging practice by a former credit manager for a Kentucky dealer.

In a Feb. 22 letter from Hancock to attorneys for KADA, Hancock states that the investigation was begun last November by members of the consumer division staff.

"After bringing it to my attention, I suggested that they contact representatives of KADA, for the purpose of asking for their help in investigating this matter. . . ." Hancock's letter states.

However, after Bullock met with the KADA board of directors on Dec. 18 and requested assistance from the trade association, KADA reported to Bullock's staff that the members of KADA "would be opposed to such cooperation and, therefore, no cooper-

ation would be given. . . ." the letter says.

The "cooperation" requested of KADA by the attorney general's office was that the trade association ask each of its members to supply the Consumer Protection Division with "complete sets of records on every sale during July and August 1973." according to Vandeventer's memo to KADA.

Vandeventer states in his memo that this would enable the consumer agency to determine whether overcharging was going on and which dealers were doing it.

When KADA refused cooperation, Hancock said, "There was no choice left to me but to authorize the investigation on a dealer-by-dealer basis."

When asked about KADA's alleged refusal to cooperate with the investigation, KADA President [Ernie] Bates said:

"I told Mr. Bullock we can't give him authority to come into a man's place of business and let him go fishing around for a mistake this man has made."

Bates added:

"We don't condone in any case any overcharging or undercharging of the automobile usage tax. It's a pretty complicated thing to compute. Surprisingly enough, there are a lot of people who don't understand it. There have probably been some mistakes made on it. I think they (dealers) are probably computing it to the best of their ability."

Bates said it is his opinion that "Mr. Bullock went on a fishing expedition in

Mr. Jones' case, and he has no law to back him up."

Hancock said:

"As far as his (Bates) saying there's no law behind us, that's going to be up to the court to decide. As far as saying,

"There's nothing wrong, but you can't see the records," that's about like (President) Nixon saying, " 'There's nothing wrong, but you can't have the tapes.' "

USED VEHICLES—VALUATION OF MOTOR VEHICLE FOR
COMPUTATION OF USAGE TAX – (KRS 138.450 & 138.460)

Passenger Cars
    1. Average retail as shown in NADA Book $ _2000.00_

    2. Less trade-in per KRS
       Ky. Registration No. _1400.00_ $ _600.00_

    3. Total   X .05 ▶$ _1400.00_
       $70.00

CASH DELIVERED PRICE OF VEHICLE ▶	1868	.00
SALES TAX	93.	40
DOCUMENTARY FEE	15.	50
TOTAL CASH DELIVERED PRICE	1976.	90

The illustration above contains segments of a bill of sale and a purchase order on an actual used-car sale in which the Kentucky attorney general's office detected an overcharge on sales tax. On top is a section of the bill of sale that lists the $1,400 "total" on which the 5 percent sales tax is computed for payment by the dealer to the county clerk. The "total" is arrived at by subtracting the trade-in allowance from the "book value" of the car being purchased. As the artist's calculation shows, the correct tax due is $70. However, as the purchase order pictured on the bottom, shows, 5 percent of the "cash delivered price of the vehicle" before subtraction of the trade-in allowance, or $93.40, was paid by the consumer to the dealer.

8

Major tax structures: Property taxes

Property taxes are the closest existing approximation to wealth taxes levied in the United States. They are not, however, true net wealth taxes because they typically omit some wealth types (individually owned personal property); they apply to gross, not net, wealth (the debt against a house or car will seldom be completely subtracted from taxable value); and they often apply twice to certain wealth forms (both corporate stock values and land and buildings owned by corporations are often taxed). To the extent that the taxes do reach wealth holdings, they add an element of redistribution from rich to poor otherwise missing from the tax structure. Because they apply to accumulated wealth, not income, they may also have less effect on work and investment incentive than do income taxes. They are not based on values from current transactions (as is usually the case for income and sales taxes), so the tax requires a hypothetical valuation process.

Property taxes are extremely difficult to categorize briefly. As Richard Almy observes:

> In the United States, "the" property tax is composed of 51 separate state-level property tax systems, each subject to numerous legal and extralegal local variations and each changing in some fashion over time—through constitutional revision, enactment of statutes and ordinances, changes in administrative procedures, court decisions and changes in the capabilities of tax administration.[1]

---

[1] Richard Almy, "Rationalizing the Assessment Process," in *Property Tax Reform,* ed. George Peterson (Washington, D.C.: Urban Institute, 1973), p. 175.

The following sections introduce several important features of property taxes and examine a group of structural issues about the tax. Because of the wide variation among the taxes, all local characteristics cannot be actually described here.

Property within reach of the tax can be categorized several ways. One important distinction is between real property (land and structures or improvements erected on that land) and personal property (property which is not real, a grouping which includes valuables ranging from factory equipment to jewelry and automobiles). Personal property is generally more easily movable than real property, but there is no general dividing line between those groupings. Each state or local government develops its own definitions, usually resorting to lists of property types which fall into one or the other at the borderline.[2] The distinction is crucial because some governments tax personal property more heavily than real.

A second distinction is between tangible and intangible personal property. Tangible personal property is property held for its own sake, including cars, machinery, inventories of raw materials and finished products, household items, etc. Intangible personal property is property valued because it represents an ownership claim on something of value. Thus, intangible properties include stocks, bonds, and other financial assets. Property taxes vary widely in the extent to which they apply to these properties. Many types of tangible personal property are both difficult to locate and, once located, difficult to value (what is the value of a 10-year-old black and white television set, after all?); intangible personal property can often be easily valued, but frequently is difficult to locate. Sometimes this property is exempt by law; sometimes, by local practice. Seldom is taxation complete.

A third distinction frequently made for taxes is between business and individual or household ownership of property. Business holdings of personal property may be fully taxable (television sets in motels, for instance), while household holdings of that same item are not taxed (a household personal property exemption). The logic of a net wealth tax would suggest that household possession is a wealth representation, probably more so than the business holding, but most structures rule in the opposite manner. Within the business class, some types are treated differently, as with public utility property which is often valued as an operating unit, not on an item-by-item basis as is the case in other assessment.

---

[2] One interesting problem concerns the treatment of mobile homes—are they real or personal property? States use rules including permanency of foundation, presence of wheels or axles, highway licensing, etc., but there is no general division.

Property tax rate setting

Most tax rates change only with special legislative action—they are the portion of the fiscal system which is strictly incremental, in the sense of small changes being made to a permanent base. Property tax rates are established, however, as a part of the annual budget process, as opposed to rates for individual income, general sales, and other major taxes which change only by special legislative action. Budgets heavily dependent on the property tax have rate setting as a normal part of the legislative process. The rate in most circumstances must be annually readopted at a level sufficient to balance operating budgets (and high enough to cover current cost of servicing budgets financed by debt). This rate setting uses these data:

1. The total of approved expenditure plans (E) included in the appropriation act or ordinance.
2. The total estimate of revenue from nonproperty tax sources, including miscellaneous charge and fee revenue, revenue from nonproperty taxes (sales or income), grants, etc. (NPR). Part of this revenue may be guaranteed state payments, but much will be estimated.
3. The total assessed value (AV) in the taxing unit established at a standard assessment date. Assessed value is the base upon which the property tax will be levied. For instance, the assessed value total on March 1, 1983, could be the figure upon which taxes were collected for a fiscal year beginning January 1, 1984. Thus, collections lag behind assessment.

The property tax rate (R) would emerge as a residual from the formula

$$R = \frac{E - NPR}{AV}$$

That rate would apply to property assessed on that earlier assessment date. For example, suppose that a village had appropriated $95,000 for the 1989 fiscal year (January 1 to December 31, 1989), expected to receive $15,000 from nonproperty tax sources during that fiscal year, and had an assessed value of $1,750,000 on March 1, 1988 (the assessment date). In that village, the property tax rate for 1989 would be 4.58 percent, or $4.58 per $100 of assessed value. A parcel valued at $8,000 for tax purposes would have a 1989 property tax bill of $366.40, possibly payable in equal installments due in May and November of 1989.

Assessment. Property taxes require a valuation process to establish a basis for distribution of the tax burden. This assessment is the heart of the real property tax system because it aligns tax burdens among properties. When properties are revalued for tax purposes, some properties will pay a higher share of the tax burden and others, lower. It is this adjustment of tax burdens to more closely match perceived capability to pay the tax—as measured by property value—that is the objective of assessment.

Valuation is done through several different schemes across the United States, but three general structures have been identified: annual assessment, mass cyclical assessment, and segmental assessment. With cyclical mass assessment, all properties in a taxing jurisdiction are valued in a particular year and that value will not change until the next scheduled mass assessment, except for new construction, demolition, or change in use of a property. A recent study found states prescribing mass cyclical assessments at intervals ranging from 2 to 10 years.[3]

Segmental assessment is a procedure by which a specified fraction of real property parcels is reassessed each year, moving through the assessing unit in sequence. Thus, if a three-year cycle is used, one third of the properties in the area would be reassessed in each year, with all properties reassessed in three years. The last valued taxpayers can complain about the inflation in their valuations which is absent from earlier-valued parcels, but administrative convenience and the fact that all parcels take their turn as last valued has preserved the method.

The third system is annual assessment, a process which presumes updated values for all real property parcels each year. Such a process is possible with EDP assistance, although revaluation with actual inventory and inspection of all parcels is not likely. More often than not, annual revaluation will employ the physical characteristics of properties as identified in earlier parcel inventories with new value weights applied to those characteristics. For instance, in earlier years, a fireplace might add $1,000 to the value of a house; this year, it is estimated to add $1,800. In that fashion, new value estimates would emerge from old physical feature data. Of course, annual reassessment can become no reassessment if last year's values are recopied on this year's forms. That process destroys the equity of the property tax because no adjustments are made for properties whose value has either fallen or increased.

The worst mutation of annual assessment is the "Welcome Stranger" system in which properties are revalued only when they are sold, and at the new transaction price.[4] This structure disrupts the property market (prospective buyers would pay a higher property tax than

---

[3] John L. Mikesell, "Property Tax Reassessment Cycles: Significance for Uniformity and Effective Rates," Public Finance Quarterly, 8 (January 1980): 23–37.

[4] This is the system forced on California by Proposition 13 in 1978.

would the prospective seller), creates a property record substructure of sales without recorded deeds as individuals seek to avoid property tax adjustments, and causes completely identical properties to pay widely different property tax.

All assessment systems but "Welcome Stranger" require estimation of values (Welcome Stranger prescribes a perverse value estimation procedure). Three general methods of assessment of real property have emerged as offshoots to private property appraisal techniques: the market data approach, the cost, or summation, approach, and the income approach.[5] The market data, or comparable, sales approach uses evidence from the real estate market to estimate values of particular property parcels. Sales of similar parcels are used to gauge buyer and seller attitudes to particular parcels to determine what the value of a parcel would be if it were to sell. A reasonably good comparison is usually possible for residential property (there are many three-bedroom split-level houses with about 2,500 square feet of living space in most cities, after all), but uniqueness can be a problem for commercial or industrial parcels.

The cost approach estimates the cost to reproduce a particular structure, considering construction type, materials, and quality of workmanship, and then subtracts depreciation which has occurred since the building was built. The approach typically proceeds by determining the cost of constructing a standard (average) grade of structure at a particular date, that is, with the labor and materials prices of that time and using the prevailing technology, in the size (square footage and number of stories) of the subject property. That cost is adjusted to account for nonstandard construction materials and workmanship—either higher or lower than standard. To that cost will be added extra features not in the standard unit—extra bathroom fixtures, fireplaces, central air conditioning, etc., for residential units; escalators, sprinkler systems, vaults, etc. for commercial units; and cranes, elevators, air circulation systems, etc. for industrial units. That final cost figure will then be adjusted for depreciation to allow for the fact that the structure is not new, but has suffered physical, technological, and economic forces which have influenced its current value. While the approach can be applied without major problems to most structures and is widely applied in mass reassessment, it obviously will not apply to land valuation.

The income approach is most applicable to value estimates for income-producing properties (apartments, stores, offices, agricultural

---

[5] International Association of Assessing Officers, *Assessing and the Appraisal Process* (Chicago: IAAO, 1973), chap. 5–7.

land, etc.). The method estimates the sustainable net income flow from the property and capitalization of that income flow at the appropriate interest rate for that investment risk. The resulting value estimates the amount a willing and knowledgeable buyer would pay for a parcel yielding that income flow.

Each method can yield uniform estimates of values when consistently applied; the first two methods are particularly amenable to the requirements of mass assessment. In many instances, the value of parcels will be estimated using all three approaches so that the assessor will have as much information as possible to form this valuation judgment. These values and the method used in their estimation will be maintained either in EDP record files or on parcel record cards. Figure 8–1 presents such a property record card: one side describes the land and the factors used in its valuation; the other side does the same for the structure. The values on these records, when summed, constitute the property tax base for the taxing unit for use in computing the property tax rate; the record information likewise is used for computation of individual tax bills from that rate, after subtraction of whatever exemptions are applicable. Figures 8–2 and 8–3 show an assessed value notice (prepared from a parcel card) to inform the property owner, and the resulting tax bill.

Exemptions. Property tax systems almost always include provisions which subtract a portion of assessed value from the taxable holdings of some individuals or institutions. Thus, if an individual holds a property with assessed value of $8,500 and qualifies for a veteran's exemption of $1,500, that person's tax bill would be computed on a net assessed value of $7,000. The exemption reduces the tax base; it is not a direct credit against tax owed. In most instances, the exemptions are additive, so if a parcel holder qualifies for exemption because of age and veteran status, for example, the property tax base would be reduced by the sum of both exemptions.

Individuals qualify for many different classes of exemption. Some of the more important in terms of use by states and size of value exemption are homestead, veterans, and old age exemptions. Homestead exemptions allow homeowners a given assessed value base before any property tax bill will be levied against property. Veteran and old age exemptions provide similar partial exemption of properties from the tax. These exemptions can dramatically reduce the base on which the tax can be applied: in Louisiana and Mississippi 18.7 and 24.7 percent of gross assessed value was exempt because of homestead exemptions in 1976; in Hawaii, homestead and disability exempted 15.7 percent of the gross base; in Oklahoma, homestead, veterans, and other exemptions eliminated 12.5 percent of the gross base. Nationwide partial exemp-

FIGURE 8-1

SE NE 7-8-1E 40A

County: Monroe   Township: Salt Creek   Corporation: ____

Property Address / Parcel Numbers: 014 027101 0071 0101   101

TRANSFER OF OWNERSHIP

DATE

MEMORANDUM

VALUATION RECORD

ASSESSMENT YEAR	1978 REVALUATION	19	19	19	19
REASON FOR CHANGE					
TRUE CASH VALUE LAND	5700				
IMPROVEMENTS	51500				
TOTAL	57200				
ASSESSED VALUE LAND	1900				
IMPROVEMENTS	17170				
TOTAL	19070				

LAND DATA AND COMPUTATIONS

LAND TYPE	SOIL I.D	ACTUAL FRONTAGE	EFFECTIVE FRONTAGE	EFFECTIVE DEPTH	DEPTH FACTOR	BASE RATE	ADJUSTED RATE	EXTENDED VALUE	INFLUENCE FACTOR	TRUE CASH VALUE
F FRONT LOT				SQ FT	FACTOR				%	
R REAR LOT				ACREAGE					%	
1 PRIMARY IND/COMM SITE		7		1.00		3000X 100	3000	3000	%	3000
2 SECONDARY IND/COMM SITE		5 100		15.00 57		450 257	3860		-60%	1500
3 UNDEVELOPED		6 100		24.00 57		450 257	6170		-80%	1200
4 OPEN TILLABLE				•					%	
5 OPEN NON TILLABLE				•					%	
6 WOOD/WASTELAND				•					%	
61 PUBLIC ROAD				•					%	
7 HOME SITE				•					%	
8				•					%	
0				•					%	

TOTAL ACREAGE 40.00   TOTAL TRUE CASH LAND VALUE 5700

TOPOGRAPHY
LEVEL	✓
HIGH	
LOW	
ROLLING	✓
SWAMPY	

PUBLIC UTILITIES
WATER	
SEWER	
GAS	
ELECTRICITY	✓
ALL	

STREET OR ROAD
PAVED	✓
UNPAVED	
PROPOSED	
SIDEWALK	
ALLEY	

NEIGHBORHOOD
IMPROVING	✓
STATIC	
DECLINING	
BLIGHTED	

INFLUENCE FACTOR
1 CORNER INFLUENCE
2 ALLEY INFLUENCE
3 TOPOGRAPHY
4 UNDER IMPROVED
5 EXCESS FRONTAGE
6 SHAPE OR SIZE
7 MISIMPROVEMENT
8 RESTRICTIONS
9 VIEW
0

PRESCRIBED INDIANA PROPERTY RECORD CARD 1978

FIGURE 8-1 (continued)

IMPROVEMENT DATA AND COMPUTATIONS

INDIANA 1978

FIGURE 8-2

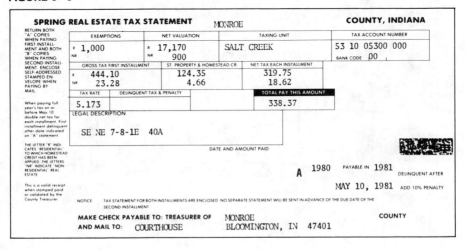

Prescribed by the State Board of Tax Commissioners

Form 11R—1976

NOTICE OF ASSESSMENT TO LAND AND *IMPROVEMENTS

DISTRICT | SECTION & PLAT | ROUTING NUMBER

Assessors are required to send this notice to the property owner whenever a change is made in assessments.

SE NE 7-8-1E 40A

You are hereby notified that the land and *improvements listed in your name in _Salt Creek_ Township Corporation and _____ Monroe County, has been assessed by me in the amount in the statement below for the year 19____. If you do not agree with the action of the assessing officer giving this notice, the COUNTY BOARD OF REVIEW will review that action if you file a petition with the County Auditor of the County in which the property is located within THIRTY (30) days of the date of this notice.

DESCRIPTION	SEC. IN-LOTS	TWP. OUT-LOTS	RANGE BLOCK	ACRES	TENTHS	VALUE OF LANDS-LOTS	VALUE OF ● IMPROVEMENTS	VALUE OF ADDITIONAL ● IMPROVEMENTS	TOTAL VALUE OF LAND-LOTS AND ● IMPROVEMENTS
						1900	17170	—	19070

*IMPROVEMENTS DESCRIBE ALL BUILDINGS, STRUCTURES OR APPURTENANCES AFFIXED TO LAND.

Witness my hand this ___27___ day of _February_ 19_79_ _____ Assessor

FIGURE 8-3

SPRING REAL ESTATE TAX STATEMENT   MONROE   **COUNTY, INDIANA**

RETURN BOTH "A" COPIES WHEN PAYING FIRST INSTALLMENT AND BOTH "B" COPIES WHEN PAYING SECOND INSTALLMENT. ENCLOSE SELF-ADDRESSED STAMPED ENVELOPE WHEN PAYING BY MAIL

EXEMPTIONS	NET VALUATION	TAXING UNIT	TAX ACCOUNT NUMBER
R 1,000	R 17,170	SALT CREEK	53 10 05300 000
NR	NR 900		BANK CODE 00

GROSS TAX FIRST INSTALLMENT	ST. PROPERTY & HOMESTEAD CR.	NET TAX EACH INSTALLMENT
R 444.10	124.35	319.75
NR 23.28	4.66	18.62

TAX RATE	DELINQUENT TAX & PENALTY	TOTAL PAY THIS AMOUNT
5.173		338.37

When paying full year's tax on or before May 10 double net tax for each installment. First installment delinquent after date indicated on "A" statement

LEGAL DESCRIPTION

SE NE 7-8-1E 40A

THE LETTER "R" INDICATES "RESIDENTIAL" TO WHICH HOMESTEAD CREDIT HAS BEEN APPLIED. THE LETTERS "NR" INDICATE "NON RESIDENTIAL" REAL ESTATE

This is a valid receipt when stamped paid or validated by the County Treasurer

DATE AND AMOUNT PAID

A 1980   PAYABLE IN 1981   DELINQUENT AFTER

MAY 10, 1981   ADD 10% PENALTY

NOTICE   TAX STATEMENT FOR BOTH INSTALLMENTS ARE ENCLOSED. NO SEPARATE STATEMENT WILL BE SENT IN ADVANCE OF THE DUE DATE OF THE SECOND INSTALLMENT

MAKE CHECK PAYABLE TO: TREASURER OF   MONROE   **COUNTY**

AND MAIL TO: COURTHOUSE   BLOOMINGTON, IN 47401

tions reduced gross assessed value by a little over 3 percent.[6] The potential revenues are not trivial.

Such exemption programs are popular politically because of their apparent tax savings and burden redistribution, but they have a number of important problems. First, the programs usually have a statewide purpose, but because property taxes primarily support local government, the revenue loss is local. They are thus a way for state legislatures to win favor with the electorate without loss of state revenue. Second, the programs do not focus tax relief on the needy. All people falling into the specific categories (homeowner or veteran) receive aid regardless of their specific needs, as there is no income test for receipt of the exemption. Despite trials and tribulations, homeowners probably are better off than renters and not all homeowners are equally well (or poorly) situated. Third, if the exemption program is sufficiently widespread, as in the case of general homestead exemption programs, the effect may be substantially higher property tax rates to recover lost revenue. For properties not completely exempted from the base, actual relief may be more psychological than real as the owner pays a higher rate on a smaller base, with about the same dollars involved. And finally, individual exemption programs ordinarily do not reach renters, many of whom are much less affluent than are property owners. This must be seen as an inherent defect in the structure of exemption programs. Overall, the political popularity of exemption programs does not reduce their substantial flaws in application.

Exemptions also apply to selected types of industrial property.[7] The exemption for a parcel may be complete and permanent or it may abate all or a portion of property tax for a specific period of time. It may also exempt particular activities at an otherwise taxable parcel, such as pollution control, property rehabilitation, solar energy use, etc. The idea is to attempt to stimulate economic activity in a particular area by luring businesses. It is, however, not clear that such property tax reductions are an effective force in industrial location. Evidence suggests things other than tax levels, particularly accessibility to markets, resource availability, transportation networks, and environmental amenities are much more significant in determining the location of commercial and industrial facilities. Thus, the expected return from such exemption is low. Possibly more important is the effect on existing property in the

[6] U.S. Bureau of the Census, *Census of Governments 1977,* vol. 2, *Taxable Property Values and Assessment-Sales Price Ratios* (Washington, D.C.: U.S. Government Printing Office, 1978), pp. 29, 42.

[7] The best general source: Steven Gold, *Property Tax Relief* (Lexington, Mass.: D. C. Heath, 1979).

area. The new industries do create a demand for public services (police protection, fire protection, planning, etc.) and new people in the area will likely demand more services than can be covered by the tax base they bring. With exemption of that new industrial property, those costs must be borne by the existing tax base. This is at, a minimum, discriminatory and, at a maximum, may eliminate some marginal businesses. Those properties not qualifying for the exemption will be facing artificially high property tax rates because of the assistance provided the new arrivals.

A final exemption group includes properties which are fully exempt because of the religious, governmental, educational, or charitable nature of the owner. An accurate estimate of the total amount of the potential tax base removed by these exemptions is not available—where the law requires assessment of these properties, officials are cavalier about the process because they recognize that no tax collections will result. Observers maintain that the taxes forgiven are substantial. As important as the lost revenue is the unequal distribution of such property among localities. Cities or counties with major state installations, for example, universities and state parks, can be particularly affected: they must provide for the peak, and special, service demands created by that facility without the power to include that facility in the tax base. Thus, the tax base of that locality must subsidize the citizenry of the state. The problem is reduced somewhat when exemption is conditioned on both ownership and use of the facility (a university classroom building is exempt, but a university-owned hotel is not), but the dual requirement is neither universal nor applied without interpretation problems. The federal government does make in-lieu-of-property-tax payments to state and local units hosting certain federal installations, but states seldom provide similar relief to their local governments. As will be discussed in a later chapter, user charges may well be an attractive option in such instances.

Circuit breakers. Property tax exemptions to individuals are flawed because they do not target property tax relief to those individuals most in need. That problem can be reduced by conditioning property tax assistance on individual income levels, as done by property tax circuit breakers. State circuit breakers pinpoint relief of property tax overload (defined in terms of the ratio of property tax payment to current family income) through integration of the local property tax and the state individual income tax structure. On the income tax return, the taxpayer reports the amount of property tax paid for the year for comparison with the taxpayer's income. If the ratio of property tax to income is excessive as defined in the circuit breaker law (an overload), some portion of that excess is returned by the state to the individual as an addition to income tax refund, as a reduction in income tax owed, or as a direct cash payment. Thus, the circuit breaker eliminates the property tax overload at state expense.

Critical structural elements for circuit breakers include age restrictions, income definition and limits, treatment of renters, and benefit formulas. Many programs limit overload relief to the elderly, at least partly to reduce program cost. Elderly individuals may, however, be especially susceptible to overload because they have accumulated property throughout their lives and now receive reduced retirement incomes. They are reluctant to reduce their household property holdings as children move away, so property tax payments take a sizable chunk of their income. The circuit breaker can reduce the need for forced sale and ease retirement. A number of states thus restrict their programs to elderly taxpayers who meet other circuit breaker criteria. Nonelderly low-income homeowners, however, may face similar overloads as well, particularly in the early years of homeownership or when a family income earner becomes unemployed. Exclusion of them is hardly defensible, but certainly does reduce the cost of the overall program.

Income limitations for the circuit breaker program are another design question. These limits imply that, beyond some income level, the state will not relieve any property tax burden. The limitation both reduces program cost and concentrates assistance at the lower end of the income spectrum, a logical structure. For these purposes, however, income should be defined more broadly than federal or state taxable income, but should include nontaxed retirement income sources as well. If it does not, individuals who are reasonably well-off because of pension, social security, and other nontaxed incomes would qualify, reducing aid available for the truly unfortunate.

Renters pose a third design problem, under the presumption that they pay a portion of the property tax on rental units. A circuit breaker limited to homeowners would provide them no assistance, even though many renters are much less affluent than the poorest homeowners. Renter relief, where given, presumes a property tax equivalent as a specified percentage of rent paid. The share is not scientifically determined because analysts have been unable to estimate the extent (if any) to which property tax is shifted to renters. With reasonable income limits, however, the program can be seen as a part of general assistance, regardless of property tax conditions.

The final design element is the choice between threshold and sliding scale relief formulas. The former approach defines a threshold percentage of income as the overload level. Property tax payments above that overload level are subject to partial relief. Relief computation follows the formula $R = t[PT - kI]$ where R = relief to be provided (subject to a lower limit of zero), t = the percentage of the overload which will be relieved, k = the overload threshold percentage, I = family income, and PT = property tax payment. Suppose a family has an income of $8,000 and pays property tax of $900. If it lives in a state which defines the overload threshold as 10 percent and grants 90 percent overload relief, the family would receive circuit breaker relief of $90. Some states further reduce their costs by reducing the threshold percentage as income is greater—a further effort to economize and focus aid.

The second formula is the sliding scale approach. In this formula, relief is a percentage of property tax payment with the percentage falling as family income is greater: $R = zPT$ where z is the percentage of property tax relieved for the income class and R and PT are as previously defined. Unless the relief percentage falls to zero at high incomes, all taxpayers receive assistance under this approach, so it is more like general property tax relief than specific relief of the property tax overload. It does differ, however, from general property tax relief because there is usually an upper limit to circuit breaker relief available to a parcel holder, taxpayers must file to obtain this relief, only homeowner property receives the circuit breaker relief (although some states extend the assistance to farm property), and relief is conditioned on income of the property owner.

Circuit breakers are flexible and easily administrable in conjunction with the state income tax. They can be focused on families in greatest need of relief and, furthermore, are financed from state, not local, revenue. They do, however, provide no incentive for improved property tax administration and may encourage greater use of local property taxes as some property tax costs are shifted to the state. Those problems are probably swamped by the contribution the circuit breaker makes to the equity of the property tax.

Deferrals. An additional relief device applicable to the special property tax problems of elderly property owners and to farmers on the borders of metropolitan areas is tax deferral. With this mechanism, individuals whose properties values have risen dramatically through no fault of their own are permitted to pay tax on the basis of historic values, with records kept on the difference between that payment and what it would have been at full property value. That difference is not forgiven, but rather is deferred to a later time. In the case of the agricultural property, it is collected when the farmland converts to a different (higher value) use. In the case of the elderly individual, the deferred tax becomes a claim against that individual's estate. These recaptures can be complete or partial and interest may or may not be changed; state approaches vary. The tax deferral relieves special property tax burdens without creating the problems that circuit breakers and special exemptions can often create; they can relieve without special subsidization—a rare combination in tax policy.

Fractional assessment and assessment uniformity. The heart of the property tax is assessment, the determination of a property value for distribution of total tax burden. Valuation may or may not be tied to current market value (defined as the transaction price for a parcel that would emerge in exchange between a willing and knowledgeable buyer and a willing and knowledgeable seller) by the prevailing property tax law and, even where it is, prevailing assessment practices may cause substantial difference between market and assessed values. For example, according to the 1977 Census of Governments the national median assessment ratio (assessed value to market value) for single-family (nonfarm houses) was 31.6 percent in 1976.[8] State medians ranged from a high of 78.1 percent in Oregon to a low of 3.1 percent in South Carolina. The former legally assesses at 100 percent of market value; the latter, at 2.5 to 4 percent of fair market value for residences (since 1976).[9]

Under normal circumstances the overall assessment ratio has little impact on absolute property tax burdens, because assessment levels can be counteracted by differences in the statutory tax rate. For instance, suppose a municipality seeks $5,000,000 from its property tax and that the market value of taxable property is $80,000,000. If the assessment ratio is 100 percent, a property tax rate of $6.25 per $100 assessed value will yield the desired money. If the assessment ratio is 50 percent, a property tax rate of $12.50 per $100 assessed value will yield the desired revenue. Low assessment ratios will produce compensating statutory rate adjustments.

Fractional assessment creates inequities and other complications, not inadequate revenue. These problems are, in fact, the major practical problems with the property tax. First, low assessment ratios increase the likelihood of unfair individual assessments, because an individual parcel holder will probably be unaware of any overassessment. Suppose the legal assessment standard is one third of market value, but the prevailing practice is 20 percent. If a parcel worth about $40,000 is assessed at $10,000, an unwary owner would believe that he has a favorable assessment: the tax assessor has valued the property far below the

---

[8] The single family, nonfarm home is used as a benchmark for assessment evaluation because almost every assessing district contains several of that class and that grouping tends to be more homogenous than other property types.

[9] U.S. Bureau of Census, *Census of Governments 1977*, vol. 2, *Taxable Property Values and Assessment-Sales Price Ratios* (Washington, D.C.: U.S. Government Printing Office, 1978).

market value and, should the parcel owner know about legal standards, even below the one third value standard. In fact, the parcel is overassessed—a 25 percent ratio compared to the prevailing 20 percent—so the parcel will bear an artificially high effective tax rate. Unless the parcel owner is sophisticated about the ways of property taxation, he will never realize the inequity.[10] As John Shannon puts it, "the lower the assessment level, the larger becomes the administrative graveyard in which the assessor can bury his mistakes."[11]

A second general problem is the impairment of overall fiscal legislation that fractional assessment can bring. Fractional assessment can make state-imposed property tax rate ceilings and debt limits linked to assessed value more restrictive than intended. Many states limit local debt to, for instance, 2 percent of assessed value. If assessment ratios have fallen over time, as is often the case, that limit becomes artificially restrictive and creates extra incentive to avoid those debt limits. Further, the practice can cause uneven distributions of any state property tax rate across local areas with differing assessment ratios. The effective state property tax rate is higher in areas with high assessment ratios than in other areas. Finally, state grant assistance is frequently distributed in formulas which are keyed to local assessed value: the lower the assessed value in an area, the greater the amount of state aid. Fractional assessment can obviously distort that distribution, so states typically develop equalization multipliers to get assessed values to a common assessment level for aid purposes: if an area has an assessment ratio of 25 percent and the statewide standard is 50 percent, its assessed value would be doubled for aid formula calculations. These equalization multipliers may or may not be applied to individual parcel values for tax bill computation. If rates are flexible and all parcels in a taxing area receive the same multiplier, the process makes no difference for those bills.

The major difficulty with fractional assessment occurs, however, when assessment ratios of parcels within a taxing area differ. When this occurs, as it does to some extent in all systems, the effective tax rate is no longer uniform and similarly situated properties bear different property tax burdens solely because of the assessment system. Thus, if property A is assessed at 30 percent of value, and property B is assessed at 20 percent, a property tax of $10.00 per $100 of assessed value translates into an effective rate of $3 per $100 of value on property A and $2

---

[10] There is an extra pitfall in the process. The legal standard is 33⅓ percent; the parcel is valued at 25 percent. Some appeal mechanisms suggest that the appropriate action is an *increase* in assessed value to the legal standard.

[11] John Shannon, "Conflict between State Assessment Law and Local Assessment Practice," in *Property Taxation —USA,* ed. Richard W. Lindholm (Madison: University of Wisconsin Press, 1969), p. 45.

per $100 on property B. No tax should be so capricious. Unfortunately, property taxes do show such dispersion in actual operation. The coefficient of dispersion (CD) provides a measure of the extent of dispersion (or the absence of uniformity) in assessment ratios and, hence, the extent to which effective property tax rates vary within a taxing unit. The CD—the average percentage by which individual assessment ratios deviate from the median assessment ratio—equals

$$CD = \left[\frac{\sum\limits_{i=1}^{n} |A_i - M|}{n} \div M \right] \cdot 100 \quad \text{where}$$

A_i = the assessment ratio for an individual property parcel, M = the median assessment ratio for all parcels sampled; and n = the number of parcels examined. The following example illustrates CD computation.

Parcels	Assessed value	Market value	Assessment ratio	Absolute dispersion
A	$15,000	$30,000	0.50	.10
B	20,000	30,000	0.67	.07
C	8,000	20,000	0.40	.20
D	30,000	40,000	0.75	.15
E	15,000	25,000	0.60	0.
				0.52

Median assessment ratio = 0.60
Sum of absolute dispersions = 0.52
Average absolute dispersion = 0.104
Coefficient of dispersion = 17.3

If all parcels were assessed at the same ratio, the CD would be zero. The CD of 17.3 means that roughly half of the properties in the sampled jurisdiction fall within a range of 17.3 percent above or below the median assessment ratio. In practical terms, it means that equally situated properties will pay substantially different effective tax rates. In the above example, property D will pay an effective tax rate which is 87.5 percent higher than the rate paid by property C, simply because of lack of uniformity in the assessment process.

Fluctuations in property market conditions make it impossible to maintain complete uniformity of assessment ratios at all times. A national investigation of property assessment by the International Association of Assessing Officers suggested performance standards:

> Coefficients of dispersion for residential properties should generally range between 5 and 15 percent. In areas of similar single-family residential properties, coefficients closer to 5 percent are attainable. In older, dissimi-

lar areas, a coefficient at the upper end of this range might indicate good performance. A similar range in coefficients of dispersion should be attainable for multifamily and other income-producing properties. The market for vacant land, however, is much more volatile and, therefore, difficult to predict. Coefficients of dispersion in the area of 20 percent may therefore indicate good performance.[12]

The most recent federal survey of assessment quality, however, shows that this standard is not regularly achieved, as Table 8–1 shows. In fact,

TABLE 8–1
Distribution of selected local areas by coefficients of intra-area dispersion based on median assessment–sales price ratios, for previously occupied single-family (nonfarm) houses: 1966, 1971, and 1976 (cumulative percentages)

Coefficient of intra-area dispersion (percent)	All selected areas			Area population 50,000 or more			Area population less than 50,000		
	1966	1971	1976	1966	1971	1976	1966	1971	1976
Less than 10.0	7.6	6.7	6.9	4.4	3.7	3.5	9.8	8.8	9.1
Less than 15.0	28.2	24.6	22.1	80.2	22.7	15.7	26.8	26.0	26.1
Less than 20.0	53.4	48.9	42.3	60.8	52.1	36.5	48.4	46.6	45.8
Less than 25.0	69.1	67.0	59.4	76.7	72.3	59.0	64.0	63.2	59.6
Less than 30.0	80.4	79.1	71.2	88.0	84.4	70.8	75.4	75.3	71.4
Less than 40.0	90.2	90.9	86.3	94.7	94.4	88.8	87.3	88.4	84.7
Less than 50.0	95.7	96.1	93.4	98.2	98.3	94.3	94.1	94.6	92.8
50.0 or more	4.3	3.9	6.6	1.8	1.7	6.7	5.9	5.4	7.2

Source: 1977 Census of Governments, vol. 2, Taxable Property Values and Assessment–Sales Price Ratios, p. 21.

success in attaining the quality goal has declined in recent years. The percentage of areas with a CD below 20 declined from 53.4 in 1966 to 42.3 in 1976. Small declines in quality appeared for small population areas, but major deterioration appeared for larger areas. In 1966, 60.8 percent of those areas had CDs better than 20; by 1976, that percentage had declined to 36.5. The median coefficient of inter-area dispersion across areas studied for the 1977 Census of Governments was 22.0. State medians ranged from a low of 12.1 in Connecticut to a high of 48.9 in Wyoming. Only 14 states (California, Colorado, Connecticut, Florida, Hawaii, Iowa, Kentucky, Maryland, Massachusetts, Michigan, New Hampshire, Rhode Island, Virginia, and Wisconsin) had median CDs below 20 in that year. This lack of uniformity is the greatest problem for operation of the property tax.

---

[12] Research and Technical Services Department, International Association of Assessing Offices, Understanding Real Property Assessment—An Executive Summary for Local Government Officials (Chicago: IAAO, 1979), p. 8.

Classification.   Several state property tax laws are structured to apply different effective rates to different types of property: their tax rates are classified, rather than uniform.[13] Classification presumes that certain property classes have superior taxpaying capability than other classes. Any validity this presumption contains has small significance for tax design because tax-bearing capability varies dramatically within classes, often to a greater extent than variation between classes. Thus, there are affluent and not so affluent homeowners, prosperous and poor farmers, and profitable and bankrupt businesses. The classification systems, however, treat each ownership class or property type as if all units in that class were alike. Furthermore, the basis of classification is more likely to be political clout or the expected ease of shifting the tax to someone else than any reasonable basis for allocation of appropriate tax burdens. Thus, agricultural and residential property receive favorable treatment while public utilities are harshly treated. There is little logic to the pattern.

Classification can be accomplished by either variation in assessment ratios or variation in statutory rates. They both can produce the same effective rate pattern, as Table 8–2 shows. Classification by statutory

TABLE 8–2
Illustration of property classification by statutory rates and assessment ratios

Classes of property	Rate classification			Ratio classification		
	Statutory rate	Assessment ratio	Effective rate	Statutory rate	Assessment ratio	Effective rate
Owner-occupied housing	2.00	50%	1.00	4.00	25%	1.00
Farms	1.00	50%	.50	4.00	12.5%	.50
Commercial and industrial	4.00	50%	2.00	4.00	50%	2.00
Public utilities	8.00	50%	4.00	4.00	100%	4.00

rate variation is more straightforward and interferes less with the assessment process. If classification is to be adopted, that approach is probably preferable.

Limits, controls, and property tax relief.   A final element in the structure of property taxes is the set of extraordinary limits and controls—beyond the normal process of rate setting—which establish a special structure for property tax operation. A categorization of controls appears in Figure 8–4. A number of the special controls date from the 1970s, although several have more lengthy heritages. The "tax revolt,"

---

[13] These taxes still presume uniformity *within* property classes.

FIGURE 8–4
Property tax control structures and their effects

Type of limit	Example	Limit effects on		
		Property tax rate	Property tax levies	Expenditures
Statutory property tax rate limit	Cities limited to rate of $5.00/$100 assessed value.	Same ceiling statewide.	Can increase with assessed value or with rate increase for units not at ceiling.	Same as levies, plus depends on other revenue sources.
Property tax rate freeze	Cities limited to rate applicable in 1978.	Ceiling varies across state.	Can increase only with assessed value.	Same as above.
Property tax levy limit	Cities 1981 property tax levy cannot exceed 105% of their 1980 levy.	Depends on assessed value change.	Constrained to limit.	Depends on use of other sources.
Local expenditure lid	City total appropriations in 1980 cannot exceed 110% of 1979 appropriations.	Depends on assessed value change and changes in other revenue.	Depends on extent of other revenue sources.	Explicitly controlled (new sources of revenue reduce property tax levy).

Source: Based on Advisory Commission on Intergovernmental Relations, State Limitations on Local Taxes and Expenditures, A-64, February 1977 (Washington, D.C.: U.S. Government Printing Office), p. 36.

especially Proposition 13 in California and related referenda in other states from 1978 through 1980, was partly the product of high and rising effective property tax rates on owner-occupied housing created by demands for local public service, waste in local government, and special exemptions provided other property types. A large part of that rebellion, however, surely reflected irritation with government in general and the feeling of powerlessness to do anything about federal or state taxes— those taxes rose without any statutory rate increase for which elected representatives were responsible. The property tax was another matter: the rate had to be established each year, so it presented an ideal focal point for those concerns. It became the lightening rod for government finance nationwide during the period of taxpayer discontent.

Property taxes have been subject to extraordinary limitations at least since the Great Depression of the 1930s. Those limits were, however, traditionally controls on statutory tax rates. These controls appeared ineffective as assessed values increased dramatically, both in total and for individual property parcels, during the inflationary 1970s. Governments could adopt property tax rates no higher than those of the prior year—certainly no higher than the legal ceilings—and obtain dramatically increased revenue because of higher assessed values. Property owners could find themselves with increased property tax bills at the stable property tax rate if their property had been reassessed to reflect the higher property values which inflation and the demand for real estate brought. Thus, the rate limit and freeze approach seemed powerless to control such increases.

The approach taken in the 1970s was the levy or expenditure limit, a control drive which capped collections, not the rate applied to the tax base. That approach does constrain the growth of government activity and prevents increases in assessed value from automatic translation into higher tax collections and individual tax bills. With a levy freeze, a general assessed value increase will require a reduction in tax rates to be consistent with that freeze. For example, suppose a control law permits 5 percent levy growth from one year to the next and that assessed value increases by 8 percent. Rate computations might look like the following table:

	Assessed value	Levy	Property tax rate
Budget year 1	$5,000,000	$250,000	$5/$100
Budget year 2	5,400,000	262,500	$4.86/$100

With this control structure, property tax levy ceilings will dominate the budget process: maximum growth in the levy establishes the budget size and total budget requests must keep within the limit. As soon as assessed value figures are known, property tax rates may be computed because law establishes the total levy. The only unknown is the manner in which that total will be appropriated among operating units. In this case the budget total is not made up of its operating components; rather, the budget total is divided among the operating components and one extra dollar provided one agency is truly a dollar not available to any other agency. The total budget cannot expand to accommodate any additions.

Limits of the 1970s are obviously more stringent than the earlier rate controls.[14] They have led local governments to adopt a rather consistent set of responses when they are applied. First, governments have reacted by trying to get other governments to take over services they have been providing or to get nonprofit organizations to accept those burdens. If the approach succeeds, the service in question will be provided, but the controlled government will retain the previously committed resources for other activities. Second, governments have sought increased intergovernmental aid (grants, shared taxes, etc.) to continue services without the use of increasingly scarce local resources. This search is particularly intense to finance mandated services, that is, services which the government provides largely because it has been required to do so by another government. If that government both restricts taxing powers and mandates services, the intergovernmental tension is especially intense. The quest for grants is particularly accelerated when spending from such revenue is placed outside any control structure, as is often the case. And finally, governments search for charge and nonproperty tax revenues outside the limits. In some instances, the charges are merely disguised property taxes (fire or police protection fees based on property characteristics, for instance), but they can be welcome additions which improve both the efficiency and the equity of service finance. Expanded use of legitimate charges is, in fact, the most attractive side effect of the new limitation movement.

Conclusion

Almost by default, the property tax is the predominant tax source of local government. While it represents an opportunity to tax accumulated wealth not offered by levies on other bases, that advantage is overshadowed by haphazard and capricious assessment of items in the tax base. Because the tax applies to values defined by the application of

---

[14] The exception is for governments experiencing assessed value decline. A levy control for these units permits the accommodating rate increases which rate control would prevent.

a regulation, not values from a market transaction, assessment will be troublesome and will require special attention. Most problems with the property tax outside of valuation can be largely resolved by circuit breakers, deferrals, and the like, so it would be unfortunate if the advantages of the tax were sacrificed solely because of unwillingness to improve administration.

CASES FOR DISCUSSION

A. The state of Kentucky provides a special assessment basis for farmland for the property tax. In essence, such land is valued not at current market value, the standard there for other property, but at its agricultural use value. The following article, excerpted from the *Louisville Courier-Journal,* describes problems with that special treatment.

Consider these questions:

1. Why did the state prescribe a special assessment basis for farmland?
2. What valuation approach would the proposed agricultural assessment process use? Why not one of the other two?
3. How did the process become a loophole? Was that surprising?

Panel Tries to Decide How to Define Farmland and How to Assess It Fairly

BY JAMES R. RUSSELL
COURIER-JOURNAL *Staff Writer*

FRANKFORT, Ky.—A legislative subcommittee struggled yesterday to assure farmers that they won't be taxed off their land and to close loopholes for the rich hobby farmer.

But two basic questions remain unanswered: What is farmland, and how do you assess it?

"Some people," said state Sen. John M. Berry Jr., D-New Castle, "are receiving the benefits of farmland as-

Source: From article in *Louisville Courier Journal,* June 13, 1975. Copyright © 1975. The Courier-Journal. Reprinted with permission.

sessments who don't deserve it, and we're trying to protect those people who are trying to make a living out of it (farming)."

And Revenue Commissioner Maurice P. Carpenter, who sat in the subcommittee meeting, added: "Frankly, I think some (farm assessments) are to high, but we took it on ourselves to implement the constitutional amendment and many PVAs (property valuation administrators) are using their own judgments, and you can imagine that out of 120 counties, what you'll come up with."

Carpenter also said, "I believe that there are no pure agricultural sales anymore—there's an investment thought in all of them."

And therein lies the problem. The constitutional amendment, passed in 1969 and implemented by the 1970 Kentucky General Assembly, made special provisions for assessing agricultural land. Its intent was to prevent farmland from being taxed for anything other than agricultural uses, as long as it was indeed, a farm.

The amendment supposedly protected farmers from artificially high land values caused by speculators, developers, weekend hobby farmers and sideline investments by wealthy professional people.

The intent of the amendment is not being carried out, Berry said yesterday, noting that fair market value based on comparable sales is being used to assess farmland. And that defeats the purpose of earlier constitutional and legislative efforts.

The "income producing capability" of farmland should be the basis for tax assessment, members of the subcommittee agreed. "And we need a law to require that it be used to determine the value of farmland," Berry said.

* * * * *

Working over a rough bill draft yesterday, agricultural land was defined—tentatively—as 10 contiguous acres, including improvements which are necessary to produce farm income. The residence would not be included in this portion of the farm assessment.

The draft also would define farmland as yielding at least $1,000 per year during the two years immediately preceding the tax year. For horticultural land, the requirements are the same, except only five acres are needed to qualify.

Tentatively—and apparently very tentatively—value would be figured this way:

Each year on Jan 1 the University of Kentucky College of Agriculture would determine a five-year average net farm income per acre on each county and give that information to the Department of Revenue.

The Revenue Department would "capitalize the net farm income per acre at a rate equal to the average interest cost for money during the previous five years." (Thus, if the average interest rate were 8 percent and the average per acre net income were $40, the land value would be $320 per acre.)

This information would be sent to the county PVAs, who would multiply the average net farm income per acre by the number of acres in a farm.

But because a county can have farmland ranging from excellent to poor, the local PVA will have discretionary power to adjust the average net farm income figure to coincide with the individual farm.

This adjustment would be determined by a number of factors, including the type of land—tillable, pasture, woodland—and the land's fertility and its risk of flooding.

But the business of getting a true picture of land value through a formula of income-producing capability is still complex and unresolved.

B. The following case describes some conditions often found in urban areas.

Consider these questions:

1. According to the standard criteria, how is this assessment system doing?
2. What sort of city program would you develop?
3. What information would you gather and how would you use it?
4. Where would you get your information?
5. What political factors must be considered?
6. What would you emphasize about the program?
7. How would you handle inquiries from the press?

The city of Western Hills is an extremely wealthy suburb with a population of approximately 40,000. It is primarily a "bedroom community" in that most workers residing in Western Hills commute seven miles to downtown Adel which is a major industrial center of the mideastern United States. Both cities are in Steele County.

Since Western Hills has long been considered a prestigious place to live, settlement came early and the city is currently 95 percent developed. This development is primarily single-family dwellings with very few retail establishments. The community borders Adel and is otherwise surrounded by other suburbs. Consequently, there is almost no chance of substantial new growth.

During the past half century, Western Hills has prided itself on its good municipal government. The city operates under the council-manager system and the current city manager has served for the past 15 years. His municipal staff is primarily young, well trained, and experienced. The finance director is quite competent.

Western Hills receives half of its revenue from the property tax. The specific breakdown follows:

Source	Percent of total revenue
1. Real estate tax revenue	50%
2. Earned income tax	20
3. Transfers from other governments	15
4. Interest, licenses, fees, service charges, etc.	12
5. Real estate transfer tax (1 percent of the sale price. All sales must be reported for proper deed transfer.)	3

The city council, city manager, and finance director are concerned with the lack of growth in the city's assessed valuation. The reason for their concern is illustrated in the following table:

Western Hills is still *the* place to live in the Adel area, and home prices have been increasing accordingly.

The county performs the assessment function for all units of government. Each parcel of property is reas-

Fiscal year	Total assessed valuation	Percent increase in the consumer price index
19X1–X2	$158,400,493	5.7%
19X2–X3	159,444,545	2.5
19X3–X4	159,705,525	4.1
19X4–X5	165,573,670	7.4
19X5–X6	165,250,000	12.6 (estimated)

This table indicates that the consumer price index is increasing at a substantially faster pace than the city's assessed valuation. With Western Hill's heavy reliance on the real estate tax, that could result in severe financial constraints.

Further investigation shows that the tax millage for the 19X5–X6 budget was increased from 13.15 mills to 16.15 mills. (The state ceiling is 20 mills per dollar of assessed value.) The 19X2 Census of Governments reports a coefficient of dispersion for single-family housing of 22.0 and a median assessment sales price ratio of 39.8 for Steele County; data for Western Hills are unavailable.

Western Hills is not suffering from any form of urban blight. Instead, property values seem to be increasing. Real estate agents maintain that

sessed every third year. The current market value is the assessment standard; by law, assessments are required to be at 50 percent of that value. Any property that sells is immediately revalued on the basis of that price, regardless of the reassessment cycle. The County Assessor's Office tries to do a good job, but it lacks skilled manpower. The office uses no electronic data processing equipment. The entire county assessment system is not likely to radically change; the assessors apparently will cooperate in any city program.

The city manager and finance director will provide reasonable funds for a program designed to improve the city fiscal structure. Temporary summer employees (college students) are available.

Tax administration

THE COLLECTION PROCESS

Collection of revenue uses resources without improving the condition of society. The objective in administration is thus to extract the desired revenues at minimum collection cost, while maintaining desired horizontal and vertical equity in the collection process, as outlined in Chapter 6. This resource use includes both administrative cost (the cost to government of collecting the tax) and compliance cost (the cost to private firms and individuals of complying with the tax law). Focus on either cost element alone may not produce desirable results for society if the relationship between those cost elements differs among taxes. Those differences can be highlighted more clearly after consideration of the general steps involved in tax administration.

Administration

Tax administration includes six general steps: inventory preparation, base valuation, tax computation and collection, audit, appeal-protest, and enforcement.[1] While the specific activities in any step vary accord-

---

[1] These operations are part of a larger system described in John L. Mikesell, "Administration and the Public Revenue System: A View of Tax Administration," *Public Administration Review,* 34 (November/December 1974).

ing to the logic of the particular tax, the common elements will be considered here. The initial step is preparation of an inventory of tax eligibles. For a real property tax system, the physical inventory includes land and structures identified within the taxing area, accompanied by ownership for those items. Particular properties are called parcels; the list of parcels (the tax roll) is the basis for valuation and bill distribution. The inventory process for sales and income taxes involves the development of a mailing list for tax forms. That list later serves as a master file for comparison with a list of those who have paid as the starting point for delinquency control. The inventory list may be on cards, on microforms, or in machine-readable form (tape or disk); modern revenue systems typically use computer storage of account or property parcel data. The inventory of eligibles provides the foundation for the administration of any tax structure. A government without such an inventory has no basis for delinquency control and probably administers a system of contribution, not taxation.

Second, individual holdings of the tax base must be valued for assignment of tax. For some taxes, particularly individual income and sales taxes, base evaluation involves a compilation of transactions (purchase or sale of goods, services, or resources) over the tax period, largely a compilation of data from accounting files. Property tax valuation, however, is much more complex as it requires construction of an exchange value for parcels of property which have not been sold in the taxing period: all values are estimates made according to some valuation standard. The process is clearly the most difficult and most critical step in the administration of a real property tax system.

Computation and remittance or collection of tax due is the third step in tax administration. For taxes following the sales or income pattern (taxpayer-active or self-assessed taxes), this step requires the taxpayer (or the taxpayer's agent, for example, employer, accountant, etc.) to apply a statutory rate schedule to the tax base previously valued and then submit a tax return, including any payment due, to the revenue collector. Returns are required at intervals ranging from annual to monthly, depending on the tax involved and, often, on the size of payment expected (large taxpayers must file returns more frequently than do small taxpayers). The cash flow profile of the collecting unit increases the opportunity for idle fund investment (see Chapter 13). Processing these returns to record and promptly deposit revenues received, ensure that return information is appropriately managed, operate delinquency control systems, and maintain account history is a critical activity for revenue departments. Figure 9–1 illustrates the general flow of returns in the collection stage. The revenue authorities compare returns received against the master file of tax eligibles to determine what accounts are delinquent; those accounts are contacted

FIGURE 9—1
Illustration of tax return processing flow

From taxpayer

Mailroom — Sorts by type of tax (sometimes by likely size of payment) according to envelope code.
Opens envelopes.
Routes sorted mail to appropriate processing flow.

Validation and batching — Verifies return agreement with check amount.
Stamps identification number on check and return.
Returns and checks split into batches.*
Returns and checks microfilmed.

Deposit — Batch totals run on checks and separated returns.
Deposits prepared and made.

Data entry — Desired data on return keyed manually.
Data entry verified (either rekeying, check digits, or computer check for internal consistency of return).
Computer audit of return.
Enter return data into main account file.
Returns either filed (by batch received or by account number) or destroyed (if microfilm or computer record is legally sufficient).

Other administrative activities: delinquency control, audit, etc.

* A batch is simply a group of returns (usually 50 or 100) which goes through the processing system together. For record control, each return has a batch and item number stamped on it: number 1050-04 might refer to the 4th return in the 1,050th batch processed.

to obtain returns and, ultimately, any tax due. Initial account contacts are often made by telephone (called "phone power" by state tax administrators). Those contacts are highly successful, but later contacts are usually made in person by field representatives.

The computation-collection process for the real property tax is substantially different.[2] Rates are computed in the balance between expenditures to be financed and the available assessed value base. Tax rates

---

[2] Personal property taxes often have taxpayer-active elements, including valuation, recordkeeping, and returns filed by the taxpayer.

must be annually established on the basis of tax base totals. The rate setting follows the simple equation

$$\text{Rate} = \frac{\text{Levy}}{\text{Tax base (or total assessed value)}}$$

where the levy is the total dollars to be extracted from the property tax (often, the total budget of the jurisdiction less estimated nonproperty tax revenue). Thus, if a city levies a property tax of $4 million on its assessed value of $38,500,000, its tax rate will be $10.39 per $100 of assessed value. The property tax operates with a lag—the property tax levy for the 1985 calendar year, to be paid by owners in April and October 1985, would be applicable to assessments made in March 1984—so official rates are not set on an estimated base, although preliminary figures may be prepared before official tallies are made. The resulting property tax rate applies to all property parcels within the taxing jurisdiction. A parcel with an assessed value of $9,500 would have a bill of $987.05 at the just-computed rate. Tax authorities compute tax bills and submit the completed bill to the taxpayer; the taxpayer simply pays the tax owed in one or two specified installments. In many instances, the owner of a residential parcel does not even see the tax bill; the mortgage lender receives the tax bill and makes payment from a tax escrow account into which the owner has made monthly payment. Thus, in the real property tax system, the taxpayer is passive. Administration by the taxing authorities eliminates compliance effort. Delinquency problems with the property tax do not involve failure to file, but rather are failure to pay a submitted bill. Delinquency thus immediately becomes an enforcement problem.

Audit, the fourth administrative stage, seeks to ensure substantial taxpayer compliance with the tax law in a voluntary compliance system. It thus protects honest taxpayers, taxpayers who have voluntarily complied with tax liability. If there were no audit process for self-assessed taxes, the premium would be on dishonesty, as taxpayers who do not submit taxes would have a competitive advantage over any taxpayers who were paying liabilities due. Audit maintains the balance between honesty and dishonesty by making it likely that the dishonest will be caught and appropriately punished. Accounts may be selected for audit for three general reasons: to obtain revenue, to enforce the voluntary compliance principle, and to measure administrative effectiveness. Because of the vast amounts of revenue which can be obtained in audits from taxpayer misinterpretation of complex tax laws, administrators are often tempted to select accounts solely on revenue production. Unfortunately, that practice will typically lead to audit of the same accounts over and over because the accounts remain large and complex. That predictability can reduce voluntary compliance by other accounts. Thus, accounts can appropriately be selected to gain notoriety for the audit, a process which could reduce audit recovery somewhat but which should improve collections produced voluntarily. Finally, some accounts may be selected at random, partly for voluntary compliance generation, partly to evaluate the success of tax administration, and partly to improve the criteria used for the selection of returns for audit. Such is the nature of the Tax Compliance Measurement Program (TCMP) of the Internal Revenue Service. There is no normal audit process in real property taxation: the real property tax system involves no compliance effort by the taxpayer. There may be performance reviews of assessment uniformity (for instance, state preparation of coefficients of dispersion), but this is different from the audit logic.

The fifth step in the tax administration is appeal or protest. Tax statutes typically contain many uncertainties (gray areas), some because the legislature slipped up and some because the legislature felt that tax administrators could better define technical points than it could. Appeals and protests help clarify these uncertainties, so they do play a valuable role in the lawmaking process. Property tax appeals, however, typically occur at a different point in the flow of administration than do appeals of other taxes. Property tax appeal is on the valuation of the property tax base, because that is the sole point ordinarily open to objection. Thus, property tax appeal follows valuation and comes before computation of liabilities and collection. Appeal after a property tax bill has been submitted to a taxpayer ordinarily is too late. Other taxes are appealed after tax payment has been made, or at least after auditors have disagreed with the payment made. Because the principal actor in these taxes is the taxpayer, not the taxing authority, appeal or protest must occur after the taxing authority objects to the manner in which the taxpayer has performed his portion of the collection process.

The final step in the process is enforcement, the step used when other remedies have not produced an appropriate payment of tax due. Most taxpayers will not reach this step, as it is the last resort for protection of the voluntary compliance system. Enforcement of sales and income taxes involves action against the income or wealth of the taxpayer: seizure and sale of assets, attachment of wages, attachment of individual or business bank accounts, closure of business establishments, and so on. Real property taxes are, however, traditionally enforced by action against the property upon which the tax is levied, not the owner of the thing (the tax is *in rem*). The enforcement remedy is sale of the property. Tax sales are politically unattractive, so many governments are understandably reluctant to conduct such sales. As a consequence, areas of older cities may contain substantial blocks of property which no one clearly owns because of substantial delinquent taxes. If assessment systems do not keep up with neighborhood decline and if tax sales are infrequent, the delinquent taxes may even exceed current market value of the property. In that case, no one will acquire the property at a tax sale because the amount required for sale is greater than the value of the property. This orphan property thus adds to the general decline of already depressed areas as it becomes a haven for derelicts, a deteriorating eyesore, and a constant fire hazard.

Total collection cost

The total cost of tax collection includes both the cost incurred by the government in administering the tax and the cost incurred by taxpayers and their agents in satisfying legal requirements of that tax (excluding taxes actually paid). Because both components of collection cost use resources, neither can be ignored. While a tax agency may reduce its budget problems by shifting greater collection cost to individuals (as with requiring individuals to pick up return forms from revenue agency offices instead of mailing them to tax eligibles), there is no reason to believe that such practices reduce collection cost. In fact, loss of specialization and scale with such practices may actually cause total collection cost to increase. The decision focus properly is on collection cost, the combination of administrative and compliance activities.

The combined costs are particularly critical when comparing real property taxes and the major nonproperty taxes. The nonproperty taxes are largely taxpayer-administered: the individual or firm maintain records of potential taxable transactions, tabulates the tax base, computes appropriate liability, and makes payments at appropriate times. Government agencies concentrate on partial coverage audits to ensure substantial compliance with the law. Administrative effort seeks voluntary compliance with the law, not direct agency collection. The taxpayer bears the bulk of total collection cost. Administration for voluntary compliance would have low administrative cost and high compliance costs.

The real property tax, on the other hand, does not rest on voluntary compliance.[3] A government agent maintains parcel records, values these property parcels for tax distribution, computes the liability for

---

[3] Property taxes could be operated on a self-assessed basis. Some states, furthermore, operate their personal property tax on a self-assessment basis with audit to ensure appropriate self-valuation. An operating concept is described in D. Holland and W. Vaughn, "An Evaluation of Self-Assessment under a Property Tax," in *The Property Tax and Its Administration,* ed. A. D. Lynn, Jr. (Madison, Wis.: University of Wisconsin Press, 1969), pp. 79–118.

each parcel, and distributes tax bills to parcel owners; the taxpayer is passive. Moreover, when property taxes are used by overlapping units of government (city, county, special districts, school districts, etc.) the taxpayer typically receives a single bill for all property taxes, to reduce even further the compliance requirement. Unless the taxpayer appeals an assessment, payment is the only taxpayer activity. In the normal scheme, total collection cost equals administrative cost. Thus, it is not appropriate to compare the cost of administering a real property tax with the cost of administering a nonproperty tax.

TABLE 9–1
Administrative cost estimates for major taxes

Tax base (fiscal year)	Administrative cost as percent of net revenue
Individual income tax:	
Federal (1978)	0.70
Colorado (1979)	0.64
Michigan (1978)	0.64
Corporate income tax:	
Federal (1978)	0.12
Michigan (single business) (1978)	0.42
Sales and use:	
Colorado (1979)	0.60
Michigan (1978)	0.37
California (1979)	0.69

Sources: California State Board of Equalization, *Annual Report, 1978–1979;* Colorado Department of Revenue, *Annual Report, 1979;* Michigan State Treasurer, *Annual Report, 1977–78;* and U.S. Internal Revenue Service, *Annual Report, 1978.* Federal estimates are computed by allocating costs to taxes according to returns filed, audits done, or—where available—directly to the tax (printing Form 1040, for instance). The reported overall federal cost to net revenue percentage is 0.49.

Table 9–1 presents administrative cost data for a selection of taxes administered in the United States. Table 9–2 illustrates similar data for a handful of other countries. Because most revenue agencies administer more than one tax and, in fact, undertake some nonrevenue functions, the joint cost allocation problem makes completely accurate cost estimates impossible. The data here must thus be viewed as simply estimates prepared through reasonably consistent allocation schemes. None of these broad-based taxes show administration costs above 1 percent of revenue produced. In comparison, the cost of administering a good quality property tax system has been estimated at around 1.5

TABLE 9–2
International comparison of tax administration costs as percentage of collections

	1973	1976–1977
United Kingdom	1.71	
Canada	0.91	1.01
Sweden	1.00	
Japan	1.87	
Philippines		1.10
Australia.....................		0.96
United States	0.48	0.56

Source: U.S., Congress, House, Committee on Ways and Means, Subcommittee on Oversight, *Underground Economy, Hearings,* 96th Cong., 1st sess., July 16, September 10, October 9 and 11, 1979 (U.S. Government Printing Office, 1980), p. 125.

percent of collections, substantially more than the cost estimates presented for other taxes.[4]

There is, however, a critical distinction between the property tax and the other major taxes. That difference is the extent to which voluntary compliance generates revenue with minimal direct government action. For the major nonproperty taxes, most revenue comes from taxpayer actions alone; very little money comes from enforcement, audit, or related revenue department actions. This pattern is illustrated in the following compilation of 1979 New Jersey data:[5]

Source	Percent of collections
Taxpayer accounting (billings for penalty/interest, bad checks)	0.30%
Contacts (delinquency phone calls, letters)	0.05
Field (delinquency investigations)	0.33
Special procedures (bankruptcies, liens, etc.)	0.68
Office audits	0.52
Field audits	0.89
Voluntary compliance..................................	97.23
	100.00%

---

[4] Ronald B. Welch, "Characteristics and Feasibility of High Quality Assessment Administration," in *Property Tax Reform,* ed. IAAO (Chicago: International Association of Assessing Officers, 1973), p. 50.

[5] New Jersey Department of Taxation, *Annual Report, 1979* and unpublished materials.

That pattern is not unusual. Thus, 2 percent of total Michigan collections, 1.69 percent of California sales and use tax collections (1975), and 1.67 percent of Internal Revenue Service collections[6] come from direct enforcement actions, including audits, penalties and interest, delinquency collection, etc. Most of the revenue comes from voluntary compliance; taxpayers—not government agencies—bear the bulk of the total collection cost (recordkeeping, return preparation, accounting and legal fees, etc.). Those compliance costs vary substantially among taxpayers, and estimates are hazardous. It is not unreasonable to expect that, for most taxpaying units, compliance cost is at least twice as large as administrative cost.[7]

For the property tax, however, administrative cost is virtually the total collection cost. After allowance for the difference between taxpayer-active and taxpayer-passive characteristics, the real property tax does not appear to be an expensive tax to collect. Relative cost of collection—compliance plus administration—does not appear to be a deterrent to better quality administration. To summarize, a comparison of administrative costs across taxpayer-active- and taxpayer-passive-type tax systems will not provide useful information for public policy consideration. The focus must be on total collection cost.

ADMINISTRATIVE STRUCTURE

The administrative structure compartmentalizes responsibility for parts of the collection process. Administration will be structured in different ways in different environments. The particular structure should fit its environment; different does not automatically mean inefficient or wrong. Two structural choices are particularly significant and will be examined here: the extent of agency centralization and arrangements for collection of several taxes by a single agency.

Centralization

Several revenue agency functions may appropriately be dispersed to regional branches of that agency. Regional offices establish a useful presence in the locality for taxpayer contact and can be vital when there are concentrations of taxed entities at several locations around the taxing area. In general, regional offices appear in major cities to service

---

[6] Same sources as Table 9–1 and California State Board of Equalization, Taxable Sales in California (sales and use tax) during 1975.

[7] John F. Due, *State and Local Sales Taxation* (Chicago: Public Administration Source, 1971), pp. 313–15.

those areas.[8] The keys to dividing functions are operating efficiency of the agency, convenience for the taxpayer, and uniformity of administration. Taxpayer convenience is especially important for taxes relying on voluntary compliance; there should be no artificial barriers to the taxpayers' collection role. Following that guide, centralized activities logically include: legal interpretations (to ensure that the effective tax structure is the same everywhere), selection of accounts for audit (to ensure equal geographic treatment), return processing (to obtain scale economies), record maintenance and retention (to ensure that the effective tax structure is the same everywhere), and provision of technical specialists for assistance with special enforcement or audit tasks beyond the ordinary capacity of decentralized offices. As travel costs rise and communication technology expands, centralized activities may increase—as with the use of a central telephone bank to make initial delinquency contacts (called "phone power" by tax administrators), use of similar systems to provide taxpayer assistance during the peak income-tax filing period, or CRT terminals in regional offices to permit direct access to taxpayer files. Penniman observes that, for these general areas, "There is little conflict between taxpayer convenience and operating efficiency."[9] Decentralized activities should include those requiring taxpayer contact or special local information. Thus, regional offices may provide full-time taxpayer assistance and information, they may provide offices for auditors when preparing reports or for meetings with taxpayers, and they may be duty stations for enforcement agents dealing with recalcitrant taxpayers. The need for numbers and distribution of district offices will depend on population, area, and transportation geography of the taxing government.[10]

Integration of activities

A second organizational question is whether the taxing department will be organized on a tax-by-tax basis or on a functional basis. That is, will there be independent divisions responsible for all administration of a particular tax (return distribution, processing, auditing, enforcement, etc.) or will those functions be the organizing units with a particular step in administration of all taxes to be done by that unit? Figure 9–2 illus-

---

[8] States increasingly establish out-of-state regional offices to serve as bases for audit operations.

[9] Clara Penniman, *State Income Tax Administration* (Baltimore: John Hopkins Press, 1980), p. 91.

[10] The central office of the Maryland Sales Tax Division is in Baltimore, not the state capital (Annapolis). This is a reasonable placement in light of the economic geography of the state.

FIGURE 9–2
General forms of organization

A. Tax - by - tax organization

B. Functional organization

trates the two forms. Staff functions (personnel, data processing, research and statistics, purchasing, etc.) are almost always integrated, as
there are almost always technical or financial economies of scale to be
achieved here; the critical decisions are about the line operations in the
collection of tax revenue, including return processing, delinquency control, auditing, and enforcement. Penniman observes that the case for
integration "rests frequently on the grounds that there is (1) a large
overlap of taxpayer clientele—the same taxpayers pay several taxes,
and (2) a large overlap in the records that constitute the basic audit

information. The argument goes on to assert that auditing is auditing, collecting is collecting, without regard to the particular tax."[11] Thus, administrative and compliance cost savings logically would result by combining processes for various taxes.

On a more specific basis, the following claims for functional organization of tax department line operations are made: (1) personnel can be better used because peak times for return filing seldom are the same for all taxes; (2) taxpayer irritation can be reduced if there is a single audit for all taxes, if the taxpayer registers once for all taxes, etc.; (3) specialization can emphasize and develop general skills of personnel; and (4) audit unification will save travel costs, permit use of the same data in audit of more than one tax, and reduce time lost in gaining access to taxpayer files.

There are, however, several important disadvantages of the functional structure: (1) no one is responsible for operation and overview of particular taxes, particularly the way individual sections of the administrative process and legal structure of the tax fit together; (2) operating data (including the cost of administration) for individual taxes are frequently lost; and (3) audits are seldom truly integrated (audit selection criteria are logically and practically not the same for all taxes, audit emphasis in record systems is not the same for all taxes, and cross-training of auditors is particularly difficult). Because full audit integration has proven so difficult—and may even be logically impossible—there are major questions about the appropriateness of process integration. Nevertheless, the Internal Revenue Service is functionally integrated and states are currently shifting heavily to that structure. Because of the differences between property and nonproperty tax administration, local governments are less likely to make that merger.

REVENUE ESTIMATION

The budget process requires an estimate of revenue to be received during the budget year. That revenue figure is never certain because the economic behavior which produces revenue is not easily predictable. Best available estimates are, however, critical for budget preparation and consideration because state and local governments generally must balance their budgets and the federal government must develop stabilitization policy plans. In addition to their budget development use, revenue estimates are crucial inputs in development of both long-range fiscal plans and cash flow forecasts for idle funds management. For

---

[11] Penniman, *State Income Tax Administration,* p. 75. Some advocates forget, however, that clientele overlap breaks down with the spread of individual, as opposed to business impact, structures.

each use, the revenue estimates must be operationally accurate, recognizing that the length of the forecast and the distance of the forecast period from the present reduces the expected accuracy of the estimate. As well as providing a forecast, the methods employed may provide insights into the functioning of the economy and may be adapted to simulate alternate public policies.

Revenue departments, as repositories of the basic data for such estimates, are the natural place for such work, but, at state and local levels, seldom have the appropriate technical staff (economists and econometricians) to develop these estimates. Accordingly, the revenue agency role is provision of usable data for those making the estimates. Furthermore, openness of process and method of estimation can focus policy debates on *policy,* not on arguments about competing estimates of revenue. Many argue that the agency implementing tax policy ought not be involved in policy formation: policy formation should not be burdened by routine administration and should rise above absorption by details.

Revenue estimation uses several different approaches; seldom will all revenue sources for a single government be estimated using the same approach. The more important approaches include (1) simplistic models, (2) multiple regression techniques, (3) econometric models, (4) microsimulations, and (5) input-output models.[12] Each method has its appropriate place and applications.

Simplistic models include trend extrapolation and pure judgment or intuition. Extrapolations may be by constant increments (collections increased by $5,000 in each of the last five years, so they are estimated to increase by $5,000 this year), constant percentage change (collections increased by 5 percent in each of the last five years, so they are estimated to increase by 5 percent this year), and linear or nonlinear time trends.[13] Thus, revenue for the budget year may be estimated as an arithmetic function of time ($R = a + bt$) or as a logarithmic function of time ($\ln R = a + bt$), where R = collections from the revenue source and t = a time index. The choice would depend on which is judged most likely to produce a reasonable estimate. Many local governments use this approach because they lack the data on the local economy requisite for the development of more complex models. States often use the ap-

---

[12] James R. Nunns and James A. Papke, "A Critical Survey of State Revenue Estimating Practices and Prospects," *National Association of Tax Administrators Conference on Revenue Estimating* (1973), pp. 28–38.

[13] Box-Jenkins and similar time series techniques would, technically, fall in this grouping, although they are not simple to apply. Their causation linkages, however, are not well developed. Their applicability to revenue forecasting may be limited by the need for lengthy data series; revenue forecasting seldom has available data series that extend for long periods with change in neither tax rate or base.

proach for minor revenue sources when improved estimates make no impact on the overall fiscal pattern. A second simplistic approach, judgment, involves informed guesses made by experienced observers of the particular revenue system. These estimates, actually based on complex but unspecified models, are often amazingly accurate. Unfortunately, most governments have more than one such "old hand" and the old hands will frequently disagree. Because there is no structure for evaluating their numbers until after the forecast year is over, their estimates often needlessly confuse budget consideration.

The multiple regression model, the most widely encountered forecasting device, estimates revenue as a function of one or more independent variables. Each equation used to estimate a part of revenue is independent of the others. Thus, retail sales tax collections and individual income tax collections for the fiscal year could both be estimated as functions of calendar year personal income, each in separate and unrelated equations. Other independent variables (the tax rate, demographic features of the economy, etc.) could also be in the equation. For use of this approach, estimates of the independent variable must be available for the forecast period: an estimating equation for sales tax collections which uses the consumer price index will not be usable if the necessary consumer price index measure is not available until three quarters of the way through the budget year. For budget preparation, the revenue estimate has to be presented well before the start of the year. The estimating equation fitted by multiple regression will ordinarily be selected on the extent to which estimates from the equation coincide with actual revenue collections in prior years. Because many alternative specifications yield similar fit to historic data, trial predictions for earlier years are also prepared: suppose data are available for 1960 to 1980— an estimate is being prepared for the 1982 budget year (the estimate is being prepared during 1981). Possible equations can be developed from 1960 to 1979 data and test "predictions" made for 1980. The alternative equation coming closest to the known 1980 result is selected. Ordinarily, separate equations are prepared for each major revenue category to allow for different responses to changes in independent variables. Careful application of multiple regression models should produce overall predictions within 1–3 percent of actual collections.

Econometric modeling estimates revenue within a simultaneous system of interdependent equations.[14] These models are particularly im-

---

[14] The independent variables used in the multiple regression approach (possibly state personal income or U.S. gross national product) often are the product of larger econometric models of the region or the nation. State and local governments obtain these estimates from numerous sources, including proprietary economic forecasting companies, universities, committees of technical advisers, and government economists.

portant when revenue sources are not truly independent (as when the
state personal income tax allows a deduction for the state sales tax) and
may provide useful insights into the way state economies operate and
the way in which they respond to external shocks. As a practical matter,
however, states have generally found that the revenue predictions from
them are little (if any) more accurate than those emerging from the
multiple regression models at lower cost and smaller data requirement.

A promising third approach is microsimulation from sample data
files, an approach used by the U.S. Treasury and experimentally by
some states.[15] Individual tax return data from a sample of returns are
stored in computer file. From this information, the effect of changes in
selected fiscal parameters can be estimated as the impact in the sample
is expanded to the entire taxpaying population. The approach is particularly valuable in the analysis of policy changes, but it can also be employed in regular estimation. Much effort is involved in selection and
preparation of the microfile, so uses beyond revenue estimation improve the economic viability of such an effort. One important other use
is in fiscal note preparation: the estimation of the revenue consequences of legal changes in the tax structure.

The final approach uses input-output models for estimation. An
input-output table, a model of interindustry sales and purchases, shows
how much each industry (steel, for instance) sells to other industries for
use in products made by those industries (automobiles, etc.) and to final
purchasers (government, households, etc.) and how much that industry
purchases from other industries (coal, etc.) and from final purchasers
(government, households, etc.).[16] The table provides great detail about
operations of an economy and can provide usable estimates of revenue
impacts of particular economic shocks and estimates of revenue
changes emerging from specified final demand changes. However, the
I-O model must exist before it can be used (the preparation of the model
is too costly for just revenue estimation) and it must be kept up to date
in the face of changes in economic structure.

Regardless of the approach taken, there are some general observations about revenue estimation. First, the hardest task in state and local
government revenue estimation—amazingly enough— is collection of a
consistent series of revenue data. Messy little transactions (tax redefini-

[15] A federal approach is described in Howard Nester, "The Corporate Microdata File
Employed by the Office of Tax Analysis," *Proceedings of the National Tax Association–Tax
Institute of America,* 70 (1977): 293–306 and Roy A. Wysecarver, "The Treasury Personal
Individual Income Tax Simulation Mode," *Proceedings of the National Tax Association–
Tax Institute of America,* 70 (1977): 306–10.

[16] Input-output analysis is described in William Miernyk, *The Elements of Input-Output
Analysis* (New York: Random House, 1966).

tion or restructuring, failure to properly record receipts for an unspecified period, failure to open mail bags at the end of a fiscal year, loss of revenue reports, inconsistent revenue accounting, etc.) confuse almost every revenue series, causing the revenue estimator to spend many hours working to obtain a clean data series. Many adjustments are possible to remedy problems with independent variables, but estimation based on a series of wrong dependent variables is nearly hopeless. Furthermore, the estimate is always subject to sabotage through a repeat of the episodes which messed up the initial data. That set of problems will haunt every revenue estimator.

Second, openness in the estimating process is a clear virtue. Both legislative and executive branches occasionally will seek to have artificially high or low revenue estimates as a part of a budget strategy to increase or reduce expenditure for political gain. An open estimation process prevents such manipulation and is quite desirable. The general public seldom wins when several different revenue estimates are strategically unveiled during budget sessions. A wrong consensus estimate will probably lead to better budget making than will a number of competing estimates, one of which is accurate.

And third, the approach selected will often depend on the tasks to be served by the model. If one seeks revenue estimates for the annual budget process, the multiple regression approach will ordinarily yield good results. If one seeks the impact of a structural change in the tax, microsimulation or input-output analysis may be more appropriate. If estimates are needed for long-range plans, trend extrapolations—sometimes adjusted for forecasted structural changes—are probably as good as anything. In sum, no single approach is ideally suited for all revenue estimation uses.

A related revenue estimation problem is that of fiscal impact statement preparation. In many instances, legislation to change tax structures must be accompanied by the amount of revenue increase or decrease produced by that action. Such statements are often difficult to prepare with any accuracy because the data required are unavailable and the size of response by taxpayers to the new tax conditions is neither known nor has been estimated by others. Because of the many estimation problems and the need for an estimate for policymaking, standard procedure requires that such statements include, along with the dollar estimate, the following additional information: the nature of the data used in the estimate; the basic estimation procedure used, including assumptions made about the level and trend of economic activity; and an appraisal of the limitations of the estimate. About all that can realistically be expected is an estimate of the relative magnitude of the revenue change.

Tax expenditure analysis

The Congressional Budget and Impoundment Act of 1974 (P.L. 93-344) requires that the President's budget report "tax expenditures" in the revenue plans contained in that budget. The act defines tax expenditures to be "revenue losses attributable to provisions of the federal tax laws which allow a special exclusion, exemption, or deduction from gross income or which provide a special credit, a preferential rate of tax, or a deferral of tax liability." The concept treats tax preferences as a mechanism for pursuit of governmental objectives, an alternative to budget outlays, credit assistance, and other policy instruments. Existing federal tax expenditures encourage selected economic activities (investment, housing, municipal borrowing, support of charities, etc.) or reduce the liability of taxpayers in special circumstances (deduction of medical expenses, casualty loss deduction, exemption for the blind and aged, etc.). Full tax expenditure budgets are limited to the federal level; there is no theoretical reason why the concept could not be extended to state and local taxes. Fiscal notes prepared by states to estimate the revenue consequences of specific tax changes require similar estimating techniques, but there has been no demand for full tax expenditure budgets at that level.

The analysis involves estimation of revenue loss from tax provisions which differ from the "normal structure" of the tax. Legislation does not define what is normal, so there is ample room for judgment and dispute. Because the concept involves computations of what the government does not collect from individuals and corporations, some observers object to the concept on philosophical grounds. Irving Kristol capably makes the point:

> The conversion of tax incentives into 'tax subsidies' or 'tax expenditures' means that 'in effect' a substantial part of everyone's income really belongs to the government—only the government, when it generously or foolishly refrains from taxing it away, tolerates our possession and use of it.[17]

Tax expenditure analysis is a tool—we hope it can be divorced from its philosophical implications because it is important to gauge the extent of the alternate system of supporting public objectives. Normal structure definition is a problem: tax expenditures would fall to zero if the current structure were taken as normal.[18]

---

[17] Irving Kristol, "Taxes, Poverty, and Equality," *The Public Interest,* 37 (Fall 1974): 15.

[18] An example of the definitional quirks: the personal exemption for individuals is part of normal structure, the extra personal exemption given the blind and aged is not. Why should they be regarded differently?

Measurement of tax expenditures is important for public policymaking because many special interests prefer them to direct cash assistance. There are two major reasons why. First, elements of the tax structure are permanent unless there is a specific expiration date attached; direct expenditure must go through an annual budget process. While programs once included in the approved budget usually have a higher probability of inclusion in later budgets, they still lack the permanence of tax provisions. Furthermore, tax provisions seldom are subject to the sunset reviews that public programs sometimes are.

The size of tax provisions is also hidden. In most instances at the state and local level, decision makers will have only the vaguest idea at best of how much money is actually involved in tax provisions being considered—and voters have no idea at all. As a result, tax relief is granted in amounts far greater than would be approved if the assistance were in the form of direct expenditure. Federal tax provisions are better measured, thanks to the Budget Act requirements, but the relative size of tax expenditures to outlays in some areas raises similar questions about the advantages of hidden tax provisions. Table 9–3 illustrates the relative size of outlays and tax expenditures for housing.[19] Would Congress approve outlays as large as the tax expenditures?

In sum, tax expenditure analysis provides a tool for evaluation of pursuit of public policy objectives through the tax structure. It is easier to agree that a tax expenditure budget is worth calculating than it is to prepare one because of the importance of defining the normal structure for comparisons.

Conclusion

Tax collection usually requires effort by both the taxpayer (compliance cost) and the collecting government (administrative cost). Both

[19] The preferences for homeowners: (1) deductions for mortgage interest and property taxes; (2) deferral of capital gains on home sales where the proceeds are used to buy another home of at least equal value; (3) exclusion of up to $100,000 of gains from the sale of a home for taxpayers 55 years of age or older; (4) the issuance of tax-exempt bonds to provide reduced mortgage interest rates for owner-occupied dwellings; (5) preferences for thrift institutions that hold residential mortgages. In the calculations presented here, these preferences for thrift institutions have been divided between owner-occupied and rental housing according to the share of single family and multifamily mortgages held by these institutions.

For rental housing, the tax preferences, in addition to those provided to thrift institutions, are: (1) accelerated depreciation for rental property; (2) expensing of construction period interest and taxes; and (3) tax-exempt financing of multifamily housing projects. See "Special Analysis G, Tax Expenditures," in *Special Analyses Budget of the United States Government Fiscal Year 1982* (Washington, D.C.: U.S. Government Printing Office, 1981).

TABLE 9–3
Housing tax expenditures and budget outlays ($ millions)

	Fiscal Year		
Description	1980	1981	1982
Housing:			
Owner-occupied housing:			
Tax expenditures (outlay equivalent)	26,840	33,170	41,655
Outlays	115	150	310
Total	26,955	33,320	41,965
Tax expenditures as a percent of total	99.6	99.6	99.3
Rental housing:			
Tax expenditures (outlay equivalent)	1,965	2,155	2,410
Outlays	6,025	7,280	8,680
Total	7,990	9,435	11,090
Tax expenditures as a percent of total	24.6	22.8	21.7
Total:			
Tax expenditures (outlay equivalent)	28,805	35,325	44,065
Outlays	6,140	7,430	8,990
Total	34,945	42,755	53,055
Tax expenditures as a percent of total	82.4	82.6	83.1

Source: Office of Management and Budget, Executive Office of the President, "Special Analysis G, Tax Expenditures," in *Special Analyses, Budget of the United States Government, Fiscal Year 1982.* (Washington, D.C.: U.S. Government Printing Office, 1981).

elements are true costs to society; government decisions must not ignore either portion. For the major nonproperty taxes, in fact, voluntary compliance—effort by the taxpayer—produces far more revenue than does direct government collection and enforcement. That points out the predominant objective of direct collection: not revenue for itself, but rather protection of the voluntary compliance system.

Revenue estimation, a portion of administration particularly vital for budget preparation, has two significant divisions: estimation of collections in future fiscal years, and calculation of revenues currently collected (or sacrificed) by existing or proposed elements of the tax law. The former activity normally produces excellent accuracy (1 to 3 percent error) when professionally done; there are few tests available for the latter.

A CASE FOR DISCUSSION

The following material is excerpted from testimony of William E. Harlton, Jr., vice president of Detroit Veterinary Supply Company, before the Senate Committee on the Judiciary. Those hearings were on a bill to provide federal judicial review of the application of jurisdictional guidelines for state taxation of interstate commerce and for the apportionment of interstate income among states—generally, to reduce state power to tax interstate and multinational business. The material provides interesting insights into the administration of a state sales tax, as well as showing some problems a small businessperson can face.

Consider these questions:

1. What would you have done differently if you had worked in the New York State Department of Taxation and Finance?
2. How could the exchange have been shortened by Mr. Harlton?
3. Would uniform jurisdictional standards necessarily have prevented this exchange?

The Detroit Veterinary Supply Company was founded by my father's uncle in 1904 and has been in business continually since them. I have been in the business since 1937 and owned it from 1954 until January 1, 1978, when I sold it to my son. I still am active in the business and am a vice president of the company.

Our business sold products all over the United States, including Hawaii and Alaska and Puerto Rico. In fact, we have made sales to all parts of the world. Now we are concentrating primarily in Michigan, Ohio, and Indiana, although we still receive a few orders from all over the country.

Ours is a small company. Our volume of sales is approximately $800,000 a year, and the average sale is somewhere between $50–$100. Some years ago, 40 percent of our sales were made

to customers outside the state of Michigan. Now, out-of-state sales are down to around 15 percent to 20 percent. We provide employment to 14 people who assist us in servicing our customers. Our only business location is in the state of Michigan; however, we do have salesmen traveling in Ohio and Indiana, and we are registered in these two states and remit the use tax to state taxing authorities.

At one time, we sent out catalogs to veterinarians regularly; however, since 1973 prices have been very unstable and we, as wholesalers of veterinary drugs, have received numerous price increases from our manufacturers. These constant changes made it difficult, and of course, the cost of printing and the cost of mailing have also skyrocketed.

Every once in awhile, we get letters from local and state taxing authorities saying we owe taxes. I guess they audited the local veterinarians and found some of our products or bills, so they write asking why we are not paying sales and use taxes. Normally, we ignore the letters, and they forget it be-

Source: U.S., Congress, Senate, Committee on the Judiciary, *Hearings on S. 2173,* 95th Cong., 1st and 2d sess. on interstate commerce, December 5, 1977, February 13 and 14, July 19 and 20, and December 20, 1978 (Washington, D.C.: U.S. Government Printing Office, 1979).

cause sales are small; however, a year ago the New York State Department of Taxation and Finance accused us of doing business in the state of New York and demanded we take out a sales tax license. As far as we can determine, they made this decision on the basis of one sale in the state of New York. I might add that we have no place of business in the state of New York, nor do we have sales persons traveling in New York soliciting sales in that state. When we did not respond, the Department of Taxation and Finance notified us that we owed the state of New York back taxes to the sum of $1,223,460. The exchange of correspondence between our company, Detroit Veterinary Supply Company, and the Department of Taxation and Finance of the state of New York is attached to the copies of this statement. You will note they arbitrarily assessed $17,000 seven times for periods ending in 1973 and 1974. Further, they assessed us $20,000 for nine more periods which ended in 1974, 1975 and 1976, for a total of $708,000. To this they added $515,460 as penalties and interest for a total of $1,223,460.

I am convinced that this type of correspondence with our company was a form of blackmail to scare us into taking out a New York sales tax license. You will note in our letter of May 19 to the state of New York we stated: "Currently we do not anticipate any future sales into New York. Under the circumstances, we believe a sales tax license will be unnecessary." Your attention is called to their response dated June 14 in which they stated they were withdrawing the demand that our firm register with the state

and canceling the assessment. In other words, the state taxing authority has been successful in halting interstate commerce. This is a frightful confrontation for a small businessman. It is my belief that there should not be walls built around the states and that business should be free to engage in interstate commerce without such threats. Perhaps this committee may wish to inquire of the Department of Taxation and Finance of the state of New York why they adopt such tactics.

The laws are constantly changing. At first, it would appear it would be a simple thing to collect sales taxes from around the country. We found it increasingly complicated for there were so many changes and more and more different exemptions. Even if we had copies of all the laws in the United States, we wouldn't be able to know what would be proper to collect or not to collect from our customers, and customers can be very touchy about the amount of tax.

An example is Ohio, where there are two levels—some counties tax 4 percent and some tax 4½ percent, and the list constantly changes.

In Indiana, we have a different problem. The law says: "The following is nontaxable in Indiana: All sales to veterinarians of drugs of a prescription type are exempt when such items are to be directly consumed in professional use."

This would seem to be simple, but it is very, very difficult to apply and determine. You have to take your customer's word. This is the type of thing you run into. An out-of-state operator can't possibly know all the exemptions and local interpretations.

Filling out forms for Michigan takes a lot of man hours. If we had to do this same job for the few dollars of sales all over the country, it would take untold hours of work and it would cost so much we would have to turn down orders to avoid the bookkeeping costs. Even if we had a computer, the computer time would be costly. And for example, if you are late filing and paying in Michigan, there is a 25 percent penalty.

We note that the bill under consideration would establish uniform jurisdictional standards for the state to follow in the collection of sales and use taxes. We believe congressional action to clarify this is long overdue. It is not in the best interests of the general public, the business community, or even the states to interfere with, restrain, or restrict commerce among the states. Only the Congress can establish uniform rules so that the States will know the limit of their taxing jurisdictional and we businessmen will be able to comply with the law, as we will wish to do.

DEPARTMENT OF TAXATION AND FINANCE

STATE CAMPUS
ALBANY, N.Y. 12227

DEC 3 1976

STATE TAX COMMISSION

SALES TAX BUREAU

FRANCIS X. MALONEY
DIRECTOR

ADDRESS YOUR REPLY TO

Mr. R. Hawkes
Audit & Review Uni
Tel. (518) 457-244

Detroit Veterinary Supply
1798 Wabash
Detroit, Michigan

Gentlemen:

It has come to our attention that your firm is selling taxable
items (veterinary supplies) in the State of New York without collecting
applicable sales taxes.

The Tax Law regarding sales to veterinarians was changed June 1,
1967. Now, any taxable items you sell to veterinarians are to be
considered retail sales, for tax purposes, and you must collect the
tax. In other words, everything you sell to a veterinarian in New
York State is taxable.

Accordingly, we request that you complete the enclosed registration forms, and return them, within ten (10) days, in the envelope
provided.

Very truly yours,

Robert S. Rightmyer
Chief, Audit & Review Unit

RH:ds
Enc: Registration Kit

STATE OF NEW YORK
DEPARTMENT OF TAXATION AND FINANCE

SALES TAX BUREAU

FRANCIS X. MALONEY
DIRECTOR

STATE TAX COMMISSION

STATE CAMPUS
ALBANY, N.Y. 12227

JAN 14 1977

ADDRESS YOUR REPLY TO

Mr. R. Hawkes
Audit and Review Unit
Tel. (518) 457-2445

Detroit Veterinary Supply
1798 Wabash
Detroit, Michigan

Gentlemen:

On December 3, 1976 we requested that you register with
the New York State Sales Tax Bureau. As of this date, we have
not received your reply.

Failure to reply within thirty days will result in the
issuance of an estimated assessment for tax, penalty and
interest in accordance with Section 1138 of Article 28, the
Sales and Use Tax Law.

Your reply should be addressed to the Audit and Review Unit
of the Sales Tax Bureau, State Campus, Albany, NY 12227.

Very truly yours,

Robert S. Rightmyer
Chief, Audit and Review Unit

RH:aa

STATE OF NEW YORK
DEPARTMENT OF TAXATION AND FINANCE
SALES TAX BUREAU
STATE CAMPUS
Albany, New York 12226

NOTICE OF DETERMINATION AND DEMAND
FOR PAYMENT OF SALES AND USE TAXES DUE

Notice Number
90,725,618

Date of Notice
3/7/77

Identification Number

Make payment promptly at your State District Tax
Office. TCB–Albany–Z

Make remittance payable to New York State Sales
Tax Bureau.

Please show notice number on face of check or
money order.

Return one copy of this notice with your payment.

NOTE: This determination shall be final unless on
application for a hearing is filed with the State Tax
Commission within 90 days from the date of this
notice or unless the Tax Commission shall redeter-
mine the tax.

Detroit Veterinary Supply
1793 Wabash
Detroit, Michigan

The tax stated below is for the periods ended: 8/31/65 –11/30/76

Explanation:

BALANCE BROUGHT FORWARD FROM ATTACHMENT

Amount Now Due

PERIOD ENDED	TAX	P & I	TOTAL
2/28/73	$17,000.00	$ 8,840.00	$25,840.00
5/31/73	17,000.00	8,330.00	25,330.00
8/31/73	17,000.00	7,820.00	24,820.00
11/30/73	17,000.00	10,880.00	27,880.00
2/28/74	17,000.00	10,370.00	27,370.00
5/31/74	17,000.00	9,860.00	26,860.00
8/31/74	17,000.00	9,350.00	26,350.00
11/30/74	20,000.00	10,400.00	30,400.00
2/28/75	20,000.00	9,600.00	29,800.00
5/31/75	20,000.00	9,200.00	29,200.00
8/31/75	20,000.00	8,000.00	28,000.00
11/30/75	20,000.00	6,800.00	26,800.00
2/29/76	20,000.00	5,600.00	25,600.00
5/31/76	20,000.00	4,400.00	24,400.00
8/31/76	20,000.00	3,200.00	23,200.00
11/30/76	20,000.00	2,000.00	22,000.00
	$708,000.00	$515,460.00	$1,223,460.00

TOTAL TAX, PENALTY AND INTEREST DUE $1,223,460.00

Taxing Jurisdiction: (0002) $1,223,460.00

Note: In order to expedite the crediting of your payment, please use the
enclosed envelope to forward your reply to the Tax Compliance Bureau, State
Campus, Albany, New York 12227.

Copy

66-690   021

The amount shown above is a balance due on your account. Prompt payment will avoid additional interest.

ATTACHMENT TO ST-570 OR ST-571

Notice Number
90,725 ,618
Identification Number

TCB—Albany—Z

3/7/77

Detroit Veterinary Supply
1798 Wabash
Detroit, Michigan

For Periods ended: 8/31/65 — 11/30/76

Explanation: Pursuant to Section 1138 of the Tax Law, the Tax Commission may
determine the amount of tax due when a return is not filed or when incorrect
or insufficient information is given. Since you failed to supply requested
information, the following taxes are determined to be due.

PERIOD ENDED	TAX	P & I	TOTAL
8/31/65	$12,000.00	$17,040.00	$29,040.00
11/30/65	12,000.00	16,680.00	28,680.00
2/28/66	12,000.00	16,320.00	28,320.00
5/31/66	12,000.00	15,960.00	27,960.00
8/31/66	12,000.00	15,600.00	27,600.00
11/30/66	12,000.00	15,240.00	27,240.00
2/28/67	12,000.00	14,880.00	26,880.00
5/31/67	12,000.00	14,520.00	26,520.00
8/31/67	12,000.00	14,160.00	26,160.00
11/30/67	12,000.00	13,800.00	25,800.00
2/29/68	12,000.00	13,440.00	25,440.00
5/31/68	12,000.00	13,080.00	25,080.00
8/31/68	12,000.00	12,720.00	24,720.00
11/30/68	14,000.00	14,420.00	28,420.00
2/28/69	14,000.00	14,000.00	28,000.00
5/31/69	14,000.00	13,580.00	27,580.00
8/31/69	14,000.00	13,160.00	27,160.00
11/30/69	14,000.00	12,740.00	26,740.00
2/28/70	14,000.00	12,320.00	26,320.00
5/31/70	14,000.00	11,900.00	25,900.00
8/31/70	14,000.00	11,480.00	25,480.00
11/30/70	14,000.00	11,060.00	25,060.00
2/28/71	14,000.00	10,640.00	24,640.00
5/31/71	14,000.00	10,220.00	24,220.00
8/31/71	14,000.00	9,800.00	23,800.00
11/30/71	17,000.00	11,390.00	28,390.00
2/29/72	17,000.00	10,880.00	27,880.00
5/31/72	17,000.00	10,370.00	27,370.00
8/31/72	17,000.00	9,860.00	26,860.00
11/30/72	17,000.00	9,350.00	26,350.00

PO BOX 577

MARCH 16, 1977

NEW YORK STATE
TAX COMPLIANCE BUREAU
STATE CAMPUS
ALBANY, NEW YORK   12227

DEAR SIRS:

IN RE NOTICE NUMBER 90,725,618 IN SUM OF $ 1,223,460,00
SINCE WE ARE A SMALL COMPANY NOT DOING BUSINESS IN NEW YORK
STATE, YOUR REQUEST FOR $ 1,223,460.00 CAME AS A SURPRISE.
WE THINK YOU HAVE THE WRONG COMPANY.   AT ANY RATE, WE DENY
BOTH LIABILITY AND ABILITY TO PAY.

YOURS,

W.F. Harlton Jr.

W.F. HARLTON JR.

STATE OF NEW YORK
DEPARTMENT OF TAXATION AND FINANCE

STATE CAMPUS
ALBANY, N.Y. 12227

STATE TAX COMMISSION

SALES TAX BUREAU

FRANCIS X. MALONEY
DIRECTOR

ADDRESS YOUR REPLY TO

Detroit Veterinary Supply Co.
1798 Wabash Avenue
Detroit, MI 48232

Attention W. F. Harlton, Jr.

Gentlemen:

We have found, during audits of veterinarians located in the State of
New York, that your firm is selling veterinary supplies without collecting applicable State and local sales taxes.

As these sales are taxable in New York State, we requested on two
occasions, that you register with this bureau and begin collecting
this tax.

Our letters were not answered – therefore, we issued an estimated
assessment for tax, penalty and interest in accordance with section
1138 of our Tax Law. (Our Notice No. 90,725,618).

If our information is incorrect, please advise. Otherwise, we will
expect to receive your application for registration within thirty
days. We will hold collection action on Notice No. 90,725,618 in
abeyance pending your reply.

Robert E. Hawkes
Central Sales Tax Section
Telephone (518) 457-2445

MAY 15 1977

REH:vlb

DETROIT VETERINARY SUPPLY CO.
1790 Wabash Avenue, Detroit, Mich. 48232

(313) 170-1-6852

POBOX577   MAY 19, 1977

MR ROBERT E HAWKES
CENTRAL SALES TAX SECTION
STATE OF NEW YORK
DEPT OF TAXATION AND FINANCE
STATE CAMPUS
ALBANY, NY   12227

SIR:

IN ANSWER TO YOUR LETTER, SEE COPY ATTACHED; AND TO YOUR
NOTICE NUMBER   90,725,618, SEE COPY ATTACHED.

YOU STATE WE HAVE NEVER ANSWERED YOUR LETTER, PLEASE SEE
COPY OF OUR LETTER MARCH 16, 1977 WHEREIN WE POINTED OUT
TO YOU YOUR REQUEST FOR

                      $ 1,223,460,00

WAS ABSOLUTELY RIDCULOUS.

WHATEVER SALES WE MAY HAVE MADE IN THE PAST INTO THE STATE
OF NEW YORK WERE PURELY ON AN OCCASIONAL BASIS.   (ONCE OR
TWICE A YEAR).   THESE WERE STRICTLY INTERSTATE
COMMERCE SALES SINCE WE HAVE NO ESTABLISHMENT IN NEW YORK,
NOR DO WE HAVE ANY SALESPEOPLE IN NEW YORK.   NOR, ARE
WE MAILING ADVERTISING INTO NEW YORK.

CURRENTLY WE DO NOT ANTICIPATE ANY FUTURE SALES INTO NEW
YORK.

UNDER THE CIRCUMSTANCES, WE BELIEVE A SALES TAX LICENSE
WOULD BE UNNECESSARY.

                         YOURS,

                         W.F. Harlton Jr

                         W.F.HARLTON   JR.

STATE OF NEW YORK
DEPARTMENT OF TAXATION AND FINANCE

STATE TAX COMMISSION

STATE CAMPUS
ALBANY, N.Y. 12227

SALES TAX BUREAU

FRANCIS X. MALONEY
DIRECTOR

ADDRESS YOUR REPLY TO

Detroit Veterinary Supply Co.
1798 Wabash Avenue
Detroit, MI   48232

Attention Mr. W. F. Harlton, Jr.

Gentlemen:

Thank you for your letter of May 19, 1977.

Based on the explanations furnished, we are withdrawing our demand that

your firm register with this Bureau. Accordingly, assessment #90,725,618

has been cancelled.

Robert E. Hawkes
Central Sales Tax Section
Telephone (518) 457-2445

JUN 14 1977

REH:ds

10

User charges

User charges are a tantalizing source of revenue at all levels of government. They can be a lucrative source of additional revenue outside public resistance to increased tax burden. Furthermore, and more importantly in less agitated fiscal conditions, they can improve both the efficiency of government resource allocation and the equity of the distribution of public service cost. Table 10–1 shows that governments continue to raise only a small percentage of their revenue from this source. Only 8.5 percent of own-source revenue for all governments came from current charges in 1978–79. Only local governments increased the relative use of that source over the 1973–74 to 1978–79 period. All local governments increased the current charge share of own-source revenue from 15.3 to 17.8 percent. The increase for cities alone was even greater: from 34.7 to 39.8 percent. Because local governments probably provide more services amenable to charge finance (as will be illustrated later) and because they were typically under greater fiscal stress in that period, those results are not surprising. The trend in local use can be expected to continue and ought to be encouraged.

For its statistical compilations, the Bureau of the Census defines charges as "amounts received from the public for performance of specific services benefiting the person charged and from sales of commodities and services. . . . Includes fees, toll charges, tuition, and other

TABLE 10-1
Use of current charges by governments, 1973-1974 and 1978-1979 ($ millions)

1973-1974	All governments	Federal	State	All local	Munici- palities*
Total revenue............	—	289,059	140,815	143,193	51,225
Own-source revenue	484,650	288,565	107,645	88,440	34,601
Current charges	41,447	18,278	9,597	13,571	11,994

1978-1979	All governments	Federal	State	All local	Munici- palities*
Total revenue............	—	500,927	247,005	234,630	84,057
Own-source revenue	829,371	499,601	189,917	139,853	56,459
Current charges	70,426	30,957	14,859	24,610	22,516

* Utility finances integrated with civil city.
Source: Bureau of the Census, *Governmental Finances in 1978-79,* and Bureau of the Census, *Governmental Finances in 1973-74,* Bureau of the Census, *City Government Finances in 1978-79,* and Bureau of the Census, *City Government Finances in 1973-74.*

reimbursement for current services, rents and sales incident to the performance of particular governmental functions, and gross income of commercial-type activities (parking lots, school lunch programs, and the like)."[1] Their tabulations exclude municipal utility (water, electric, gas, etc.) and state liquor-store revenue because such revenues are separately reported in their statistics. *Those* excluded sources do fit the general concept of charge revenue, however. License taxes imposed to regulate specific activities for the benefit of the general public (massage parlor licenses might be an example) are also excluded from the Census definition but are *not* charges.

A license tax is a fee—flat rate, graduated by type of activity, related to business receipts, etc.—levied by a government as a condition for exercise of a business or nonbusiness privilege. Without the license, one or more governments forbid the activity. The license is a necessary condition for operation, but does not "purchase" any specific government service. It may thus be distinguished from a user charge, which may be avoided if an individual or firm chooses not to purchase the supplied item or service and the payment of which entitles the individual or firm to a commodity or service, and from fees that are indirectly related to particular privileges.

The license tax must also be distinguished from franchise fees. The latter involve contracts detailing rights and responsibilities of both franchisee and the issuing municipality, entail requirement of service to all

---

[1] U.S. Bureau of the Census, *Governmental Finances in 1978-79,* series GF79, no. 5. (Washington, D.C.: U.S. Government Printing Office, 1980) p. 97.

in the service area, and bring a presumption of rate and quality of service regulation. A license simply permits a holder to undertake an activity otherwise forbidden and involves no contractual or property rights.[2] In general, franchises are provided in very limited numbers, while licenses are made available to virtually all applicants.

The definitions usually do not differentiate between licenses for revenue and for regulation. Both varieties are based on the inherent authority of a state to exercise all elements of police power, with state delegation of this power to municipalities by constitution, statute, or city charter grant. Revenue and regulation motives may often be hopelessly entangled. Nevertheless, a tentative separation may be suggested: a license ordinance which does not require inspection of the business or of the articles sold or fails to regulate the conduct of business in any manner is a pure revenue license, particularly if license applications are never denied. If such controls apply or if licenses are difficult to obtain (not just expensive), the license is of the regulatory variant. While the differences may not always be sharp, the distinctions are serviceable. Some states require that license charges be reasonably related to the cost of issuing, policing, or controlling the thing or activity being licensed. When that stipulation applies, it is especially important to review costs and adjust charges frequently.

Both user charges and fees attempt to relieve burdens placed on the general revenue system by extracting greater contribution from service beneficiaries, but the former more closely resembles private enterprise pricing. Fees can compensate government for extra costs incurred in the provision of special services to identifiable entities or for administrative paperwork done for individuals. Thus, governments often apply fees for traffic direction or crowd control and charge fees for many legal filings. Fees, however, seldom involve the direct sale of a good or service, but involve payment for some privilege granted by government. The exercise of that privilege may cause government to incur a cost which the fee seeks to recoup in part or in total.

User charges apply prices for services provided so that only those receiving the service bear the cost of its provision. The charge is voluntary: an individual can choose not to receive the service and, accordingly, not to pay for its finance. Thus, there is no burden on the general public or on the general tax system. The individual would receive no service if the user charge were not paid. Taxes are by their nature compulsory and are not linked to any government services, individually or separately. A dramatic difference of individual choice divides taxes and

---

[2] Charles S. Rhyne, *Municipal Law* (Washington: National Institute of Municipal Law Officers, 1957), p. 655 further develops this logic.

user charges and can influence all resulting attributes of agency operation. Sometimes, individuals are given no right to refuse a service—a city may require all to pay a garbage collection charge. Whether this finance structure is a true user charge is debatable. It may better be viewed as a residential unit tax with proceeds dedicated to garbage collection. It clearly lacks the incentive effects of true user charges.

Necessary conditions for user charge application

User charges can induce production and consumption efficiency while gauging citizen preferences and demand for government services. Unfortunately, they can only work when activities financed have two necessary conditions: benefit separability and chargeability. These are the features absent from pure public goods (Chapter 1); the farther a good or service departs from publicness and the closer it approximates a private good, the more feasible are user charges.

First, user charges are feasible when identifiable individuals or firms, not the community as a whole, benefit from the service. Services to a narrow segment of the community financed by general revenues provide an opportunity for that segment to profit at the expense of others. Those using the service will benefit, but pay no more than similarly situated citizens who do not benefit. A user charge would prevent that systematic subsidization. If recipients of benefits cannot be identified or if the community in general benefits, a user charge is neither feasible nor desirable. Thus, charges for elementary education would be inappropriate; they would be quite desirable for an adult auto mechanics course. Voluntarism in the first instance would be foolish—Milton benefits if his neighbor's children receive an elementary education because they help rationally choose his government, they read traffic signs, they do not go on welfare which Milton must help provide, and so on. In the latter instance, the mechanic does help the community, but that help is for a fee: if Milton's car is repaired, he directly pays the bill—there are no uncompensated community benefits.

Second, user charges require an economical method for excluding from service benefits those who do not pay for the service. If exclusion cannot be accomplished, the charge cannot be collected. Furthermore, resource allocation gains will be greatest if service use can actually be metered, as with water meters, toll booths, and the like. Thus, heavy users would pay more than light users, although both pay more than nonusers. Some discretion is needed here, however, because everything gaugeable may not be worth gauging: city street usage could be metered using the tollgate technology of turnpikes and toll bridges. The costs involved, including the time waiting in lines, make that option untenable. Administrative cost—measurement of customer service use (metering), calculation of charges according to service cost, and billing and collection of computed charges—and compliance cost must not be excessive. Many services can, however, be gauged and controlled by meters, fences, turnstiles, decals, and the like. Others may be indirectly measured—many cities gauge residential sanitary sewer use by water use, a reasonable proxy for volume in the drain. Without enforceable charge barriers, user charges are inappropriate.

Charges are particularly appropriate when substantial waste would occur if the individually identifiable service were unpriced. Such would undoubtedly result if, for instance, water were provided through property tax financing. Under that system, efforts to economize on water use would yield the individual consumer no direct return. Payments for water would be determined by property holdings, not the amount of water used. Usage would be much inflated. Investment in supply facilities would have to be abnormally great and artificially expanded amounts of water would have to be treated. Appropriate user charges could substantially reduce water waste and total water supply cost.

Advantages of user charges

When a user charge can be applied, it has advantages beyond the naked pragmatism of additional revenue for government functions. These strengths include both the important efficiency effects of appropriately designed charge structures and improved equity from direct pricing. First, user charges can register and record public demand for a service. Suppose a city is considering support of extensive summer softball leagues for adults. If these leagues are financed by user charges (either team sponsors or individual participants), the city receives important information for choices about service type, quality, and quantity. Without charge finance, there will be continual—and inconclusive—debate about program advisability and structure. That need not occur with appropriate charges. Furthermore, a program which, through user charges, covers its cost of provision is not likely to be eliminated and places no burdens on other governmental activities. Not incidentally, citizens who do not want the service do not have to receive it and do not have to pay for it. Thus, a user charge system not only provides a tangible way for citizens to register their preference for particular services but also provides some funds for provision of the services.

Those extra funds can be a problem, however, when the program does not cover all costs it generates, but does provide *some* revenue.

During periods of tight finances, decision makers are tempted to expand the activities generating revenue, often reasoning that any revenue will help with the fiscal problem. Unfortunately, such expansion can actually increase the total subsidy required for that service and worsen the overall budget condition. For example, a city may expand its summer tennis instruction program because it generates $25 per person in charge revenue. If recreation department cost increases by $30 per person enrolled in the program, the expanded revenue produced will actually increase any city deficit. The difficulty is prevented if the design of the charge system ensures that charges for programs at least cover the additional cost caused by the program, an important condition for the demand-registering advantage attributed to user charges.

Second, the user charge can dramatically improve equity of financing selected services. If the service is of a chargeable nature, its provision by general tax revenues will undoubtedly subsidize the service recipient group at the expense of the general taxpaying public. User charges can obviously prevent that problem. Less obvious but equally significant are two related equity problems that direct pricing can reduce: the problems created by nonresident service recipients and by tax-exempt entities. Many urban services, particularly cultural and recreational, can easily be used by anyone in the region. General revenue finance permits a subsidy to any nonresident consumer; a user charge prevents that subsidy. The approach is a simple and direct way to reduce burdens placed on one government by citizens of neighboring governments. A user charge similarly provides a mechanism for obtaining financial support from tax-exempt institutions. Many cities, for example, finance refuse collection with property tax revenue. Charitable, religious, or educational institutions exempt from property taxes would contribute nothing to finance refuse collection, even though they receive refuse collection service. The cost of this service must be borne by the general taxpaying body. If, however, refuse collection were financed by user charges, that cost shifting would not occur. Just as these entities must pay for gasoline purchased from a private firm, they would pay the refuse collection charge: tax exemption does not exempt institutions from paying for goods or services obtained on the open market. For both nonresidents and exempt institutions, the user charge allows governments to extract revenue from entities outside their tax network; if they use, they pay.

Third, a user charge program may improve operating efficiency, as agency staff must respond to client demand. Agencies usually operate with funds obtained by request to, and justification prepared for, a legislative body. That justification will elaborate need as determined by the agency staff and defended according to performance criteria established by that staff. User charge finance, however, requires a shift to preferences articulated by consumer demand. The agency must provide services which are desired by consumers or it will fail the financial test for survival. It cannot define what clients *should* want in its budget defense: it must provide the services which clients *do* want or it will not survive.

Finally, a user charge may correct cost and price signals provided in the private market. Suppose a manufacturing plant placed extraordinary demand on traffic conditions in a neighborhood. That special demand requires additional police officers to be assigned traffic direction duties at a handful of intersections in that area during shift changes at the factory. The way the plant operates thus produces substantial extra costs for the community. If the plant must pay for the extra traffic control costs its operations require, its management has a direct financial incentive to consider whether the current operating pattern (with attendant traffic control charges) or patterns with lower peak flow traffic produced by staggered shifts, van pooling, subsidies for mass transit use, and so on (and no traffic control charge) are less expensive. The user charge makes the decision unit recognize and respond to the true social cost of its action. In the example cited, without the user charge the additional traffic control costs the plant nothing; no one can be expected to conserve a resource which appears to be free. This is exactly the same logic which applies in the application of effluent charges to the discharge of environmental pollutants.

The efficiency arguments are most important in the continuing federal effort to apply substantial deep draft and inland waterway user fees. David Stockman made that case as director of the Office of Management and Budget:

> When the federal government renders a service directly to economic enterprises at less than cost, the service amounts to a subsidy. Subsidies not only increase the size of the federal budget, but almost inevitably distort the workings of our free market economy. Such distortions decrease economic efficiency.
>
> The imposition of user fees will increase overall national economic efficiency. If a plant locates in one region rather than another because the decision was biased by the presence of a subsidy, the nation's overall economic efficiency is reduced and the nation's output is smaller. Because the decision-maker does not consider the cost of the subsidy when he makes a decision—only his own costs—he may locate where it costs him less, but you and I, the taxpaying public, end up paying the difference.[3]

---

[3] Testimony before the Senate Subcommittee on Environment and Public Works, reported in *Rail News Update,* no. 2327, July 29, 1981.

User charges closely tied to the cost of providing a service thus prevent the misallocation of resources which can result from general tax financing of specific services.

Limitations of user charges

User charges cannot be substituted generally for taxes in the finance of government services because many public services, in fact most services provided by most governments, simply do not fit the full requirement for finance by price. First, activities which have substantial benefits extending beyond the principal recipient are not candidates for user charge finance. Basic fire protection in an urban area could not, for example, be considered for charge finance because fire tends to spread; extinguishing a fire in one building will protect those surrounding units. Thus, protection financed by one individual will automatically protect others; nonpayers are not excludable, so the service cannot be financed by charges. There is a corollary to the external benefit problem: the ability to charge for particular services can distort agency decision making. Thus, there is the scenario of magnanimous resources for a high school football team, because gate receipts are sizable, while the girls' volleyball team gets hand-me-downs. The question for resource allocation is contribution to the purposes of the community (or social benefits); cash flow is appropriately ignored in such an instance.

Second, services may intentionally subsidize low-income or otherwise disadvantaged recipients. Charges for these services could be counterproductive.[4] Beneficiaries ought not pay if the service has welfare elements. In a related fashion, some have argued that user charges in general are unfair because they often produce a regressive burden pattern, taking a larger percentage of a low-income consumer's income than from higher-income consumers.[5] That argument is not a convincing attack on user charges for several reasons. For one thing, not all low-income families would use many priced services, even if the services were tax-financed and priced at zero. They would thus share in the payment for the service without receiving any benefits from it. Thus, low-income families not using the service clearly are better off with the user charge system. A further reason is that tax financing devices may have a more regressive burden than user charges, even if the service is widely used by disadvantaged citizens. Local revenue systems often are

---

[4] There are, of course, more efficient ways of redistributing income in society than providing government services. But once that method is selected, it ought not be thwarted by charges.

[5] Willard Price, "The Case against the Imposition of a Sewer Use Tax," *Governmental Finance,* 4 (May 1975): 38–41.

very regressive, so it is not unlikely that a shift to charges could reduce regressivity from its level with general tax finance. Finally, it may be possible to design "payability" tests for the charges, because the services are received by identifiable individuals.[6] Suppose a city charges an admission fee to swimming pools: benefits are primarily individual (to the swimmer and family), prices can be enforced using fences and turnstyles (safety requires access control, regardless of financing technique), and overcrowding may otherwise result when children are dumped at the facility for "free" babysitting. Charge opponents argue that free pools are a significant recreation option for low-income families; a charge would harm that redistributive function. Charges can, however, function equitably and efficiently if disadvantaged families receive season passes at no cost or if pools located in low-income areas are free while charges apply at other pools. In general, protection of the disadvantaged ought not be an excuse for subsidizing the well-to-do.

Guides for user charge application

Governments differ in the extent to which they charge for services, partly because of the different services they provide (national defense, welfare, and highway patrol are, for instance, hardly priceable) and partly because of political attitude toward pricing of public goods. Outside those constraints, there are some guides for charge preparation and manipulation. Any service showing the features described earlier (individual benefit, susceptibility to excluding nonpayers, and absence of redistributive elements) are reasonable candidates for charge finance. The short list in Table 10–2 provides some suggestions. Bird and Mushkin nominate for charge (1) household support functions (water, refuse collection, sewerage); (2) industrial development support (airports, parking, special police or fire services, etc.); (3) "amenities" (specialized recreation facilities, cultural facilities, etc.); and (4) services provided to tax-exempt entities.[7] The list and their classification should give ample direction.

Some governments, often in response to property tax limits, controls, or freezes, have applied general police or fire protection charges based on the value of property protected. These are not true charges because they are not voluntary; they are simply an escape mechanism around the control. A related charge does have greater logical appeal.

---

[6] Mushkin and Vehorn coined the "payability" phrase. Selma J. Mushkin and Charles L. Vehorn, "User Fees and Charges," *Governmental Finance,* 6 (November 1977): 46.

[7] Selma J. Mushkin and Richard M. Bird, "Public Prices: An Overview," in *Public Prices for Public Products,* ed. S. J. Mushkin (Washington, D.C.: Urban Institute, 1972): 8–9.

278

TABLE 10-2
Selected government services amenable to user charges

Special police work—service for stadium or auditorium events, alarm servicing.
Parking—garage, meters.
Refuse management—collection, disposal.
Recreation—golf courses, tennis courts, swimming pools, park admissions, concessions.
Cultural—museum or gallery admissions, special library services.
Water and sewer charges.
Electric and gas utilities.
Health and hospitals—ambulance charges, inoculations, hospital rates.
Transportation—transit fares, bridge and highway tolls, airport landing/departure fees, hangar rentals, lock tolls.
Education—rentals of special books, equipment, or uniforms; college or technical school.
Resource management and development—surveys, extension service inquiries, tree nursery stock.

That is the assignment of service costs in relation to physical characteristics of a property, according to an estimate of how those characteristics produce demand for a service. There has been more discussion of this approach than actual adoption, but—as a response to the reduction in property taxes required by California's Proposition 13—Inglewood, California, adopted a "fire-flow assessment fee" in 1978. The fee was "based on the relative fire risk of each structure and the amount of water, personnel, and equipment that would be needed to extinguish a blaze there."[8] Single-family residences with some simple fire protection device (a smoke detector) paid no levy. Other structures (multiple family dwellings, commercial/industrial units, etc.) paid an assessment based on service need criteria, including construction type, structure use, and fire protection equipment sprinklers).

The Inglewood fee survived only one year. A court challenge questioned whether it was a tax and, hence, adopted by means in violation of Proposition 13; the city council repealed the fee. It was not a good revenue raiser, possibly because of the challenges to it, and state assistance substantially restored lost property tax revenue. Citizen response at a public hearing also halted plans for a similar assessment for street maintenance based on property foot frontage and street type (neighborhood, commercial, thoroughfare, etc.).

[8] Stephen J. Sansweet, "Californians Discover Tax-Cut Mania Has a Corollary: Fee Fever," *Wall Street Journal*, 59 (June 1, 1979): 16. Fire service fees in Inglewood increased from $188,000 in fiscal 1978 (pre-Proposition 13) to $911,000 in fiscal 1979. Over that same period, property taxes fell from around $3.5 million to about $1.4 million, because of Proposition 13. (California State Controller, *Financial Transactions Concerning Cities of California, 1978–79 Annual Report* and *1977–78 Annual Report.*)

That variety of fee should not be considered a true user charge because it cannot be voluntary. Because unchecked fires in urban areas will spread, voluntary decisions about purchase of fire protection are untenable. Protection for one unit will protect its neighbors and an unprotected unit will endanger its neighbors. Thus, these financing devices must be structured as taxes (nonvoluntary), but they are taxes based on a concept other than the ability of an economic unit to afford the designated tax burden. The burden of financing that municipal service is allocated among economic units according to the physical attributes of those units which require service cost to be incurred. As such, it could have desirable development effects; it could provide structure owners an extra financial reward for installing private fire control devices (smoke alarms, sprinklers, fire walls, etc.) in older units and could also cause owners of particularly deteriorated structures to raze them. The fees, of course, would not be related to firm profitability: some marginal businesses housed in deteriorated, high-fire-risk structures could face substantial fees. On the whole, however, a rigid structure of fire-risk fees could significantly accelerate the process of structural modernization and, over time, could reduce the total cost of fire protection, even though they are not user charges.

When a government does decide that a particular service can be financed by a charge, the question of appropriate level for that charge remains. Answering that question is not simple. Stocker reports:

> Evidence suggests that pricing policies used by municipal governments are often fairly unsophisticated, perhaps understandably so in light of the difficulty of determining price elasticities, marginal costs, distribution of benefits and other things that enter into economic models of optimal pricing.[9]

The municipality may, however, derive reasonable, if not optimal, prices with fairly simple concepts about service cost.[10] In particular, the government should separate its service costs into two categories: those that change as a result of the service being provided (incremental cost)

---

[9] Frederick D. Stocker, "Diversification of the Local Revenue System: Income and Sales Taxes, User Charges, Federal Grants," *National Tax Journal*, 29 (September 1976): 320.

[10] Downing maintains that appropriately designed user charges would have three components: a portion which reflects the short-run cost of production and varies with output consumed, a portion which reflects the cost of plant and equipment used in production (possibly allocated as an individual's share of its designed capacity), and a portion based on the cost of delivering the service to a specific customer location. The first portion may vary by time of day, depending on whether the system is at peak utilization or not. If so, the charge would be increased. These principles are particularly important for utility operation. (Paul Downing, "User Charges and Special Districts," in *Management Policies in Local Government Finance*, ed. J. Richard Aronson and Eli Schwartz (Washington, D.C.: International City Management Association, 1981), pp. 191–92.

and those that do not change with provision of that service. The latter include any cost which would continue, regardless of decisions concerning that service. The pricing objective can then be, at least initially, recovery of those costs incurred because of the particular service. If that price is collected, the provision of the charge-financed service is no burden for the normal functions of government.[11] Prices above that level are possible, subject to the demand for the service and the conscience of the government as reflected in its desire to subsidize other governmental activities. There is no reason why a charging government cannot experiment with different prices for its service to see what happens to demand and its net revenue; there is no special virtue in stable prices.

A final consideration about user charges concerns their method of application. Alfred Kahn writes, in an analysis of public utility pricing: "The only economic function of price is to influence *behavior. . . .* But of course price can have this effect on the buyer's side only if bills do indeed depend on the volume of purchases. For this reason, economists in the public utilities field are avid meterers."[12] A similar principle applies in the application of user charges: buyer behavior will not change unless changes influence payments made. If a refuse collection customer pays $25 per year for that service, regardless of whether two or five cans of trash are collected per week, customers cannot be expected to change the number of trash cans they set out for collection. A charge sensitive to usage, however, will induce behavior changes by some customers. To obtain the full benefits of user charge finance, then, the service must be metered and made usage-sensitive: dividing estimated total cost by the number of entities served and presentation of a bill to each entity will not produce the desired effects of a user charge.

Conclusion

User charges can be an attractive alternative to tax finance. They avoid citizen resistance to taxes and can improve both equity and efficiency of service provision. Of the various governmental levels, cities make greatest use of them currently. Charges have the advantage of

---

[11] Johnson has identified six elements in existing municipal sewerage service charges: water use (a volume proxy), flat charges, number of plumbing fixtures used by the customer, size of water meter or sewer connection, property characteristics (assessed value, square footage, front footage), and sewage strength. Water use is the most frequently encountered charge element. (James A. Johnson, "The Distribution of the Burden of Sewer User Charges under Various Charge Formulas," *National Tax Journal,* 22 (December 1969): 472–85.)

[12] Alfred E. Kahn, "Can An Economist Find Happiness Setting Public Utility Rates?" *Public Utilities Fortnightly,* January 5, 1978, p. 15.

voluntarism not found with taxes, but only services with some degree of benefit separability and chargeability are reasonable candidates for charge finance. Services provided by government usually lack those features. Most governments could increase their user charge revenues, but seldom can true charges (not disguised taxes) constitute a major portion of financial support.

A SELECTION FOR DISCUSSION

California voters approved a dramatic reduction in property taxes in 1978. While a state surplus provided substantial funds to replace reduced local property tax revenue, many local governments had to seek additional revenue sources to continue services desired by the public. As the following selection from the *Wall Street Journal* reports, many localities sought to replace property tax revenue with user charges and fees.

Consider these questions:

1. What distinguishes user charges and fees from taxes? Do any of the charges and fees described here seem to be taxes? Explain.
2. Does the logic of user charge finance (pricing for public services) *require* a link between cost of service and level of the charge? Explain.

Californians Discover Tax-Cut Mania Has A Corollary: Fee Fever

BY STEPHEN J. SANSWEET
Staff Reporter of THE WALL STREET JOURNAL

Students in Glendale, California, who need to brush up on their skills at summer school this year will have to pay as much as $110 for the sessions. Last year they were free.

Los Angeles art and nature lovers put up with recently imposed admission charges of up to $1.50 for once-

free visits to county museums and botanic gardens.

Builders in the San Diego suburb of La Mesa find that the cost of fees and permits for an average house has rocketed to $1,283 from just $43 in early 1978.

In the year since Californians voted themselves a deep cut in property-tax payments under Proposition 13, they have been increasingly confronted with new or rapidly escalating fees, charges and other costs for services and programs local governments previously paid for from general revenue. So far, the average homeowner is still coming out ahead, but the gap is narrowing. And the non-tax-deductible fees are a particular blow for the large number of renters in the state who received little, if any, benefit from last year's initiative.

Prostituting 13

"The real meaning of Proposition 13 is being prostituted right and left by local government," charges Paul Gann, cosponsor of the initiative that ignited national tax-cutting fever when California passed it last June 6. "We got the property taxes cut, but they immediately took the dough back in another way."

Mr. Gann's response has been to join in several suits challenging fees, as well as to sponsor a new initiative, the "Spirit of 13," that would limit spending by the state and local governments. The measure will be on the ballot by June 1980 at the latest, and political observers think it has a good chance of enactment.

But regardless of whether the "Spirit of 13" passes, the original "13" has wrought a fundamental and probably irreversible change in the way Californians pay for services, programs, and facilities provided by the state's 58 counties, 417 cities, and 4,750 special districts. While many have praised the new "pay as you go" approach, others fear its possible negative effects on such groups as low for fixed-income people and first-time home buyers.

Cities Recoup 19 Percent

Proposition 13, which limited property taxes to 1 percent of the 1975–76 assessed market value and restricted assessment increases, cut about $550 million from city revenues. According to the latest available statistics, compiled last fall, the cities made up 19 percent of this, or $103 million, from new or higher fees and service charges in the months just before and after Proposition 13 took effect. (Much of the rest was made up by bail-out legislation that distributed surplus state revenue.)

Counties, which lost nearly $1.5 billion in property-tax revenue, added only $22 million in fees. An incomplete survey of special districts, each of which is set up to raise money for a purpose such as sewers or hospitals, showed higher fees and charges of around $70 million, compared with a property-tax loss of $291 million.

Most observers believe that the initial rush to impose fees was only the beginning. "If state bail-out funds decrease as projected . . . local government officials will be increasingly tempted to raise existing fees and create new ones," a state task force that studied the situation predicts. "Fees are one of the few mechanisms open to local governments for raising added revenues."

Fees for Sidewalk Repair

After lengthy debate and several changes of mind, the Los Angeles city council recently passed a residential trash-collection fee ranging from $1.50 to $5 a month. There wasn't any agonizing earlier when the city imposed or raised fees for such things as dog licenses, use of recreation facilities, emergency ambulance transportation, fire-safety inspections and repair of cracks in sidewalks, to name a few.

Besides Mr. Gann's "Spirit of 13" and the numerous lawsuits, other attempts are being made to stem the upward spiral of fees. Several bills pending in the California legislature would restrict the kinds of fees that could be levied and limit each fee to the cost of the service provided. Also, state attorney general George Deukmejian has just issued an advisory opinion that several new fees are actually special taxes and thus require approval of two thirds of the electorate under terms of Proposition 13.

The residential-construction industry has been hit with an especially large number of fee increases. Prior to Proposition 13, existing homeowners in a community, in effect, partially subsidized new development, because their property taxes helped pay for such things as sewer hookups and new streets. With the taxes reduced, localities have switched the cost of new developments to builders, who, in turn, have passed it on to home buyers. Fees are up in more than a dozen items, ranging from filing of plans to on-site inspections.

* * * * *

The California Building Industry Association says the median bill for construction related fees and service charges across the state has risen 26 percent in the last year, but the range is all the way from zero to $3,000 for an average three-bedroom house. "Builders are in a difficult position," says Norman Jachens, spokesman for the trade group. "We don't want to be

blamed for local governments being unable to fund improvements for new housing. But we don't want to be easy pickings to make up for Proposition 13 losses either."

Even simple modifications or additions to existing homes "have become a rich man's game," says Donald E. Cunningham, a Los Angeles land-use consultant. "It costs $1,200 to $1,500 in fees before you even walk up to the counter with your final plans, and the city and county are about to raise the fees again."

Focus on Sales Taxes

Some communities are using the fund crunch to further their "no-growth" policies. One state survey concludes that many localities aren't any longer interested in luring residential or industrial development because of the low property-tax revenue relative to the cost of capital improvements and services. Instead, they are competing more vigorously for commercial establishments, which generate sales-tax revenue.

Raymond Jallow, senior vice president and economist at United California Bank, is concerned at what he sees as a rush to impose or raise business and licensing fees without knowing the consequences. Beverly Hills businessmen, for example, are faced with business-fee increases of up to 1,800 percent, and Los Angeles County is raising license fees for everyone from weed eradicators to "massage technicians."

"While the economy is still expanding, there might not be much impact," says Mr. Jallow. "But in any slowdown, many of the fees will prove detrimental because they will drive away business and professional people. Some fees haven't been changed in 100 years and certainly should be raised, but others are going up without any direct justification, just to raise revenue."

Effects on the Poor

Many officials concede that tying the level of a fee to the cost of the service performed would often be guesswork. Because of archaic accounting and bookkeeping systems and the difficulty in allocating overhead expenses, service charges frequently bear little relation to service costs, UCLA's Professor [Fred] Case says. "They usually err on the high side, and the money just goes to the general fund anyway," he says. "Los Angeles raised building-permit fees but still laid off people in the department, so we're paying more money for less service."

A major concern of a state Commission on Government Reform, appointed by Gov. Edmund G. Brown, Jr., to suggest ways to cope with Proposition 13, is the effect of new and higher fees on the quality of life, particularly that of the lower-income groups that tend to use public facilities the most.

"Low-income residents may find fees prohibitive to the enjoyment of a park or a community swimming pool as these fees are increased," a commission task force warns. Attempts to set a rate structure subsidizing such groups would require a bureaucracy that in itself would lead to even higher costs, the report adds.

"We don't want to turn parks and swimming pools into country clubs for the middle-class and the rich," says Larry Naake, executive director of the California Park and Recreation Society, a professional group. "Fees may increase total revenue, but already attendance is down everywhere, from the Sacramento zoo to inner-city pools and parks." Mr. Naake says a recent survey by his group shows that 85 percent of the park and recreation agencies in the state have raised fees, the boosts ranging from 30 percent to 400 percent.

Money-Raising Strategies

Fees have been instituted at previously free museums, while charges at beaches and campgrounds are up substantially and fines for overdue library books have doubled or tripled in many cases. Community colleges, almost wholly dependent on property-tax revenue, have started charging for formerly free classes and services. As a result, attendance at noncredit courses—mainly recreation, crafts and courses for senior citizens—dropped 26 percent this past semester. Some 20 percent of 4,600 noncredit courses were shelved.

Localities have come up with some innovative ways to replenish their coffers. Oakland enacted an employe [sic] license fee based on salary earned in the city. Inglewood has instituted a fire-service fee based on the relative fire risk of each structure and the amount of water, personnel, and equipment that would be needed to extinguish a major blaze there. Pasadena's board of directors enacted an ordinance that will adjust all taxes, fees, and charges annually based on the preceding year's consumer price index. The directors retain the option to veto any particular increase.

Theoretically, communities could raise fees and charges to cover all their property-tax losses. But political realities, strong lobbying by interest groups and public opinion have helped to mitigate the increases. When put to the test of advisory or actual votes, proposed fee increases have failed in cities ranging from San Francisco to Palos Verdes Estates.

The ultimate tool of the angry taxpayer, the recall election, also has been used successfully. Voters recalled two members of the Simi Valley city council who were identified as leaders of the move that raised the annual sanitation service charge to $96 a home from $60. And voters in Sacramento County recalled four members of the San Juan Unified School District who had voted to contribute $1,000 in district funds for a lawsuit challenging Proposition 13.

11

Intergovernmental fiscal relations: Diversity and coordination

Federal, state, and local governments provide and finance public services in the United States, sometimes independently, sometimes cooperatively. No level operates as a regional department of another, although the extent of control and independence varies by level (as considered in Chapter 1). Each level is distinct and separate from the others, each with prescribed powers and authorities. Governments of each level are selected by their own electorates; even though local electorates sum to a state electorate and state electorates sum to the federal electorate, the balance of choices differs among localities in a state and among states in the nation. Because of that diversity of choice possible in a federal system, state and local governments have an important role in provision and finance of government services.

In spite of the important role performed by state and local governments, completely independent operation of these levels would, most argue, produce untenable results. Such a posture would undoubtedly leave the public without desired and affordable services, would inflict severe burdens on some unluckily placed individuals and businesses, and would leave some lower-level governments in chronic fiscal crisis outside their control. Those problems create the importance for fiscal interrelationships among governments.

DIVERSITY

Subnational governments provide what Justice Louis Brandeis called "insulated chambers of experimentation" for public action, but this diversity itself requires an allocation of the government functions among operating levels, an allocation which includes both questions of delivery and of financing that delivery. While only the federal government provides national defense in a meaningful sense,[1] few other public services show dominance by only one level. What establishes the appropriate level for predominant provision and how should intergovernmental financing be arranged?

Spillovers

The initial and probably the most important factor involved in choosing level of government for service delivery is the extent of benefit spillover. Because governments exist to provide collective, or public, goods, there is logic behind the attempt to match the extent of spillover with the jurisdictional extent of the government making decisions about that activity. This structural idea is called the *correspondence principle.* [2] Making the spillover area and the decision unit coincide serves to concentrate the government attention on the matters of most importance and prevents the convoluted patterns of decisions which otherwise occur when beneficiaries do not pay for a service.

A mismatch of spillover extent and government jurisdiction can produce significant misallocation of public resources. Suppose a city can construct a local sports complex which would cost $1 million with only $50 thousand of its own resources, the difference being financed by the federal government. The city will reasonably behave as if the full cost of the project is $50,000, even though the project uses up $1 million of resources. If the project has minimal beneficial impact beyond the city, there is no significant spillover which the project financing from the federal government corrects. Thus, the lack of correspondence causes the city to behave as if $1 million of resources have a value of only $50,000. Had the city been required to finance the project itself, it would have been unwilling to pay the $1 million (the project wasn't worth $1 million to the community). Resources get wasted and costs get exported to federal taxpayers only because of correspondence principle failure.

---

[1] In spite of state names, the various National Guard units are federally financed.

[2] Wayland Gardner, *Government Finance* (Englewood Cliffs, N.J.: Prentice-Hall, 1978), p. 276.

In all likelihood one can draw out a hierarchy of public services by the geographic extent of primary spillovers. A completely private good would have no spillovers; no distortions result from permitting private individuals decisions on the provision of purely private goods. Local recreation facilities—neighborhood parks—involve benefit spillovers extending beyond the family unit but certainly seldom involve spillovers far outside the immediate geographic area. Police and fire protection both involve some extent of spillover through movement of individuals across boundaries and the mobility of business transactions. Provision of these services purely at the individual or neighborhood level would generally lead to underprovision, as significant service spillovers would be ignored in decisions. Primary and secondary education, at least through welfare drains created by interregional mobility, involves concerns over a fairly wide area. At the furthest extreme is national defense, with a range of spillover extending throughout the geographic extent of the nation, and possibly even beyond. Failure to match spillover range and provision range can produce substantial misallocations. These can be reduced by either reallocation of decisions to other governments or through construction of intergovernmental aid programs which compensate lower governments for benefits spilled over to other units. Such corrections represent a major focus of fiscal federalism.

Under different circumstances, federal financing could correct misallocations from spillovers. Suppose the sports complex primarily benefited those from outside the city. In that case, the city decision would be made on the comparison of returns to its residents (only a small portion of total returns) against the full complex cost—a comparison biased against the project. In this case, federal financing of a large share of project cost is justified. That financing would allow the city to pay only to the extent its residents receive benefits, while federal taxpayers pay for returns received by outsiders.

Fiscal imbalance

A second influence in intergovernmental service delivery questions is fiscal imbalance between governments of a given level. Within the nation, per capita income of states ranges significantly—from $6,508 in Mississippi to $12,406 in Alaska in 1980.[3] Similar differences occur among local units in any state. While there is no one-to-one relationship, similar differences occur in the tax base available to governments.

---

[3] "State Personal Income," *Survey of Current Business,* 61 (April 1981): 38. National per capita personal income was $9,458.

If there is a disparity of fiscal resources among governments, equally situated individuals will be treated differently because of the affluence of the government in which they are located. Possibly the simplest method for demonstrating the problem uses the property tax as an example. Suppose two property owners, Smith and Jones, each own and live in houses valued at $10,000 for property tax purposes. Smith lives in a community with a property tax base of $40,000 per pupil; Jones lives in a community with a property tax base of $20,000 per pupil. If a quality education uses resources costing $1,500 per pupil, Smith's community need only levy a property tax of $3.75 per $100 assessed value to meet that cost while Jones's community would require a tax of $7.50 per $100. When both communities spend the same amount per pupil, the Jones property must pay property tax twice as high as the Smith property for the quality education previously described ($750 versus $375). Thus, services rendered from a given tax rate—or level of tax effort—will be greater where the capacity endowment is greater. Because there often is a mismatch between need for government service and capacity to finance those services, higher governments intervene by providing various fiscal assistance.

COORDINATION

Revenue relationships

Fiscal relationships between levels of governments can involve adjustments in revenue structures to provide both financial and administrative assistance. Revenue side assistance will not bring new resources into a government but it can improve access to resources already there. That can be valuable help, as it can reduce higher level involvement in the affairs of the unit, permitting substantial local freedom in government decisions. The two general classes of revenue relationship are relief in use of the tax base and assistance in lower-level revenue administration and compliance.

Revenue relief includes both deductions and credits granted the taxes of one unit in tax computations made for another unit. The two devices are both significant, but their operation and power are different. Deductibility means that the tax base for one tax is reduced by the amount of tax paid to a supported unit. For example, the federal individual income tax permits deduction of selected state and local taxes in computing the base upon which the federal rates are levied. Not only does this procedure free tax capacity for the lower units, but it also serves as an incentive for the adoption of the deductible taxes. The power of deduction may be demonstrated: suppose a taxpayer is in the

30 percent federal tax bracket. If his state income tax increases by $100, that taxpayer's net tax burden will increase by only $70 because the deduction of that state tax will reduce his federal liability by $30. Thus, the deduction provides both an incentive to coordination and aids lower units of government. In the pre-1964 tax reduction period—when federal marginal rates were as high as 90 percent—deductibility prevented taxpayers from encountering marginal rates above 100 percent, but that era has ended. Of course, the coordination effects are not extraordinarily strong (states continue to use nondeductible taxes) and deductibility will not equalize wealth between lower units.

 Deductibility creates a curious effect on state tax reductions—the loss of state tax revenue will be greater than the increase in disposable income available to its taxpayers. The other beneficiary is the federal government. For example, an individual pays $1,000 state income tax and is in the 30 percent marginal bracket for federal taxes. If his state tax is cut in half (to $500), his federal tax base will increase by $500 (because his deduction for state income tax paid is $500 lower) and his federal tax will increase by $150. Thus, the $500 state tax reduction increases his aftertax income by only $350—increased federal income tax accounts for the remainder. Estimates suggest, for instance, a federal revenue increase of $1−1.7 billion in 1979 as a result of California's Proposition 13 property tax reduction.[4]

A stronger device is the tax credit, an arrangement in which the tax levied by one unit of government acts as full or partial payment of the liability owed to another unit of government. One of the best examples is the federal tax on transfer at death: payments under a qualifying state tax act as an 80 percent credit of liability owed on the federal tax.[5] This creates an almost overwhelming incentive for state units to adopt the tax at least up to the maximum credit limit and obviously frees resources for subunit use. The credit does involve loss of revenue for the unit that grants the credit and the credit does not alter the basic distribution of resources among states of localities: affluent units remain affluent and poor units remain poor. In general, the credit does involve substantial implicit control of the lower unit by the higher unit.[6]

---

[4] Report to the Comptroller General of the U.S., *Will Federal Assistance to California be Affected by Proposition 13?,* GGD-78-101, August 10, 1978.

[5] Death taxes (estate and inheritance) are levied on the value of property transferred to another at the death of the property owner. The transfer must be gratuitous, or not in payment for services rendered. Estate taxes apply at the benefactor level; inheritance taxes apply to the heir.

[6] The power of the credit can be easily shown. Property can be transferred on death or during the benefactor's life. There are both federal death and gift taxes, but the credit applies only to the former. While only Nevada has no state death tax, only 15 states apply gift taxes.

Both deduction and credit of lower level taxes free up resources for lower level use and provide incentive for use of "approved" tax forms. They do not assist lower levels with administration and do not reduce the burden of compliance with taxes by multiple governments encountered by businesses and individuals. Another set of revenue tools can assist with that part of the intergovernmental fiscal problem. These devices include source separation, cooperative administration, coordinated tax bases, tax supplements, and centralized administration, arrayed in order of high to low amounts of lower-level government involvement in operations.

Separation of tax sources will avoid the problem of tax overlapping. Tax overlapping occurs vertically when governments at different levels (say, federal and state) apply a tax to exactly the same base, and horizontally when more than one government at the same level (say, two different states) applies a tax to the same base. Problems can be merely the nuisance of multiple taxpayer filings, or it can cause economic dislocation. If each level of government were guaranteed an exclusive use of particular tax bases, the vertical overlap problem would be effectively eliminated. The federal government, however, would likely continue with the individual income tax—a lucrative, generally viewed as equitable, source—which responds well to changes in economic activity. State and local units would be left with their traditional sales and property tax sources, an unhappy bargain for them.

TABLE 11–1
Tax source separation, 1959 and 1979

	Share of source (percent)					
	Federal		State		Local	
Source	1959	1979	1959	1979	1959	1979
Taxes on property	0%	0%	3.78%	3.83%	96.22%	96.16%
Taxes on income	94.75	85.25	4.85	13.46	0.40	1.30
Taxes on sales	52.06	26.46	42.66	63.06	5.28	10.48

Source: Computed from Bureau of the Census, *Summary of Governmental Finances in 1959* (G-GF59-no. 1) and *Governmental Finances in 1978–1979* (GF79-no. 5) (Washington, D.C.: U.S. Government Printing Office, 1980), p. 17.

Table 11–1 illustrates the mixed separation of source responses over the past 20 years. In 1959, local government dominated the property tax source, as it has for as long as records are available. The federal government has been excluded from the source by the constitution. State government once obtained a large portion of its revenue from the source (40 percent of state revenue in 1922 came from general property taxes, for example),[7] but the overall state role was small relative to that of local government. As state activity increased, those governments resorted to other sources than the property tax, so the state share of property tax revenue has never been high. Data for 1979 show continued local dominance of that source.

The federal government nearly monopolized the income base in 1959—95 percent of total collections (individual and corporate) were by the federal level. The highest federal marginal rate was 90 percent at that time, so neither states nor localities were much inclined to add any tax to that rate, even though very few individuals would have been subject to such punative rates. More states had corporate income taxes, but there was reluctance among the states to appear to discourage business. In all, the income base was nearly preempted by the federal government. In the early 1960s, the federal government substantially reduced its individual income tax rate structure. That action made heavier state and local use of the base more palatable; by 1979, the federal share of income taxes had fallen 10 percentage points (to 85 percent), the state share had risen 9 percentage points (to 13 percent), and the local share had increased to 1 percent. Federal dominance continues, but source separation is not nearly so complete as it had been 20 years earlier.

The pattern of sales tax separation over the past 20 years is not so easily summarized. The federal government was the dominant user (52 percent) in 1959, but the state revenue share was nearly as great (43 percent); local use was minimal (only 5 percent). From that time to the present, the federal government has dramatically reduced its use of selective excises (taxes on motor fuel and alcoholic beverages constitute over half of such revenue), state governments have increased their use of general sales taxes, and local governments have added both general sales and selective excise taxes. State use dominates (63 percent), while the federal share has fallen by half (to 26 percent) and the local share has doubled (to 10 percent). General sales taxation has long been dominated by state government. There has never been a federal general sales tax. Some have argued, however, that the federal government should adopt a value-added tax, clearly a movement away from base separation.[8]

Overall, governments show little taste for source separation as a

---

[7] Bureau of the Census, *Wealth, Public Debt, and Taxation: 1922. Taxes Collected Compiled as a Part of the Deciennial Report on Wealth, Public Debt, and Taxation* (Washington, D.C.: U.S. Government Printing Office, 1924), p. 12.

[8] It is not clear why any federal consumption tax should not be simply piggybacked on state sales taxes. Certainly that linkage would have the advantage of familiarity in compliance and administration.

response to vertical coordination problems. Only sources viewed rightly or wrongly as inferior (like the property tax) are likely to be separated to any level of government—and those governments can be expected to seek other sources traditionally used by other levels. While source separation would be an orderly solution, practical problems make its use not especially practical or likely.

The other coordination approaches all entail use of a single tax base by more than one level of government (source separation is not attempted) and leave lower levels of government with varying amounts of involvement in administration. The arrangements include cooperative administration, coordinated tax bases, tax supplements, and centralized administration.[9] *Cooperative administration* involves continued contact and exchange of information among taxing units. Sales tax administrators may inform their peers when a firm is found to be violating their tax laws in a manner which would generate liability in other states. Income tax administrators may exchange information about audits performed: the Internal Revenue Service may inform a state about audit findings for an individual living in that state. Business tax administrators may exchange information about contractors who should be registered to pay taxes in other states. Coordination is weak, but profitable for the administering parties: work done by one administration can generate revenue for another with little or no additional work. Base, rates, and rates structures need not coincide among governments for this cooperation, but all governments can gain from the exchange.

The next level of tax coordination is the *coordinated tax base,* an arrangement in which one government begins its tax from some stage in the structure of the tax levied by another government. Thus, several states key their individual income tax to adjusted gross income in the federal system and a number of localities begin their local sales tax ordinances with definitions taken from their state sales tax. Other elements of the tax may differ from that point—different exemptions, rate patterns, rate levels, etc.—but the higher- and lower-level taxes do have common elements. As a result, taxpayer compliance problems are reduced (one set of records can be used for both taxes and some of the computations need not be replicated) and administrative cooperation is simplified. Usually substantial differences between the taxes will, however, prevent the full gains from coordination in compliance or administration.

Greater coordination results with *tax supplements,* either through application of a lower-level rate on the base used by the higher level

---

[9] George Break, *Financing Government in a Federal System* (Washington, D.C.: Brookings Institution, 1980), p. 34.

(many state sales taxes have supplements added by local action) or application of a lower-level rate as a percentage of tax paid to the higher unit (a few states have determined their tax as a percentage of federal liability). This method dramatically reduces compliance requirements for taxpayers and cuts administration expenses when the supplementing unit refrains from making numerous changes in the tax used by the higher unit. Few units can refrain from at least a few changes and each change cuts the saving to taxpayers.

The final coordination system is central administration of a *supplemental, or "piggyback," tax rate:* the lower governmental unit applies its own rate on a tax base used by a higher unit of government. Full piggybacking would have the higher unit doing all administrative and enforcement work for the tax—the tax is paid on a single form to the higher unit, which records and remits collections for the lower unit. Lower units must adopt the tax (it is not simply a system of tax sharing) but they cannot select a base substantially different from that used by the state. Administrative economies are possible with single unit administration and the taxpayer can comply with multiple obligations at one time. Supplemental tax rates, however, do not permit a redistribution of resources among lower units. Most local sales taxes are piggybacked on the state sales tax—many times the local tax return consists simply of some extra lines on the state sales tax return—and local income taxes in Maryland, Indiana, and Iowa are similarly supplements to the state return. Most local income taxes are are not related to either federal or state taxes. States that continue a state property tax do apply them to the locally administered base, an example of piggybacking from state to local.

Grants

Grants transfer spending power (command over resources) from one government to another. A significant amount of the money spent by state and local government comes from assistance provided by other levels of government. In 1978–79, 23 percent of state revenue and 40 percent of local revenue was assistance (grants) from other levels of government. These funds were raised by other governments for use by the recipient government. The general pattern of intergovernmental aid since 1957 appears in Table 11–2. During that period, the growth of intergovernmental assistance to these governments exceeded that of total revenue: in 1957, state and local intergovernmental revenue was 21 percent of total revenue; in 1979, it was 32 percent of total revenue. Within that overall increase are some important developments.

TABLE 11–2
Sources of Intergovernmental Assistance, 1957 to 1979 ($ millions)

Recipients	Total revenue	Intergovernmental revenue*			
		Total	Federal	State	Local
1957:					
State	24,656	3,928	3,500	—	427
Local	28,896	7,539	343	7,196	—
Cities	12,047	1,756	105	1,489	162
School districts	8,914	3,733	117	3,390	227
1962:					
State	37,595	7,480	7,108	—	373
Local	43,147	11,642	763	10,879	—
Cities	16,797	2,674	330	2,134	210
School districts	14,199	5,769	204	5,267	298
1966–67:					
State	61,082	14,289	13,616	—	673
Local	64,608	20,188	1,753	18,434	—
Cities	24,096	5,081	803	4,001	277
School districts	22,787	10,064	522	9,103	439
1971–72:					
State	112,343	27,981	26,791	—	1,191
Local	114,791	39,694	4,551	35,143	—
Cities	42,114	11,528	2,538	8,434	556
School districts	39,364	17,653	749	16,471	433
1976–77:					
State	204,426	169,126	45,890 (2,217)	—	2,737
Local	196,458	76,831	16,554 (4,397)	60,277	—
Cities	73,527	24,062	8,910 (2,390)	14,093	1,059
School districts	62,938	31,501	952 (—)	29,659	891
1977–78:					
State	225,011	53,461	50,200 (2,255)	—	3,262
Local	214,518	84,053	19,393 (4,556)	64,661	—
Cities	80,125	25,833	10,234 (2,487)	14,482	1,117
1978–79:					
State	247,005	57,087	54,548 (2,261)	—	2,539
Local	234,630	94,777	20,616 (4,591)	74,162	—
Cities	86,864	25,598	10,837 (2,501)	15,472	1,288
1957–79 average annual growth rate:					
State	11%	13%	13%	—	10%
Local	10	12	20	11	—
Cities	9	13	23	11	10
School (to 1977)	10	11	11	11	7

Note: Comparable school district data are not available for the last two years.
* Amounts in parentheses indicate revenue sharing.
Source: U.S. Bureau of the Census, *Census of Governments: Compendium of Government Finances.* Censuses of 1957, 1962, 1967, 1972, 1977. U.S. Bureau of the Census, *Governmental Finances in 1977–1978* and *1978–1979,* and *City Government Finances in 1977–1978* and *1978–1979.*

There has been a healthy growth of aid to each level by each providing level. As Table 11—2 shows, the average annual growth rate of aid to each level exceeds the growth rate of total revenue in all instances. Aid growth from each level exceeds total revenue growth in all instances except from local government. The greatest difference between aid growth and total revenue growth appears with federal aid to local government and to cities only. Those aid growth rates—respectively 20 and 23 percent—are double the total revenue growth rates. Further, the federal aid growth rate exceeds the rate from any other level of government, often by several percentage points.

States continue as the primary source of intergovernmental aid for local government, both overall and to cities and school districts. States provided 78 percent of total aid to local government in 1978—79, compared to 95 percent in 1957. The major increase in federal assistance came in the decade of between 1967 and 1977. School districts did not fare well during the expansion: their share of federal assistance to local units fell from 30 percent in 1967 to 6 percent in 1977.

Overall, intergovernmental assistance plays a significant role in governmental finance. State and local dependence on these revenues is sufficient that their loss would create substantial fiscal pressure if they were stopped. In terms of assistance, at least, things have changed since President Coolidge's observation: "If the Federal Government should go out of existence, the common run of people would not detect the difference in the affairs of their daily life for a considerable length of time."[10] Recent estimates suggest a "cresting of federal aid flows to states and localities."[11] and recent growth rates of federal aid clearly do not approach those of the expansion decade before 1977. The evidence suggests greater attention to intergovernmental revenue relationships as subnational governments seek stronger indigenous tax sources.

The federal grant system includes three types of assistance: categorical grants, block grants, and general revenue sharing. State grant systems have some elements similar to federal, although each state has its own peculiar mix. Overall there is much hybridization of grant styles, making clear classification more and more difficult. In general, federal grants have moved gradually from a narrow categorical grant structure to broader, general-purpose assistance. Between 1972 and 1978, the proportion of block or general grants increased from 8.4 to 14.7 percent of the federal total.[12] State grants have always been for relatively broad

---

[10] Quoted in Arthur Schlesinger, *Crisis of the Old Order* (Boston: Houghton Mifflin Company, 1957), p. 57.

[11] Advisory Commission on Intergovernmental Relations, *Significant Features of Fiscal Federalism, 1978—1979* (Washington, D.C.: ACIR, May 1979), p. 1.

[12] Break, *Financing Government in a Federal System,* p. 167.

purposes, sometimes involving specified percentages of certain state taxes distributed for any local purpose.

Categorical grants. Categorical grants provide assistance for a particular program purpose, usually limited to spending for certain activities. These grants intend "to stimulate and support state and local programs in areas of specific national interest".[13] Their intention is to induce state or local governments to behave in a fashion other than the way they would behave without the aid—the grants seek to encourage recipient units to shift expenditures to particular functions or to guarantee provision of certain recipient government services in a manner consistent with national interest. In these areas, local interest and national interest presumably do not coincide. The grant alters local interest by making certain activities more attractive—the federal share makes the aided activity cheaper for the lower government—so that local actions are consistent with national interest.

Categorical assistance has four forms: formula-based, project, formula-project, and open-end reimbursement. The Advisory Commission on Intergovernmental Relations describes the varieties:

> Formula grants are those for which funds are allocated among recipients according to factors specified in legislation or in administrative regulations. Project grants are nonformula grants for which potential recipients submit specific, individual applications in the form and at the times indicated by the grantor. The third or mixed type of categorical grants are project grants for which a formula specified in statutes or regulations is used to determine the amount available for a state area. Distribution takes place in two stages, with the first stage involving state area allocations governed by formula and the second entailing project applications and discretionary awards. For open-end reimbursement grants—often regarded as formula grants—the federal government commits itself to reimbursing a specified proportion of state-local program costs, thus eliminating "competition" among recipients as well as the need for an allocational formula.[14]

While two thirds of the categorical grants in fiscal 1975 were project, 69 percent of categorical grant outlays are formula-based.

Project grants are the realm of the modern grantsman, the person assigned by many state and local governments and nonprofit agencies to make application for external assistance. (Formula and reimbursement categoricals plus the block and revenue sharing assistance, to be

---

[13] John Shannon, "Federal Revenue Sharing—Time for Renewal?" *National Tax Journal,* 27 (December 1974): 496.

[14] Advisory Commission on Intergovernmental Relations, *Summary and Concluding Observations, The Intergovernmental Grant System: An Assessment and Proposed Policies,* Washington, D.C.: ACIR, 1978, p. 3.

examined shortly, do not require competitive application.) This individual becomes familiar with the activities of federal agencies and private foundations (state government tends not to use project grants) and watches announcements of project funding available published in sources such as the *Federal Register*. When project requirements and the activities of the grantsman's employer coincide, the grantsman manages the preparation of a project proposal. The funding agency awards go to proposals evaluated as best according to the constraints of legislation and regulations. While political influence may sometimes be important, more often the decision will depend on factors like these:

1. Does the project meet goals of legislation?
2. Is the project within restrictions of the legislation?
3. Does the proposer demonstrate capacity to implement the project?
4. Does the project address a significant problem area?
5. Does the project demonstrate creativity?
6. Does the project have results transferable to other local governments?[15]

One peculiarity of the categorical grant must be recognized. For the recipient, the grant is most valuable if it will support an activity the unit was going to undertake even without the assistance. In that case, there is minimal disruption of local interest and resources are released for use in accord with local priorities. For the donor, the grant is most powerful when it supports activities not ordinarily undertaken by the recipient, at least at levels consistent with the donor's interest. Thus, there will consistently be some divergence of interest between recipient and donor in a well-designed categorical grant. Many do, in fact, have matching requirements to get greater spending for a granted donor dollar.

Critics of the categorical grant system emphasize three particular difficulties. First is the administrative complexity of the categorical grant system. In an effort to ensure that federal policy objectives are met as nearly as possible by state and local activities financed by federal funds, federal programs establish elaborate control mechanisms to monitor and shape actions taken by the recipient. Systems usually have different planning, application, reporting, and accounting requirements—none of which coincides with those ordinarily used by the recipient government. Not only are these controls an irritation but they also divert state and local resources to the administrative process.

A second criticism is the program overlap and duplication which has emerged in the federal grant system. An Advisory Commission on In-

---

[15] Reported by Charles A. Morrison, "Identifying Alternative Resources for Local Government", *Management Information Service Report,* 9 (July 1977).

tergovernmental Relations count found, for instance, 24 agencies administering 52 separate grant-in-aid programs related to control and prevention of fires in 1979.[16] That pattern almost inevitably means that some communities will not participate, leaving their residents less well served than would be desirable, while others will aggressively seek funds, producing extraordinary assistance for their residents. Governments may even use funds from one program to meet matching requirements of another, thus thwarting the intention of matching to stimulate local expenditure.

Finally, critics fault the distortion of local priorities that categorical grants produce. While the recognition of national interest is the predominant logical reason for the existence of such grant structures, the distortion may exceed any justified by the traditional spillover of local action argument. Furthermore, the aid may not be reliable. Aid often is eliminated after a few years, leaving state and local government with a responsibility but no resources. The combination of these criticisms has been instrumental in movement toward block and general-purpose assistance.

Block grants. Block grants are distributed, usually to general-purpose governments (categorical grants often go to special-purpose governments or nongovernments), according to a statutory formula to finance activities in a broad functional area. Much of the expenditure is left to the discretion of the recipient institution. To the early 1980s, the federal government had established five block grant programs:

1. Partnership for Health (Comprehensive Health Planning and Public Health Service Amendments of 1966) consolidated nine grant programs to reduce categorization of public health and improve the quality of health care funded by the programs.
2. Safe Streets (Omnibus Crime Control and Safe Streets Act of 1968) grants established a broad program of assistance for crime prevention and the administration of justice.
3. Comprehensive Employment and Training Program (CETA, 1973) consolidated 17 categorical programs generally related. It did not include all federal manpower programs (47 authorizations administered by 10 federal departments or agencies continued in 1978) and CETA likewise had sizable categorical programs along with the block program.[17]
4. Community Development Block Grants (1974) combined six urban

---

[16] Cited in Sarah Scott, "Fighting Fires from Washington," *National Journal,* (January 3, 1981): p. 8.

[17] ACIR, *Summary and Concluding Observations, The Intergovernmental Grant System,* pp. 10–11.

aid programs. The grants, while distributed partly by formula, also have a discretionary funding component and the legislation includes 13 eligible activities for funding. The program thus rests somewhere between a categorical and a block grant.

5. Social Services (Social Services Amendments of 1974) block grants brought together several social service programs that had been troublesome to operate.

A sixth program, the Public Works Employment Act of 1976, sometimes is classified as a block grant: funds are allocated by formula and there is no matching requirement. They fail to be true block grants because state and local governments compete on the basis of project application.

The Omnibus Reconcilation Act of 1982 (August 1981) consolidated into nine block grants 57 existing grant programs. The new programs and the number of consolidated programs in each are social services (2), home energy assistance (1), community development (1), elementary and secondary education (33), alcohol, drug abuse, and mental health (3), maternal and child care (6), community services (1), primary health care (1), and preventive health and health services (9). Social services and community development grants were already in block form and only four contain more than one earlier program, so substantial consolidation still awaits.

The Advisory Commission on Intergovernmental Relations states the case for block grants with "well-designed allocation formulas and eligibility provisions" to ensure that funds go to the appropriate units. These grants:

[1.] Provide aid to those jurisdictions having the greatest programmatic needs, and give them a reasonable degree of fiscal certainty.
[2.] Accord recipients substantial discretion in defining problems, setting priorities, and allocating resources.
[3.] Simplify program administration and reduce paperwork and overhead.
[4.] Facilitate interfunctional and intergovernmental coordination and planning.
[5.] Encourage greater participation on the part of elected and appointed generalist officials in decision making.[18]

The block grants should not be expected to stimulate new initiatives by recipient governments and should be confined to activities for which a broad national consensus already exists. They are not well designed to bend local choices in a direction more consistent with national interest or to cause local units to change their methods of operation. They can

---

[18] Ibid., p. 24.

be useful as replacements for groups of similar categoricals which have established local clienteles during their operation.

General revenue sharing. The third variety of federal grant is general revenue sharing, a formula distribution with few or no restrictions on the use of funds provided. The federal revenue sharing program, started in 1972, distributes, by formula, money which has been appropriated on a multiyear basis to that use. Similar (and older) state tax sharing programs typically dedicate a given share of selected taxes, e.g., one percentage point of the state sales tax rate, to a local aid formula. The federal approach provides some greater certainty of aid during the life of the appropriation (unforeseen changes in federal revenue do not influence distributed shares), but the funds have to be appropriated again when the period of appropriation expires and each renewal raises questions about continuation of the program (states were excluded for at least fiscal 1981—clearest evidence of that danger).

Revenue sharing distributes an appropriated amount of money to general-purpose governments according to formula. Because the Senate and House were not able to agree on a distribution formula, the present system uses a complex hybrid of two formulas. The Senate formula combines three factors: population, tax effort, and per capita income. The House formula add two more factors: extent of urban population and state income tax collections. Each state's share is computed according to each formula; the higher of the two shares is the one used for each state. Because using the higher for all states would cause more than 100 percent of available money to be distributed, the share for each state is reduced by the constant proportion needed to reduce totals to 100 percent. Resulting fractions are multiplied by the total revenue sharing appropriation for the year to determine the amount for each state. One third of that amount goes to state government (not 1981); two thirds is distributed to local governments in the state, usually according to the three-factor formula. Checks are sent to each eligible government without application and with only minimal restrictions concerning use (there must be a publicized appropriation process, there can be no discrimination in hiring or compensation, funds cannot be used for grant matching, use must be subject to external financial audit, etc.), but there are no controls on activities for which the funds are used.[19]

---

[19] When states return to the revenue sharing system in fiscal 1982 and 1983, they will be required to surrender $1 of categorical aid for each $1 of revenue sharing they accept, a requirement which will prove almost impossible to enforce and which sadly fails to recognize the difference in purpose between categoricals and revenue sharing. The categoricals induce states to recognize a national purpose by carefully controlling program use. Because of those national controls, $1 of general aid is more valuable to a recipient than $1 of categorical aid, so states will ordinarily be willing to make the trade, with attendant loss of contribution to the national purpose. If the categoricals really were sensible, this is a silly trade for Congress to propose.

General revenue sharing can strengthen local spending power and reduce intergovernmental fiscal disparities (the great differences in fiscal capacity that exist among governments at the same level across the nation). It does not shape local priorities to make them more consistent with national interest and it is not particularly effective as a way to aid disadvantaged groups. The former results because of the lack of controls placed on the assistance; the latter, because advantaged and disadvantaged tend, with few exceptions, to live in the same political jurisdictions. General aid to the jurisdiction will produce improved capability to provide services (or reduce taxes with no change in services) for anyone—and probably the advantaged will do better because they usually have greater political clout. It is simply not reasonable to expect revenue sharing (or block grants) to achieve the targeting and revision of public action that categorical programs can produce. Revenue sharing is suited for reducing fiscal disparity among governments at a given level and to strengthen the expenditure capability of units with constrained taxing powers. That is its position in the grant system.

Mandates

A mandate is a constitutional provision, statute, administrative regulation, or judicial ruling which places an expenditure requirement on a government, that requirement coming from outside the government forced to take the action.[20] Mandates are much like regulations of operation that governments place on private industry to regulate workplace safety, environmental quality, and so on. A state government can mandate local spending, the federal government can mandate either state or local spending, and the judiciary—the branch of government outside the normal flow of budgeting and appropriation—can mandate spending at any level. Most concern about mandates emerges from the local level because these units typically lack the overall size needed to respond flexibly to external expenditure shocks (few individual mandates would be sufficiently large, relative to overall expenditure, to significantly disrupt the federal or a state government). And these units lack the access to revenue sources of the other levels.

Mandates seek to cause governments to behave in some manner other than the way they would ordinarily behave. This changed behavior can be directed either toward services and programs or toward inputs used (normally personnel). Examples of the former include such things as

---

[20] Advisory Commission on Intergovernmental Relations, *State Mandating of Local Expenditures* (Washington, D.C.: ACIR, July 1978), p. 2.

hours libraries will be open, provision of special education by local schools, jail condition standards, water temperature in hospitals, provision of legal defense for indigents,[21] etc. Each requirement or regulation directs some expenditure, unless existing action already fulfills the requirement. Input use requirements encompass levels of compensation which must be paid resources acquired, the quality and/or quantity of input to be used and the conditions under which the input will be employed. All potentially change the cost of providing any given level of service. Examples include state determination of local welfare department salaries, requirement of local collective bargaining or compulsory arbitration, required employee training, funding requirements for pension systems, required participation in unemployment insurance or workman's compensation systems, regulation of wages, hours, and working conditions, and so on. Of course, several of this latter group are simple extensions of requirements applied to private employers.[22]

There are many other state controls on local government action beyond the mandates. States establish the "rules of the game" for localities: election frequency, budget and finance structures, permissible forms of government, due process definitions, etc. Many of these standards cause extra expenditure, but we accept them as reasonable cost of an informed democracy. "Rules of the game" are, however, often designed to reduce local government costs by limiting competition among local units, restricting direct democracy initiatives and elections for officials, constraining salaries of elected officials, or defining tax processes on a statewide basis. They are clearly of a different nature than the earlier group of mandates. Other interventions determine the distribution of tax burdens as the permissible scope of local taxation is defined (e.g., residential electricity may be removed from the local sales tax base). Because these actions directly restrict revenue-raising capability only in conjunction with tax rate limitations, they are not of the same concern as service or input mandates. Furthermore, these controls, along with control of the rules of the game, are best considered with the issue of home rule and the balance between local power and state sovereignty.

The case for mandates has two logical elements. First, the benefit of a lower unit action (or the cost of inaction) may spill beyond the bound-

---

[21] *Gideon* v. *Wainwright,* 372 U.S. 335 (1963) and *Argersinger* v. *Hamlin,* 407 U.S. 25 (1972).

[22] Governments also pick up restrictions as a result of accepting grants from federal or state governments. Grant controls create fewer logical problems than ordinary mandates: the recipient government accepts obligations as a condition of accepting the funds. There is no compulsion to enter the system.

aries of the lower unit. Thus, an irresponsible action by one unit can reduce the expenditures of that unit (and the taxes paid by those in that unit) while producing harm to residents of adjacent units. The state government may choose to mandate correcting service levels to prevent that damage to innocent bystanders. Second, statewide uniformity may be seen as essential by the legislature or the judiciary. The state may require equal expenditure per unit for schools, sanitation, etc., to prevent individuals from having low service levels solely because of their residence. Expenditure correction thus is mandated.

Against these arguments for mandates are a strong countercase. First, many argue that the mandating unit should be responsible for financing the mandate. The mandate can become a mechanism for producing political credit for the higher unit while the lower unit bears the burden of finance—a condition not conducive to careful decisions. Second, mandates can threaten other government programs. If limits rest on a government's ability to raise revenue, mandates for certain expenditures can endanger the provision of other desirable services. Third, mandates are characteristically enacted without cost awareness. While the result of the mandate may be desirable, the cost of its achievement may be excessive, particularly when compared with the return from other uses of the government resources. Mandates seldom are imposed in an environment favorable to comparisons of return and cost. This is particularly true when mandates emerge from the judiciary. Twenty-five states estimate in fiscal notes the cost to localities of state mandates,[23] but there is seldom any effort to identify cost to individual units—the point where expenditures must be financed. Finally, mandates restrict any autonomy provided under other legal provisions. They are clearly an uneasy companion where home rule has been provided.

For decisions about mandates, the appropriate comparison would appear to be whether the resource cost created by the mandate is worth the return generated by the mandate. Inflicting costs on other units may not be a likely way to generate that comparison. Some suggest that mandates without financial assistance sufficient to cover their costs are a violation of intergovernmental fair play. Others are skeptical, pointing out that governments do not finance mandated activities for private firms or individuals (minimum wage requirements, safety regulations, etc.), so while mandates may raise questions of appropriate government roles, they do not logically require accommodating fiscal transfers.

---

[23] Advisory Commission on Intergovernmental Relations, *Intergovernmental Perspectives,* 5 (Winter 1979).

Conclusion

Multiple levels of government provide public services in the United States. That diversity allows greater individual choice, but service delivery cannot be entirely uncoordinated because of two factors: intergovernmental spillovers and fiscal imbalance. Spillovers occur when an action by one government has impacts (good or bad) on its neighbors. Intergovernmental intervention can induce that government to allow for those external effects. Imbalance emerges because fiscal capacity is unevenly distributed across the nation and within states. Without an intergovernmental response, some individuals will be unduly penalized by the public sector simply because of where they live.

Those intergovernmental problems can be reduced by four different varieties of coordination: revenue relief (deductibility, credits), assistance in administration (source separation, coordinated use of a single revenue base), grants (categorical, block, revenue sharing), or mandates. The devices together help retain the advantages of multilevel government without some associated problems.

A CASE FOR DISCUSSION

The following selection appeared in *The Wall Street Journal.* No questions about it are necessary.

The Squirrel Memo

Many releases and handouts that cross newspaper desks each day could be offered as prime exhibits for hiking the postal rates on unsolicited mail. But occasionally there's gold in them thar hills, and we offer as evidence a recent item from the news bureau of Washington and Lee University in Lexington, Va.

It seems that one Frank Parsons,

assistant to the university president, was struggling with a lengthy application for federal funds to be used in building the university's proposed new library. Among other things, HEW wanted to know how the proposed project "may affect energy sources by introducing or deleting electromagnetic wave sources which may alter man-made or natural structures or the physiology, behavior patterns, and/or activities of 10 percent of a human, animal or plant population." The questions go on and on, but you get the idea.

Assistant Parsons plugged away, dutifully answering as best he could. And then he came to the section on animal populations, where he was asked to list the extent to which the proposed library would "create or precipitate an identifiable long-term change in the diversity of species within its natural habitat."

"There are some 10 to 20 squirrels living, or appearing to live, in the site proposed for the new library," he wrote. "Some trees that now provide either homes or exercise areas for the squirrels will be removed, but there appear to be ample other trees to serve either or both of these purposes. No major food source for the squirrels will be affected. It is likely that the squirrels will find no difficulty in adjusting to this intrusion. . . . They have had no apparent difficulty in adjusting to relocations brought on by non-federally supported projects."

To the question of whether the proposal will "create or precipitate an identifiable change in the behavior patterns of an animal population," he assured HEW the squirrels and such would have to make some adjustments but "it will be difficult to tell if they're unhappy about having to find new trees to live in and sport about."

Eventually the application was shipped off to Washington, and lo and behold before long HEW official Richard R. Holden actually wrote the president of the school. He said: "Perhaps bureaucracy will tremble, but I salute Washington and Lee University. . . . The mountain of paperwork which confronts me daily somehow seemed much smaller the day I read about the squirrels in Lexington. May they and your great university co-exist in harmony for many, many years." As copies of the correspondence zipped throughout federal agencies, with all the speed of a confidential memo destined for Jack Anderson, bureaucrats from all over telephoned their congratulations to the "squirrel memo man."

We're still not sure exactly what lesson is to be drawn from all this. Our initial reaction was surprise that anyone actually reads these exhaustive applications, and even now we're undecided whether that's cause for comfort or dismay. Yet while we never doubted that HEW possessed a sense of humor—indeed, we've gotten some of our biggest laughs from proposals emanating from the vicinity of 330 Independence Ave., S.W.—it's nice to know that an occupational devotion to red tape has not completely eroded the agency's ability to laugh at itself.

A CASE FOR DISCUSSION

State revenue sharing can be a major vehicle for equalizing local government ability to provide public services. Such a plan is far superior for that purpose than categorical assistance, an approach appropriate for stimulation of spending on specific local services. The following case, excerpted from an Advisory Commission on Intergovernmental Relations report describes the development of state revenue sharing in Wisconsin, a state providing much heavier general support to local government than is typical in the United States.

Measures of general support for local governments (1978)

	Wisconsin	All states
General state-local support ($000)	$701,598	$6,716,418
Per capita	$149.82	$30.87
Percent of local government general-purpose general revenue	23.3%	5.7%
Percent of total state expenditure	14.8%	3.3%

Source: ACIR, *The State of State—Local Revenue Sharing,* p. 18.

Consider these questions:

1. Why did Wisconsin revenue sharing drift away from an origin basis?
2. Explain the conflict between urban and rural areas on the aid formulas. Would that be a problem in other states?
3. How does equalization affect the willingness of localities to accept industries?

State-local revenue sharing in Wisconsin dates from 1905 when the state legislature exempted utility property (mainly railroad property at that time) from local property taxation. Using a state gross earnings tax instead, part of the proceeds were used to reimburse communities for their lost tax base. These utility aids have continued, in a much altered form, to the present.[1]

In 1911 Wisconsin initiated the first state individual and corporate income taxes. Their primary purpose was to enable the state to exempt all intangible personal property from the local property tax. To compensate localities, 70 percent of the proceeds of the state income taxes went to municipalities,

Source: ACIR, *The State of State—Local Revenue Sharing* (Washington, D.C.: ACIR, 1980).

20 percent went to county governments, and only 10 percent was retained by the state.[2]

Both the utility aids and shared income taxes initially, and for many years, were origin-based revenue sharing. Utility aids went to communities in proportion to their amount of utility property, while personal income tax receipts were disbursed in proportion to the amount of taxes paid by residents of each county and municipality. Since the individual income tax applied only to high incomes, and the exempted property was financial wealth, the new tax base was distributed among localities much like the old base. The origin method of sharing served well as a reimbursement to localities for lost tax base. The proceeds of the corporate income taxes were also distributed according to where corporate income was generated.

As the state's role in the provision of state and local services grew, the proportion of the income tax revenues earmarked for localities was decreased. For example, in 1925 the legislature lowered the shares of income tax from 70 percent to 50 percent for municipalities and from 20 percent to 10 percent for counties. Dollar levels did continue to rise because the income tax base and rates were increased. As other types of personal and business property were removed from the tax roles, the state earmarked new funds to reimburse local governments. A portion of state motor vehicle license charges and highway user taxes was allocated to communities to replace local property taxes on automobiles. A portion of the liquor tax was distributed to cities and towns, based on population.

After 1925 the legislature obtained additional revenues solely for state purposes by attaching surcharges to the income tax and making deductions prior to the local sharing distribution. The state abandoned these subterfuges in 1962 and adopted the principle that the state would receive all the additional revenue that would result from tax rate increases. Localities would continue to benefit from the growth in revenues resulting from increases in income. In order to implement this change, the legislature reduced the percentage of income tax revenues going to local government as the tax rate was increased.[3] Despite the growth in state revenue sharing money, the structure of the sharing continued to reflect the original plan to reimburse localities for property exempted from their tax rolls.

Wisconsin was an innovator not only in revenue sharing, but also with other actions related to property taxes. In 1949 the state introduced an aid formula for school districts that recognized the lack of district property taxing ability compared to a minimum guaranteed valuation per pupil. In the early 1960s Wisconsin instituted a sales tax and used much of the early proceeds to finance a new general property tax relief program. Under this program the state paid a portion of the real estate property taxes for all taxpayers in communities where the mill rate exceeded a state-specified rate. The aid is in proportion to that part of the property tax levy due to a rate in excess of the state-specified rate. A separate, personal property tax relief credit was created for the taxes paid on merchants' stock-in-trade, manufacturers' inventories, and farmers' livestock. A proportional credit was given everywhere, regardless of tax rate. The state also enacted a property tax "circuit breaker" for the elderly called the homestead credit. In 1973 the homestead credit was extended to include all individuals with low incomes.[4]

1969: THE TARR COMMISSION

Dissatisfaction with the state-shared revenue policy led to creation of the Task Force on Local Government Finance and Organization in 1969. Known as the Tarr Commission for its chairman, Curtis W. Tarr, the main conclusion of this commission's studies was that the then current system of origin-based aids were needlessly complex and inequitable.

The Tarr Commission said that the revenue sharing system was complex because of the various separate funds involved which necessitated the mailing of 8 to 10 checks a year to roughly 1,900 units of local government.

The commission found that the origin-based distribution of corporation income tax receipts was a particular administrative burden. Corporations had to maintain special records of income by municipality. Localities were concerned about the accuracy of these records and the accounting practices used to derive them since in 1966 shared corporate income taxes amounted to nearly $42 million.

The Tarr Commission emphasized a second weakness in the Wisconsin revenue sharing program: The method of distributing aids led to inequities, as communities that needed aid did not get enough of it and communities that did not need aid received too much. The origin-based system led to local governments with adequate property tax bases being rewarded by disproportionate shared aids, because they were the homes of higher-income families and corporations whose taxes were the primary sources of the aids. The Tarr Commission cited examples of communities that received aids many times the size of their property tax levy and noted that "one municipality has sufficient resources to offer two-year scholarships to all of its young people attending college."[5]

The Local Need Discussion

To remedy the defects of the origin-based formula, the commission considered two different approaches to measuring needs. The commission studied but rejected a local expenditure-related formula that would have provided aid to communities which spent above a certain per capita amount for essential services such as police and fire. The commission rejected this approach because it felt that the theory of causation of expenditure levels was insufficiently developed, and the methods of municipal accounting sufficiently varied, as to make this approach unworkable. Instead, the commission described its preferred alternative—a tax rate—type of formula:

> A second alternative seems more suitable as a representation of community needs: to assume that the tax rate itself expresses local requirements. This alternative stipulates that a municipality determines its expenditure level, subtracts the revenue it receives from state payments and special charges, and raises the remainder from property taxes. The underlying assumption is that the local elected governing body knows best the requirements of the local government and can balance these against the tax capacity of the community.[6]

* * * * *

The Tarr Commission advocated a consolidated revenue sharing fund from which the new aid distributions would be made and which would replace the general aids then provided on an origin and population basis (that is, personal and corporate income taxes, utility and liquor taxes, and motor vehicle registration fees). The size of the fund was to be based on percentages of the same taxes that were shared before. The system for allocating shared taxes was to have three components. The first part was a payment to communities to be determined by multiplying a state-set mill rate by the value of certain types of utility property. There was to be a maximum or cap put on the amount that could be received under this part of the formula. The logic was that utility property paid no property taxes and yet certain utility property received local services, particularly fire protection. It had been argued that the old origin formula provided excessive aid to communities with utility property.

A second part of the formula was to be a per capita payment to all localities, with the amount determined by the state. The logic here was that need for expenditures is primarily, although not exclusively, a function of population.

The final component was to incorporate the new need measure into the formulas, by providing aid to communities in proportion to the excess taxes caused by having a total tax rate for all purposes higher than a state-specified mill rate. The commission suggested that communities with tax rates below 20 equalized mills should receive no aid; this would have excluded 7 percent of the communities in the state. This part of the formula was referred to as the "percentage of levies payment." The statewide total payment to offset excess taxes, however, would be limited to the remainder of the revenue sharing money after the special utility and per capita payment had been distributed.

The distribution of aid between counties and municipalities was handled by having each county receive a percentage of what was determined by the formulas for each municipal area in the individual county; the commission suggested 16 percent of the municipal area amount be given to the county. This arrangement roughly preserved the historic county share. To ease transition problems, the Tarr Commission also advocated that the formula be phased in.

Legislative Response

At the urging of newly elected Gov. Patrick Lucey, the Wisconsin legislature, in 1971, adopted nearly all of the shared revenue recommendations made by the Tarr Commission. One change, however, was that added annual payments for general property tax relief were provided and funded by deductions from the municipal and county shared tax account. When the new redistributive formulas were enacted, "hold-harmless" guarantees were also superimposed on the system to prevent injury to any locality.

This new need-related formula system did not dramatically increase the amount of revenue sharing and it was not intended to. While total property tax relief—related state payments rose after 1971, most of the growth through 1977 came in general property tax relief, which also used an excess tax—type formula.

1975: CLOSER TARGETING FOR THE NEED CONCEPT

During its 1975 session, and again at the urging of Governor Lucey, the Wisconsin legislature further developed its revenue sharing system. The major change was to replace the percentage of levies formula with a new one that better recognized differences in local taxing ability rather than tax effort alone. The new formula also keyed municipal or county government aid to its respective taxing status alone, not including the level of school or other taxes.

The new formula was aidable revenues (a three-year average of most revenues raised by the recipient government) multiplied by a measure of taxing capacity. Taxing capacity was determined by subtracting from one a fraction equal to the ratio of actual full-value local tax base divided by a state standard for per capita property valuation. This latter amount was set at $30,000, over twice the 1976 state average. Communities with per capita property valuation over $30,000 received no aid under this part of the formula, although new hold-harmless provisions prevented actual reductions in aid.

For example, if a community had aidable revenues of $1 million, a local property tax base of $75 million full value, and a population of 5,000, its aid factor would equal $500,000. The formula multiplied aidable revenues by 0.5 because the locality was 50 percent short of the standard set for taxing ability. An otherwise identical community, with a larger property tax base of $100 million would have a smaller aid factor, because it was only 33 percent short of the standard set for taxing ability. The actual aid was subject to proration because the sum of the aid factors exceeded the total available funds.

Also associated with the move from a "percentage of levies" to "aidable revenues" formula was a redetermination of the county share. Rather than having county funds set by the municipal shares, the counties began to compete on their own for aidable revenue aids, although only 25 percent of their aidable revenues were counted in the formula.

CURRENT ISSUES
The Formula

By 1979 the percentage of levies formula had been changed to aidable revenues, the per capita formula aid had been frozen for three years, hold-harmless payments were no longer fully funded, and general property tax relief growth had been stopped in favor of added direct sharing. These circumstances combined to increase rapidly the money to be distributed under the aidable revenues portion of the formula.

The move to aidable revenues and the consequent greater targeting to low tax base urban areas have not been greeted with enthusiasm by officials in many rural areas and suburbs. Table 1 shows why. Rural areas are largely unincorporated and the town is the primary unit of local government. Roughly 59 percent of Wisconsin citizens live in cities, 11 percent in villages, and 30 percent in towns. All three are mutually exclusive.

Towns received over $16 million, or 18.4 percent of the aid allocated in 1975 under the percentage of excess levies portion of the aid formula. They received just over $4 million in 1977 under the aidable revenues portion of the aid formula. The towns' 18.4 per-

TABLE 1
"Percentage of levies" and "aidable revenue" aids (by type of recipient municipal government, 1975 and 1977)

	Percentage of levies aids 1975	Percent	Aidable revenue aids 1977	Percent
Cities	$62,704,644	71.2%	$73,118,706	86.8%
Villages	9,189,917	10.4	7,096,320	8.4
Towns	16,186,354	18.4	4,035,035	4.8
Total	88,080,915	100.0%	84,250,061	100.0%

Source: Wisconsin Department of Revenue, Bureau of Local Fiscal Information and Analysis, *Taxes, Aids, and Shared Taxes in Wisconsin Municipalities, 1975, 1977* (Madison, Wis.: Department of Revenue, 1977, 1979), p. 103.

cent share had shrunk to 4.8 percent in 1977. The losses in total aids were largely offset by the various hold-harmless elements or the formula. It was originally the intent of the legislature to phase out the hold-harmless clauses, but it has renewed them several times.

Nevertheless, further equalization and aid to cities was recommended in January 1977, by the Commission on State-Local Relations and Financing Policy, empaneled by Gov. Patrick J. Lucey:

> The commission recommends that the shared tax program be revised to more nearly equalize disparities between municipalities in the relationship between their available revenue sources and their financial requirements. The shared tax formula should take into account the burden imposed upon central cities in providing services to commuters.[7]

Members of the Wisconsin legislature representing rural districts who were on the commission took exception to this policy statement. They filed a minority report concerning state-shared revenues which said:

> We do not believe it is equitable to the rural areas of the state that state-shared tax payments emphasize the aidable revenue portion of the formula to the detriment of the per capita payment portion. This, in essence, rewards big spenders and penalizes those municipalities which have been efficient or even frugal. . . .
>
> We hasten to add that many services in rural areas, e.g., sewage, water, and garbage, are handled by the individual and require little, if any, public expenditures. Nonetheless these persons are entitled to state-shared tax payments inasmuch as they are also a point source of the revenue collected by the state income and sales tax.
>
> If the rural areas are to lose their per capita payments, at the very least those monies should go to expand substantially the homestead tax credit program rather than be consumed by those municipalities which benefit greatly from the aidable revenue portion of the formula.[8]

The change from the percentage of levies to the aidable revenue formula increased aids to urban areas at the expense of rural sectors partly because the aidable revenues for municipalities are based only on revenues raised locally by a municipal government and partly because rural property values rose faster than urban values between 1975 and 1977. The percentage of levies formula gave aids to municipalities based on total county, school, and municipal property tax levies. Since urban areas typically spend much more for municipal services than rural areas, but not much more or equal amounts on schools and county services, switching only to municipal revenues to determine aid acted to the disadvantage of rural areas.

The rural versus city debate illustrates the different aspects of need, and the difficulty associated with its definition. Although schools are aided separately from municipalities in Wisconsin, rural areas feel that school and overall property tax burdens from any given tax rate are more of a hardship than in urban areas. There is more hardship because of lower rural incomes and because the rapid increases in rural property values lowered their share of aid but did not provide increased ability to pay taxes. Urban areas, while acknowledging a relative shift in aid to their favor, could argue that their needs remained inadequately met. Table 2 shows that the average per capita amount of shared taxes from all formulas going to towns declined between 1971 and 1977 relative to the amount going to the City of Milwaukee.

Despite the increase that favored Milwaukee and other cities, the municipal property tax rate difference between urban and rural areas of the state continued between 1971 and 1977 (see Table 3).

One way of measuring the equalizing effect of state-shared revenues is to calculate how much property tax and shared revenues a municipality obtained per person, relative to its property tax effort. Municipalities can be compared by examining these ratios of revenue per person to mills of property

TABLE 2
Average shared taxes per capita indexed to amount received by Milwaukee, 1971 and 1977

	1971	As a percentage of Milwaukee's allocation	1977	As a percentage of Milwaukee's allocation
Milwaukee	$54.27	(100)	$72.19	(100)
Cities*	36.16	(67)	56.44	(78)
Villages	55.70	(103)	53.49	(74)
Towns	40.90	(75)	43.70	(61)
State	50.55	(93)	54.46	(75)

* Excludes Milwaukee.
Source: ACIR staff calculation based on Wisconsin Revenue Department data.

TABLE 3
Municipal purpose mill rates,* 1971 and 1977

	Municipal mill rate levy 1970 (payable 1971)	Municipal mill rate levy 1976 (payable 1977)
Milwaukee	15.34	14.36
Cities†	7.21	8.48
Villages	4.00	5.14
Towns	1.44	1.19
State	6.34	6.11

* As equalized to adjust to varying levels of property assessments.
† Excludes Milwaukee.
Source: ACIR staff calculations based on Wisconsin Revenue Department data.

tax rate. When this is done (as Table 4 shows), Milwaukee remains disadvantaged in 1977 as well as in 1971. While the relative advantage of towns declined between 1971 and 1977, towns still obtained over three times the tax and shared revenue per capita for each mill of tax effort than was obtained by Milwaukee. Put differently, Milwaukee's 1977 tax rate was nearly 12 times the average for towns, but it obtained less than four times as much revenue per person. The relative advantage of other areas over Milwaukee, and of towns and villages over cities, was still substantial in 1979, but the equalizing trend accelerated in the years 1977 to 1979.

The decision of the legislature to continue to increase the aidable revenues portion of the formula represented a commitment to decrease the difference in revenue raising ability among municipalities. In the future, the governor and legislature will be called upon to reconsider this policy in light of rural and suburban complaints that too many state tax dollars have to be taken from them in order to equalize the ability of higher spending cities to obtain local revenue. In 1979 new Governor Lee Sherman Dreyfus called for a study by the Wisconsin Department of Revenue on the fairness of the aid formulas.

The Impact of Equalization on Industrial Location

The emphasis on equalization, which has characterized Wisconsin public finance not only for general-purpose local government finance but also for school finance, has raised an interesting issue: Does equalization, substantial or otherwise, mistreat communities with industrial property and cause communities not to accept or seek an industrial tax base? That is, are localities now so insulated from tax base changes that they can be indifferent or opposed to attracting new industry?

Wisconsin business groups and legislators from districts with high concentrations of industrial property gave the answer, yes. The 1979 legislature and Governor agreed that action

TABLE 4
Equalization in Wisconsin, 1971, 1977, 1979

	Levy and shared taxes per capita per property tax mill	As a percent of Milwaukee
1971 total:		
Milwaukee	$10.55	100%
Cities*	15.44	146
Villages	22.22	211
Towns	36.61	347
Total State	15.85	150
1977 local:		
Milwaukee	$16.16	100%
Cities*	19.78	122
Villages	24.04	149
Towns	54.37	336
Total State	23.14	143
1979 total:		
Milwaukee	$23.78	100%
Cities*	28.12	118
Villages	31.84	134
Towns	62.49	263
Total State	32.90	138

* Excludes Milwaukee.
Source: ACIR staff calculations based on Wisconsin Department of Revenue data.

was necessary. Manufacturing property, which makes up 5 percent of the state's property tax base, was excluded from calculations of a community's tax capacity in the aidable revenues portion of the shared revenues formula. Roughly 250 communities with high concentrations of manufacturing property gained aid because of this change. The loss was spread among the remaining 1,600 localities, so the loss to any individual community was not significant.

The legislature had passed a bill excluding 50 percent of industrial valuation from the calculation of fiscal capacity, but the governor vetoed the

50 percent clause, thereby excluding all industrial valuation.

The Wisconsin Revenue Department Study

In 1978–79, the Wisconsin Department of Revenue studied the issue of equalization and industrial location and focused on two questions:

1. Are there local government costs associated with concentrated industrial development which are not recognized in the shared revenue formulas?
2. Does the existence of equalization formulas for school and local gov-

ernment aids cause communities not to seek or to oppose industrial development to the detriment of the economic health of the state?[9]

The aidable revenue portion of shared revenues formula is based on the principle that differences among local property tax rates should be a function of service levels, but not tax bases. What this system did not take into account, critics maintained, was that industrial properties cause a need for additional revenue to be raised per resident because of the cost of municipal services for industry. Further, it was contended that the burden was unfairly placed on the community's residents because the aid formula allows their tax rate to be higher, regardless of where the beneficiaries from industry live.

The revenue department found some empirical evidence to substantiate this claim. Using a multiple regression analysis, the department found that higher than average per capita local spending could be statistically explained in part by high industrial concentration when the latter was one independent variable in a statistical model with other explanatory factors such as total tax base wealth and intergovernmental aids. These other factors were included to control for the possibility that higher per capita spending in industrial communities was due to past fiscal advantages rather than industry per se. The revenue department's analysis further found that the aidable revenue portion of the formula could result in higher tax rates for industrial communities

than for nonindustrial communities of similar per capita tax base. The additional aid that they would receive through the formula due to higher expenditure was more than offset by the aid they lost due to their having a higher tax base. This would be unfair if the residents of industrial communities did not themselves benefit substantially from industry-related government spending.

It is difficult to empirically determine the answer to the second issue—whether formula equalization discourages communities from accepting new manufacturing plants. Wisconsin and Minnesota have gone further than other states in equalization of local government finance. Even in these states, however, equalization is not dollar for dollar. Communities do not lose a dollar in aid for each dollar increase in potential tax revenue that comes from tax base growth. The move in Wisconsin from a pro-industrial area aid system to a partly equalizing aid system was also accompanied in 1974 by a property tax exemption for manufacturers' machinery and equipment and, in 1977, by legislation to also exempt inventories over a five-year period. The end result of the exemptions will be to eliminate nearly two thirds of taxable manufacturing property. Thus, the potential tax base gain from industrial development was considerably diluted over the 1970s. There are no documented cases, however, of a community planning to refuse future permission to industry to build because of a possible adverse effect on state aids.

This problem is in one sense ironic.

The intent of state programs to equalize revenue raising abilities has been to create "tax base neutrality," i.e., to make tax rates less influenced by tax base, and to reduce the advantages that high tax base places had in attracting more tax base. As a result some Wisconsin officials now fear that if the local tax base is guaranteed, the willingness of communities to accept industrial development will substantially diminish.

Footnotes

1. James R. Donohue, "Local Government in Wisconsin," *Wisconsin Blue Book 1979– 1980* (Madison, Wis.: Madison Legislative Reference Bureau), p. 214.
2. Wisconsin Commission on State-Local Relations and Financing Policy, *The Final Report of the Commission on State-Local Relations and Financing Policy* (Madison, Wis.: 1977), p. 1–8.
3. Wisconsin Task Force on Local Government Finance and Organization, *The Report of the Task Force on Local Government Finance and Organization* (Madison, Wis.: 1969), pp. vi–1,4.
4. *Ibid.*, pp. vi–2–3.
5. *Ibid.*, p. vii–1.
6. *Ibid.*, p. vii–1.
7. Wisconsin Commission on State-Local Relations and Financing Policy, *The Final Report of the Commission,* p. 19.
8. *Ibid.*, p. MR–8.
9. Wisconsin Department of Revenue, Division of Local Fiscal Analysis, internal department document, "Technical Supplement: Aidable Revenues Formula and Local Cost Impacts from Industry" (Madison, Wis.: March 24, 1978.

1. Patterns and structures of revenue for state and local government are important policy concerns because they establish the level and distribution of the burden of public service provision. Revenue revision can only begin with a clear understanding of where revenue policy leaves the state and its localities now, and what options available have not been selected. Furthermore, it is useful to understand what conditions are like in surrounding areas. Evidence for such discussions can be drawn from sources like the Department of Commerce's *Survey of Current Business* (monthly); the Census Bureau's *Census of Governments* (quinquiennial), *Governmental Finances* (annual), *State Tax Collections* (annual), *State Finances* (annual), and *City Finances;* the Advisory Commission on Intergovernmental Relations' *Significant Features of Fiscal Federalism* (biennial); and state tax handbooks published annually by Prentice-Hall and Commerce Clearing House. From those and similar sources, prepare answers to these questions about the revenue system in your state:

   a. How does the burden of state, local, and state–local taxation in your state compare with that of the nation and region? (Comparisons are often made as percentages of state personal income and per capita.) How does the local share of state and local taxes compare?
   b. Prepare an estimate of the relationship between business and individual tax shares for your state. Where are there allocation problems?
   c. How rapidly have state and local taxes grown in your state during the past five years? Is that faster or slower than growth in state personal income and the rate of inflation? Have there been tax rate increases (decreases) affecting that growth?
   d. What are the major revenue sources used by governments in your state? How does relative use of those sources compare with the nation and the region? Does your state have any major taxes not common to other states (severance, business and occupation, local income, etc.)? Are some typical taxes not used?
   e. Identify the important elements of the income tax in your state: what governments levy the tax, does the tax apply to individuals and corporations, how is the tax linked to federal income taxes, are the rates graduated, and is the tax indexed?
   f. Identify the important elements of the general retail sales tax in your state: what governments levy the tax, what commodity sales are exempt, are credits used, what is the nominal rate, and what are the brackets?
   g. Identify these elements of the property tax in your state: who assesses property, what valuation standard is used, when was the latest reas-

sessment of real property, what classification system (if any) is used, and what circuit breaker–type (if any) is used?

2. Mr. and Mrs. Knight, an elderly couple, had $3,500 income from taxable sources and $4,500 social security. They own property assessed at $12,230 (with a market value of $49,000) and pay a tax rate of $6.50 per $100 of assessed value. Their state has a threshold-type circuit breaker, with the threshold set at 5 percent of total money income, subject to an upper limit for relief of $800. Relief is given as a refundable credit under the state income tax. Compute their gross property tax liability before circuit breaker relief, the amount of property tax relief for which they are eligible, and their net property tax liability (after relief).

3. John Smith has an adjusted gross income of $26,000 and a taxable income of $19,000. Using the information in Table 7–2, compute Smith's average and marginal effective tax rates. Smith's income (adjusted gross and taxable) increases by $5,000. Compute his average and marginal effective rates. Is Smith in a higher tax bracket? Does Smith have higher after-tax income with the extra $5,000 or without it?

4. A midwestern state aids its institutions of higher education by giving a credit against its income tax equal to 50 percent of any gift to those institutions (subject to a limit of $50 credit per person). Two residents of that state, Mr. Blue (in the 20 percent federal tax bracket) and Ms. Jones (in the 40 percent federal tax bracket), each contribute $100 to an eligible state university.

    a. How much will state tax liabilities of each change as a result of their gifts?
    b. State income tax payments and contributions to charitable organizations (such as universities) are both deductible from the base used to compute federal tax liability. How much will federal tax liability change for Mr. Blue and Ms. Jones as a result of their contributions?
    c. Considering both changes in federal and state tax liability, what is the net after-tax cost of their gifts to Mr. Blue and Ms. Jones? (Hint: subtract the changes in state and federal liability from $100.)
    d. Compute the federal tax liability change for both without including the deduction for state income tax. The difference between the answers here and in question (b) equals the increase in federal revenue resulting from reduced state tax revenue—the difference between reduced money for state government to spend and increased disposable income for residents of the state.
    e. Suppose the state changed from a credit to a deduction. If the state tax rate were a flat 2 percent, how much would state liability for Mr. Blue and Ms. Jones change?
    f. From the computations in question (e), which approach (credit or deduction) do you suppose universities in the state would favor? Why?

5. According to the brackets presented in Table 7–5, is it possible in Maryland to make a single purchase of a taxable item with a quarter and receive five cents change? Explain.

6. Suppose a state applies a 5 percent sales tax to consumer purchases of many items. The following display presents data about the purchasing characteristics of two families which are generally representative of similar units in the state.

	Low-income family	High-income family
Income.....................................	$5,500	$22,000
Family size	3	4
Purchases of taxed items...................	$4,300	$12,000
Purchases of food for at-home use..........	$2,500	$ 5,000

a. What is the statutory sales tax rate paid by each family?
b. What is the effective sales tax rate on income paid by each family?
c. Is the tax progressive, regressive, or proportional? Why?
d. Suppose the state decides to exempt food purchased for at-home use from the tax. What will be the effective rate for each family? Does the exemption change the progressivity or regressivity of the tax? Explain.
e. Suppose the state provides a rebate or credit of $40 per person, instead of exempting food. (Notice that $40 per person is about equal to the sales tax paid on food by the lower-income family.) Answer the questions of part (d). Compare the impact on state revenue of the two approaches.

7. Compute property tax statistics as directed:

a. A city has assessed value of $55,000,000 and levies a property tax of $7,500,000. An individual property is valued at $15,000. What is the property tax rate in dollars per $100 assessed value and what is the bill for the parcel of property?
b. If assessed value increases by 5 percent and levies can increase by 6 percent, what is the maximum-allowed property tax rate and what would be the bill for the parcel?
c. If assessed value increases by 10 percent and property tax rates are allowed to increase by $1.50 per $100 assessed value, what is the maximum-allowed levy and what would be the bill for the parcel?

8. Randolph County includes four townships (Lincoln, Madison, Wayne, and Indian Creek) and one city, Fairview. It is served by two independent school districts: Tecumseh United (Lincoln and Madison Townships) and Randolph Southern (Wayne and Indian Creek Townships). The county assessor reports the following true cash values for the units in the county:

Wayne Township	$ 67,000,000
Indian Creek Township....................	71,000,000
Lincoln Township—in city	65,000,000
Lincoln Township—remainder	43,000,000
Madison Township—in city	38,000,000
Madison Township—remainder	34,000,000
County total	318,000,000

Each government in the county levies a property tax to finance its activities and no other revenue sources are available. Rates are applied to assessed value, defined to be 50 percent of true cash value. The county tax does apply within Fairview. The following table presents the amounts that each taxing unit seeks to finance from its property tax:

Randolph County	$5,500,000
City of Fairview	3,000,000
Lincoln Township	750,000
Madison Township	700,000
Wayne Township	600,000
Indian Creek Township	650,000
Tecumseh United Schools	2,500,000
Randolph Southern Schools	1,500,000

    a. Determine the property tax rate for each taxing unit. Compute the rate in dollars per $100 of assessed value.

    b. The Jones family owns property with a true cash value of $40,000 in the Madison Township part of Fairview. Prepare an itemized tax bill for them. The Smith family owns $40,000 of property in Wayne Township. Prepare an itemized tax bill for them.

    c. There are 5,500 pupils in the Randolph Southern school district and 15,000 pupils in the Tecumseh United district. How many dollars per pupil would a tax rate of $1.00 per $100 yield in each district?

9. There have been complaints about assessment practices in Garfield County. Each of the three townships in the county assesses property independently, using an elected assessor. State law dictates that assessed value equal one third of true cash value; the state constitution contains a clause requiring uniform property tax rates. The state agency of which you are an employee judges assessment quality in counties, recommends multipliers to produce overall balance among townships, and can recommend general reassessments where needed.

    You have obtained a random sample of assessed values and selling prices of the residential properties that have sold during the last quarter in the county. All prices are arm's length transactions, none involve special financial arrangements, and none involve substantial amounts of personal property. The attached list presents these data.

a. Prepare a preliminary opinion of assessment quality in Garfield County. Compute all important statistics.

b. The Garfield County Board of Equalization wants multipliers to get each township AV/MV ratio up (or down) to the state-required one third ratio. What multipliers would you apply in each township? Will the application of these multipliers increase or reduce measured equality of assessment in each township? What would their impact be on measured equality in the county?

c. Total property tax rates by township are:

Buchanan Township	$6.15 per $100 AV
Arthur Township	$6.00 per $100 AV
Coolidge Township	$5.75 per $100 AV

(1) What properties pay the highest and lowest nominal tax rates?
(2) What properties pay the highest and lowest effective tax rates?

Parcel	Assessed value	Selling price
Coolidge Township:		
1 – 1	$ 6,730	$ 38,500
1 – 2	13,020	65,000
1 – 3	22,230	120,000
1 – 4	4,610	28,000
1 – 5	13,240	67,000
1 – 6	7,850	75,000
1 – 7	5,550	29,500
1 – 8	5,290	27,700
1 – 9	10,970	36,900
1 – 10	7,020	34,750
1 – 11	6,580	23,000
1 – 12	9,540	39,500
1 – 13	4,640	24,900
1 – 14	6,790	37,000
1 – 15	6,430	30,500
1 – 16	4,000	16,900
Arthur Township:		
2 – 1	$ 4,730	$ 20,500
2 – 2	19,900	15,500
2 – 3	3,130	15,000
2 – 4	6,720	38,500
2 – 5	6,420	28,750
2 – 6	3,140	27,000
2 – 7	4,740	22,000
2 – 8	3,280	15,500
2 – 9	3,920	19,500
2 – 10	3,240	18,500
2 – 11	4,670	17,500
2 – 12	4,500	27,100
2 – 13	3,790	25,000

Parcel	Assessed value	Selling price
Arthur Township:		
2−14	2,640	12,724
2−15	3,770	26,000
2−16	2,930	15,500
2−17	5,120	28,500
Buchanan Township:		
3−1	$13,360	$ 62,400
3−2	8,720	45,000
3−3	5,680	28,500
3−4	13,080	54,600
3−5	3,400	15,000
3−6	3,460	18,000
3−7	5,040	23,600
3−8	6,850	36,000
3−9	8,180	41,900
3−10	3,580	20,500
3−11	4,590	21,900
3−12	5,050	33,000
3−13	5,470	29,000

10. The Indiana intangibles tax is levied on the holders of intangible personal property in the state. The tax base is market value of the item of property on the last day of December; for most taxpayers, intangible holdings in December will establish tax due by April 15 of the next year (paid with the annual income tax return). Tax rates have been 0.0025 percent, but a phase-out of the tax begins in calendar year 1982. In that year, the rate will be 0.00233 and in the following year, 0.00217.

Fiscal year (July 1 to June 30) collections for the tax from 1973 through 1980 follow, along with estimates previously prepared for fiscal 1980 and 1981 and calendar year data on Indiana personal income. Both income and collections are in millions.

Year	Collections	Personal income
1973	$15.6	$26,158
1974	17.8	27,776
1975	15.7	29,816
1976	17.1	33,206
1977	16.6	37,132
1978	18.4	41,487
1979	22.2	46,279
1980 (estimated)	18.0	n.a.
1981 (estimated)	18.5	n.a.

n.a. = not available.

Estimate revenue from the tax for fiscal years 1981, 1982, and 1983, using any method that is appropriate. (An independent commission has estimated Indiana personal income for the three years to equal $52,660 million in 1981, $59,800 in 1982, and $67,500 million in 1983.) Describe the method you use and indicate why it is better than other alternatives available.

11. The Indiana General Assembly is considering a bill to permit Marion County (Indianapolis) to impose a 1 percent tax on sales by restaurants and bars. The tax would be collected with the 4 percent state sales tax. The lawmakers need to know the amount of revenue the tax would generate. Furthermore, the city intends to use the revenue as support for a bond issue to construct a domed stadium and will require a revenue estimate for that issue. The following data are available:

Sales tax data for SIC Code 58—eating and drinking places
(4 percent state tax)

	Calendar 1976	Calendar 1979
Marion County		
Taxable sales	$ 228,962,065	$ 325,478,215
Receipts	9,110,890	13,066,175
State		
Taxable sales	1,352,036,319	1,929,639,993
Receipts	54,207,562	77,516,374

Sales data from 1972 and 1977 census of retail trade

	1972	1977
Marion County		
SIC 58: eating and drinking places	$181,237,000	$ 289,238,000
State of Indiana		
SIC 58	904,181,000	1,519,522,000

Census definitions of sales seldom coincide with the base for sales tax purposes. Indiana uses consolidated reporting of sales tax collections: all outlets of a restaurant chain would report their sales through the single home office county.

Use the data provided here to estimate the yield for the tax in calendar 1981 and 1982. Clearly describe your estimation procedure and indicate each assumption you make in the derivation.

12. The Fernwood Wastewater District—at the gentle insistence of both state and federal agencies—is changing methods of financing the operating and maintenance costs of its system. Presently, all users of the system (residential, commercial, agricultural, industrial, etc.) pay for the system by a property tax: payments to the district are assigned according to individual holdings of property value. If a car wash has 0.0001 of total property in the

district, the car wash pays 0.0001 of the operating and maintenance cost of the system. The proposed effluent charge system would assign cost on the basis of estimated toxic waste quality and quantity introduced into the system. The structure could easily be applied, because a federal agency has data on the amount and type of waste that production and consumption processes generate annually, based on national data. These data would then be used to assign an annual effluent charge to each user, based on the costs of the system.

How do the two systems differ in terms of incentive to reduce wastewater quantity and toxicity?

PART THREE

Administration of public debt and idle fund management

ART

12

Debt administration

Public debt, whether federal, state, or local, results from borrowing money from an individual or institution with the promise of repayment at a later date. Borrowing changes the pattern of purchasing power between the lender and the borrower: the lender forgoes purchasing power now for the promise of repayment later, the borrower receives purchasing power now and makes repayment later. Government debt results from the necessity to cover deficits (annual expenditures greater than annual revenues), from the finance of capital project construction, and from coverage of short periods within a fiscal year in which needed disbursements for payment of bills exceeds cash on hand. Governments borrow for different purposes, depending on the level of government. For that reason, those causes will be briefly considered before a more intense examination of debt policy and administration by state and local units. Federal debt is largely a product of national economic stabilization and war finance; those policies are outside the scope of this work.

SOURCES OF PUBLIC DEBT

The federal government debt, shown in Table 12–1, is largely the product of war finance and of actions taken to stabilize the macroeconomy of the nation, that is, to deal with problems of unemploy-

TABLE 12–1
Ownership of the public debt of the United States Treasury (billions of current dollars, end of year)

	1939	1946	1960	1970	1975	1977	1978	1979	1980	Compound annual growth rate, 1970–1980
Total gross public debt	$41.9	$259.1	$290.4	$389.2	$ 576.6	$ 718.9	$ 789.2	$ 845.1	$ 930.2	9.1%
Held by U.S. government agencies and trust funds	6.1	27.4	55.1	97.1	139.1	154.8	170.0	187.1	192.5	7.1
Held by Federal Reserve Banks	2.5	23.4	27.4	62.1	89.8	102.5	109.6	117.5	121.3	6.9
Held by private investors	33.4	208.3	207.9	229.9	347.7	461.6	509.6	540.5	616.4	10.4
Held by foreign and international	0.2	2.1	13.0	20.6	66.5	109.6	137.8	123.8	134.3	20.6
Gross national product			504.0	992.7	1,549.2	1,918.0	2,156.1	2,413.9	2,627.4	10.2

Source: *Federal Reserve Bulletin* (several issues) and *Economic Report of the President*, January 1981.

ment and inflation. Greater deficits are presumed to stimulate the economy, with accompanying boosts to employment and production. The
table shows that, over the years, the federal government has seen fit to
increase its debt by sizable amounts. There is no meaningful linkage of
borrowing to particular federal capital expenditure projects; the debt
levels are the accumulated totals of deficit outcomes not masked by the
methods described in Chapter 3. This nonproject orientation is reflected
in the shortness of maturity of federal debt: almost 50 percent of the
federal debt matures within one year. The debt is for cash, not for
projects, and must be regularly refinanced at the same time new borrowing is done. Gross public debt grew at an annual rate of 9 percent
through the 1970s.[1] It did not, however, grow as rapidly as did gross
national product (slightly over 10 percent rate), so the absolute claim on
federal debt repayment at the start of the 1980s was somewhat less than
it was at the beginning of the 1970s.

Not all the federal debt is, however, a net requirement for resource
transfer outside government. Sizable portions of that debt are held by
federal agencies or federal trust funds (21 percent of gross debt in 1979)
and by Federal Reserve Banks (13 percent in 1979). Trust funds and
agencies acquire the debt in their cash management programs—what
safer place to invest funds than in U.S. Treasury debt?—so this debt is
not truly a net claim on government resources. Federal Reserve Banks
buy and sell federal debt in the practice of monetary policy (transactions
with the public and the commercial banking system to change the supply of money in the economy). As the Federal Reserve Banks legally
must return to the U.S. Treasury sizable portions of interest received
and as they are, at least loosely, government agencies, this debt likewise is not truly an outside claim on the government. For most analytic
purposes, then, it is the debt held by private investors—that debt outside federal agencies, federal trust funds, and Federal Reserve Banks—
that is the major concern for federal debt policy. During the 1970s, that
debt held by investors did increase as a share of gross public debt (from
50 percent in 1970 to 66 percent in 1979), as agency and trust fund
investments were less important (their investable balances were less as
most experienced overall cash outflows).

The amount of debt in private investor hands thus depends on accumulated federal deficits (gross public debt), monetary policy actions
by the Federal Reserve, and trust fund investable cash balances.
Investor-held debt grew at a rate slightly greater than did gross debt in

---

[1] Following Federal Reserve System reporting, these debt figures exclude guaranteed
agency securities and includes issues of the Federal Financing Bank. The former totals
around $200 billion.

the 1970s and matched the rate of growth of the economy. Thus, the ratio of investor-held debt to gross national product was about the same in 1980 (24 percent) as it was in 1970 (23 percent). Probably more significant, however, is the remarkable growth of debt held by foreign and international investors; during the decade this ownership grew at a 20.6% annual rate, a dramatic increase in the extent to which federal debt holders are outside the United States economy. Thus, repayment of that portion of federal debt and interest represents a transfer of resources outside the economy, and the federal debt can no longer be casually dismissed as a problem because "we owe it to ourselves." About 22 percent of debt in private investor hands is owed, not to ourselves, but to foreign individuals and institutions. Servicing that debt involves transfer of resources from American taxpayers to foreign bondholders, a condition with substantially different standard of living implications for the United States than the traditional situation of American taxpayers making payment to American bondholders.[2] As long as foreign entities build up dollar reserves in international trade and world investors regard United States government debt as yielding a high rate of return without significant risk of the sort of political upheaval which leads to debt repudiation and seizure of foreign assets, such investment is not likely to diminish.

Debt of state and local governments has likewise grown rapidly through the 1970s, from $143.6 billion in 1970 to $259.7 billion in 1977, an annual growth rate of 8.8 percent. This debt, the product of states, counties, municipalities, townships, school districts, and special districts as shown in Table 12–2, is generically called municipal debt, distinguishing it from corporate or federal issues. The preponderance of this debt is long term (95 percent of the total), particularly in comparison with the federal debt, and most is issued for construction of identifiable, long-life assets, such as schools, highways, housing projects, and so on. The purposes are indicated in Table 12–3, which shows the heavy state–local debt emphasis on education and utilities. Such an identification of purposes would, of course, not be possible for federal debt.

The state–local debt figures distinguish between *full faith and credit* debt and *nonguaranteed,* or *limited-liability,* debt. Full faith and credit obligations "have an unlimited claim"[3] on the taxes of the issuing unit;

---

[2] A compilation of foreign held debt (November 30, 1978) shows it heavily concentrated in Germany (36 percent), Japan (22 percent), and Switzerland (9 percent). Further, it is heavily concentrated in the under one-year maturity structure: 66 percent of the total holdings mature in less than a year.

[3] Roland I. Robinson, "Debt Administration," in *Management Policies in Local Government Finance,* ed. J. Richard Aronson and Eli Schwartz (Washington, D.C.: International City Management Association (ICMA), 1975), p. 231.

TABLE 12–2
Indebtedness of state and local governments, by type of government, 1976–1977 ($ millions and percent distribution)

Item	State and local, total	State government	Total	Counties	Munici- palities	Town- ships	School districts	Special districts
Debt outstanding, total	$259,658	$90,200	$169,458	$22,663	$71,792	$4,128	$28,411	$42,464
Long-term	246,816	87,184	159,632	21,443	67,251	3,413	27,267	40,258
Full faith and credit	136,409	42,913	93,496	15,293	39,131	3,197	27,267	8,609
Nonguaranteed	110,407	44,271	66,136	6,151	28,120	216	—	31,649
Short-term	12,842	3,016	9,826	1,220	4,541	715	1,144	2,206
Percent distribution								
Debt outstanding, total	100.0%	34.7%	65.3%	8.7%	27.6%	1.6%	10.9%	16.4%
Long-term	100.0	35.3	64.7	8.7	27.2	1.4	11.0	16.3
Full faith and credit	100.0	31.5	68.5	11.2	28.7	2.3	20.0	6.3
Nonguaranteed	100.0	40.1	59.9	5.6	25.5	0.2	—	28.7
Short-term	100.0	23.5	76.5	9.5	35.4	5.6	8.9	17.2

Source: *1977 Census of Governments* (Compendium, p. 35)

TABLE 12–3
Long-term debt of state and local governments outstanding at end of fiscal year, by purpose, 1976–1977 ($ millions and percent distribution)

Item	State and local	State	Local	State and local	State	Local
Total	$246,816	$87,184	$159,632	100.0%	100.0%	100.0%
Education	57,314	19,348	37,966	23.2	22.2	23.8
State institute of higher education	12,041	12,041	—	4.9	13.8	—
Local schools	37,963	4,048	33,915	15.4	4.6	21.2
Other	7,310	3,259	4,051	3.0	3.7	2.5
Highways	19,317	16,663	2,654	7.8	19.1	1.7
State toll facilities	6,203	6,203	—	2.5	7.1	—
Other	13,114	10,460	2,654	5.3	12.0	1.7
Housing and urban renewal	16,495	6,913	9,582	6.7	7.9	6.0
Sewerage	7,894	1,746	6,148	3.2	2.0	3.9
Hospitals	5,952	3,269	2,683	2.4	3.7	1.7
Airports	3,370	268	3,102	1.4	0.3	1.9
Parks and recreation	3,199	1,379	1,820	1.3	1.6	1.1
Water treatment and terminals	2,287	566	1,721	0.9	0.6	1.1
Utilities	40,160	3,325	36,835	16.3	3.8	23.1
Electric power	17,986	3,186	14,799	7.3	3.7	9.3
Water supply	16,906	135	16,770	6.8	0.2	10.5
Transit system	4,993	4	4,989	2.0	—	3.1
Gas supply	276	—	276	0.1	—	0.2
Other and unallocable	90,830	33,708	57,122	36.8	38.7	35.8

Note: Because of rounding, detail may not add to totals. A dash represents zero or rounds to zero.
Source: *1977 Census of Governments* (Compendium, p. 35)

nonguaranteed debt issues lack that assurance and are sold on the basis of repayment from revenue proceeds from particular sources. Types of nonguaranteed debt include:

1. Revenue bonds: revenue from the project financed (toll bridge, water plant, etc.) redeem the debt.
2. Lease-rental bonds: facilities (office building, computer equipment, etc.) constructed from the debt proceeds are leased to a government at a rent sufficient to cover debt service and operating cost.
3. Lease-purchase bonds: public works (school, hospital, etc.) constructed by a private firm from debt proceeds are leased to a government (the government receives title to the property when the debt is retired).
4. Industrial development and pollution control bonds: private facilities—ultimately owned by their user—are constructed by the municipal debt with rental payments by the users servicing the debt.
5. Special revenue bonds: projects financed by bonds serviced from special revenues (parking garages financed by a special property tax on downtown property or sidewalks financed by a special assessment on property owners in the affected area).
6. Tax increment bonds: bonds financing area redevelopment which are serviced from the additional taxes generated in the redeveloped region.

Another type, mortgage revenue bonds, will be prohibited after 1983. State and local governments used their tax-exempt borrowing power to obtain funds for home mortgage lending at rates lower than otherwise available.

Because purchasers of public debt (the individuals and institutions lending money to state-local governments) regard the claim on all tax resources as offering greater likelihood that bond principal and interest payments will be made on time, full faith and credit debt bears a lower interest rate than does equivalent nonguaranteed debt. (Later sections will suggest why many governments use nonguaranteed debt, in spite of its greater cost.) Long-term state government debt is over half nonguaranteed; long-term local government debt is more heavily full faith and credit. Short-term debt at both levels is almost completely full faith and credit.

Nonguaranteed debt is outside limits frequently placed on municipal government debt by state statute or constitution. Interest on such debt is, however, granted the same exclusion from federal taxation received by municipal debt. That creates a logical consistency:

> In order to invoke tax immunity, the agency which issues those bonds must show that they are the obligations of a state or subdivision; but in order to provide that they are revenue bonds and not subject to the usual debt limitations it must show that they are *not* the obligations of any such unit.[4]

Creating and defending the appropriate distinctions is the source of substantial income for bond counsel. The convenience of having the debt interpreted both ways is usually worth the price. Much revenue bond debt is issued by public authorities, entities with public powers outside normal constraints placed on government. Governments form authorities to build a public project (bridges, power projects, highways, etc.) and pay off bonds used to finance the construction with tolls from users. The authority may or may not go out of existence when the bonds are retired.[5]

Table 12–2 provides extensive detail on the nature of local government debt. Of particular importance are the following features. First, municipalities are the largest local user of debt markets. Second, special districts are the heaviest users of nonguaranteed debt. This is not surprising because many special districts (waste management, transit, water, etc.) are established on a semicommercial basis, i.e., they are financed by user fees and have no taxing power. Thus, they have revenue generated by capital projects and lack the tax base for guarantee. And third, school districts are heavy users of full faith and credit debt, with no nonguaranteed debt, according to the Census Bureau classification. School districts traditionally have not been operated from user fees, so there is no project revenue available to support borrowing. Tax and intergovernmental aid revenue are the sole sources for repayment, so full faith and credit issues are the fiscal devices used by schools.

Table 12–4 identifies the patterns of state–local debt growth in the past 20 years. While all sectors of debt have risen substantially, local nonguaranteed debt shows the greatest increase in relative terms, from around 30 percent of the local total to 40 percent. This shift emerges from substantial use of local credit to obtain funds for private firm financing (industrial development bonds, pollution control equipment financing) and a desire to avoid the legal restrictions placed on full faith and credit issues. The trend is troubling for larger cities: "The economic

---

[4] B. U. Ratchford, "Revenue Bonds and Tax Immunity," *National Tax Journal,* 7 (March 1954): 42.

[5] For a fascinating view of public authority operation, see Robert Caro, *The Power Broker: Robert Moses and the Fall of New York* (New York: Vintage Books, 1975), chap. 28.

TABLE 12-4
State and local debt outstanding by character of debt ($ millions)

Year	State long-term		Local long-term	
	Full faith	Nonguaranteed	Full faith	Nonguaranteed
1977	$42,913	$44,271	$94,837	$62,126
1972	25,228	25,314	70,585	37,654
1967	13,558	17,627	49,204	27,232
1962	10,313	11,300	38,008	17,923
1957	6,490	7,032	26,210	10,803

Source: Bond Buyer's *Municipal Finance Statistics,* 1978. (Periods not strictly comparable with data in Tables 12–2 and 12–3.)

advantage of cities lies in making the marginal maintenance and repair expenditures that can keep the basic elements of their present infrastructure in adequate working order.''[6] Nonguaranteed bonds are not easily adapted to generate financing for reconstruction or maintenance, so the shift indicates special problems to confront those cities. If the infrastructure (streets, water and sewage systems, etc.) is not maintained, the economic advantage of newer cities becomes overwhelming.

APPROPRIATE DEBT POLICY

Debt yields resources for public use now to be repaid (plus interest) in the future. Borrowing thus commits future budgets. Because of that contractual rigidity, debt must be issued with care: improper use can disrupt lives of those paying taxes and expecting services in the future as debt service costs can impair the ability of the borrower to operate normally. The fundamental rule of debt construction is: do not issue debt for a maturity longer than useful life of the project it is financing. If the debt life exceeds useful life, the true annual cost of the project has been understated and people will continue to pay for the project after the project is gone. If the useful life exceeds the debt period, the annual cost has been overstated and people will receive benefits in periods in which no payment is made. The timing of payment question is particularly significant across generations and, at the local level, across a citizenry which is frequently changing with mobility in society.[7]

---

[6] George E. Peterson, "Capital Spending and Capital Obsolescence—The Outlook for Cities," in *The Fiscal Outlook for Cities,* ed. Roy Bahl (Syracuse, N.Y.: Syracuse University Press, 1978), p. 49.

[7] Temporary cash needs should be covered by short-term borrowing liquidated within the fiscal year. Carrying short-term cash borrowing across a fiscal year (rolling over) would violate the fundamental principle.

Long-term borrowing is appropriately done for long-life capital facilities. Economic growth does require expanded public capital infrastructure, often before any associated expansion of public revenue, so a strong case can be made for use of debt: the future revenue stream will be adequate to service debt expansion, to borrow a concept from corporation finance. Some governments have, however, elected to employ "pay as you go finance," paying for capital facilities only from current year operating surpluses. Such a policy can produce both inefficiency and inequity. First, with population mobility, users would not pay an appropriate charge for those facilities. Those in taxing range would pay when the facility is built; they may not be there when the facility for which they have paid is actually providing services. Second, the high single-year ticket price of a major project may discourage construction, even when the project is sound and feasible. Finally, pay-as-you-go financing can produce substantial tax rate instability, with artificially high rates during the construction phase and artificially low rates during operation. Such instability is unlikely to be helpful in development of the local economy. Furthermore, debt finance produces annual debt service charges which are fixed by contract. Therefore, when the area tax base grows, the property tax rate for debt service for a project will decline over time.

Debt commits resources for extended periods and can be misused by public officials who seek to postpone the time when costs of public actions are felt. Potential for misuse, however, does not preclude debt finance. When properly handled, debt is an appropriate financing medium. In fact, strict "pay as you go" can be as unsound as careless use of debt. Both financing methods can be appropriate tools in the fiscal arsenal.

DEBT STRUCTURE AND DESIGN

After the decision to finance a project by borrowing has been made, a number of debt structure decisions remain. They will be considered here, along with some institutional detail about municipal bond markets.[8] Characteristics should ideally be designed to assure least cost marketability of the issue, to simplify debt management, and to provide appropriate cost signals to fiscal decision makers.

One initial decision involves the type of security and its term to maturity (i.e., the period for which the money will be borrowed). Markets respond differently to full faith and credit bonds as opposed to

---

[8] The jargon of the market lumps all state and local government borrowing under that label.

revenue bonds. The greater security behind the former debt typically will cause a lower interest rate to be paid on an equivalent offering. The latter form of debt may be desired, however, because of legal restrictions placed on full faith and credit debt[9] or because revenue debt is appropriate as a means for allocating costs to the users of a project. For instance, a city may enter capital markets to obtain funds for pollution control equipment for a private electric utility. There can be no logic to full faith and credit finance here: charges paid by the utility should be the sole service source.

Maturity of the debt should roughly coincide with project life to ensure that the project will be paid for and the debt liquidated before replacement or major repair is required. This maturity-matching principle both prevents debt finance of operating expenditures and permits financing the use of the improvement by those receiving benefits from that improvement. Debt service costs along the life of the project roughly represent a rental (or depreciation) charge for the facility: users pay charges or taxes to cover those annual costs. The total charge can thus more accurately reflect annual cost of the service, including both capital and operating costs.

A given issue with 30 years overall maturity, for example, can be of either *term* or *serial* nature. A term issue would have all bonds in the issue timed to mature at the end of 30 years. Funds to repay principal would be obtained through the life of the bond issue (along with interest charges along the way) and placed into a sinking fund maintained by the bond issuer. At maturity of the issue, sinking fund accumulations would be sufficient to repay the principal. A serial issue contains multiple maturities in a single issue. Thus, some bonds would be for a 30-year term, some for a 20-year term, and so on. Portions of the project cost would be paid through the overall term of the issue. The serial issue may improve marketability of many municipal issues. Thin secondary markets for municipal debt cause most purchasers of that debt to hold the bond to maturity.[10] With serial issues, the issuing government can sell its debt to purchasers with funds available for several different periods of time. Either term bonds with sinking funds or serial

---

[9] Full faith and credit debt may be limited to a maximum total amount, to a maximum percentage of the tax base (usually assessed value), or by a requirement that voters approve the debt at a referendum. Reserve bond debt generally escapes all these limits. Limits are reported by state in Tables 61–63 of Advisory Commission on Intergovernmental Relations, *Significant Features of Fiscal Federalism, 1976–77*, vol. 2, *Revenue and Debt* (Washington, D.C.: ACIR, 1977).

[10] Corporate bond purchasers can purchase a bond with reasonable assurance that the bond can be sold to another person if funds are needed prior to maturity: a strong secondary market exists. Thus, these bonds will ordinarily not be serial.

bonds spread the financing of the project over the life of the project and provide financing on a "pay as you use" basis.[11]

Maturity of the debt will play an important role in determining what the ultimate interest cost of the issue will be because there is a relationship between the term to maturity of debt and the interest rate required. This relationship, the "term structure of interest rates," is influenced by economic conditions at the time of borrowing and will often, but not always, be upward sloping. That is, the longer the term to maturity, the higher the interest rate required to borrow for that period of time. Figure 12–1 illustrates the term structure prevailing in late 1980. The maturity-matching principle dictates, however, that maturities not be shortened to reduce the overall interest rate paid.

FIGURE 12–1
The term structure of interest rates (selected recent dates)

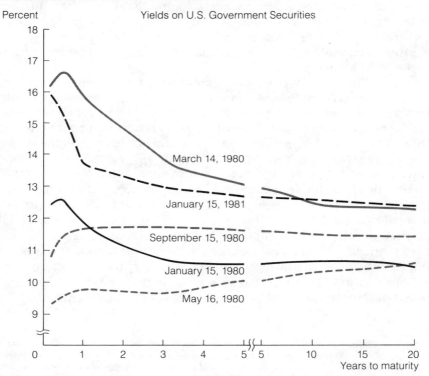

Source: Prepared by Federal Reserve Bank of St. Louis (released: February 13, 1981).

---

[11] "Pay as you go" would have current payment for purchases with no debt. Payment occurs as facilities are acquired, not as they are used.

RATINGS

The extent of risk to lender attached to a particular bond issue will be critical in determining the interest rate paid by the borrowing government. Credit worthiness opinions are prepared by a few rating firms, including Moody's Investor Service, Standard and Poor's, and Fitche, to list the more widely known firms. These agencies, for a fee paid by the bond issuer, prepare an opinion of the credit quality of the borrower (for full faith and credit issues) or of the particular bond issue (for revenue bond debt). These rating opinions are widely distributed to the investment community and are nationally used to form portfolio strategy. An issue without a rating will seldom sell on national markets, but issues can be unrated if local markets will buy them. These ratings have a major influence on borrowing cost, as Table 12–5 shows. Notice that

TABLE 12–5
Bond ratings (Moody's) and yield, 1940–1980
(end of year)

	Aaa	Aa	A	Baa
1980	9.44	9.64	9.80	10.64
1979	6.50	6.69	6.89	7.42
1978	5.91	6.01	6.51	6.76
1977	5.07	5.23	5.46	5.79
1976	5.07	5.50	6.42	6.73
1975	6.50	6.94	7.78	7.96
1974	6.65	6.81	7.14	7.50
1972	4.91	5.04	5.19	5.39
1970	5.21	5.33	5.60	5.80
1965	3.39	3.47	3.60	3.78
1960	3.12	3.35	3.60	4.03
1955	2.29	2.46	2.81	3.25
1950	1.42	1.60	1.92	2.17
1945	1.11	1.27	1.62	1.91
1940	1.56	1.78	2.11	2.60

Source: Moody's Investors Services, *Moody's Municipal and Government Manual.*

about a full percentage point separates highest grade (Aaa) and lower investment grade (Baa). Lower grades fare less well because many financial institutions are forbidden to hold lower rates securities because of the speculative elements associated with that debt. Table 12–6 relates the ratings of the two major services and suggests the general risk factors associated with each rating.

The precise manner in which borrowing unit characteristics contribute to a rating is not estimable. However, Moody's Investor Service,

TABLE 12–6

Credit risk	Moody's	Standard & Poor's
Prime........................	Aaa	AAA
Excellent.....................	Aa	AA
Upper medium	A-1, A	A
Lower medium	Baa-1, Baa	BBB
Speculative	BA	BB
Very speculative	B, Caa	B, CCC, CC
Default	Ca, C	D

Note: Moody's hyphenated A-1 and Baa-1 ratings indicate better quality credits in those ratings. A plus or minus attached to a Standard & Poor's rating indicates upper or lower segment of that rating category.

probably the most prominent firm in municipal debt rating, reports that the following information is used in a full faith and credit rating:

1. Debt policy: the uses, purposes, and planning of debt issuance, as well as the type instruments used.
2. Debt structure: adequacy of plans for debt retirement—the relation between rate of retirement and purpose of debt, resources of the community, and existing and future debt needs.
3. Debt burden: gross and net debt related to resources and a comparison with other communities—overlapping debt and pyramiding.
4. Debt history and trend: the record as to defaults, refunding of maturing bonds and funding of operating deficits—rapidity of debt growth relative to purposes for which it has been incurred.
5. Prospective borrowing: authorized and unissued bonds—adequacy of capital programming—obsolescence or inadequacy of capital plant—existing debt structure.

Financial analysis:

6. The current account: the year-end relation of current liabilities to available cash—promptness in disposing of casual deficits—devices to keep deficits from accumulating—if accounting is revenue accrual, the adequacy of reserves for uncollectible accounts—the liquidity of current account cash and uncollected taxes should equal demand liabilities outstanding.
7. Revenue system: adequacy of property tax base—trend of assessed value, equalization ratio, levy, and collections—other components of revenue system—source, base rates, yields—diversity, cyclical stability and adequacy of aid from other governments.
8. Expenditure analysis: vulnerability to mandated expenditures—relation of debt service to total expenditures.
9. Budget analysis: adequacy of planning—appraisal of past performance on revenue and expenditure estimates—current trend of financial operations.

10. Financial administration: assessment practices—tax collection procedures—financial planning as evidenced by budgeting, reporting, services.

11. History of financial operations: long-term trend of revenues and expenditures—secular and cyclical patterns.

Government:

12. Organization: diffusion of responsibility—degree of professionalism—sufficiency of powers to discharge functions.

13. Services: provision for essential services to perpetuate economic base.

14. Intergovernmental factors: the pyramid of governmental units, conflicts and duplications—complementarity—other units which drain off resources or impede planning.

15. Administrative performance: conscientious administrators who promote confidence through standing and experience—availability of audits, budgets, annual reports, capital planning documents, land use plans.

Economic:

16. Identity and natural resources: geographic and locational advantages—natural catastrophe—natural resources—size and land use characteristics.

17. Population, welath, and labor factor: population characteristics—wealth level (family income and per capita full value)—housing characteristics—new construction values.

18. Economic structure and capital: types of employment industry and occupation—major employers—relation to SMSA (Standard Metropolitan Statistical Area)—evidences of industrial decline or population shifts—transportation and its relation to the economic structure.

19. Economic performance and prospects: the secular trends of the economy—cyclical trend—seasonal and random variations.[12]

No explicit formula produces the ratings, as they are house opinions based on forecasts of the borrower's ability and willingness to repay the debt as shaped by the economic, financial, and governmental environment. Accumulations of report summaries are published annually as a guide to investors. Figure 12–2 illustrates with the Moody's report for Ashtabula, Ohio.

Revenue bond analysis is primarily concerned with the revenue potential of the enterprise and legal protection of bondholders in the covenants in the bond resolution. There is little concern with the government, as there is no precedent requiring bail out of revenue bonds. For

---

[12] Moody's Investors Service, Inc., *Pitfalls in Issuing Municipal Bonds* (New York: Moody's, 1977), pp. 14–15.

FIGURE 12–2
Moody's summary of Ashtabula, Ohio, fiscal conditions and debt rating

ASHTABULA

City in Ashtabula County. Incorporated in 1828.
Population: 1970, 24,313; 1960, 24,559.

Assessed Value, etc. ($000)

Year:	Real property	Utility property	All property
1979–80	n.a.	n.a.	126,037
1978–79	75,665	20,353	125,305
1977–78	n.a.	n.a.	111,483

Tax Rate Per $1,000 (in $):

Year	Debt	Total	Overall
1979–80	2.10	10.11	49.11
1978–79	2.72	10.705	49.85
1977–78	3.13	11.15	51.28

City Income Tax: 1.2% under present ordinance to Dec. 31, 1980.

Bonded Debt, Jan. 1, 1980: General, $2,396,150; special assessment, $92,446; urban renewal revenue, $1,505,000. Due within one year: Gen., $227,575; sp. assess., $46,635.

Tax Collections, Real & Utility ($000)

Year:	Taxes levied	Collected (Amt.)	%
1977–78	897	937	104.5
1976–77	899	810	90.1
1975–76	876	786	89.7

Accum. delinq., Dec. 31, 1978, $618,406.

Schedule of Bonded Debt, Jan. 1, 1980
Limited Tax Issues

Street Improvement

4½s	'66	Ser. to 12-	1-81	J & D1a	$17,150
4⅞s	'72	Ser. to 12-	1-92	J & D1a	600,000

Urban Renewal

5¾s	'75	Ser. to 12-	1-85	J & D1a	635,000

Unlimited Tax Issues

Sewage Treatment Plant

1 5½s	'73	Ser. J&J 1 to 97		J & J 1b	1,144,000

Special Assessments

Street

4½s	'66	Ser. to 12-	1-81	J & D1a	52,850
4⅛s	'72	Ser. to 12-	1-81	J & D1a	20,000

Also outstanding, $19,596 other special assess. bonds.

Revenue Bonds

Urban Renewal

2 6½s	'73	Ser. to 12-	1-03	J & D1c	840,000
2 5s	'73	Ser. to 12-	1-03	J & D1c	665,000

1 Held by O.W.D.A.
2 Callable, details not reported.
RATING: General obligations .... **A 1**
Interest Paid: As follows:
a Farmers National Bank & Trust Co., Ashtabula.
b City Treasurer.
c Not reported.

Source: *Moody's Municipal and Government Manual, 1981,* vol. 2, p. 2680.

instance, in two well-publicized incidents, neither the City of Chicago nor the State of West Virginia prevented default of associated revenue bond issues (Chicago Skyway and West Virginia Turnpike). Thus, revenue bond analysis presumes the project must stand on its financial merits.

The impact of ratings on borrowing cost for an issuer has been altered recently with the development of insurance for new municipal bond issues. This insurance, purchased by the bond issuer, guarantees timely payment of principal and interest on that issue. Thus, a lower rated issue can sell at roughly the same interest rate as a better quality issue if the former issue is insured. The insurance is a sound purchase for a borrower when the premium paid for the insurance is less than the interest savings resulting from greater market acceptance of the insured issue. The major insurance carriers are Municipal Bond Insurance Corporation, a pool of major casualty insurance companies, and the American Municipal Bond Assurance Corporation/MGIC Indemnity Corporation of the MGIC Investment Corporation. The former insures new issues; the latter insures some new issues, but primarily insures portfolios held by individuals and institutions. By risk pooling, new issue insurance should improve markets for smaller units and increase the range of markets for many borrowers.

UNDERWRITING

Bond issues are usually too large to be bought by a single investor and the issuer cannot effectively handle marketing of the issue to large numbers of individual investors.[13] Thus, bonds are typically sold to an underwriter, a firm which purchases the entire issue and hopes to resell them at a profit to investors. The gross profit (or "spread") will be the difference between the price the firm pays for the bonds and the price the firm receives from their sale to investors. From that spread, the firm will pay all costs of distribution involved in the transaction.

Underwriting firms are selected either by negotiation or by competitive bid. In the former case, the underwriter is selected as the bond issue is being designed. An interest rate is established in negotiation between the borrowing unit and the underwriting firm. The underwriter will be engaged in pre-sale marketing and will assist the borrower with such organization services as preparation of official statements, structuring the bond issue, and securing credit ratings. Negotiated offerings are particularly common with revenue bond offerings, especially when they

---

[13] Some experiments with "mini-bonds" sold directly to investors were tried in Massachusetts and East Brunswick, N.J. in 1978. (*The Wall Street Journal,* September 29, 1978, and January 1, 1978.) There has been no rush to follow these examples.

are large or involve novel uses of bonding. Some states (Vermont is an example) have bond banks which underwrite municipal offerings; these sales are also negotiated.

Two important documents must be prepared during the sale of bonds: the official statement and the legal opinion. The official statement, a requirement when the underwriter will be selected by competitive bid, contains two sections providing information prospective underwriters and investors need before committing funds to the borrower. One section provides information about the ability of the borrower to repay its borrowing: a description of the community and its industries, its major taxpayers, debt currently outstanding, a record of tax collections and bond repayments in the last five years, and future borrowing plans. The other section describes the proposed bond issue: purpose, amount, and type of issue, its maturity structure and interest payment schedule, call provisions, date and place of bidding, whether a bond rating has been applied for, the name of the counsel preparing the legal opinion (described later), and where bonds will be delivered. The statement will also indicate any maximum interest rate and discount. Most statements will include a disclaimer indicating a right to refuse any and all bids, even though that right will seldom be used by units intending to maintain good relations with underwriters.

The second document is the legal opinion prepared by a bond counsel, a certification that the bond issuer has complied with all federal, state, and local legal requirements governing municipal debt. Seldom will local law firms do this work; underwriters and large private investors require opinions of specialist law firms. The bond counsel assures that the issuer has legal authority to borrow, that the revenue source for repayment is legal and irrevocable, and that the community is legally bound by provisions of the bond. The counsel also indicates whether interest paid on the debt will, in his opinion, be exempt from federal and state income tax. The counsel offers no judgment about the capacity of the borrower to repay the debt; his concern is with how tight the contract to repay binds the borrower. Without a satisfactory opinion, the bond issue is virtually worthless.

Competitive bid is the typical method of selecting underwriters for full faith and credit bonds and for many revenue issues. In this method, the issuer selects the amount of principal to mature at various years through the life of the issue, and underwriters bid on the interest rate which the issuer would have to pay. The rates, of course, need not be the same for different maturities but would be the same for all bonds in a single maturity. The issuer chooses the underwriter bidding the lowest interest rate for the total issue.

Two methods are used to evaluate bids, net interest cost (*NIC*) and true interest cost (*TIC*). (The complexity emerges because of the serial nature of municipal bonds.) The *NIC* method computes cost according to the formula

$$NIC = \frac{\text{Interest payable (less premium or plus discount)}}{\text{Principal} \times \text{average maturity}}$$

and produces an average annual cost of the debt as a percentage of the outstanding principal of the debt. *NIC* is computed in the following formula:

$$N = \sum_{i=1}^{n} C_i \cdot A_i \cdot Y_i + D$$

where N = net dollar interest costs
n = number of different maturities in issue
C = coupon rate on each maturity
A = par amount in each maturity
Y = number of years to maturity
D = bid discount (bid premium is negative discount).

This result, N, is the total dollar cost of coupon payments over the life of the bond. *NIC* equals N divided by bond year dollars:

$$NIC = N \Big/ \sum_{i=1}^{n} (A_i Y_i).$$

The TIC (or Canadian) method is more complicated because it takes into account the time profile of interest payment flows. If two bids have the same net interest cost, but one bid involves higher interest payments in the early maturities of the issue and lower interest payments in the later maturities (front loading), then that bid would be less attractive: it requires the issuer to surrender resources earlier and, thus, to lose the return that could have been received from use of those resources. Thus, the other bid is, in present-value terms, lower than this bid. *TIC* is the interest rate which equates the amount of dollars received by the bond issuer with the present value of the flow of principal and interest payments over the life of the issue. The *TIC* formula is:

$$B = \sum_{i=1}^{m} \frac{A_i}{(1 + TIC)^i} + \sum_{i=1}^{m} \frac{I_i}{(1 + TIC)^i}$$

where b = aggregate dollar amount received by issuer; i = number of years to cash payment; m = number of years to final maturity; A_i = annual principal in \$ repaid in period i; *TIC* = true interest cost; and I_i = aggregate interest payment in period i (assuming one interest payment

TABLE 12–7
Example *TIC* and *NIC* computation worksheet

Bonds sold July 1, 1981, and interest payable on July 1 thereafter

(Bid amount = $39,920)

Maturity dates	Amount	Bid interest rate	Annual interest paid	Bond years	Bond dollar years
July 1, 1985	$ 5,000	6.00%	$ 300	4	20,000
July 1, 1986	5,000	6.50	325	5	25,000
July 1, 1987	5,000	7.00	350	6	30,000
July 1, 1988	5,000	8.00	400	7	35,000
July 1, 1989	10,000	9.00	900	8	80,000
July 1, 1990	10,000	10.00	1,000	9	90,000
Total	$40,000				

Schedule of payments by dates paid

	Interest	Principal	Total
July 1, 1982	$ 3,275	—	$ 3,275
July 1, 1983	3,275	—	3,275
July 1, 1984	3,275	—	3,275
July 1, 1985	3,275	$ 5,000	8,275
July 1, 1986	2,975	5,000	7,975
July 1, 1987	2,650	5,000	7,650
July 1, 1988	2,300	5,000	7,300
July 1, 1989	1,900	10,000	11,900
July 1, 1990	1,000	10,000	11,000
Total	$23,926	$40,000	$63,926

a. Solving for *NIC:*

$$NIC = \frac{23,926 + 80}{280,000} = 8.573571\%$$

b. Solving for *TIC:*

$$\$39,920 = \frac{3275}{1 + TIC} + \frac{3275}{(1 + TIC)^2} + \frac{3275}{(1 + TIC)^3} + \frac{8275}{(1 + TIC)^4} + \frac{7975}{(1 + TIC)^5} +$$
$$\frac{7650}{(1 + TIC)^6} + \frac{7300}{(1 + TIC)^7} + \frac{11900}{(1 + TIC)^7} + \frac{11000}{(1 + TIC)^8}$$
$$TIC = 9.00\%$$

per year). In a *TIC* computation for municipal bond sale, the bid price or amount to be paid by the underwriter to the issuer (B) and the stream of debt service payments (I_i) are specified by the bidder. The number of years to future payments were defined in the offering. The implied interest rate (*TIC*) is solved for. Larger offerings require computer assistance for *TIC* calculation, but smaller issues can be handled using standard methods for approximating the internal rate of return. Table 12–7 illustrates *TIC* and *NIC* computation.

The successful underwriting firm or syndicate (a group of firms) then sells the bonds to investors. Underwriters cover their costs and make any profit from the difference between the price the underwriters pay the issuer and the price they receive from purchasers (the spread). If increases in market rates cause a substantial decline in the value of the issue before the firm has the bonds sold, that spread can be negative. Table 12–8 reports the type of entities holding municipal bonds. Own-

TABLE 12–8
Entities holding state and local government securities (end of 1975)

Entity	Holdings as percent of total
Households	32.2%
Nonfinancial corporate business	1.9
State–local government general funds	1.9
Commercial banks	44.6
Savings and loan associations	0.5
Mutual savings banks	0.7
Life insurance companies	2.0
State–local government retirement funds	1.1
Other insurance companies	14.9
Brokers and dealers	0.3

Source: Federal Reserve Board, *Flow of Funds Accounts, 1946–1975* (no date), p. 145.

ership is concentrated in any class among units in higher tax brackets—those are the purchasers to whom the tax-exempt status of municipal bond interest is especially attractive.

CASES FOR DISCUSSION

A. The following selection from *The Wall Street Journal* reports on municipal bond insurance.

Consider the following questions:

1. Who gains from municipal bond insurance?
2. Explain why the insurers avoid large borrowers.
3. If the estimated interest saved over the life of the Dade County issue was $4.3 million and the insurance premium was $920,000, why is the real interest saving listed as only $1 million?

Insured Issues Attract Top Rating, Buyers, But Not All Borrowers Can Get Coverage

BY BYRON KLAPPER
Staff Reporter of THE WALL STREET JOURNAL

NEW YORK—When Dade County, Fla., needed $43 million last month to buy a water system, it let Wall Street decide whether to bid on revenue bonds backed by certain taxes, or those covered by municipal bond insurance.

Without exception, dealers selected insured bonds carrying Standard & Poor's triple-A rating, instead of the county's uninsured medium grade triple-B credit.

The higher bond rating slashed Dade's borrowing fees by more than $1 million over 20 years based on current-value dollars. And it allowed dealers to avoid a 6¾ percent interest ceiling, above which bids may have been rejected.

The offering had one other distinction. It was the largest issue accepted for coverage since Municipal Bond Insurance Association began guaranteeing tax-exempt bonds in 1974.

A Bitter Reality

Such a program would have enormous benefits for such cities as New York, Detroit, Cleveland, Philadelphia, and Boston. But before their mayors try to sign up for an insurance policy, they should be aware of a bitter reality.

"If they need it badly, we don't want them," said John R. Butler, president of Municipal Issuers Service Corp., the insurance group's managing agent.

Last year, 159 local governments and agencies sold $1.05 billion of insured bonds, up 9 percent from 1977. Insurance premiums jumped 31 percent to $17.5 million. Nevertheless, MBIA reported $2 million of losses, reflecting "substantial underwriting costs associated with conducting the business," Mr. Butler said. Part of that is the way insurance companies account for profits and losses, and certain funds which must be kept in reserves.

As the nation's largest bond insurer, MBIA guarantees $6.6 billion of principal and interest payments. The liability is spread among four underwriters. They are Aetna Casualty & Surety Co., with 40 percent; Fireman's Fund Insurance Co. 30 percent, and 15 percent each by Aetna Insurance Co. and U.S. Fire Insurance Co.

Guaranteed Payment

Holders of insured bonds are guaranteed payment on tax-exempt issues as they come due. The concept attracted investors after default by New York's Urban Development Corp. in 1975, and a moratorium on $1.6 billion of New York City notes. Noteholders waited more than a year for payment while the moratorium bought time for New York to devise a plan to keep from going bankrupt. Currently, insured issues account for just over 2 percent of the $45.9 billion of tax-exempt bonds sold last year. MBIA said there haven't been any missed payments among bonds it insures.

"Insurance throws a security blanket over the issues come hell or high water," says Mr. Butler. "It's an unconditional, irrevocable guarantee that we will make payment. There isn't a Proposition 13, a New York City, or any other disaster for a municipal government which isn't covered."

Such ironclad protection doesn't come cheaply once MBIA's credit tests are met. Last year more than twice as many applicants were rejected as accepted. Those that qualified paid $9 to $20 as insurance premiums for each $1,000 face amount of bonds sold. Fees depend on credit quality and marketability, and are payable when bonds are sold.

Reasons for Rejection

Issues are rejected where revenue sources aren't considered reliable, if there are doubts over certain legal aspects of a security, or where debt service is backed by revenue of a private corporation, to name a few.

Says Mr. Butler: "We're established to assist creditworthy communities with a good history and a promising future who want to obtain money at a lower interest rate."

That goal is largely achieved as a result of the automatic triple-A rating from Standard & Poor's. Moody's Investors Service, another agency, views it differently.

"We choose to rate issuers on their own credit-worthiness," said Frieda Ackerman, a Moody's vice president of municipal research. In its credit analysis, Moody's says it recognizes insurance coverage. The service said it won't revise its rating, however, because it doesn't "want to confuse the public" by departing from its accepted rating methods. As a result, insured issuers rarely apply for a Moody's rating.

Absence of Large Borrowers

Of all insured bonds sold last year, 55 percent were general obligations, 42 percent were water, sewer and electric revenue issues, and the remaining 3 percent were other revenue bonds. Most policies were written in nine states, led by Florida, Pennsylvania, New Jersey, Michigan, Kansas, New York, Connecticut, Tennessee, and Georgia. No states or large cities are among the insured. The absence of large borrowers reflects the limits of the municipal insurance industry.

"If we accept major cities which sell substantial volumes of bonds, we'd be insuring very little else," Mr. Butler says. "From an insurance point of view, it would create undue concentration and risk."

Smaller government units with high-grade or premium bond ratings also would find little benefit in insurance. The interest difference on their uninsured bonds and those with MBIA coverage wouldn't justify the insurance fee.

For Dade County, however, the $920,000 insurance premium was more than offset by the $4.3 million interest-rate reduction. That saving, taken over the 20-year average life of the bonds, will be reduced by inflation. After making an up-front payment of the insurance premium, Dade's "present value" interest saving is estimated at about $1 million.

"We advise clients that the difference between insured and uninsured interest should take into account present-value cost and future-value savings," says Arthur L. Greenfield, first vice president of Loeb Rhoades, Hornblower & Co., Dade's fiscal adviser.

B. As Table 12–7 shows, insurance companies—particularly casualty insurers—are heavy holders of municipal debt. This case from *The Wall Street Journal* reports on the investment of one company.

Consider these questions:

1. Explain why State Farm is in the municipal market when other similar insurers are not.
2. Explain how an interest rate increase would create a paper loss for State Farm. Why might the firm, as compared with an underwriter or dealer, be unconcerned about that loss?

State Farm Bets Day Will Come For Municipals

BY DAVID P. GARINO
Staff Reporter of THE WALL STREET JOURNAL

BLOOMINGTON, Ill.—In the long-term municipal bond market, or what's left of it, they call State Farm Insurance Company's financial vice president Rex J. (Jim) Bates the Lone Ranger. That's because other corporate and institutional buyers of new municipal bond issues have become so scarce. Day in and day out, State Farm is one of the few that continues to buy new issues.

On paper, the big insurer's persistence has cost it a bundle. As interest rates have risen and stuck at record levels, the market value of the com-

pany's bonds has sunk. The full face value of its portfolio of tax-exempts stands at some $8.4 billion. "Unfortunately," Mr. Bates says, "that's not the market value"—which has fallen to about 70 percent of face value from 98 percent at the end of 1977.

Still, the company is sticking with its strategy of buying high-grade tax-exempts. "We don't plan to change anything," Mr. Bates says. "We'll go on our own naive way." He does concede, "You have to fight the human tendency to leave when things don't work out."

That has made State Farm exceedingly popular among underwriters and dealers in municipal bonds. Last month, only 40 percent of a $105 million offering of revenue bonds by Washington Suburban Sanitary District, Md., sold on the first day, and State Farm was practically the only buyer. On some days State Farm's municipal securities departments get more than 200 telephone calls from dealers trying to peddle bonds; often all the department's five direct lines are busy.

Casualty insurers such as State Farm historically bought municipal bonds for the same reason other investors did, to earn tax-free income. But as claims payoffs exceeded premium income in recent years, the insurer's big underwriting losses cut their cash income and made income taxes an academic problem. In addition, institutional investors of all kinds have backed away from the bond market because of the inflationary threat to principal and the market losses created by high interest rates.

But State Farm—which rarely discusses its investment strategy publicly—committed $692 million to the tax-exempt market in the first half of 1981, compared with $580 million in 1980's first half. For one thing, State Farm had cash. It outperformed the casualty industry last year. Its underwriting ratio—the percentage of premium income paid out in claim losses and expenses—came to 95.3 percent, producing a profit of $269.7 million. For the industry, the ratio was a losing 103 percent. "Fortunately, we had the cash flow for municipals as the markets slid into new depths," Mr. Bates says.

Waiting It Out

For another thing, the company has bought for the long term and isn't greatly concerned about an adverse market meantime. "We've learned you can't outguess the market," Mr. Bates says, although he adds, "We used to think we could."

If interest rates do fall, bond prices will rise, and, a municipal bond analyst says, "They"—State Farm—"will look good. If the rates are 20 percent, they don't look so good. You have to give State Farm credit for sticking its neck out." A trust officer at a Midwest bank says, "Unless they need to liquidate, all they have is a paper loss. If they've selected the right issues, they'll come out all right. In the meantime, they're getting a hell of a yield."

The yield on State Farm's tax-exempt portfolio amounted to 10.15 percent for the first half this year, up from 8 percent a year before, Mr. Bates says.

Only the Best

The company buys only high-grade issues. Clifford F. Steinkraus, vice president of municipal securities, says the average rating on the bonds the company buys is double-A. Such high-grade issues have become relatively more attractive, he says, because the difference in yields between higher-grade and lower-grade issues has narrowed. Thus, the additional reward in yield for buying lower-grade issues is small in terms of the additional risk in those issues. That narrowing in spread has come about largely because of the demand for high-yielding, lower-grade issues by bond funds that pool individual investors' money to buy maximum-yield securities.

State Farm's municipal bond staff does its own research; staffers even drive through communities whose bonds the company may buy, inspecting residential, commercial, and industrial areas to get impressions of the communities' economic health, and tape their observations on recorders. But the company has found state obligations particularly attractive lately. State governments, Mr. Bates says, "have potential resources to make the bonds secure." Of the first half's bond investments, $305 million went into state general obligation bonds.

State Farm is also a big buyer of industrial revenue bonds sold to raise money for pollution control. Such bonds are sold by communities to build nonpolluting facilities that are leased out to corporations. The corporate lease rentals supply the cash to pay interest and principal on the debt. Because interest on the obligations is tax-exempt, interest costs to the corporation are less than they would be on the corporation's own securities.

There are some bonds that the company dislikes. "We don't own any hospital revenue bonds for philosophical reasons," Mr. Steinkraus says. "We don't feel they serve a public purpose, and they're often promoted by investment houses" with little regard for any surplus of hospital beds in a community, he says.

In the bond market, State Farm gets high marks for its accessibility. "The best thing is that they're good people," says a New York municipal bond dealer who complains that many institutional bond investors shut their doors to all but a favored clique.

Mr. Bates says, "Life's too short to be nasty to people, so we try to talk to them." Not long ago, however, a visiting bond dealer kept "telling us how great we were," Mr. Bates says, and complimented the company's "super advertising." The dealer cupped his hand and said, "You're in good hands"—part of the tag line of a commercial for Allstate Insurance Co., State Farm's arch competitor.

13

Cash management and investment

Cash management encompasses the collection and disbursement of public money and the use of those funds between receipt and disbursement in the public interest. Treasury operations should be managed to ensure the safety of public resources, to maintain liquidity when needed,[1] to increase funds available for investment, and to obtain the highest feasible yield on public funds. The funds are a valuable public resource which should work for the community. Leaving them idle in a checking account, for instance, provides safety and liquidity but no yield. Such a strategy would increase profits of the favored bank by providing a low-cost source of short-run investable funds, but would provide the government with no return. Idle deposits neither keep down the loan cost in the community nor stimulate the local economy, as both are determined largely by national economic activity.[2] The government fiscal officer must thus seek investment of these funds in money markets to utilize this community resource.

---

[1] Liquidity is "the ease of converting an asset into money." (Basil J. Moore, *An Introduction to the Theory of Finance,* New York: Free Press, 1968, p. 12.) Some items may be valuable (land or antiques) but their value cannot be used directly to pay bills; they must be sold to obtain money before payment can be made (and market conditions may make it difficult to sell them quickly or at their normal value). Those items are illiquid.

[2] Kerry S. Cooper, "The Economics of Idle Public Funds Policies: A Reconsideration," *National Tax Journal,* 25 (March 1972): 97–99.

TABLE 13–1
Financial assets of state and local government general funds, 1946–1976 ($ millions)

Year	Demand deposits and currency	Time deposits	Credit markets instruments	Percent in demand deposits and currency
1946	4.6	0.7	6.5	39%
1950	6.5	1.4	9.0	38
1955	8.0	2.4	14.6	32
1960	8.4	4.6	18.8	26
1965	12.1	12.2	23.7	25
1970	12.5	23.2	32.5	18
1972	15.2	37.2	37.9	17
1974	14.2	50.1	49.6	12
1975	14.4	48.1	53.7	12
1976	13.1	50.2	67.0	10

Sources: Board of Governors of the Federal Reserve System, Flow of Funds Accounts, 1946–1975 (December 1976) and *Annual Statistical Digest, 1972–1976* (December 1977).

Table 13–1 reports recent patterns of state and local general fund investment. Such governments held almost 40 percent of their financial assets in cash and checking accounts as recently as 1950. While interest rates were far lower then than they are now, that management meant sacrifice of potential interest earnings. Since that time, there has been a significant and continuing trend toward interest-yielding assets: only 10 percent of financial assets were in cash and checking accounts by 1976. That movement represents several influences, including the lure of higher interest rates, greater sophistication of government fiscal officers, and public demand for better use of government resources.[3] Because idle fund investment provides revenue without additional burden on taxpayers, no government can afford to ignore its potential.

A public cash manager will invest cash available from daily flows, not simply an annual surplus. The investment opportunity results because governments typically receive revenue in lumps at tax due days, while expenditures occur in relatively smooth outflows. Figure 13–1 illustrates such a cash balance pattern. That government receives major cash inflows at two dates in the year, the start of April and the start of October. These may be property tax due dates, payment dates for a sales tax, receipt dates for intergovernmental assistance, or whatever. The government spends from the fund at a relatively constant rate through the year. The requirements of the budget-appropriation-disbursement process make these outflows predictable and controllable. (It should be

---

[3] State and local governments were estimated to have lost $453 million in 1972 because of excess idle cash. (George M. Blankenbeckler, "Excess Cash Management at the State and Local Levels," *State and Local Government Review,* 10 (January 1978): 2–7.)

FIGURE 13–1
Cash balance through year for a fund

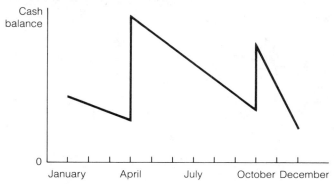

apparent that, for the unit depicted in Figure 13–1, the first cash inflow is larger than the second and that spending exceeds receipts during the fiscal year shown here.) The cash manager will invest available lumps as fully as is feasible. Thus, investment is of the daily—not just annual—surplus for as many days as possible.

ELEMENTS OF PUBLIC CASH MANAGEMENT

Public cash management involves three elements: collection, processing, and deposit of receipts; control of disbursements; and investment of otherwise idle cash balances. Much emphasis is on investment, but the other two elements are important for success of the overall program. The cash manager seeks deposit of all revenues owed to any part of the government as quickly as possible. That presumes a prompt billing for any funds owed, rapid processing of remittances with an accurate accounting of funds to maintain fiscal records and control nonpayment, and immediate deposit of funds into an account controlled by the cash manager.[4] Some governments use lockbox systems with regional banks as collection agents; Figure 13–2 suggests such a framework. Taxpayers mail payments to a local or nearby postal box. A bank in that city immediately empties the box, deposits checks, and transmits details to the government cash manager. The funds are ready for government use—investment or disbursement. Other governments use their own postal box system to gain quick control over funds. High

---

[4] Cash managers in some large Texas cities fly to the state capital to pick up the check for the state-collected city sales tax and deposit it immediately. The interest for the extra few days more than covers the travel cost.

FIGURE 13–2
A postal lockbox collection system

quality systems have deposits made within 24 hours of receipt. Not only do quick collection and control provide longer investment pools, but rapid deposit also prevents questions that taxpayers rightly have about the quality of any administration which leaves checks undeposited for extended periods.

The other end of the cash management flow requires control over disbursements. Among the special features here, beyond the normal internal audit to verify validity of claims before payment, are care to avoid late payment penalties and a balancing of early payment discounts against the interest that could be earned from cash investment. Slow payment, as has been pointed out earlier, is a technique used to conceal budget imbalance. The objective here is not to conceal but rather to maximize return from a public resource.[5]

Investment of idle cash, the intermediate element of cash management, seeks to maximize yield within the constraint of full safety of principal and liquidity when cash is required. These constraints indicate several potential investments which are not appropriate. First, default risk—the risk of loss of principal because of failure of the investment

---

[5] Examples of these cash management practices are reported in Executive Office of the President, Office of Management and Budget, *Report on Strengthening Federal Cash Management* (Washington, D.C.: U.S. Government Printing Office, 1980). Savings available there were estimated at $450 million per year.

activity or of changing market conditions—must be avoided, so cash will not be invested in the acquisition of physical properties or in commercial stocks and bonds. Public pension funds may invest in such assets because of their long-term focus, but they remain inappropriate for cash management. Second, the constraints dictate that credit market risk—loss in the value of a fixed-dollar return asset which results when market interest rates rise[6]—be avoided, so long-term debt instruments will not be in the idle fund management portfolio. And third, debt issued by state or local governments will be avoided by the public cash manager because the tax-exempt nature of interest paid by these bodies permits them to bear artificially low interest rates. Governments ordinarily are exempt from the federal income tax on all their activities, so this exclusion is of no value to them. The lower interest rate received on state and local bond holdings would simply penalize the investing government for its investment mistake.

Beyond the constraints established by sound financial management, public cash management must operate within the special limits placed by federal, state, and local laws. Those controls can limit the places where deposits can be held, establish shares of total financial assets which may be placed with a particular depository, establish what securities and maturities can be purchased, define formulas for determining what interest rate will be paid on public fund deposits, limit the funds from which investment can be made, and so on.[7] While the tendency has been toward greater freedom and expanded options, it is unlikely that public cash managers will have all the options available to corporate cash managers because of potential conflict of interest problems which can emerge in the management of government resources.

Investment instruments available to state and local governments are usually defined by state law, local ordinances, or both. Some instruments permitted are, by the standards of cash management previously outlined, inappropriate. Available instruments may include:

a. Demand deposits at commercial banks (checking accounts).
b. Time or savings deposits at commercial banks and, sometimes,

---

[6] That loss occurs in the following fashion. Suppose a 10-year bond sells for $1,000 and pays its purchaser $100 at the end of each of the 10 years. If market interest rates rise to, say, 20 percent, the holder of that bond would be able to sell the bond for only $500—the flow of $100 payments has a lower market value because competing investments have a higher yield. None would accept a 10 percent yield when 20 percent yield with no greater risk is available.

[7] A list of recent state actions on how governments may manage idle cash appears in Advisory Commission on Intergovernmental Relations, *Understanding State and Local Cash Management* (Washington, D.C.: ACIR, 1977), pp. 47–58.

similar accounts with related financial institutions (savings and loan associations, credit unions, savings banks).[8]

c. Certificates of deposit (CDs) issued by commercial banks and similar financial institutions.[9]

d. United States government securities of all maturities, including Treasury bills, bonds, and notes.

e. Debt instruments issued by U.S. government agencies, including Federal National Mortgage Association notes, Federal Home Loan Bank obligations, etc.

f. State and local debt.

g. Repurchase agreements or REPOS (agreements for purchase and resale of U.S. government securities with commercial banks).

h. Commercial paper (short-term promissory notes issued directly by large corporations).

Several features of the instruments which may be unfamiliar appear in Table 13–2.

The heart of most public cash management programs includes United States treasury bills, certificates of deposit issued by commercial banks, and repurchase agreements. These instruments are attractive because they offer high interest rates, safety, and liquidity. High-denomination certificates of deposit will usually not be fully covered by federal insurance (negotiated rates typically begin with CDs of $100,000, the current insurance limit). Thus, some states require pledging of particular assets by banks to guarantee the security of public funds: if the bank fails, those pledged assets would ensure that the public funds were not lost.[10] Commercial paper from large corporate borrowers offers high rates but because of their greater risk typically will be avoided in most public cash management programs. Furthermore, they offer substantially greater potential exposure to political problems than do ordinary money market instruments.[11]

---

[8] Savings and loan associations are primarily long-term lenders. It is likely that funds received by them from short-term CDs would simply be arbitraged, that is, relent on a short-term basis through some other money market instrument. Short-term government cash is unlikely to finance local home construction, in other words.

[9] Banks issue a certificate of deposit against funds deposited for a contracted period. The deposit earns a contracted rate of interest for that period, regardless of any other rate changes during the period.

[10] Pledging is not popular with banks because it reduces profitability and the amount of credit a bank can extend. (James A. Verbrugge, "The Effects of Pledging Regulations on Bank Asset Composition," *Journal of Bank Research*, 4 (Autumn 1973): 168–76.)

[11] Corporate bonds and corporate stocks are to be avoided because of both default risk and credit market risk. Because pension funds are more concerned with long-term investment, public pension funds do frequently acquire high-grade corporate bonds or stocks.

TABLE 13–2
Selected characteristics of major investment instruments

Instrument	Issuer	Maturities	Markets	Denominations
Repurchase agreements	Commercial banks	Overnight minimum	Primary by demand; no secondary	$100,000 minimum (usually)
Federal securities				
Bills	U.S. Treasury	91,182,270,360 days	Primary: weekly auction; very active secondary	$10,000–$1,000,000
Notes	U.S. Treasury	1–10 years	Primary: periodic; active secondary	$1,000 minimum $1,000,000 normally
Bonds	U.S. Treasury	10–30 years	Primary: periodic; active secondary	$1,000 minimum
Agency securities	Federal Loan and Loan Guarantee Agencies	Various	Primary: various; active secondary	$1,000 minimum
Negotiable certificate of deposit	Commercial banks	30-day minimum	Primary by demand; active secondary	$100,000 minimum
Certificates of deposit	Commercial banks and savings & loan	30-day minimum	Primary by demand; limited secondary	$1,000 minimum
Time deposits	Commercial banks and savings & loan	30-day minimum	Primary by demand; no secondary	No minimum
Commercial paper				
Finance paper	Finance companies	5–270 days	Primary: daily; no secondary	$100,000–$5,000,000
Prime industrial paper	Major industrial firms through dealers	5–270 days	Primary: daily; no secondary	$100,000–$5,000,000

Source: Frank M. Patitucci and Michael H. Lichtenstein, *Improving Cash Management in Local Government: A Comprehensive Approach* (Chicago: *Municipal Finance Officers Association, 1977), p. 60.*

TECHNIQUE

In establishing a cash management program the manager must initially determine what cash is available and for what period of time that cash will be available. Money market conditions are often such that longer-term interest rates are higher than short-term interest rates. Larger commercial banks typically issue money market conditions memos, at least weekly, as a guide to money managers. Figure 13–3 provides an illustration. When the six-month treasury bill rate is higher than the three-month rate, cash available for six months can profitably be directed to the longer instrument. The manager can invest without fear of actual capital loss from interest rate fluctuations if the manager matches the term of the security to the time that the cash will be available. Matching is possible only if cash flows have been estimated through the fiscal year. Thus, *forecasting* of revenue and expenditure flows is a critical first step in a cash management program. Those forecasts will be keyed to experience of recent fiscal years and actions in the current year budget.

A second step is *pooling* as many cash sources as possible to obtain the largest possible cash pot for investment. Figure 13–4 illustrates a pooled cash estimate for a small government. Financial institutions negotiate rates and conditions of certificates with larger pool investors (as well as pay higher interest rates), so such pooling should generate a larger return for the investing unit. Pooling is not commingling of funds: sources of the cash are recorded and the invested money will be returned to the originating fund as the investment instruments mature. Interest from the investment pools may or may not be returned to the source fund, depending on state law and local investment orders. The simplest practice returns total interest from the investment pool to the general fund for reappropriation by the governing body.

Pooling can, in fact, extend beyond the funds held by a single government. A number of states, including California, Connecticut, Florida, Illinois, Massachusetts, Montana, New Jersey, Oklahoma, Oregon, Utah, West Virginia, and Wisconsin, have formed local government investment pools to enable local units to combine funds for short-term investment. The pools offer professional management, wider markets for investment, and the return advantages of larger investment blocks, but participation by eligible governments has not been high.[12] Overall, these pools ought to be most attractive for smaller governments; their use should grow with tight budgets and fiscal sophistication.

---

[12] Timothy Q. Cook and Jeremy G. Duffield, "Short-term Investment Pools," *Economic Review of Federal Reserve Bank of Richmond,* 66 (September/October 1980): 6.

FIGURE 13–3

Money Market Rates	Sales 317 266-6829 Federal Funds 317 266-6826 Incoming WATS 1 800 382-1102

September 18, 1981

Indiana National

Investment

Maturity	Municipal Market Project Notes	This Week	Last Week	Last Year	Treasury This Week	Last Week	Last Year	Agencies This Week	Last Week	Last Year
3 mos	10-02-81	9.25	9.00	5.25	14.24	14.95	10.50	--	--	--
6 mos	01-08-82	9.25	9.75	5.60	14.28	15.26	11.23	15.58	16.70	11.06
9 mos	04-05-82	9.40	9.90	6.05	14.26	15.10	11.46	15.98	16.94	11.39
1 year	06-05-82	9.35	9.90	6.15	14.02	14.72	11.62	--	--	--
	Aaa	Aa	A	A(Ind)						
1983	9.75	10.00	10.20	10.20	16.04	16.69	11.77	16.25	16.80	11.90
1984	10.00	10.20	10.40	10.40	15.97	16.58	11.77	15.94	16.42	11.81
1985	10.20	10.40	10.60	10.60	15.64	16.44	11.72	16.25	16.76	11.92
1986	10.40	10.60	10.75	10.75	15.50	16.14	11.50	15.47	16.68	11.75
1987	10.60	10.80	10.90	10.90	15.14	15.60	11.55	15.39	15.90	11.66
1988	10.80	11.00	11.10	11.10	15.26	15.88	11.46	15.46	16.02	11.66
1989	11.00	11.25	11.35	11.35	14.97	15.41	11.48	—	—	--
1990	11.25	11.50	11.60	11.50	14.90	15.35	--	—	—	—
1991	11.50	11.75	11.85	11.75						
1992	11.75	12.00	12.10	12.00						
1993	11.90	12.25	12.30	12.20						
1994	12.00	12.40	12.50	12.40						
1995	12.15	12.60	12.75	12.60						
1996	12.30	12.80	12.90	12.80						
1997	12.50	13.00	13.10	13.00						
1998	12.75	13.10	13.40	13.15						
1999	12.90	13.25	13.50	13.30						

INB Certificates of Deposit ($100,000 and Over)

Maturity	This Week	Last Week	Last Year
30 days	15 1/2	16 3/4	10
60 days	15 5/8	17	10 3/8
90 days	15 3/8	16 1/2	10 3/4
120 days	16	17 1/4	11 1/8
150 days	15 3/4	17	11 1/8
180 days	15 3/4	17	11 1/4
210 days	15 3/4	16 1/2	11 1/4
270 days	15 3/4	16 1/2	11 3/8
365 days	15 3/4	16 1/2	11 3/8

	This Week	Last Week	Last Year
Bond Buyer Index	12.79	13.12	8.98
Indiana Index	11.62	11.49	7.25
Blue List ($ Million)	559	584	690
30 Day Supply ($ Million)	14.08	15.92	2155

	This Week	Last Week	Last Year
Prime Rate	20	20 1/2	12 1/2
Discount Rate	14	14	10
Federal Funds	15.66	16.32	10.63
90 Day Commercial Paper	15.25	15.75	10.63

Commentary   STOCK MARKET REVIEW FROM THE TRUST DIVISION

In spite of the stock market's weakness during the past month the immediate outlook can be classified as no better than neutral. Interest rates continue to provide powerful competition to the typical equity. Without substantial relief in the money and bond markets stocks have nowhere to go on the upside and indeed could be subjected to further downward pressure. In addition to interest rates, the market has become increasingly concerned about the potential for cyclical erosion of corporate earning power over the next several quarters. If the Standard and Poor's 500 should fall to the general area of 110, we would view the longer term opportunities as more than offsetting any remaining cyclical risk. Should this event materaliza a more positive approach to equities would be warranted. Within the framework of near term defensiveness, portfolio policy should continue to stress quality and larger capitalization companies with a high degree of self financing. Leveraged companies and smaller capitalizations have a larger amount of market risk at this point in the cycle. Many institutional quality companies appear to be positioning themselves for future market leadership by demonstrating the first signs of relative strength after declining to longer term price support areas. Consequently our policy is to overweight companies possessing these characteristics in the Consumer, Interest Sensitive and to a lesser degree the Capital Spending sectors.

FIGURE 13–4
Illustration of pooled cash flow—investable fund estimate

Cash, beginning of year	General fund			Parks fund			Total investable $185,000
	Revenue	Expenditure	$125,000 investable	Revenue	Expenditure	$60,000 investable	
Week 1	0	$10,000	$115,000	$ 5,000	$15,000	$ 50,000	$165,000
Week 2	0	10,000	105,000	5,000	20,000	35,000	140,000
Week 3	0	10,000	95,000	5,000	15,000	25,000	120,000
Week 4	$400,000	10,000	485,000	105,000	20,000	110,000	595,000
Week 5	0	10,000	475,000	5,000	15,000	100,000	575,000
. . .							
Week 52	0	10,000	100,000	5,000	20,000	40,000	140,000
Cash, end of year			100,000			40,000	140,000

The third stage in cash management is investment of idle cash in the pool for appropriate terms at the highest return. All cash not needed in the investment period should be invested. Cash needs may be computed according to minimum balance requirements at banks, by some rule of thumb, or according to some rough application of the economic ordering quantity model.[13] The traditional problem with state and local governments is not holding cash balances that are too small, rather it is the problem of maintaining cash balances that are substantially too large. Corporate cash managers frequently operate with zero balances, so the appropriate position is ordinarily one of maintaining a balance that is as low as is feasible within prevailing banking requirements.

The final step of cash management is *maintenance of a rolling score card* for the program. The score card would contain the data required to evaluate the success of the program and to improve operation of the program. At a minimum the score card would have on weekly basis:

1. Estimated total financial assets (cash and investments) held by unit (from the forecast).
2. Actual total financial assets held.
3. Demand deposit and currency total.
4. Interest received to date, this year.
5. Interest received to date, last year.
6. Six-month treasury bill rate, this week.
7. Six-month treasury bill rate, same week last year.

A comparison of interest rate profiles is important because substantial differences in investment income can occur from one year to the next from fluctuations in money market conditions, not because of cash management efforts. The data thus can feedback to improve forecasting models as well as gauge the benefits from the program.

Conclusion

Idle cash in public accounts should be invested at the highest yield consistent with safety of principle and liquidity. While many investment media are legally available to governments, U.S. Treasury bills, certificates of deposit, and repurchase agreements are the heart of most cash management programs. Cash management involves four critical steps: forecasting daily cash balances, pooling available funds to maximize investable balances, investment in the most attractive instruments, and

---

[13] Various cash demand models are applied to a municipal government in Rita M. Maldonado and Lawrence S. Ritter, "Optimal Municipal Cash Management: A Case Study," *Review of Economics and Statistics,* 47 (November 1971): 384–88.

366

maintenance of a score card for the program. Nationally, state and local governments have made great improvements in cash management over the past 30 years.

SELECTION FOR DISCUSSION

The following article about state investment pools appeared in *The Wall Street Journal.*

Consider these questions:

1. What advantages do state pools provide, compared with individual local government investment? What units are most likely to gain from such pools?
2. What are the arguments against such pools? What validity are they likely to have?
3. Why do banks oppose the pools?

Cities Earn Extra Interest by Pooling Investment Of Surplus Funds, but Banks Fight to Halt Trend

BY BYRON KLAPPER
Staff Reporter of THE WALL STREET JOURNAL

Since the beginning of the year, Robert Schwab, finance director of Milpitas, Calif., has pulled $4 million of the city's money out of banks paying 4.5 percent interest and put it in a special investment account yielding 5.8 percent.

For the city of 27,000 people, the extra income ($52,000 on an annual basis) doesn't add up to much. But, says Mr. Schwab, "I'd be remiss if I didn't get the highest interest on investments of city funds."

Mr. Schwab put the Milpitas money in California's Pool Money Investment Account, one of a half-dozen cash

Source: *The Wall Street Journal,* October 11, 1977. Reprinted by permission of The Wall Street Journal, © Dow Jones & Company, Inc. (1977). All rights reserved.

pools that have sprung up in the past five years to enable cities and public agencies to earn higher interest on surplus funds. The idea behind the pools is simple enough. A small town can't shop for the high interest rates that banks and companies pay on large, short-term investments. But combine the cash from many localities, and the doors open at money centers like New York and San Francisco.

While the state pools aid investment officers like Milpitas's Mr. Schwab, they are heartily disliked by banks fearful of losing deposits. Stiff opposition by bankers has already knocked out one proposed state pool and almost scuttled two others. Moreover, some public officials also are concerned about the idea of sending local funds off to state capitals for investment. "It's a form of state-run bank to bypass other banks," says Elinor M. Ray, treasurer of the island community of Nantucket, in referring to Massachusetts's new Municipal Depository Trust.

Free Service Cited

Bankers contend that they earn the deposits of governmental units with free services like handling city payrolls and giving market advice when treasurers sell bonds and notes. They also argue that large-scale withdrawals would impair a region's fiscal health, particularly in rural areas. "Money drawn out of the community to any degree damages the local economy by reducing funds available for lending," says Truman Jeffers, executive secretary of the Minnesota Bankers Association.

Last spring, two Minnesota state senators, Wayne Olhoft and Earl W. Renneke, drew up a bill to form a state investment pool. But after intensive lobbying by bankers, the two legislators removed their names from their own bill and helped vote it down. Says Sen. Olhoft, "My banker in Herman (population 600) saw it as a threat. He didn't like the idea that funds raised locally would be sent off to the big city."

Wisconsin started a cash pool last year over objections of the Wisconsin Bankers Association. It was approved by the legislature only after it was tacked onto a bill to cope with a state cash-flow crisis.

In New Jersey, the legislature passed a bill this summer to create a state Cash Management Fund, but the measure carried in the senate by only a two-vote margin above the 40 necessary for passage due to "considerable opposition from banks," says Roland M. Machold, head of the state's investment division. "Banks were concerned about money leaving the state and were wary of losing deposits," he says. The bill now is awaiting Gov. Byrne's signature.

A Warning Sign

The defeat of the state pool in Minnesota and opposition in other states signal trouble for state treasurers willing to lend their market savvy to help local-government units. It also shows that bankers will fight to keep public deposits that might earn higher interest elsewhere (in Minnesota, in fact, about 30 percent of idle local government funds sit in bank accounts paying no interest at all, bank sources say).

Opposition to the pooled funds has continued even in states where they are already operating. Mattoon, a city of 24,000 in central Illinois, won't send surplus cash to the state fund in Springfield regardless of rates. "It's a matter of policy," says City Treasurer Frank McFarland, who also happens to be senior vice president of Central National Bank in Mattoon. "We support area financial institutions and, if possible, keep money invested locally," he says.

Some city officials, such as Theodore L. Scafidi, treasurer of Newton, Mass., don't think the extra return provided by some of the securities in state pool portfolios is worth the risk. While cities and towns often are limited to investing in U.S. government securities and collateralized bank certificates, a state pool may also buy corporate bonds, short-term trade bills (bankers' acceptances) and unsecured corporate IOUs (commercial paper). "If there's another Penn Central, we share the loss," Mr. Scafidi says. (Penn Central Transportation Co. filed for reorganization under federal bankruptcy laws in June 1970 and left investors with nearly worthless commercial paper.)

Pressure from Banks

In states with pooled funds, banks sometimes try to discourage communities from using them. "Make us your bank, and when you need money, we'll bid on your bonds," is the tactic banks commonly use, says Harry V. Keefe Jr., president of Keefe, Bruyette & Woods Inc., a dealer in bank securities. Small towns without access to national credit markets are most vulnerable to such pressures since there are few sources other than local banks to finance projects like school construction and road repair.

Nantucket Treasurer Ray says the community's bank balances help it get favorable terms on its bonds. "My impression from banks is that their willingness to bid is based somewhat on past business relationships," she says. "If we pull out our balances, rates may not be so attractive."

In California, however, banks have taken a benign view of the state's investment pool, according to the state's chief investment officer, Terry A. Brown. "We don't act in lieu of banks," he says. "We help small people with-

out market access or expertise." As a consequence, California municipalities have $1.3 billion on deposit in Sacramento, where the money is commingled with the state's own $6.5 billion of short-term funds.

A typical user is June Stevens, treasurer of Larkspur, just south of San Francisco. "We don't leave funds lying in idle checking accounts over the weekend," she says. "I wire $25,000 to the state pool on Friday, withdraw it on Monday, and get the same interest rate as the state gets on its billions of dollars." In some states, deposits may be as small as $5,000 for periods ranging from one day to a year.

Flexible Operation

Even in states where investment pools are available, city officials don't automatically use them for excess funds. Darien, Conn., City Treasurer Earl Johnson says his state's Short Term Investment Fund (STIF) gives him "flexibility to get the best return on the city's money." But recently, 70 percent of the city's reserves were in Connecticut banks' certificates of deposit, which at the time were yielding half a percentage point more than STIF.

While investment pools are proving to be useful for smaller communities, they are also helping some states manage their funds. With the advent of STIF in 1972, the first such cash pool to get started, Connecticut keeps just enough interest-free deposits, known as compensating balances, to cover banks' costs of services to the state, such as handling payroll, welfare and vendor checks (the state figures $1 million of interest-free deposits is worth about $152 a day to a bank, based on the going rate on U.S. Treasury bills). A monthly cost analysis of the banks' services is sent to the state treasurer's office, which then adjusts state balances in the banks to meet the cost. Excess funds are invested through STIF.

EXERCISES
FOR PART THREE

1. What restrictions are placed on state and local government debt in your state? What methods are used to avoid those limits?

2. What was the debt rating on the most recent bonds issued by your city? Was that debt full faith and credit or limited liability? Do all outstanding issues have the same rating?

3. A city advertised for bids for the purchase of $2,000,000 principal amount of Sewage Works Revenue bonds. Bonds will be delivered on April 1, 19X0; interest will be payable annually on April 1 of the following years. The bonds mature as follows:

Maturity date	Amount
April 1, 19X5	$ 50,000
April 1, 19X6	50,000
April 1, 19X7	50,000
April 1, 19X8	100,000
April 1, 19X9	100,000
April 1, 19Y0	100,000
April 1, 19Y1	150,000
April 1, 19Y2	150,000
April 1, 19Y3	150,000
April 1, 19Y4	550,000
April 1, 19Y5	550,000

Two bids were received:

a. From Five Points Securities:
   Pay $2,104,314 or $105.2157 for each $100 bond.
   The interest rates for each maturity:
   19X5 through 19Y3 .... 8.50%
   19Y4 through 19Y5 .... 9.25

b. From Wellington-Nelson:
   Pay $2,000,000. The interest rates for each maturity:
   19X5 through 19X7 .... 8.25%
   19X8 through 19Y3 .... 8.75
   19Y4 through 19Y5 .... 9.25

For each bid, compute the net interest cost (*NIC*) and the true interest cost (*TIC*). Which bid is most advantageous to the city?

4. From tables in *The Wall Street Journal* or other papers which carry quotations on U.S. Treasury bonds, notes, and bills, determine the general shape of the term structure of interest rates.

5. Grantsville is a medium-sized midwestern town, not quite rural, not quite urban, and not quite a willing participant in the 20th century. As the new Clerk-Treasurer, you are eager to bring new aggressiveness to the city administration, so long as none of the "Old Guard" gets mad. You suspect that a nonirritating first step would be the development of a cash plan and short-term investment strategy for the city. You further believe that an appropriate start would be with the four largest funds in the city financial structure: General, Parks and Recreation, Motor Vehicle, and Cumulative Capital. The following data emerge from your research. (A 19X7 calendar is shown)

```
        JANUARY                                                        JULY
S   M   T   W   T   F   S          IMPORTANT                 S   M   T   W   T   F   S
                        1            DATES                                       1   2
2   3   4   5   6   7   8                                    3   4   5   6   7   8   9
9  10  11  12  13  14  15        JANUARY                    10  11  12  13  14  15  16
16  17  18  19  20  21  22        1  New Year's Day          17  18  19  20  21  22  23
23  24  25  26  27  28  29       15  Martin Luther King's    24  25  26  27  28  29  30
30  31                               Birthday               31

       FEBRUARY                  FEBRUARY                          AUGUST
S   M   T   W   T   F   S        12  Lincoln's Birthday      S   M   T   W   T   F   S
            1   2   3   4   5    14  Valentine's Day                     1   2   3   4   5
6   7   8   9  10  11  12        16  Ash Wednesday           7   8   9  10  11  12  13
13  14  15  16  17  18  19       21  Washington's           14  15  16  17  18  19  20
20  21  22  23  24  25  26           Birthday - Obsvd.       21  22  23  24  25  26  27
27  28                           22  Washington's Birthday   28  29  30  31

                                 MARCH
        MARCH                    17  St. Patrick's Day
S   M   T   W   T   F   S        27  Palm Sunday                   SEPTEMBER
            1   2   3   4   5    29  Passover Begins         S   M   T   W   T   F   S
6   7   8   9  10  11  12        APRIL                                           1   2   3
13  14  15  16  17  18  19        1  Good Friday             4   5   6   7   8   9  10
20  21  22  23  24  25  26        3  Easter Sunday          11  12  13  14  15  16  17
27  28  29  30  31               MAY                        18  19  20  21  22  23  24
                                  8  Mother's Day           25  26  27  28  29  30
        APRIL                    21  Armed Forces Day
S   M   T   W   T   F   S        23  Victoria Day (Canada)
                        1   2    30  Memorial Day                  OCTOBER
3   4   5   6   7   8   9        JUNE                        S   M   T   W   T   F   S
10  11  12  13  14  15  16       14  Flag Day                                           1
17  18  19  20  21  22  23       19  Father's Day            2   3   4   5   6   7   8
24  25  26  27  28  29  30       JULY                        9  10  11  12  13  14  15
                                  1  Dominion Day (Canada)   16  17  18  19  20  21  22
        MAY                       4  Independence Day        23  24  25  26  27  28  29
S   M   T   W   T   F   S        SEPTEMBER                   30  31
1   2   3   4   5   6   7         5  Labor Day
8   9  10  11  12  13  14         8  Rosh Hashanah
15  16  17  18  19  20  21       17  Yom Kippur                   NOVEMBER
22  23  24  25  26  27  28       OCTOBER                     S   M   T   W   T   F   S
29  30  31                       10  Thanksgiving Day                    1   2   3   4   5
                                     (Canada)               6   7   8   9  10  11  12
                                 10  Columbus Day - Obsvd.   13  14  15  16  17  18  19
        JUNE                     12  Columbus Day            20  21  22  23  24  25  26
S   M   T   W   T   F   S        24  United Nations Day      27  28  29  30
                1   2   3   4    31  Halloween
5   6   7   8   9  10  11        NOVEMBER                         DECEMBER
12  13  14  15  16  17  18        8  Election Day            S   M   T   W   T   F   S
19  20  21  22  23  24  25       11  Veterans Day                            1   2   3
26  27  28  29  30               24  Thanksgiving Day        4   5   6   7   8   9  10
                                 DECEMBER                   11  12  13  14  15  16  17
                                  1  Hanukkah               18  19  20  21  22  23  24
                                 25  Christmas Day          25  26  27  28  29  30  31
```

(1) *Fund balances for January 1, 19X7*

General fund	$520,860
Parks and recreation	52,968
Motor vehicle	104,015
Cumulative capital	739,611

(2) *Revenue estimates*

    a. *Property Tax.* Collections are received by the city on May 1 and November 1. Because of a discount for early payment, ⅝ of the collections come in the first installment. Delinquency has historically been about 2 percent of the levy.

        Levy: General fund $2,965,200
                    Parks and recreation   718,300
                    Cumulative capital   385,400

    b. *Parking meters* (General Fund). Revenues run about $6,000 per month, except September and October (football season) run about 5 percent higher, December about 10 percent higher, and July 15 percent lower.

    c. *Building permits, inspection fees* (General Fund). Estimated at $130,000 for the year. The Engineer's office transmits collections to you at the end of each quarter. You estimate the seasonals as QI, 85.0; QII, 105.0; QIII, 125; QIV, 85.0.

    d. *Traffic fines* (half to General Fund, half to Motor Vehicle). Estimated at $6,500 per month. Court remits at end of month.

    e. *Swimming pool admissions* (Park and Recreation). Estimates based on prior years.

        May . . . . $ 800
        June   950
        July 1,750
        August 2,500
        September   750

    f. *Community auditorium rental* (Parks and Recreation). Estimates based on prior year.

        July 4 Freedom Celebration . . . . $ 400
        Labor Day Custom Car Show   1,500
        Casual rentals (square dances,
           Rotary, etc.) bring in about . . . . $150 per month.

    g. *State shared tax* (Motor Vehicles). Data provided by state department of revenue:

        March 31 . . . . $109,000
        June 30   120,000
        September 30   110,000
        December 31   108,000

(3) *Expenditures, as appropriated by city council*

    a. *Payrolls.* Paydays are every other week. The first payday is January 7.

        General fund . . . . $95,000 biweekly
        Parks & recreation . . . .   15,000 biweekly
          Also, temporary summer lifeguards,
          playground supervisors, etc., from
          May 15 to September 10 . . . .   20,000 biweekly
        Motor vehicle fund . . . .   10,200 biweekly

b. *Other regular expenditures.* Checks to suppliers and other non-employees only on alternate Thursdays. The first such date is January 13, 19X7

General fund .... $25,000 per disbursement
Parks and recreation .... 4,000 per disbursement
    Additional summer payments (May 10–
    September 15) are about $3,000 per
    disbursement.
Motor vehicle .... 7,000 per disbursement
Cumulative capital
    Bond retirements due May 15 ($150,000)
    and November 15 ($125,000).

c. *Special expenditures*

    General fund .... 2 police cars @ $4,500 to be paid for August 15.

    Motor vehicle fund .... Dump truck with sand–salt distributor and snowplow @ $14,000 to be paid for October 1.

With these data, do the following:

(1) Prepare a complete cash plan for 19X7 and include end-of-year balances. Estimate what amounts are available for investment and what your investment strategy will be. Estimate what funds shortages occur and how you intend to cover them. Base your estimates and strategies on current money market conditions and local bank costs and policies.

(2) After this work is completed, you wonder what the Utilities Service Board (water and sewerage), which has independent control of its financial affairs, does with its available cash. The USB manager is a registered professional engineer. A bookkeeper does all financial and accounting work. One Board member comments, "Oh sure, we try to invest every extra penny we get as soon as we get it. We have a couple $30,000 CDs, maybe a $40,000, and a $70,000 one, but nothing larger. We also make a few Treasury bill investments. The banks have been very cooperative and even waived the commission charge. We're happy to see that extra cash come to use." This member is likely to be more familiar with utility finances than any other members. What does your investigation suggest to you about USB cash management? Do you have any recommendations?

(3) On the basis of your efforts, do you have any special financial or operating reports to the council? What investment income do you suspect that you can generate?

(4) How might the success of a municipal cash management program be evaluated?

APPENDIXES

A. Three managerial concepts
B. Overview of the federal budget process
C. Municipal bond disclosure guidelines

Three managerial concepts

Modern fiscal administration makes extensive use of three concepts taken from applied microeconomics: discounting and the time value of money, opportunity cost, and incremental analysis. Without an understanding of these analytical tools, fiscal managers are likely to make decisions detrimental to their community. The following sections provide an elementary overview of these concepts and their application in public decision making.

DISCOUNTING AND TIME VALUE

Decisions made today often have impacts for several years into the future. The standard approach for comparing such impacts in personal, business, and public finance is *discounting,* a process of converting a stream of returns or costs incurred over time to a single *present value.* The present value takes account of both the absolute size and the timing of impacts of a proposed action.

Why is a payment of $100 received at the end of one year not equivalent to $100 received now? If inflation's erosion of purchasing power and the uncertainty of the future seem to make the answer obvious, assume that the $100 is certain to be received and has been adjusted for price level changes: the reason for discounting is related neither to inflation nor to uncertainty. The reason is simply that the $100 available now can yield a flow of valuable services (or interest) through the year. At the end of the year, the holder could have $100 *plus* the services received from use of the $100 during the year. The $100 plus services is greater than $100, so $100 now has greater value than does $100 received at the end of the year. Furthermore, as the date of receipt is more distant, the present value of a given dollar amount is lower: the flow of services between now and then would be greater.

While the principle of discounting and time value applies to any resource or service, the mechanics most often are done using market exchange equivalents (dollar values) of those returns and the analysis uses investment for interest as the earned service flow. Thus, $X available now (the principal) will become $X plus $X times the rate of interest (the principal plus interest earned on that principal) at the end of one year. The mechanics of discounting are easier to understand after working through the more familiar process of compounding. Suppose the rate of interest is 9 percent: if $1,000 is invested today, it will accumulate to $1,090 at the end of the year. Thus,

$$\$1,090 = \$1,000 + (\$1,000 \times 0.09)$$

or

Amount at end of year = Original principal + Interest earned

Algebraically, if r = the rate of interest, PV = the present amount, and FV_1 = the amount at the end of a year, then

$$FV_1 = PV + PV\,r \qquad \text{or} \qquad FV_1 = PV\,(1 + r)$$

FV_1 equals the original principal (PV) plus accumulated interest ($PV\,r$).

Many policy and management questions involve multiple-year decisions—where the returns are permitted to compound over several years. In other words, the principal plus accumulated interest is reinvested and allowed to accumulate. An example would be calculation of the amount to which $1,000 would accumulate at the end of five years with 9 percent annual interest. Annual account balances follow.

Initial deposit, $1,000	Interest earned (interest rate × previous balance)	Account balance
End of year:		
1	$ 90.00	$1,090.00
2	98.10	1,188.10
3	106.93	1,295.03
4	116.55	1,411.58
5	127.04	1,538.62

Obviously there must be an easier way to compute compound interest than going through all the year-end balance computations. Using the symbols previously introduced for values now and values at the end of a year,

$$FV_1 = PV \ (1.09)$$

At the end of the second year, the account balance would increase from interest earned:

$$FV_2 = FV_1 \ (1.09) = (PV \ (1.09))(1.09) = PV \ (1.09)^2$$

The same increase from interest earned occurs at the end of the third year:

$$FV_3 = FV_2 \ (1.09) = ((PV \ (1.09))(1.09))(1.09) = PV \ (1.09)^3$$

For the fourth year:

$$FV_4 = FV_3 \ (1.09) = (((PV \ (1.09))(1.09))(1.09))(1.09) = PV \ (1.09)^4$$

The same process applies, regardless of the number of years. In general, if PV = the present amount, r = the appropriate interest rate, n = the number of periods of compounding, and FV_n = the account balance at the end of the periods,

$$FV_n = PV \ (1 + r)^n$$

From the previous example,[1]

$$FV_n = 1,000 \ (1.09)^5 = 1,538.62$$

Interest is often compounded more frequently than once a year. The compounding formula can easily be adjusted to allow for semiannual, quarterly, or any other regular scheme of paying interest. For example, suppose interest is paid twice a year. With an annual rate of 9 percent, that system would mean that 4½ percent interest is paid for the first half of the year and 4½ percent is paid for the second half year. Thus, principal plus interest amounts at the end of *half years* would be

$$FV_1 = PV \ (1.045) \quad \text{(balance at end of one half year)}$$
$$FV_2 = PV \ (1.045)^2 \quad \text{(balance at end of two half years)}$$
$$FV_3 = PV \ (1.045)^3 \quad \text{(balance at end of three half years)}$$

and so on. Thus, at the end of n years,

$$FV_n = PV \ (1.045)^{2n}$$

---

[1] For electronic calculators, use the y^x key: $y = 1.09$ and $x = 5$. Thus, $(1.09)^5 = 1.53862$.

In general, if interest is added x times per year, and other definitions are as before,

$$FV_n = PV \left(1 + \frac{r}{x}\right)^{nx}$$

Discounting simply adjusts sums to be received in the future to their present-value equivalent, the amount which will accumulate to that future sum if invested at prevailing interest rates. Recall that FV, the accumulated balance at the end of one year, equals $PV (1 + r)$, the balance at the start of the year multiplied by one plus the rate of interest. That formula can be rearranged to become

$$PV = \frac{FV_1}{(1 + r)}$$

The amount PV invested at interest rate r will grow to FV_1 at the end of the year.

Suppose $1,000 will be received at the end of one year ($FV = 1,000$): if the interest rate that could be earned is 9 percent, what sum today (PV) would accumulate to $1,000 at the end of the year? That present value emerges from operation of the present-value formula:

$$PV = \$1,000/(1 + .09) = \$917.43$$

That means that $917.43 now plus 9 percent interest earned for one year ($917.43 × .09 = $82.57) equals $1,000: the present-value equivalent of $1,000 received at the end of one year when the prevailing interest rate available is 9 percent is $917.43. That prevailing rate is called the discount rate.

What happens if the return is received more than one year into the future? The same logic of adjusting for interest which could have been earned still applies, but the computations look messier because the interest earnings would compound. In other words, interest earned during the first year would be able to earn interest in the second year, and so on through the years. The general formula for compounding, $FV_n = PV (1 + r)^n$, may be rearranged in the same way that the single-year compounding formula was to produce the general present-value formula:

$$PV = \frac{FV_n}{(1 + r)^n}$$

where PV = the present-value equivalent, FV_n = a value received in the future, r is the discount rate, and n is the number of years into the future that the sum is received. For example, $800 received 10 years in the future, assuming a 10 percent discount rate, would have a present value of $308.43 (or $800/(1 + .10)^{10} = 800/2.5937$). That means that $308.43 invested at 10 percent per year for 10 years will accumulate to $800; when the discount rate is 10 percent, $308.43 is the present-value equivalent of $800 received at the end of 10 years.

With that technique, projects yielding dramatically different returns over time can be compared. Suppose an agency has two projects under consideration. Each costs $1,900 (all occurring at the present) but the profile of returns from the projects differs substantially:

Received at end of year	Returns	
	Project A	Project B
1	$1,000	$480
2	300	480
3	1,000	480
4	0	480
5	0	480

Neither project lasts beyond the fifth year. Which project yields greater net benefits? Recognize that simple addition of returns—$2,300 for A and $2,400 for B—will not be appropriate because the timing of those returns is not the same.

An appropriate comparison requires that both streams be converted to their present-value equivalents. Suppose that prevailing interest rate conditions indicate that resources should be able to earn a 10 percent return: 10 percent is then a reasonable discount rate to use, with the following results.

Received at end of year	Discount factor	Project A returns		Project B returns	
		Current	Discounted	Current	Discounted
1	$1/(1.1) = .909$	$1,000	$ 909	$480	$ 436
2	$1/(1.1)^2 = .826$	300	248	480	396
3	$1/(1.1)^3 = .751$	1,000	751	480	360
4	$1/(1.1)^4 = .683$	0	0	480	328
5	$1/(1.1)^5 = .621$	0	0	480	298
Total present value			$1,908		$1,818

Under those conditions, the present value of A is $1,908 and of B, $1,818. Of the two projects, only A has a value exceeding its cost.

What happens if 3 percent were the appropriate discount rate? As the following display shows, the present value of both projects increases and both now have present values above the cost of the project.

Received at end of year	Discount factor	Project A returns Current	Project A returns Discounted	Project B returns Current	Project B returns Discounted
1	1/(1.03) = .971	$1,000	$ 971	$480	$ 466
2	1/(1.03)² = .943	300	283	480	453
3	1/(1.03)³ = .915	1,000	915	480	439
4	1/(1.03)⁴ = .888	0	0	480	426
5	1/(1.03)⁵ = .863	0	0	480	414
Total present value			$2,169		$2,198

In fact, project B now has a present value greater than project A because returns in the future make greater contribution to present value when the discount factor is lower. Choice of the appropriate discount rate clearly matters for public decisions—an artificially high or low rate can lead to wasteful choices.

Analysts sometime compare alternatives by determining what discount rate would cause the present value of projects under consideration to be equal. Thus, the present value of A and B would be the same at a rate around 4 percent. If the rate is above that level, A is better; if below, B is better. Rates probably are above 4 percent, so A is quite likely the better choice, regardless of what the exact discount rate is.

OPPORTUNITY COST

The principle of cost applicable to managerial decisions is that of opportunity cost: "By the opportunity cost of a decision is meant the sacrifice of alternatives required by that decision . . . [O]pportunity costs require the measurement of *sacrifices.* If a decision involves no sacrifices, it is cost free."[2] The cost that matters for decisions is the value of paths not taken; that is the true cost of any decision. The previous section on discounting used the opportunity concept without a label. The discount rate is the interest rate which could have been earned if the flow were available now and invested. Present-value computations implicity are always based on opportunity cost values.

Opportunity cost of a resource may not equal the amount actually paid for that resource (its historical cost). For example, if a municipality

---

[2] William Warren Haynes, *Managerial Economics* (Plano, Tex.: Business Publications, Inc., 1969), p. 32.

invests $1.5 million in a new incineration plant that will not burn the refuse mix generated by the city, the value of the plant clearly is less than $1.5 million and, unless there is some salvage value for the facility, approximates zero. Decisions are appropriately based on opportunity costs, not historical costs.

The concept may best be understood by use of a simple illustration. Suppose a wealthy alumnus bequeaths $800,000 to a university for construction of an office building to house its public relations staff. If the bequest were not honored, the money would go to a home for stray cats in another state. The university will construct the building on land it already owns next to a busy highway. In a simple accounting or financial sense, the cost of the building would equal $800,000, the construction cost plus nothing for the land already owned by the university. Opportunity cost, however, focuses on the sacrifice of alternatives required by the decision. Thus, the opportunity cost to the university for the facility would be zero for construction (the university does not have the $800,000 available for any other use) plus the value of the land in its best alternative use. The university could have used the land for something else—the land had alternative uses sacrificed when the building was built.

In sum, decisions require that alternatives sacrificed be the focus. Opportunities forgone are the basis of decisions. Amounts paid in the past (historical cost) have no necessary influence on cost in present decisions. Opportunities now gauge the cost that matters for choice.

INCREMENTAL ANALYSIS

The heart of incremental analysis is the principle that decisions must focus on the factors that are different in the options under consideration. Nothing can be gained by examination of factors that will happen regardless of the decision. The principle seems too simple to matter, except that much policy argument does take place around elements that will not change regardless of choice.

Some elements of the incremental approach may be demonstrated in this example. Suppose a town is contemplating a newspaper recycling project: its garbage truck will be fitted with a rack to collect bundles of newspapers along the collection route. Cost and revenue estimates prepared by the town clerk appear on the next page.

While the estimates are consistent with accounting principles which require that each activity bear its share of entity operation cost, the conflict is with the incremental principle—that only costs or revenue which change because of a decision should be considered in making the decision. In the illustration, there is nothing logically wrong with reve-

Annual cost:	
Labor (one extra worker to gather and process papers)	$ 9,600
Purchase and installation of rack (one-year useful life)	400
Apportioned share of truck operation and maintenance	1,500
Apportioned share of Public Works Department administrative expense	2,000
Total	13,500
Annual revenue:	
480 tons of paper at $25 per ton	12,000
Annual loss (or required subsidy)	1,500

nue, labor cost, or rack cost: none of those would exist without the recycling, so they are incremental to the decision. There are problems, however, with the administrative, operation, and maintenance cost figures: will any of these costs be different because of the recycling program? If not (which is probably the case), they should be *excluded* in making the decision. When the adjustment to incremental reasoning is made, the program actually will subsidize the general government ($2,000 incremental revenue over incremental cost), rather than require subsidization.

EXERCISES FOR APPENDIX A

1. Ms. LaRue has $10,000 to invest for three years. Two banks offer a 10 percent interest rate, but bank A compounds quarterly and bank B compounds semiannually. To what value would her money grow in each of the two banks?

2. Penn Central Railroad had not paid local taxes since 1969, under federal bankruptcy court protection. Some years later, the court required Penn Central to offer municipalities a choice of two payment options to clear this liability. (Penn Central, of course, has been absorbed by Conrail, so there are no future tax liabilities involved.) The choices were: (a) immediate payment of 44 percent of total liability or (b) immediate payment of 20 percent of the liability, 10 percent paid at the end of each of the next three years, and 50 percent paid at the end of 10 years. Which alternative would you recommend to a municipality and why?

3. "A logical estimate of the current opportunity cost to the community of destroying the Parris-Dunning House (a structure built in the early 1800s and lived in by an early Governor of Indiana) for construction of a traffic corridor in Bloomington, Indiana, could be prepared by using the formula: $C_p = C_o (1 + r)^n$ where C_p = current opportunity cost, C_o = the original construction cost of the house, r = the appropriate interest rate available on

investments over the period, and n = the number of years between construction and the present." Do you agree? Explain.

4. The irrigation system a farmer uses cost $10,000 8 years ago. It will last another 25 years without additional investment. With that system, he produces crops valued at $3,000 per year at a cost of $1,000 per year. A new system would cost $15,000 to install, but would increase production to $7,000 per year. Operating cost would be $2,500 per year. The farmer would have to refurbish the new system 12 years after installation at a cost of $5,000. Assume that investment in the new system occurs at the start of the first year, that the increases in output and operating cost occur immediately and last for 25 years without change, and that both systems have a salvage value of $1,000 at the end of 25 years. Assume a 12 percent discount rate. Should the farmer replace his existing system?

APPENDIX B

Overview of the federal budget process

The federal budget, like all public budgets, reflects what is proposed to be done for a specific period of time in the future, usually 12 months. It is a plan concerned with managing public funds, and it deals with how much government will spend and how those expenditures will be financed. When passed by Congress and signed by the president, the budget becomes law. The amount of funds specified in the legislation is then legally binding for all federal agencies for a given fiscal year. Agencies cannot spend more than is specified unless they are able to get supplemental or deficiency appropriations through the same legal channels as the original budget.

The budget, of course, is much more than a legally binding financial plan. Since funds are always limited, the act of budgetmaking becomes a process of choosing among alternative expenditures, and the budget document itself becomes a description of national goals and priorities. The budget process, then, entails political decisions (choices) as well as financial and economic analyses. In the United States that process is lengthy and complex. What our federal budget actually contains in any given fiscal year is the result of the interplay between the executive branch, and its many departments and agencies, and Congress, with its system of committees and subcommittees.

Source: Adapted from *A Glossary of Terms Used in the Federal Budget Process,* 3d ed., PAD-81-27 (Washington, D.C.: U.S. General Accounting Office, 1981).

Although the Constitution (Article I, Sect. 1) gives Congress the responsibility for budget decisions, by law the executive branch is charged with preparing and submitting the budget. Under the Budget and Accounting Act of 1921, every year the president transmits a proposed federal budget to Congress within 15 days after it convenes in the new calendar year. Until 1976, the president's annual budget message contained the proposed budget for the fiscal year that began July 1 and ended June 30. The Congressional Budget and Impoundment Control Act of 1974 (P.L. 93–344) changed those dates. The federal fiscal year now runs from October 1 through September 30. The act has not directly altered the executive budget process—agency officials continue to channel their budget requests through the cabinet level, and in turn through the Office of Management and Budget which reviews the requests in light of the president's proposed budget initiatives—but the act has strengthened the legislative side of budgetmaking by introducing changes that have helped Congress form a clearer perspective of fiscal policy requirements.

Although federal budgeting is a continuous process, it can be understood and studied in terms of four phases: (1) executive preparation and submission, (2) congressional action or the congressional budget process, (3) implementation and control of the enacted budget, and (4) review and audit. Our discussion of these phases augments Figure 1,

Executive branch budget timetable

Timing	Action to be completed
April–June (March)	Conduct spring planning review to establish presidential policy for the upcoming budget.
June	OMB sends policy letters to the agencies.
September 1	Smaller agencies submit initial budget request materials.
September 15	Cabinet departments and major agencies submit initial budget request materials.
October 15	Legislative branch, judiciary, and certain agencies submit initial budget request materials.
September–January (September)	OMB and the president review agency budget requests and prepare the budget documents.
January	The president transmits the budget during the first 15 days of each regular session of Congress.
January–February	OMB sends allowances letters to the agencies.
April 10 (February)	The president transmits an update of the budget estimates. (Note: transmittal is often requested to be made earlier than the required date.)
July 15 (June)	The president transmits an update of the budget estimates. (Note: transmittal is often requested to be made earlier than the required date.)

Source: OMB Circular no. A-11, rev., June 3, 1980.

FIGURE 1
The federal budgetmaking process

Summary of major steps in the budget process

Period before the fiscal year			Fiscal year	Beyond fiscal year
March	November	January	October	September 30	November 15

Phase 1. Executive preparation and submission. (Beginning 19 months before fiscal year.)*

Phase 2. Congressional budget process. Includes action on appropriations and revenue measures. (Beginning 19½ months before fiscal year.)†

Phase 3. Implementation and control of enacted budget. (During fiscal year.)

Phase 4. Review and audit

FIGURE 1 (continued)

Phase 1-Executive preparation and submission

Approximate timing	Agency	Office of Management and Budget	The president
Budget policy development			
March (or earlier in some agencies)	Reviews current operations, program objectives, issues, and future plans in relation to up-coming annual budget. Submits projections of requirements that reflect current operations and future plans, supporting memoranda and related analytic studies that identify major issues, alternatives for resolving issues, and comparisons of costs and effectiveness.	Develops economic assumptions. Obtains forecasts of international and domestic situations. Prepares fiscal projections.*	
April May		Issues policy guidance on material to be developed for spring planning review.	Discusses budgetary outlook and policies with the director of OMB and with the Cabinet as appropriate.
May		Discusses program developments and management issues, and resulting budgetary effects, with agencies.	
		Compiles total outlay estimates for comparison with revenue estimates. Develops recommendations for president on fiscal policy*, program issues, and budget levels.	Discusses with the director of OMB and others as necessary, general budget policy, major program issues, budgetary planning targets, and projections.
June	Issues internal instructions on preparation of annual budget estimates.	Issues technical instructions for preparation of annual budget estimates.	Establishes general guidelines and agency planning targets for annual budget.
Compilation and submission of agency estimates		Conveys president's decisions to agency heads on government-wide policies and assumptions, the application of policies, and budgetary planning targets to individual agencies.	
July – September 30	Allocates budgetary planning target to agency programs. Develops and compiles detailed estimates.	Advises and assists agencies on preparation of budget submissions.	
Office of Management and Budget review and presidential decisions		Analyzes budget submissions. Holds hearings with agency representatives on program, budget, and management issues in preparation for director's review.	
September October November	Submits formal estimates for annual budget, including projections of requirements for future years and supporting materials.	Reexamines economic assumptions and fiscal policies. *Discusses program developments with agencies. In light of outlook and policy discussion with president, prepares budget recommendations for the president.	Reviews budget recommendations and decides on agency budget amounts and on overall budget assumptions and policies.
	Revises estimates to conform to president's decisions.	Notifies agency heads of president's decisions.	
December January February		Again reviews economic outlook and fiscal policy for discussion with president of economic policies.*	Revises and approves budget message.
		Drafts president's budget message; prepares budget with summary tables, budget appendix, special analyses, and budget-in-brief. Arranges printing of budget documents.	Transmits recommended budget to Congress within 15 days after Congress convenes.
			Congress

* In cooperation with the Treasury Department and Council of Economic Advisers.

FIGURE 1 (continued)

Phase 2. Congressional Budget Process

FIGURE 1 (*concluded*)

Phase 3.   Implementation and control of enacted budget

Approximate timing

Treasury-General Accounting Office	Agency	Office of Management and Budget

Funds made available
August – September

On approval of appropriation bill, appropriation warrant is drawn by Treasury, countersigned by the General Accounting Office, and forwarded to agency.

Revises operating budget in view of approved appropriations and program developments.

Prepares requests for apportionment by August 21 or within 10 days after approval of appropriations, whichever is later.

Makes apportionment by September 10 or within 30 days after approval of appropriations, whichever is later.

May reapportion at any time, on own initiative or on agency request.

Control over funds
Continuous

Allots apportioned funds to various programs or activities.

Obligates money. Receives and uses goods and services. Makes monthly or quarterly reports to OMB on status of funds and use of resources in relation to program plans. Reports periodically to OMB on management improvements and actions affecting personnel requirements and costs.

May withhold funds through the apportionment process as a deferral or as an amount withheld pending rescission. Such withholding requires transmittal by the president of special messages to Congress for its approval or disapproval.

Examines reports on status of funds in relation to apportionments. Analyzes reports on use of resources and relationship of accomplishments and costs. Reports to the president periodically on budget and program status, personnel, management improvements, and cost reductions.

Expenditure of funds

As bills become payable

Treasury issues checks (except for certain agencies which issue their own) and reports on financial transactions in Monthly Treasury Statement, Treasury Bulletin, and Combined Statement of Receipts, Expenditures and Balances of the United States Government.

Prepares and certifies vouchers and invoices for payment.

Phase 4 — Review and audit

Approximate timing

Treasury-General Accounting Office	Agency	Office of Management and Budget

Program evaluation, management appraisal, and independent audit

Periodic

General Accounting Office performs independent audit of financial records, transactions, and financial management, generally. "Settles" accounts of certifying and disbursing officers. Makes reports to Congress including reports on special messages on deferrals and proposed rescissions.

Reviews compliance with established policies, procedures, and requirements. Evaluates accomplishment of program plans and effectiveness of management and operations.

Reviews agency operations and evaluates programs and performance. Conducts or guides agencies in organization and management studies. Assists president in improving management and organization of the executive branch.

Source: Office of Management and Budget, January 1977.

which describes and identifies the activities and actors in the federal budget process. Most of our discussion is devoted to phase 2 because, with the passage of the 1974 Budget Act, Congress acquired a new budget process. Rather than acting on the executive's budget proposals in a piecemeal fashion, as had been done in the past, Congress now has a system for looking at the budget as a unified proposal early in the budget cycle. The act has given both Houses the opportunity to determine if the budget is consistent with national priorities.

PHASE 1: EXECUTIVE PREPARATION AND SUBMISSION

Preparing the President's budget starts many months before it is submitted to Congress in late January. Formulation begins at the agency level, where individual organizational units review current operations, program objectives, and future plans in relation to the upcoming budget. Throughout this preparation period, there is a continuous exchange of information among the various federal agencies, OMB, and the president. Agency officials receive help in the form of revenue estimates and economic outlook projections from the Treasury Department, the Council of Economic Advisers, the Departments of Commerce and Labor, and OMB. The budget timetable [included here] highlights the key steps involved in preparing the president's budget and transmitting it to Congress. The months in parentheses indicate when agencies are expected to submit review materials to OMB.

PHASE 2: THE CONGRESSIONAL BUDGET PROCESS (AN ILLUSTRATIVE OVERVIEW)

The Budget of the United States Government, published early January, contains the president's proposals for the federal government's outlays and budget authority for the ensuing fiscal year. Congress can act as it wishes on these proposals. It can change funding levels, modify or eliminate programs, or add new ones not requested by the president, and it can act on legislation determining tax rates. The final outcome of Congress' actions is the expenditure (outlay) of federal funds. However, Congress does not act (vote) on outlays directly, but rather on requests for budget authority. Through the appropriations bills it passes, Congress grants budget authority to agencies, which permits them to incur obligations and hence to spend federal funds.

Before a request for budget authority can be considered, Congress must first enact legislation authorizing an agency to carry out a particular program, such as revenue sharing or food stamps. Authorizing legislation can set a limit on the funds for a given program or call for "such sums as may be necessary," but it cannot stipulate the dollar amount to be spent on the program. Some major programs, like space, defense procurement, and foreign affairs, are reauthorized by the standing legislative committee every year, while other programs are authorized for several years in advance.

How much money each department, agency, or program receives is determined by the House and Senate Appropriations Committees and their subcommittees, each of which has jurisdiction over specific numbers of federal agencies. Money bills (i.e., appropriations) may be for one year (the most common form), which allows an agency to spend only during one fiscal year, or they may be multiyear appropriations. The Constitution requires that all revenue (tax) bills originate in the House, and by custom the House also originates appropriations measures.[1]

Since appropriations are not usually considered until authorizing legislation is passed, in recent years many federal agencies have received their appropriations after the new fiscal year has begun. When an agency does not receive its appropriation before the old one lapses, it operates under a continuing resolution passed by Congress. A continuing resolution usually allows an agency to spend at the previous year's rate.

The 1974 Budget Act has introduced the following changes into the congressional budget process:

1. It requires Congress, before it enacts any appropriation bills, to adopt concurrent budget resolutions. The first resolution sets target totals for budget authority, outlays, receipts, and the public debt. These targets serve as a guide for Congress' subsequent considerations of appropriations and tax measures. The resolution also subdivides the targets into 17 functional spending categories, such as defense and health, which represent broad national priorities.
2. It established the House and Senate Budget Committees and has charged them with the responsibility of reporting the concurrent budget resolutions. The committees also keep track of individual authorization, appropriations, and revenue decisions that Congress makes during the budget process.
3. By creating the Congressional Budget Office (the congressional counterpart to OMB) and granting it broad authority to obtain data from executive agencies, the act has provided Congress with a

---

[1] Passage of revenue bills follows the same general procedure as appropriation bills, except that revenue measures are reported by the Ways and Means Committee in the House and by the Finance Committee in the Senate.

mechanism for obtaining impartial policy and cost analyses and five-year budget projections. CBO provides Congress with all available information related to the budget and conducts budget-related studies at Congress' request. It also monitors individual spending bills and issues periodic scorekeeping reports showing the status of congressional action on these bills.

4. It has provided Congress with a firm budget timetable that coordinates the authorization and appropriations cycles with the overall congressional budget as embodied in the concurrent budget resolutions.

5. It has changed the rules on presidential impoundment of funds by establishing a procedure for congressional involvement. The act requires that any money not spent must be reported to Congress in rescission or deferral messages. Impoundments take effect unless they are disapproved by both Houses within 45 days of the president's notification. Deferrals (temporary withholding of funds from obligation) are effective until overturned by either House.

The congressional timetable laid down in Title III of the act is illustrated in Figure 1. Congress' activities with respect to the timetable are summarized below.

CONGRESSIONAL BUDGET TIMETABLE

November 10

Congressional review of the budget begins when the president submits estimates of the current services budget, a five-year projection of federal spending based on current programs and existing funding levels, exclusive of any new programs. The Joint Economic Committee assesses these estimates, spelling out the economic assumptions (inflation, unemployment, rate of economic growth) that underlie them, and reports its evaluation to Congress by December 31. Congress uses the current services budget as a basis for examining the president's January budget submission.

January (15 days after Congress convenes)

Following the submission of the president's budget, the Senate and House Budget Committees begin hearings to examine the president's economic assumptions and spending priorities in preparation for drafting the first concurrent resolution on the budget.

March 15

Authorization and appropriations committees report to the Budget Committees their views and estimates of new budget authority to be enacted for the ensuing fiscal year. Some committees hold formal markup sessions to draft these views and estimates. The reports are used by the Budget Committees to gauge the total and functional spending estimates contained in the first concurrent budget resolution.

April 1

The Congressional Budget Office submits its report detailing alternative spending patterns and revenue levels associated with different budget options and their budgetary implications to the Budget Committees. The CBO report, which in theory is used in drafting the first budget resolution, presents Congress with spending scenarios above and below the president's.

April 15

The Budget Committees of both Houses report the first concurrent budget resolution to Congress. This initial resolution establishes targets for: (a) the appropriate level of total outlays (money to be spent in the ensuing fiscal year) and total new budget authority (money to be spent in the ensuing fiscal year and in future fiscal years) both in the aggregate and by functional category, (b) the appropriate budget surplus or deficit, (c) the recommended level of federal revenues, and (d) the appropriate level of public debt.

May 15

Budget Committees report legislation proposing new budget authority to the House and Senate. If a committee fails to meet this deadline, the legislation cannot be considered by the House or Senate unless a waiver is reported by the House Rules Committee or the Senate Budget Committee.

May 15

Congress completes action on the first budget resolution. Until the first budget resolution has been finalized, setting a "target" spending ceiling and revenue floor for the fiscal year, neither House can consider any spending or revenue measures that would take effect in that fiscal year.

September (7th day after Labor Day)

Congress completes action on all regular authorization and appropriations measures. The only exception to this rule is consideration of bills that have been delayed because necessary authorizing legislation has not been enacted in time. When this happens, federal departments and agencies exist on "continuing resolutions"—the prior year's funding levels—until their regular appropriations are passed.

September 15

There is no deadline for reporting the second budget resolution, but it normally occurs before the annual August recess (or immediately after), and it must be made final by September 15. In the first resolution, the total and functional spending levels are "targets," but in the second resolution they are "binding." This has the effect of "locking in" a congressional spending ceiling and revenue floor. Once the second budget resolution is in place, no legislation can be passed that would breach these limits, unless Congress passes a subsequent budget resolution.

September 25

Congress completes final actions on reconciliation for second budget resolution, which either affirms or revises the budget targets set in the first resolution. The House and Senate Budget Committees report any changes to the floor in the form of a reconciliation bill. Congress cannot adjourn for the year until the reconciliation legislation is passed.

October 1

The fiscal year begins.

PHASE 3: IMPLEMENTATION AND CONTROL OF THE ENACTED BUDGET

After the budget is approved by Congress, the president is responsible for executing it. Under law, most of the budget authority granted to the agencies of the executive branch is converted into outlays through an apportionment system regulated by the Office of Management and Budget. The director of OMB apportions (distributes) budget authority to each agency by time periods (usually quarters) or by activities over the duration of the appropriation. This ensures both the economical and effective use of funds and obviates the need for agencies having to ask for supplemental authority. However, changes in law or economic conditions during the fiscal year may necessitate the enactment of additional budget authority. When this happens, supplemental requests are sent to Congress for its consideration. On the other hand, the executive branch, under the Antideficiency Act (31 U.S.C. 665), may establish reserves to fund contingencies or to effect savings made possible by more efficient operations or by changes in requirements.

Title X of the 1974 Budget Act permits the president to withhold appropriated funds for fiscal or other policy reasons, or because the president has determined that all or part of an appropriation is not needed to carry out a program. When these circumstances arise, the president sends a special message to Congress requesting that the budget authority be rescinded. If Congress does not pass a rescission bill within 45 days of continuous session, the budget authority is made available for obligation.

In order to defer—temporarily withhold—budget authority, the president must also send a special message to Congress indicating the reasons for the proposed delay in spending. Either House may, at any time, pass a resolution disapproving the president's request for deferral of budget authority, thus requiring that the funds be made available for obligation. When no congressional action is taken, deferrals may remain in effect until, but not beyond, the end of the fiscal year. If continued deferal is desired into the new fiscal year, the president must transmit a new special message to Congress.

PHASE 4: REVIEW AND AUDIT

Individual agencies are responsible—through their own review and control systems—for making sure that the obligations they incur and the resulting outlays adhere to the provisions in the authorizing and appropriations legislation, as well as to other laws and regulations governing the obligation and expenditure of funds. OMB exercises its review responsibility by appraising program and financial reports and by keeping abreast of agencies' efforts to attain program objectives.

In addition, the General Accounting Office, as an agency responsible to Congress, regularly audits, examines, and evaluates Government programs. Its findings and recommendations for corrective action are made to Congress, to OMB, and to the agencies concerned. GAO also monitors the executive branch's reporting of messages on proposed rescissions and deferrals. It reports to Congress any differences it may have with the classifications (i.e., rescissions or deferrals) of the president's requests for withholding funds. Should the President fail to make budget authority available in accordance with the 1974 Budget Act, GAO may bring civil action to obtain compliance.

THE FEDERAL BUDGET DOCUMENTS

The official data and analyses relating to the federal budget are published in four documents:

The Budget of the United States Government
The United States Budget in Brief
The Budget of the United States Government, Appendix
Special analyses, Budget of the United States Government

The Budget of the United States Government contains the president's budget message and an overview of the president's budget proposals. It explains spending programs in terms of national needs, agency missions, and basic programs, and it analyzes estimated receipts and discusses the president's tax program. This document also describes the budget system and presents summary tables on the budget as a whole.

The United States Budget in Brief is designed for the general public. It provides a more concise, less technical overview of the budget than the full *Budget.* Summary and historical tables on the federal budget and debt are provided, together with graphic displays.

The Budget of the United States Government, Appendix contains information on the various appropriations and funds that compose the budget. For each agency the *Appendix* includes the proposed text of appropriation language, budget schedules for each account, new legislative proposals, explanations of the work to be performed and the funds needed, proposed general provisions applicable to the appropriations of entire agencies or groups of agencies, and schedules of permanent positions. Supplementals and rescission proposals for the current year are presented separately. Information is also provided on certain activities whose outlays are not part of the budget total.

Special Analyses, Budget of the United States Government highlights specific program areas and other significant presentations of federal budget data. It presents alternative views of the budget, that is, current services and national income accounts; economic and financial analyses of the budget covering government finances and operations as a whole; and government-wide program and financial information for federal civil rights and research development programs.

These documents are for sale in paper covers only, by the Superintendent of Documents, U.S. Government Printing Office, Washington, D.C. 20402.

Municipal bond disclosure guidelines

DISCLOSURE GUIDELINES OUTLINE

Section I
Described in cover page of the Official Statement

1. Total principal amount.
2. Name of issuer.
3. Type or title of issue (e.g., general obligation).
4. Date of obligations, interest payment dates, and date from which interest is paid.
5. Denominations of securities.
6. Registration and exchange provisions.
7. Trustee and paying agents.
8. Redemption features, if any, including sinking fund provisions.
9. Maturity date and principal amount by maturity in columnar form.
10. Statement of tax status or interest.

Source: The voluntary disclosure guidelines have been proposed by the Municipal Finance Officers Association. The outline, from Philip Rosenberg et al., *A Debt Management Handbook for Small Cities and Other Governmental Units* (Chicago: MFOA, 1978), condenses the more lengthy M.F.O.A. disclosure document.

Also may include:

11. Ratings.
12. Designation of new issues.
13. Buy statement of authority for issuance.
14. Anticipated date and place of delivery.
15. Summary statement of security or source of payment.

Section II
Briefly describe in Introduction to the Official Statement

1. Description of issuer.
2. Purpose of securities, including application of proceeds.
3. Security and source of payment.

Section III
Describe securities being offered

1. Amplification of items 1–9 in Section I.
2. Pertinent provisions of state constitution, statutes, resolutions, and other documentation as appropriate.
3. Purposes for which net proceeds are to be used.
4. Security provisions and sources of payment.
5. Provisions regarding (*a*) flow of funds, (*b*) creation of reserves, (*c*) maintenance or insurance of properties, (*d*) any proposed investment of the proceeds, (*e*) and parties who will control the proceeds.
6. Purposes for which additional debt may be issued.
7. Name and responsibilities of trustee or fiscal agent, if any; any indemnification trustee or fiscal agent may require before enforcing the rights of securities' holders.
8. Pertinent state constitution provisions, statutes or judicial decisions that could affect the status of or priority for the bondholder.
9. Terms of securities which may be modified.
10. Events which constitute defaults and the remedies for default.

Section IV
Describe issue and the enterprise

A. Issuer

1. Year in which issue was established; name of state; form of government; powers and organization of issuer.

2. List of executive officials, way chosen, length of term, and the method and authority for making decisions.
3. Principal services; services required; revenue sources for services; extent of performing services with other governments; any recent changes in such services.
4. General character of principal facilities.
5. Historical and current socioeconomic data.
6. Historical and current community financial information.
7. Information about principal industries: number of persons employed, economic stability, economic effects of any recent addition or loss of employers.
8. Number of persons employed by issuer.

B. Enterprise

1. Year organized; form of organization; cities, counties, and states in which enterprise is located.
2. Executive of the enterprise, manner chosen, terms, authority and method by which decisions are made.
3. Location and general character of principal facilities.
4. New facilities to be constructed.
5. Reference to any relevant engineers or financial feasibility reports. If no report, make statement of this with an explanation.
6. Operations to be performed by new facility including: principal services rendered; whether position in service area is exclusive; number of current and projected customers; parties responsible for determining rates and any rate covenant; source of needed raw materials; status of licenses, permits, and franchises to be held; any governmental regulation of the operations and its effect; number of persons employed and to be employed; plan of operations if no revenue have been received one fiscal year prior to date of sale.

Section V
Description of debt structure

1. Category, amount of debt authorized, and amount outstanding within the previous 120 days.
2. Debt service schedule of outstanding indebtedness, including required payments of principal and interest.
3. Indebtedness of overlapping governmental entities.
4. At end of each of last five fiscal years: (a) debt per capita, (b) debt as a percentage of total assessed valuation, (c) debt per capita.

5. Amount of long- and short-term debt at end of each of last five fiscal years.
6. Securities in default in the last 25 years together with circumstances for default.

Section VI
Description of financial information

A. General description of financial practices and recent results of operations

 1. Summary of operations: beginning and ending fund balances; for enterprise or intragovernmental service funds—operating revenues, expenses, interest income, extraordinary items, effects of changes in accounting principles, changes in retained earnings, and amount of retained earnings; material trends; facts which would alter financial information presented.
 2. Accounting practices.
 3. Budgetary process.
 4. History of particular receipts to pay securities if applicable.
 5. History of taxes pledged to pay securities if applicable.
 6. At end of each of last five fiscal years: assessed valuation of taxable real property; estimated true valuation of taxable real property; assessed valuation of taxable personal property; assessed valuation of taxable real property as a percentage of estimated true valuation.
 7. Ten largest taxpayers, amount of taxes paid, percentage of total tax levy, assessed valuation of taxable real property of each taxpayer.
 8. Revenue or tax anticipation notes.
 9. Any use of securities for current operating expenses in last 10 years.
 10. Any payment of securities met through loans from other government fund sources.
 11. Public employee retirement or pension plans: adverse trends, unfunded liabilities.

B. Financial statements

 1. Balance sheets, statements of revenues and expenditures, changes in fund balance, income, retained earnings, changes in financial position.

Section VII
Description of legal matters

1. Pending legal proceedings which may materially affect the ability of the issuer to perform its obligations.
2. With consent of bond counsel, include or summarize approving legal opinion. Name of bond counsel.
3. Tax status of securities and interest.
4. Certificate that no litigation is pending.

Section VIII
Miscellaneous

1. All ratings obtained or refused, changes in any ratings of any securities during the preceding two years.
2. Certain persons named in official statement employed on a contingent basis.
3. Investors' specimens of copies of any indenture and any other authorizing or governing instruments.

Terms used in public finance and budgeting

A number of the following definitions are taken from three publications of the federal government: U.S. General Accounting Office, *A Glossary of Terms Used in the Federal Budget Process and Related Accounting, Economic, and Tax Terms,* 3d ed., PAD-81-27 (Washington, D.C.: General Accounting Office, 1981); Bureau of the Census, *State Government Finances in 1979,* GF79, no. 3 (Washington, D.C.: U.S. Government Printing Office, 1980); and Bureau of the Census, *City Government Finances in 1978–79,* GF79, no. 4 (Washington, D.C.: U.S. Government Printing Office, 1980). Because of language differences from state to state, most definitions stay with the federal system.

Ability to pay The principle that the tax burden should be distributed according to a person's affluence. It is based on the assumption that as a person's affluence increases, the person can and should contribute a larger percentage of his/her affluence to support government activities.

Accounting system The procedures which record, classify, and report on the finances and operations of a business, government, individual, or other entity.

Accrual basis of accounting Accounting basis which records revenues when they are earned (whether or not cash is received then) and expenditures when goods and services are received (whether or not cash payments are made then).

Activity A specific and distinguishable line of work performed by one or more organizational components of a governmental unit for the purpose of discharging a function or subfunction for which the governmental unit is responsible. For example, food inspection is an activity performed in the discharge of the health function.

Advance appropriation Budget authority provided in an appropriation act to become available in a fiscal year, or more, beyond the fiscal year for which the appropriation act is passed. The amount is not included in the budget totals of the year in which the appropriation bill is enacted but it is included in the budget totals for the fiscal year in which the amount will become available for obligation. For examples and further discussion of this term, see Part V of *The Budget of the United States Government, Appendix.*

Advance funding Budget authority provided in an appropriation act to obligate and disburse funds during a fiscal year from a succeeding year's appropriation. The funds so obligated increase the budget authority for the fiscal year in which obligated and reduce the budget authority of the succeeding fiscal year. Advance funding is a device for avoiding supplemental requests late in the fiscal year for certain entitlement programs should the appropriations for the current year prove to be too low. For examples and further discussion of this term, see Part V of *The Budget of the United States Government, Appendix.*

Agency missions Responsibilities assigned to a specific agency for meeting national needs.

Agency missions are expressed in terms of the purpose to be served by the programs authorized to carry out functions or subfunctions which, by law, are the responsibility of that agency and its component organizations. In contrast to national needs, generally described in the context of major functions, agency missions are generally described in the context of subfunctions. (*See also* Functional classification; Mission budgeting; National needs.)

Allotment An authorization by the head (or other authorized employee) of an agency to his/her subordinates to incur obligations within a specified amount. An agency makes allotments pursuant to the requirements stated in OMB Circular no. A-34. The amount allotted by an agency cannot exceed the amount apportioned by the Office of Management and Budget.

Anticipation notes or warrants Short-term debt issued in anticipation of collection of taxes, the proceeds of a bond sale, or other revenue, and retirable from the collections they anticipate.

Antideficiency act Legislation enacted by Congress to prevent the incurring of obligations or the making of expenditures (outlays) in excess of amounts available in appropriations or funds; to fix responsibility within an agency for the creation of any obligation or the making of any expenditure in excess of an apportionment or reapportionment or in excess of other subdivisions established pursuant to 31 U.S.C. 665(g); and to assist in bringing about the most effective and economical use of appropriations and funds. The act is sometimes known as Section 3679 of the Revised Statutes, as amended.

Apportionment A distribution made by the Office of Management and Budget of amounts available for obligation, including budgetary reserves established pursuant to law, in an appropriation or fund account. Apportionments divide amounts available for obligation by specific time periods (usually quarters), activities, projects, objects, or a combination thereof. The amounts so apportioned limit the amount of obligations that may be incurred. In apportioning any account, some funds may be reserved to provide for contingencies or to effect savings, pursuant to the Antideficiency Act; or may be proposed for deferral or rescission pursuant to the Impoundment Control Act of 1974 (Title X of the Congressional Budget and Impoundment Control Act, P.L. 93-344, 31 U.S.C. 1400, et seq.).

The apportionment process is intended to prevent obligation of amounts available within an appropriation or fund account in a manner that would require deficiency or supplemental appropriations and to achieve the most effective and economical use of amounts made available for obligation. In this regard, federal agency obligations may not be incurred in excess of the amount of budget authority apportioned.

Appropriation act A statute, under the jurisdiction of the House and Senate Committees on Appropriations, that generally provides authorization for federal agencies to incur obligations and to make payments out of the Treasury for specified purposes. An appropriation act, the most common means of providing budget authority, generally follows enactment of authorizing legislation unless the authorizing legislation itself provides the budget authority.

Currently, there are 13 regular appropriation acts enacted annually.

From time to time, Congress also enacts supplemental appropriation acts. Similar relationships apply to state and local governments.

Assessed value The value placed on property, usually by a government employee, for the purpose of distributing property tax burden. That value may or may not be directly related to market value.

Assets Property with economic value owned by an entity.

Audit An examination of evidence, including records, facilities, inventories, systems, etc., to discover or verify desired information. A written report of findings will normally result and findings will normally be based on investigation of a sample of agency operations.

Authorizing committee A standing committee of the House or Senate with legislative jurisdiction over the subject matter of those laws, or parts of laws, that set up or continue the legal operations of federal programs or agencies. An authorizing committee also has jurisdiction in those instances where backdoor authority is provided in the substantive legislation.

Authorizing legislation Substantive legislation enacted by Congress that sets up or continues the legal operation of a Federal program or agency either indefinitely or for a specific period of time or sanctions a particular type of obligation or expenditure within a program.

Authorizing legislation is normally a prerequisite for appropriations. It may place a limit on the amount of budget authority to be included in appropriation acts or it may authorize the appropriation of "such sums as may be necessary." In some instances authorizing legislation may provide authority to incur debts or to mandate payment to particular persons or political subdivisions of the country.

Backdoor authority Budget authority provided in legislation outside the normal (appropriations committees) appropriations process. The most common forms of backdoor authority are authority to borrow (also called borrowing authority or authority to spend debt receipts) and contract authority. In

other cases (e.g., interest on the public debt), a permanent appropriation is provided that becomes available without any current action by Congress. Section 401 of the Congressional Budget and Impoundment Control Act of 1974 (31 U.S.C. 1351) specifies certain limits on the use of backdoor authority.

Balance sheet A statement of the financial position of an entity which presents the value of its assets, liabilities, and equities on a specified date.

Balloon maturity Bond issue with substantially more late maturities than early maturities. Some or all of the late maturities are often callable to allow for early redemption.

Basis point One one-hundredth of one percent. Ten basis points equal 1/10 of one percent.

Benefits received The principle that the tax burden should be distributed according to the benefits an individual receives from government. It is a logical extension of the exchange relationship of private markets.

Bond Contract to pay a specified sum of money (the principal or face value) at a specified future date (maturity) plus interest paid at an agreed percentage of the principal. Maturity is usually longer than one year. Notes have shorter maturities and are issued with less formality.

Bond discount The excess of the face value of a bond over its price (or underwriter bid).

Bond premium The excess of the bond price (or underwriter bid) over its face value (excluding any accrued interest).

Budget A financial plan, including proposed expenditures and estimated revenues, for a period in the future.

Budget authority Authority provided by law to enter into obligations that will result in immediate or future outlays involving federal government funds, except that budget authority does not include authority to insure or guarantee the repayment of indebtedness incurred by another person or government. The basic forms of budget authority are appropriations, authority to borrow, and contract authority. Budget authority may be classified by the period of availability (one-year, multiple-year, no-year), by the timing of congressional action (current or permanent), or by the manner of determining the amount available (definite or indefinite).

Forms of budget authority

Appropriations. An authorization by an act of Congress that permits federal agencies to incur obligations and to make payments out of the Treasury for specified purposes. An appropriation usually follows enactment of authorizing legislation. An appropriation act is the most common means of providing budget authority, but in some cases the authorizing legislation itself provides the budget authority. (*See* Backdoor authority.) Appropriations do not represent cash actually set aside in the Treasury for purposes specified in the appropriation act: they represent limitations of amounts that agencies may obligate during the period of time specified in the respective appropriation acts. Several types of appropriations are not counted as budget authority, since they do not provide authority to incur additional obligations. Examples of these include: Appropriations to liquidate contract authority—congressional action to provide funds to pay obligations incurred against contract authority; Appropriations to reduce outstanding debt—congressional action to provide funds for debt retirement; Appropriations for refunds of receipts.

Authority to borrow. Also called borrowing authority or authority to spend debt receipts. Statutory authority that permits a federal agency to incur obligations and to make payments for specified purposes out of borrowed monies.

Contract authority. Statutory authority that permits obligations to be incurred in advance of appropriations or in anticipation of receipts to be credited to a revolving fund or other account. (By definition, contract authority is unfunded and must subsequently be funded by an appropriation to liquidate obligations incurred under the contract authority, or by the collection and use of receipts.) (*See also* Backdoor authority.)

Determination of amount

Definite authority. Authority which is stated as a specific sum at the time the authority is granted. This includes authority stated as "not to exceed" a specified amount.

Indefinite authority. Authority for which a specific sum is not stated but is determined by other factors, such as the receipts from a certain source or obligations incurred. (Authority to borrow that is limited to a specified amount that may be outstanding at any time, i.e., revolving debt authority is considered to be indefinite budget authority.)

Period of availability

One-year (annual) authority. Budget authority that is available for obligation only during a specified fiscal year and expires at the end of that time.

Multiple-year authority. Budget authority that is available for a specified period of time in excess of one fiscal year. This authority generally takes the form of two-year, three-year, etc., availability, but may cover periods that do not coincide with the start or end of a fiscal year. For example, the authority may be available from July 1 of one year through September 30 of the following fiscal year (15 months). This type of multiple-year authority is sometimes referred to as "forward funding."

No-year authority. Budget authority that remains available for obligation for an indefinite period of time, usually until the objectives for which the authority was made available are attained.

Extensions of budget authority

Reappropriations. Congressional action to continue the obligation availability, whether for the same or different purposes, of all or part of the unobligated portion of budget authority that has expired or would otherwise expire. Reappropriations are counted as budget authority in the year for which the availability is extended.

Continuing resolution. Legislation enacted by Congress to provide budget authority for federal agencies and/or specific activities to continue in operation until the regular appropriations are enacted. Continuing resolutions are enacted when action an appropriations is not completed by the beginning of a fiscal year. The continuing resolution usually specifies a maximum rate at which the obligations may be incurred, based on the rate of the prior year, the president's budget request, or an appropriation bill passed by either or both Houses of the Congress.

Timing of congressional action
Current authority. Budget authority enacted by Congress in or immediately preceding the fiscal year in which it becomes available.
Permanent authority. Budget authority that becomes available as the result of previously enacted legislation (substantive legislation or prior appropriation act) and does not require current action by Congress. Authority created by such legislation is considered to be "current" in the first year in which it is provided and "permanent" in succeeding years.
Budget calendar The timetable a government follows in budget preparation and adoption, either by law or by administrative regulation.
Callable bond A bond which permits the issuer to redeem it before maturity according to terms and price (the call price) stipulated in the bond agreement.
Capital assets Assets with a useful life of several years (also called fixed assets).
Capital budget A plan for investment in capital assets separate from current or operating expenditures.
Capital. improvement program A plan for future capital expenditures which identifies each capital project, its anticipated start and completion, the amount to be spent in each year, and the method of finance.
Capital outlay Direct expenditure for acquisition of capital assets by contract or direct construction of buildings, roads, or other improvements, and purchase of equipment, land, and existing structures. The work may be addition, replacement, or major alteration, but not simply repair.
Cash and security holdings Cash and deposits (including demand and time deposits) and governmental and pri-

vate securities (bonds, notes, stocks, mortgages, etc.) held by a government.
Cash basis of accounting Accounting basis which records revenues when received in cash and expenditures when paid.
Cash budget An estimate of receipts and disbursements during a given period, usually as a cash management guide. The projection usually covers a year with estimates made for periods within the year (month, week, day).
Certificate of deposit Deposit with a financial institution for a contractual period at a contracted interest rate.
Concurrent resolution on the budget A resolution passed by both Houses of Congress, but not requiring the signature of the president, setting forth, reaffirming, or revising the congressional budget for the United States government for a fiscal year.

Two such resolutions are required before the start of a fiscal year. The first, due by May 15, establishes the congressional budget targets for the next fiscal year; the second, scheduled to be passed by September 15, sets a ceiling on budget authority and outlays and a floor on receipts. Additional concurrent resolutions revising the previously established budget levels may be passed by Congress at any time.
Congressional budget The budget as set forth by Congress in a concurrent resolution on the budget. By law the resolution includes:
The appropriate level of total budget outlays and of total new budget authority.
An estimate of budget outlays and new budget authority for each major functional category, for undistributed intergovernmental transactions, and for such other matters relating to the budget as may be appropriate to carry out the purposes of the 1974 Congressional Budget and Impoundment Control Act.
The amount, if any, of the surplus or deficit in the budget.
The recommended level of federal receipts.
The appropriate level of the public debt.
Continuing resolution Legislative resolution to permit government agencies

to continue activities requiring authority to spend beyond the end of a fiscal year, even though no appropriation bill has been passed.

Controllability The ability of Congress and the president to increase and decrease budget outlays or budget authority in the year in question, generally the current or budget year. Relatively uncontrollable refers to spending that the federal government cannot increase or decrease without changing existing substantive law. For example, outlays in any one year are considered to be relatively uncontrollable when the program level is determined by existing statute or by contract or other obligations.

Controllability, as exercised by Congress and the president, is determined by statute. In the case of Congress, all permanent budget authority is uncontrollable. For example, most trust fund appropriations are permanent, as are a number of federal fund appropriations, and interest on the public debt, for which budget authority is automatically provided under a permanent appropriation enacted in 1847. In the case of the president, relatively uncontrollable spending is usually the result of open-ended programs and fixed costs (e.g., social security, medical care, veterans benefits—outlays generally mandated by law), but also includes payments coming due resulting from budget authority enacted in prior years, such as entering into contracts.

Corporation net income taxes Taxes on net income earned by business organized as a corporation. Net income is gross earnings less expenses.

Cost–benefit analysis An analytical technique that compares the social costs and benefits of proposed programs or policy actions. All losses and gains experienced by society are included and measured in dollar terms. The net benefits created by an action are calculated by subtracting the losses incurred by some sectors of society from the gains that accrue to others. Alternative actions are compared, so as to choose one or more that yield the greatest net benefits, or ratio of benefits to costs.

The inclusion of all gains and losses to society in cost–benefit analysis distinguishes it from cost-effectiveness analysis, which is a more limited view of costs and benefits.

Cost-effectiveness analysis An analytical technique used to choose the most efficient method for achieving a program or policy goal. The costs of alternatives are measured by their requisite estimated dollar expenditures. Effectiveness is defined by the degree of goal attainment, and may also (but not necessarily) be measured in dollars. Either the net effectiveness (effectiveness minus costs) or the cost-effectiveness ratios of alternatives are compared. The most cost-effective method chosen may involve one or more alternatives.

The limited view of costs and effectiveness distinguishes this technique from cost–benefit analysis, which encompasses society-wide impacts of alternatives.

Coupon Detachable portions of a bond presented by its holder to bond issuer's paying agent to document interest due. The coupon rate is the rate of interest on face value that the coupons reflect.

Coverage The number of times by which earnings of a revenue bond–financed project exceed debt service payable in a period. It gauges the margin of safety offered the bondholder.

Crosswalk Any procedure for expressing the relationship between budgetary data from one set of classifications to another, such as between appropriation accounts and authorizing legislation or between the budget functional structure and the congressional committee spending jurisdictions.

Current charge revenue Amounts received from the public for performance of specific services benefiting the person charged, and from sales of commodities and services, except liquor store sales. Includes fees, assessments, and other reimbursements for current services, rents and sales derived from commodities or services furnished incident to the performance of particular functions, gross income of commercial activities, and the like. Current charges are distinguished from license taxes, which relate to privileges granted by the government or regulatory measures for the protection of the public.

Current operation expenditure Direct expenditure for compensation of own officers and employees and for the purchase of supplies, materials, and contractual services, except amounts for capital outlay.

Current services estimates Presidential estimates of budget authority and outlays for the ensuing fiscal year based on continuation of existing levels of service. These estimates reflect the anticipated costs of continuing federal programs and activities at present spending levels without policy changes, that is, ignoring all new initiatives, presidential or congressional, that are not yet law.

These estimates of budget authority and outlays, accompanied by the underlying economic and programmatic assumptions upon which they are based (such as the rate of inflation, the rate of real economic growth, the unemployment rate, program caseloads, and pay increases) are required to be transmitted by the president to the Congress with the president's budget. (For a more detailed discussion of this term, see Special Analysis A of the *Special Analyses, Budget of the United States Government.*)

Death and gift taxes Taxes imposed on transfer of property at death, in contemplation of death, or as a gift. The death tax may be either on the *estate* (the undivided holdings of the decedent) or on the *inheritance* (the share received by the heir).

Debt Comprises long-term credit obligations of the government and its agencies, and all interest-bearing short-term (i.e., repayable within one year) credit obligations. Includes judgments, mortgages, and "revenue" bonds as well as general obligation bonds, notes, and interest-bearing warrants. Excludes noninterest-bearing short-term obligations, interfund obligations, amounts owed in a trust or agency capacity, advances and contingent loans from other governments, and rights of individuals to benefits from employee-retirement funds. Non-

guaranteed federal agency debt is excluded from total long-term balances. *Full faith and credit debt* is long-term debt for which the credit of the government, implying the power of taxation, is unconditionally pledged. Includes debt payable initially from specific taxes or nontax sources, but representing a liability payable from any other available resources if the pledged sources are insufficient. For the federal government, includes *Public debt* (subject to Public Law 94-3 statutory limitations) and *Agency debt* (issued outside the above federal statutory restrictions). *Nonguaranteed debt* consists of long-term debt payable solely from earnings of revenue-producing activities, from special assessments, or from specific nonproperty taxes. *Net long-term debt* is total long-term debt outstanding minus *long-term debt offsets.*

Debt, federal There are three basic tabulations of federal debt: gross federal debt, debt held by the public, and debt subject to statutory limit.

Gross federal debt

Consists of public debt and agency debt and includes all public and agency debt issues outstanding.

Public debt. That portion of the federal debt incurred when the Treasury or the Federal Financing Bank (FFB) borrows funds directly from the public or another fund or account. To avoid double counting, FFB borrowing from the Treasury is not included in the public debt. (The Treasury borrowing required to obtain the money to lend to the FFB is already part of the public debt.)

Agency debt. That portion of the federal debt incurred when a federal agency, other than the Treasury or the Federal Financing Bank, is authorized by law to borrow funds directly from the public or another fund or account. To avoid double counting, agency borrowing from Treasury or the FFB and federal fund advances to trust funds are not included in the federal debt. (The Treasury or FFB borrowing required to obtain the money to lend to the agency is already part of the public debt.) Agency debt may be incurred by agencies within the federal budget (such as the Tennessee Valley Authority) or by off-budget federal entities (such as the Postal Service). Debt of government-sponsored, privately owned enterprises (such as the Federal National Mortgage Association) is not included in the federal debt.

Debt held by the public
Part of the gross federal debt held by the public. (The Federal Reserve System is included in "the public" for this purpose.) Debt held by government trust funds (e.g., Social Security Trust Fund), revolving funds, and off-budget federal entities is excluded from debt held by the public.

Debt subject to statutory limit
As defined by the Second Liberty Bond Act of 1917, as amended, it currently includes virtually all public debt. However, only a small portion of agency debt is included in this tabulation of federal debt.

Under Public Law 96-78, approved September 29, 1979, an amendment to the Rules of the House of Representatives makes possible the establishment of the public debt limit as a part of the congressional budget process.

Debt limit The maximum debt a governmental unit may incur under constitutional, statutory, or charter requirements, either in total or as a percentage of assessed value. Limits typically encompass only full faith and credit debt.

Debt management Operations of the U.S. Treasury Department that determine the composition of the federal debt. Debt management involves determining the amounts, maturities, other terms and conditions, and schedule of offerings of federal debt securities and raising new cash to finance the government's operations. The objective of debt management is to raise the money necessary for the government's operations at least cost to the taxpayer and in a manner that will minimize the effect of government operations on financial markets and on the economy.

Debt outstanding All debt obligations remaining unpaid on the date specified.

Debt service Expenditure to pay interest and repay principal to owners of debt issued by an entity.

Decision package In zero-base budgeting, a brief justification document containing the information that managers need to judge program or activity levels and resource requirements. Each decision package presents a level of request for a decision unit, stating the costs and performance associated with that level. Separate decision packages are prepared for incremental spending levels:
Minimum level—performance below which it is not feasible for the decision unit to continue because no constructive contribution could be made toward fulfilling the unit's objectives.
Intermediate level—performance between the minimum and current levels. There may be more than one intermediate level.
Current level—performance that would be reflected if activities for the budget year were carried on at current-year service or output levels without major policy changes. This level permits internal realignments of activities within existing statutory authorizations.
Enhancement level—where increased output or service are consistent with major objectives and where sufficient benefits are expected to warrant the serious review of higher authorities.

A series of decision packages are prepared for each decision unit. Cumulatively, the packages represent the total budget request for that unit.

Default Failure to pay a bond's principal and/or interest when due.

Deferral of budget authority Any action or inaction by an officer or employee of the United States government that temporarily withholds, delays, or effectively precludes the obligation or expenditure of budget authority, including authority to obligate by contract in advance of appropriations as specifically authorized by law. Deferrals consist of (*a*) amounts reserved for contingencies pursuant to the Antideficiency Act (31 U.S.C. 665), and (*b*) amounts temporarily withheld for other reasons pursuant to the Congressional Budget and Impoundment Control Act of 1974 (P.L. 93-344; 31 U.S.C. 1403).

Deferrals may not extend beyond the end of the fiscal year in which the message reporting the deferral is transmitted and may be overturned by the passage of an impoundment resolution by either House of Congress.

Deficiency apportionment A distribution by the Office of Management and Budget of available budgetary resources for the fiscal year that anticipates the need for supplemental budget authority. Such apportionments may only be made under certain specified conditions provided for in law (Antideficiency Act, 31 U.S.C. 665(e)). In such instances, the need for additional budget authority is usually reflected by making the amount apportioned for the fourth quarter less than the amount that will actually be required. Approval of requests for deficiency apportionment does not authorize agencies to exceed available resources within an account.

Deficit The amount by which expenditures exceed revenues during an accounting period.

Demand deposit Checking account; claims against a bank (or similar financial institution) which may be transferred to another individual or firm by an order to pay (usually a check).

Deobligation A downward adjustment of previously recorded obligations. This may be attributable to the cancellation of a project or contract, price revisions, or corrections of estimates previously recorded as obligations.

Direct expenditure Payments to employees, suppliers, contractors, beneficiaries, and other final recipients of government payments—i.e., all expenditure other than *intergovernmental expenditure.*

Document and stock transfer taxes Taxes on the recording, registering, and transfer of documents such as mortgages, deeds, and securities, except taxes on recording or transfer of motor vehicle titles, which are classified elsewhere.

Employee–retirement system A government-administered contributory plan for financing retirement and associated benefits for government employees. Does not include noncontributory plans.

Encumbrances Purchase orders, contracts, or salary commitments which must be covered by an appropriation and for which part of the appropriation is reserved. When paid, they are no longer encumbrances.

Entitlements Legislation that requires the payment of benefits (or entitlements) to any person or unit of government that meets the eligibility requirements established by such law. Authorizations for entitlements constitute a binding obligation on the part of the federal government, and eligible recipients have legal recourse if the obligation is not fulfilled. Budget authority for such payments is not necessarily provided in advance, and thus entitlement legislation requires the subsequent enactment of appropriations unless the existing appropriation is permanent. Examples of entitlement programs are social security benefits and veterans compensation or pensions. Section 401(b) of the Congressional Budget and Impoundment Control Act of 1974 (P.L. 93-344, 31 U.S.C. 1351[b]) imposes certain limits on the use of entitlements.

Expenditure All amounts of money paid out by a government—net of recoveries and other correcting transaction—other than for retirement of debt, investment in securities, extension of credit, or as agency transactions. Note that expenditure includes only external transactions of a government and excludes noncash transactions such as the provision of perquisites or other payment in kind.

The cost of goods received or services rendered whether cash payments have been made or not (accrual basis); payment of cost of goods received or services rendered (cash basis).

Financial administration Activities involving finance and taxation. Includes central agencies for accounting, auditing, and budgeting; the supervision of local government finance; tax administration; collection, custody, and disbursement of funds; administration of employee-retirement systems; debt and investment administration; and the like.

First concurrent resolution on the budget The resolution, containing government-wide budget targets of receipts, budget authority, and outlays that guides Congress in its subsequent consideration of appropriations and revenue measures. It is required to be adopted by both Houses of Congress no later than May 15, pursuant to the Congressional Budget and Impoundment Control Act of 1974 (P.L. 93-344, 31 U.S.C. 1324).

Fiscal year The 12-month period at the end of which a government determines its financial condition and the results of its operations and closes its books.

The fiscal year for the federal government begins on October 1 and ends on September 30. The fiscal year is designated by the calendar year in which it ends; for example, fiscal year 1980 is the year beginning October 1, 1979, and ending September 30, 1980. (Prior to fiscal year 1977, the federal fiscal year began on July 1 and ended on June 30.) The following conventions are followed:

The *budget year* is the fiscal year for which the budget is being considered (the fiscal year following the current year).

The *current year* is the fiscal year in progress.

The *prior year* is the fiscal year immediately preceding the current year.

Float Value of checks written but not yet presented for payment to the bank upon which the check was written.

Full faith and credit debt Long-term debt for which the credit of the government, implying the power of taxation, is unconditionally pledged. Includes debt payable initially from specific taxes or nontax sources, but representing a liability payable from any other available resources if the pledged sources are insufficient.

Full funding Provides budgetary resources to cover the total cost of a program or project at the time it is undertaken.

Full funding differs from incremental funding, where budget authority is provided or recorded for only a portion of total estimated obligations expected to be incurred during a single fiscal year. Full funding is generally discussed in terms of multiyear programs, whether or not obligations for the entire program are made in the first year. For further discussion of this term, see U.S. General Accounting Office, *Further Implementation of Full Funding in the Federal Government,* PAD-78-80, September 7, 1978.

Functional classification A system of classifying budget resources by function so that budget authority and outlays of budget and off-budget federal entities, loan guarantees, and tax expenditures can be related in terms of the national needs being addressed.

Budget accounts are generally placed in the single budget function (e.g., national defense, health) that best reflects its major end purpose addressed to an important national need, regardless of the agency administering the program. A function may be divided into two or more subfunctions, depending upon the complexity of the national need addressed by that function.

For budget presentation purposes, each budget function is described in the context of national needs being served, and the subfunctions are described in the context of the major missions devoted to meeting national needs. (For distinction, *see* Object classification.)

Functions Public purposes served by governmental activities (education, highways, public welfare, etc.). Expenditure for each function includes amounts for all types of expenditure serving the purpose concerned.

Fund An accounting device established to control receipt and disbursement of income from sources set aside to support specific activities or attain certain objectives. In the accounts of individual governments, each fund is treated as a distinct fiscal entity.

Fund accounting The legal requirement for federal agencies to establish accounts for segregating revenues and other resources, together with all related liabilities, obligations, and reserves, for the purpose of carrying on specific activities or attaining certain objectives in accordance with special regulations, restrictions, or limitations. Fund accounting, in a broad sense, is required in the federal government to demonstrate agency compliance with requirements of existing legislation for which Federal funds have been appropriated or otherwise authorized.

One of the most important laws requiring federal agencies to adhere to fund accounting concepts is the Antideficiency Act.

Funding Issuance of bonds or other long-term debt in exchange for, or to provide funds to retire, outstanding short-term debt.

General obligation debt Long-term full faith and credit obligations other than those payable initially from nontax revenue. Includes debt payable in the first instance from particular earmarked taxes, such as motor fuel sales taxes or property taxes.

General revenue All revenue of a government except utility revenue, liquor stores revenue, and insurance-trust revenue. All tax revenue and all intergovernmental revenue even if designated for employee-retirement of local utility purposes, is classed as general revenue.

General revenue sharing Funds distributed to states and local general-purpose governments by the federal government under the State and Local Fiscal Assistance Act of 1972.

General sales or gross receipts taxes Sales or gross receipts taxes which are applicable with only specified exceptions to all types of goods, all types of goods *and* services, or all gross income, whether at a single rate or at classified rates. Taxes imposed distinctively upon sales or gross receipts from selected commodities, services, or businesses are separate.

Grants Assistance awards in which substantial involvement is not anticipated between the federal government and the state or local government or other recipient during the performance of the contemplated activity.

The two major forms of federal grants are block and categorical. **Block grants** are given primarily to general-purpose governmental units in accordance with a statutory formula. Such grants can be used for a variety of activities within a broad functional area. Examples of federal block grant programs are Omnibus Crime Control and Safe Streets Act of 1968, Comprehensive Employment and Training Act of 1973, Housing and Community Development Act of 1974, and the 1974 Amendments to the Social Security Act of 1935 (Title XX).

Categorical grants can be used only for a specific program and are usually limited to narrowly defined activities. Categorical grants consist of formula, project, and formula-project grants.

Formula grants allocate federal funds to states or their subdivisions in accordance with a distribution formula prescribed by law or administrative regulation.

Project grants provide federal funding for fixed or known periods for specific projects or the delivery of specific services or products.

Impoundment Any action or inaction by an officer or employee of the United States government that precludes the obligation or expenditure of budget authority provided by Congress.

Impoundment resolution A resolution by either the House of Representatives or the Senate that expresses disapproval of a proposed deferral of budget authority set forth in a special message transmitted by the president as required under Sec. 1013(a) of the Impoundment Control Act of 1974 (P.L. 93-344, 31 U.S.C. 1403).

Whenever all or part of any budget authority provided by Congress is deferred, the president is required to transmit a special message to Congress describing the deferrals. Either House may, at any time, pass a resolution disapproving this deferral of budget authority, thus requiring that the funds be made available for obligation. When no congressional action is taken, deferrals may remain in effect until, but not beyond, the end of the fiscal year. If the funds remain available beyond the end of a fiscal year and continued deferral of their use is desired, the president must transmit a new special message to Congress.

Incremental funding The provision (or recording) of budgetary resources for a program or project based on obligations estimated to be incurred within a fiscal year when such budgetary resources will cover only a portion of the obligations to be incurred in completing the program or project as programmed. This differs from full funding, where budgetary resources are provided or recorded for the total estimated obligations for a program or project in the initial year of funding. (For distinction, *see* Full funding.)

Indirect cost Any cost incurred for common objectives and therefore cannot be directly charged to any single cost objective. These costs are allocated to the various classes of work in proportion to the benefit to each class. Indirect cost is also referred to as overhead or burden cost.

Individual income taxes Taxes on individuals measured by net income, including distinctive taxes on income from interest, dividends, and the like.

Industrial development bonds Municipal bonds which finance private industrial plant construction. Lease payments by the private firm service the bonds.

Insurance trust system A government-administered program for employee retirement and social insurance protection relating to unemployment compensation, workmen's compensation, Old Age, Survivors', Disability, and Health Insurance, and the like. *Insurance trust revenue* comprises amounts from contributions required of employers and employees for financing these social insurance programs, and earnings on assets of such systems. *Insurance trust expenditure* corresponds with the character and object category, *Insurance benefits and repayments,* and comprises only cash payments to beneficiaries (including withdrawals of contributions). These categories exclude costs of administering insurance trust systems, which are classed as general expenditure. Insurance trust revenue and expenditure do not include any contributions of a government to a system it administers. Any amounts paid by a government as employer contributions to an insurance trust system administered by another government are classed as general expenditure for current operation, and as insurance trust revenue of the particular system and receiving government.

Intergovernmental transactions *Intergovernmental revenue* and *Intergovernmental expenditure* comprise, respectively payments from one government to another as grants-in-aid, shared revenues, payments in lieu of taxes, or reimbursements for governmental services. Excludes amounts for the purchase of commodities, property, or utility services, any tax levied as such on facilities of the payer, and employer contributions by the government for social insurance (e.g., employee-retirement and OASDHI insurance).

Investment Asset purchased and held to generate interest, dividend, or rental income.

Joint resolution A joint resolution requires the approval of both Houses of Congress and the signature of the president, just as a bill does, and has the force of law if approved. There is no real difference between a bill and a joint resolution. The latter is generally used in dealing with limited matters, such as a single appropriation for a specific purpose.

Joint resolutions also are used to propose amendments to the U.S. Constitution. These do not require presidential signature, but become a part of the Constitution when three fourths of the states have ratified them.

Level debt service Serial maturities arranged so that the volume of maturing bonds increases at approximately the same rate as interest payments decline with reduced outstanding debt. Thus, total debt service remains almost constant, even as debt is retired.

License taxes Taxes enacted (either for revenue raising or for regulation) as a condition to the exercise of a business or nonbusiness privilege, at a flat rate or measured by such bases as capital stock, capital surplus, number of business units, or capacity. Excludes taxes measured directly by transactions, gross or net income, or value of property except those to which only nominal rates apply. "Licenses" based on these latter measures, other than those at nominal rates, are classified according to the measure concerned. Includes "fees" related to licensing activities—automobile inspection, gasoline and oil inspection, professional examinations and licenses, etc.—as well as license taxes producing substantial revenues.

Limited liability bonds Bonds which do not pledge the full faith credit of the jurisdiction, but do usually dedicate a specific revenue source for repayment.

Liquidity The ease with which an asset can be converted to money.

Long-term debt Debt payable more than one year after date of issue.

Long-term debt issued The par value of long-term debt obligations incurred during the fiscal period concerned, including funding and refunding obligations. Debt obligations authorized but not actually incurred during the fiscal period are not included.

Maturity The date on which the debt principal is to be repaid.

Mission budgeting A budget approach that focuses on output rather than input and directs attention to how well an agency is meeting its responsibilities. By grouping programs and activities according to an agency's mission or end purposes, mission budgeting makes it easier to identify similar programs. Missions at the highest level in the budget structure represent basic end-purpose responsibilities assigned to an agency. Descending levels in the budget structure then focus more sharply on the specific components of the mission and the programs needed to satisfy them. At the lowest levels are line items—that is—the supporting activities necessary to satisfy the missions. For further discussion of this term, see U.S. General Accounting Office, *A Mission Budget Structure for the Department of Agriculture—A Feasibility Study*, PAD-80-08.

Multiyear budget planning A budget planning process designed to make sure that the long-range consequences of budget decisions are identified and reflected in the budget totals. Currently, multiyear budget planning in the executive branch encompasses a policy review for a three-year period beginning with the budget year, plus projections for the subsequent two years. This process provides a structure for the review and analysis of long-term program and tax policy choices.

Municipal bond A bond issued by a state or local government, including cities, towns, villages, counties, special districts, states, and state agencies.

Nominal interest rate The contractual interest rate appearing on a bond and determining the amount of interest to be paid to a holder.

Nonguaranteed debt Long-term debt payable solely from pledged specific sources—e.g., from earnings of revenue-producing activities (university and college dormitories, toll highways and bridges, electric power projects, public building and school building authorities, etc.) or from specific and limited taxes. Includes only debt that does not constitute an obligation against any other resources of the government if the pledged sources are insufficient.

Object classification, object-of-expenditure classification A uniform classification identifying the transactions of the government by the nature of the good or services purchased (such as personnel compensation, supplies and materials, and equipment), without regard to the agency involved or the purpose of the programs for which they are used.

Obligational authority The sum of (*a*) budget authority provided for a given fiscal year, (*b*) balances of amounts brought forward from prior years that remain available for obligation, and (*c*) amounts authorized to be credited to a specific fund or account during that year, including transfers between funds or accounts.

Off-budget federal entities Certain federally owned and controlled entities whose transactions (e.g., budget authority or outlays) have been excluded from budget totals under provisions of law. The fiscal activities of these entities, therefore, are not reflected in either budget authority or budget outlay totals. However, the outlays of off-budget federal entities are added to the budget deficit to derive the total government deficit that has to be financed by borrowing from the public or by other means. Off-budget federal entities are discussed in Part 6, Perspectives on the Budget, of *The Budget of the United States Government*. Schedules and financial statements are presented in Part IV of *The Budget of the United States Government, Appendix*.

Operating budget A financial plan which presents proposed expenditures for a given period (typically a fiscal year) and estimates of revenue to finance them. Excludes expenditures for capital assets.

Outlays Obligations are generally liquidated when checks are issued or cash
disbursed. Such payments are called
outlays. In lieu of issuing checks, obligations may also be liquidated (and
outlays occur) by the maturing of interest coupons in the case of some bonds,
or by the issuance of bonds or notes (or
increases in the redemption value of
bonds outstanding).

Outlays during a fiscal year may be
for payment of obligations incurred in
prior years (prior-year outlays) or in the
same year. Outlays, therefore, flow in
part from unexpended balances of
prior-year budget authority and in
part from budget authority provided
for the year in which the money is
spent.

Total budget outlays are stated net
of offsetting collections, and exclude
outlays of off-budget federal entities.

The terms *expenditure* and *net disbursement* are frequently used interchangeably with the term *outlays.*

Oversight committee The congressional
committee charged with general oversight of the operation of an agency or
program. In most cases, but not all, the
oversight committee for an agency is
also the authorizing committee for that
agency's programs.

Par value The face value of a security.
For bonds, the amount that must be
paid at maturity. A quotation of 100
means selling at par; below 100, at a
discount (95 = $950 for a $1,000 par
value bond); above 100, at a premium
(105 = $1,050 for a $1,000 bond).

Personal services and benefits Amounts
paid for compensation of officers and
employees of the government. Consists
of gross compensation before deductions for taxes, retirement plans, or
other purposes.

Personnel benefits
Comprises cash allowances paid to civilian and military employees incident
to their employment and payment to
other funds for the benefit of employees. Perquisites provided in kind, such
as uniforms or quarters, and payments
to veterans and former employees resulting from their employment are excluded.

Benefits to former personnel
Pensions, annuities, or other benefits

due to former employees or their survivors, based (at least in part) on the
length of their services to the government, other than benefits paid from
funds financed from employer and/or
employee contributions and premiums.
Includes federal payments to funds that
provide benefits to former employees.
Excludes benefits provided in kind, such
as hospital and medical care, and in-
demnities for disability or death of
former employees.

Personnel compensation
Comprises gross compensation (before
deduction for taxes and other purposes) for services of individuals, including terminal leave payments. This
classification covers all payments
(salaries, wages, fees) for personal services rendered to the government by its
officers or employees, either civil or
military, and compensation for special
services rendered by consultants or
others.

Poll taxes Capitation taxes levied as
specific amounts, uniform or graded,
against persons, or as ad valorem taxes
on an arbitrary valuation of polls.

Program Generally defined as an organized set of activities directed toward
a common purpose, or goal, undertaken or proposed by an agency in order
to carry out its responsibilities. In practice, however, the term program has
many uses and thus does not have a
well-defined, standard meaning in the
legislative process. Program is used to
describe an agency's mission, programs, functions, activities, services,
projects, and processes.

Program evaluation In general, the process of assessing program alternatives,
including research and results, and the
options for meeting program objectives
and future expectations. Specifically,
program evaluation is the process of
appraising the manner and extent to
which programs (1) achieve their stated
objectives, (2) meet the performance
perceptions and expectations of responsible Federal officials and other interested groups, and (3) produce other
significant effects of either a desirable
or undesirable character.

Progressive tax A tax with effective
rates that are higher for families with
high affluence than they are for families
with low affluence.

Property taxes Taxes conditioned on ownership of property and measured by its assessed value. Includes general property taxes relating to property as a whole, real and personal, tangible or intangible, whether taxed at a single rate or at classified rates; and taxes on selected types of property, such as motor vehicles or certain or all intangibles.

Proportional tax A tax with *effective* rates that do not change across families with different affluence levels.

Rating Grading by analysts or investors' services of quality (safety of principal and interest payment) of a bond.

Reapportionment A revision by the Office of Management and Budget of a previous apportionment of budgetary resources for an appropriation or fund account. Agency requests for reapportionment are usually submitted to OMB as soon as a change in previous apportionment becomes necessary due to changes in amounts available, program requirements, or cost factors. A reapportionment would ordinarily cover the same period, project, or activity covered in the original apportionment.

Reconciliation process A process used by Congress to reconcile amounts determined by tax, spending, and debt legislation for a given fiscal year with the ceilings enacted in the second required concurrent resolution on the budget for that year. Section 310 of the Congressional Budget and Impoundment Control Act of 1974 (P.L. 93-344, 31 U.S.C. 1331) provides that the second concurrent resolution on the budget, which sets binding totals for the budget, may direct committees to determine and recommend changes to laws, bills, and resolutions, as required to conform with the binding totals for budget authority, revenues, and the public debt. Such changes are incorporated into either a reconciliation resolution or a reconciliation bill. (*See also* Concurrent Resolution on the Budget.)

Reconciliation bill
A bill, requiring enactment by both Houses of Congress and approval by the president, making changes to legislation that has been enacted or enrolled.

Reconciliation resolution
A concurrent resolution, requiring passage by both Houses of Congress but not the approval of the president, directing the clerk of the House or the secretary of the Senate to make specified changes in bills or resolutions that have not yet reached the stage of enrollment.

Refunding The issuance of long-term debt in exchange for, or to provide funds for, the retirement of long-term debt already outstanding.

Regressive tax A tax with effective rates that are lower for families with high affluence than they are for families with low affluence.

Rescission The consequence of enacted legislation that cancels budget authority previously provided by Congress before the time when the authority would otherwise lapse (i.e., cease to be available for obligation).

The Congressional Budget and Impoundment Control Act of 1974 (P.L. 93-344, 31 U.S.C. 1402) specifies that whenever the president determines that all or part of any budget authority will not be needed to carry out the full objectives or scope of programs for which the authority was provided, the president will propose to Congress that the funds be rescinded. Likewise, if all or part of any budget authority limited to a fiscal year—that is, annual appropriations or budget authority of a multiple-year appropriation in the last year of availability—is to be reserved from obligation for the entire fiscal year, a rescission will be proposed. Budget authority may also be proposed for rescission for fiscal policy or other reasons. Generally, amounts proposed for rescission are withheld for up to 45 legislative days while the proposals are being considered by Congress.

All funds proposed for rescission, including those withheld, must be reported to Congress in a special message. If both Houses have not completed action on a rescission proposed by the president within 45 calendar days of continuous session, any funds being withheld must be made available for obligation.

Rescission bill A bill or joint resolution that cancels, in whole or in part, budget authority previously granted by Congress.

Rescissions proposed by the president must be transmitted in a special message to Congress. Under Section 1012 of the Congressional Budget and Impoundment Control Act of 1974 (P.L. 93-344), unless both Houses of Congress complete action on a rescission bill within 45 days of continuous session after receipt of the proposal, the budget authority must be made available for obligation.

Revenue All amounts of money received by a government from external sources—net of refunds and other correcting transactions—other than from issue of debt, liquidation of investments, and as agency and private trust transactions. Note that revenue excludes noncash transactions such as receipt of services, commodities, or other "receipts in kind."

Revenues represent the increase in assets (or decrease in liabilities) that result from operations. Revenues result from (1) services performed by the federal government, (2) goods and other tangible property delivered to purchasers, and (3) amounts becoming owed to the government for which no current performance by the government is required.

Contingencies that might result in gains should not be recorded in the accounts since to do so would recognize revenue prior to its realization. Contingencies that might result in gains should be carefully explained in financial statements.

The term *revenues* is commonly used interchangeably with the term *collections.*

Revenue bond Limited liability bond whose debt service requirements are paid only from the earnings of a public project.

Revenue elasticity A coefficient measuring the percentage increase in revenue from a given source resulting from a one percent increase in economic activity.

Sales and gross receipts taxes Taxes, including "licenses" at more than nominal rates, based on volume or value of transfers of goods or services, upon gross receipts therefrom, or upon gross income, and related taxes based upon use, storage, production (other than severance of natural resources), importation, or consumption of goods.

Scorekeeping Procedures for tracking the status of congressional budgetary actions. Examples of scorekeeping information include up-to-date tabulations and reports on congressional actions affecting budget authority, receipts, outlays, surplus or deficit, and the public debt limit, as well as outlay and receipt estimates and reestimates.

Scorekeeping data published by the Congressional Budget Office (CBO) include, but are not limited to, status reports on the effects of congressional actions (and in the case of scorekeeping reports prepared for the Senate Budget Committee, the budget effects of potential congressional actions), and comparisons of these actions to targets and ceilings set by Congress in the budget resolutions. Periodic scorekeeping reports are required to be produced by the CBO pursuant to Section 308(b) of the Congressional Budget and Impoundment Control Act of 1974 (P.L. 93-344, 31 U.S.C. 1329).

Second concurrent resolution on the budget The resolution adopted by Congress containing budget ceilings classified by function for budget authority and outlays and a floor for budget receipts. This resolution may retain or revise the levels set earlier in the year, and can include directives to the appropriations committees and to other committees with jurisdiction over budget authority or entitlement authority. The second resolution may also direct the appropriate committees to recommend changes in budget receipts or in the statutory limit on the public debt.

Changes recommended by various committees pursuant to the second budget resolution are to be reported in a reconciliation bill (resolution, in some cases) on which Congress must complete action by September 25, a few days before the new fiscal year commences on October 1.

Selective sales and gross receipts taxes Sales and gross receipts taxes imposed on sales of particular commodities or services or gross receipts of particular businesses, separately and apart from the application of general sales and gross receipts taxes.

Serial bond A bond in an issue that contains multiple maturities.

Severance taxes Taxes imposed distinctively on removal of natural products—e.g., oil, gas, other minerals, timber, fish, etc.—from land or water and measured by value or quantity of products removed or sold.

Short-term debt Interest-bearing debt payable within one year from date of issue, such as bond anticipation notes, bank loans, and tax anticipation notes and warrants. Includes obligations having no fixed maturity date if payable from a tax levied for collection in the year of their issuance.

Sinking fund Fund used to accumulate periodic payments toward redemption of bonds at maturity: payments on schedule plus interest earnings will accumulate to par value of the bonds.

Special assessment bond Bond serviced from special assessments; a local tax against certain property to cover the cost of improvements giving special benefit to that property (sidewalks or street paving in an area, for instance). The bonds may be supported either by the special assessment alone or by full faith and credit as well.

Spending authority As defined by the Congressional Budget and Impoundment Control Act of 1974 (P.L. 93-344, 31 U.S.C. 1323), a collective designation for appropriations, borrowing authority, contract authority, and entitlement authority for which the budget authority is not provided in advance by appropriation acts. The latter three are also commonly referred to as backdoor authority.

Spending committees The standing committees of the House and Senate with jurisdiction over legislation that permits the obligation of funds. For most programs, the House and Senate Appropriations Committees are the spending committees. For other programs, the authorizing legislation itself permits the obligation of funds (backdoor authority). When this is the case, the authorizing committees are then the committees with spending responsibility.

Spending legislation (spending bill) A term used in the budget scorekeeping of the Congressional Budget Office to indicate legislation that directly provides budget authority or outlays. Spending legislation includes (1) ap-

propriations legislation, (2) legislation that provides budget authority directly without the need for subsequent appropriations action, and (3) entitlement legislation which, while requiring subsequent appropriations action, essentially "locks in" budget authority at the time of authorization (except legislation that establishes conditional entitlements, where recipients are entitled to payments only to the extent that funds are made available in subsequent appropriations legislation).

Spread A bond underwriter's gross profit: the price received by the underwriter on sale of the bonds less the price paid by the underwriter for those bonds.

Substantive law Statutory public law other than appropriation law; sometimes referred to as basic law. Substantive law usually authorizes, in broad general terms, the executive branch to carry out a program of work. Annual determination as to the amount of the work to be done is usually thereafter embodied in appropriation law.

Supplemental appropriation An act appropriating funds in addition to those in an annual appropriation act. Supplemental appropriations provide additional budget authority beyond the original estimates for programs or activities (including new programs authorized after the date of the original appropriation act) in cases where the need for funds is too urgent to be postponed until enactment of the next regular appropriation bill. Supplementals may sometime include items not appropriated in the regular bills for lack of timely authorizations.

Supplemental summary of the budget (mid-year or mid-session review) A supplemental summary of the budget for the ensuing fiscal year transmitted to Congress by the president on or before July 15 of each year pursuant to the Budget and Accounting Act of 1921, as amended (31 U.S.C. 11[b]). With respect to that ensuing fiscal year, the summary reflects (a) all substantial alterations in or reappraisals of the estimates of expenditures and receipts, (b) all substantial obligations imposed on that budget after its transmission to Congress, (c) the actual or proposed appropriations made during the fiscal year in progress, and (*d*) the estimated condition of the Treasury at the end of the fiscal year if the financial proposals contained in the budget are adopted. The summary also contains any information the president considers necessary or advisable to provide the Congress, and a complete and current estimate of the functions, obligations, requirements, and financial condition of the government for that ensuing fiscal year.

Tax credits Tax credits include any special provision of law that results in a dollar-for-dollar reduction in tax liabilities that would otherwise be due. In some cases, tax credits may be carried forward or backward from one tax year to another, while other tax credits lapse if not used in the year earned. Tax credits may result in a reduction of tax collections or an increase in the value of tax refunds.

Tax expenditures Revenue losses attributable to provisions of the federal income tax laws that allow a special exclusion, or deduction from gross income, or that provide a special credit, preferential tax rate, or deferral of tax liability.

Tax expenditures may be considered federal government subsidies provided through the tax system to encourage certain activities and to assist certain groups. For example, capital formation is encouraged by permitting businesses to claim some portion of the cost of an investment as a credit on their income taxes, and the unemployed are aided by excluding unemployment benefits from taxable income. Tax expenditures involve no transfer of funds from the government to the private sector. Rather, the U.S. Treasury Department forgoes some of the receipts that it otherwise would have collected, and the beneficiary taxpayers pay lower taxes than they otherwise would have had to pay.

Tax expenditures budget A list of legally sanctioned tax expenditures for each fiscal year which the 1974 Congressional Budget and Impoundment Control Act (P.L. 93-344, Sec. 601 [e]) requires be part of the President's budget submission to Congress. (See Special Analysis G of the *Special Analyses, Budget of the United States Government.*)

Tax rate limit The maximum legal rate at which a government may levy a tax. The limit may apply to a single tax applied by a single government for a single purpose, to a single tax applied by a single government for any purpose, to a single tax applied by any government, or class of governments, or to all taxes applied by any government or class of governments.

Taxes Compulsory payments to a government based on holdings of a tax base.

Treasury bills The shortest term federal security. Treasury bills have maturity dates normally varying from 3 to 12 months and are sold at a discount from face value rather than carrying an explicit rate of interest.

Underwriter Investment firm that buys an entire bond issue from an issuing government with the intention of reselling to the public.

Unemployment compensation system A state-administered plan for compulsory unemployment insurance through accumulation of assets from contributions collected from employers or employees for use in making cash benefit payments to eligible unemployed persons. Does not include distinctive sickness or disability insurance plans carried out in conjunction with unemployment insurance programs by certain states. Unemployment insurance contributions collected by the state are deposited in the U.S. Treasury in a trust account maintained for the state; interest is credited by the U.S. Treasury on balances in state accounts; and funds are withdrawn by the state as needed to make unemployment compensation benefit payments.

Unified budget The present form of the budget of the federal government adopted beginning with the 1969 budget, in which receipts and outlays from federal funds and trust funds are consolidated. When these fund groups are consolidated to display budget totals, transactions that are outlays of one fund group for payment to the other fund group (i.e., interfund transactions) are deducted to avoid double counting. By law, budget authority and outlays of off-budget entities are excluded from the unified budget, but data relating to off-budget entities are displayed in the budget documents.

Warrant An order drawn by a government officer directing the treasurer of that government to pay a specified amount to the bearer after a specified date. Some state and local governments issue warrants rather than checks in order to strengthen internal expenditure control.

Workmen's compensation system A state-administered plan for compulsory accident and injury insurance of workmen through accumulation of assets from contributions collected from employers for financing cash benefits to eligible injured workmen.

Zero-base budgeting A process emphasizing management's responsibility to plan, budget, and evaluate. Zero-base budgeting provides for analysis of alternative methods of operation and various levels of effort. It places new programs on an equal footing with existing programs by requiring that program priorities be ranked, thereby providing a systematic basis for allocating resources. Formally adopted at the federal level in 1977 and formally abandoned in 1981.

INDEX

This book has been set VIP, in 10 and 9 point Univers 55, leaded 2 points. Part numbers are 36 point Eurostile Bold and part titles are 24 point Univers 55. Chapter numbers are 36 point Eurostile Bold and chapter title are 24 point Univers 45 Light. The size of the type page is 28 by 46 picas.

STUN
Delivery Tape
Career Planning